THE INITIATIVE AND REFERENDUM
IN CALIFORNIA, 1898–1998

# The Initiative and Referendum in California, 1898–1998

John M. Allswang

STANFORD UNIVERSITY PRESS

STANFORD, CALIFORNIA

Stanford University Press
Stanford, California

© 2000 by the Board of Trustees of the
Leland Stanford Junior University

Printed in the United States of America
on acid-free, archival-quality paper

Library of Congress Cataloging-in-Publication Data

Allswang, John M.
    The initiative and referendum in California, 1898–1998/
John M. Allswang.
        p.   cm.
    Includes bibliographical references (p.      ) and index.
    ISBN 0-8047-3811-4 (alk. paper) —
ISBN 0-8047-3821-1 (pbk. : alk. paper)
    1. Referendum — California — History — 20th century.
I. Title.

JF495.C2 A45 2000
328.2794'09'04 — dc21                          99-044068

Original printing 2000

Last figure below indicates year of this printing:
08   07   06   05   04   03   02   01   00

Typeset by Keystone Typesetting, Inc., in 10/12.5 Sabon.

*Once again, for S, E, & Y*
*and in memory of BKK*

# Contents

# Tables

# Preface

Like most historians of my generation, I long assumed that what was important in American history began at the Atlantic Ocean and ended at the Mississippi River. Even after I had come to live and work in California, my academic mind remained well to the east. But over time I became increasingly interested in, and often bemused by, my adopted state. As a political historian I found its politics a bit odd, but obviously important, reflecting the increasingly influential position California was playing in all aspects of our national life. Nowhere was this so evident as in the direct intervention of the people in the political process, ignoring the principles of representation and disdaining the role of party.

This book is about that popular participation in political decision making. Specifically, it deals with direct legislation, a process whereby the people at large can ignore or confound their elected representatives by directly enacting or revoking statutes and constitutional amendments. The process began in what is generally called the Progressive Era, at the turn of the century, a time when middle-class business and professional people began to use the power of government to shape society to their emerging values. And it has grown in significance well beyond the expectations of that era. Direct legislation as process has never existed apart from substance; that is, the social, political, economic, and cultural issues being addressed have always been at least as important as the way they were being decided by the public.

California has been more important than any other state in the development of this form of democratic politics. Particularly since the "Proposition 13 Revolution" of 1978, California has influenced other states not only to use direct legislation, but also to apply it to specific contemporary issues. Thus, a focus on California projects, to some degree, well beyond the state's borders. This phenomenon has been sometimes impressive, sometimes disturbing, and sometimes screwy; its development and effects over a century's time are the subject of this book.

The book is the result of a much lengthier process than I had ever anticipated. I began the research in the early 1990s, working on the origins of direct legislation and data collection for the whole period. This resulted in an article or two, and a book which was designed primarily as a reference source and guide to research. Then, in the middle of the decade, my work on the topic came almost to a halt, interrupted by almost four years of administrative duties and a few other things. Only in the last few years have I been able to get back to it and complete what I had long anticipated. The delay was not without value, however, since the second half of the 1990s has been an important period in the development of initiative democracy.

Over this long period of time, and inquiry into three hundred elections spanning nearly a full century, I have benefited from the assistance and graciousness of a very large number of institutions and individuals — more, indeed, than I may remember. The Special Collections and Map & Government Documents libraries at UCLA, as well as the Institute of Governmental Studies and Bancroft libraries at UC Berkeley, were most welcoming. This was true also at the Huntington Library, Stanford University Library, and at my own institution, California State University, Los Angeles. The staffs of the California State Archives and the California State Library in Sacramento also helped with my repeated searches for various kinds of rarely used information. The Office of the Secretary of State of California, particularly the Political Reform Division, and the California Fair Political Practices Commission, were very helpful with voting and campaign contribution information.

My tenure as Field Institute Faculty Fellow in 1997–1998 permitted me to formulate my own questions, in collaboration with Professor Ted Lascher of California State University, Sacramento, for the Field ("California") Poll of August 1997. I am grateful to Mark DiCamillo of the Field Research Institute for his assistance with those questions. The early stages of research for this book were supported by two grants from California State University, Los Angeles, which I am pleased to acknowledge.

At various times, a number of individuals have read and commented upon parts of this manuscript. Tom Sitton of the History Division of the Natural History Museum of Los Angeles County provided some helpful advice early in the project, and then, as reader for Stanford University Press, made numerous suggestions, great and small, that improved the quality of the manuscript. Martin J. Schiesl of California State University, Los Angeles, frequently shared with me his extensive knowledge of California history. Bruce M. Stave of the University of Connecticut, as usual, provided insightful comments and support. Thomas Goebel of the German Historical Institute and Helmut Klumpjan of Universität Erlangen-Nürnberg also provided useful suggestions based on their own work on direct legislation.

Norris Pope and Stacey Lynn of Stanford University Press, and copy editor Ruth Steinberg, were all very helpful in the development of the manuscript.

Suzanne Allswang has, despite her limited English, proved to be a most effective copy editor. Yael and Justin Prough, and Eden Allswang Bruner and Marc Bruner provided latent support that helped establish overall perspective.

Dealing with hundreds of elections and such a wide variety of information and data seems to produce a copious quantity of errors, no matter how high the quality of one's assistance. While I would like to blame others for the blunders that remain, I fear that the responsibility is mine.

J.M.A.
LOS ANGELES, CALIFORNIA
SEPTEMBER 1999

THE INITIATIVE AND REFERENDUM
IN CALIFORNIA, 1898–1998

# Introduction

The process of direct democracy, including the initiative, the referendum, and the recall, has played an important and controversial role in American city and state politics and government since the end of the nineteenth century. The initiative allows voters to originate, by petition, statutes or constitutional amendments, which are submitted directly to the electorate for approval or rejection. In the referendum, voters by petition can demand that a statute passed by the state legislature be put on the ballot for popular approval or revocation.[1] And in the recall, voters can petition to place on the ballot a proposal to remove an officeholder.

The terms *direct democracy* and *direct legislation* are often used synonymously, although, strictly speaking, the former term includes the recall whereas the latter does not. Because there have been no statewide recalls in California, however, we can ignore the fact that the terms were often used interchangeably. To confuse matters a bit more, the term *referendum* has often been used, especially but not exclusively in the past, not only as the name of a particular process but also as a synonym for "direct democracy" in general. Here, the term will be used only in its specific sense.

The initiative and referendum were originally adopted to serve as a lifeboat of sorts—to provide a way for the public to directly intervene in the legislative process when the state legislature was unresponsive to public concerns. Somewhere along the way direct legislation moved well beyond its original intent, to the point that it has often overwhelmed the governing processes it was designed to monitor, becoming in effect a "fourth branch" of state government. Consequently, the impact of direct legislation on the structure and operation of California politics and government is as worthy of study as is its role in deciding important issues in the state's life.

The idea of direct popular participation in governmental decision making, as opposed to representative government, is a modern one that nonetheless has ancient roots. It is based on the related idea of the collective popular wisdom, albeit with "the people" defined in often restrictive terms. Supporters of the ideal of popular governance have often pointed to its origins in ancient Athens, and it is true that Athens and other Greek city-states did permit all adult male citizens to meet and participate in government decisions. In a way, Athenian democracy was more "direct" than what we call direct democracy today, since the people did not assert their influence from discrete polling places but rather met and discussed and decided issues face to face.[2]

In the Athenian capital, the practice of democracy often entailed as many as six thousand people at a time engaging in such direct participation; no wonder oratory became a Greek virtue. These six thousand represented about one-fifth of those qualified to vote, suggesting that "low turnout" is not an exclusively modern phenomenon. Moreover, that total of 30,000 qualified participants was only about one-third of all citizens, given that women and minors had no political rights. And citizens made up only about 10 percent of the entire Athenian population, foreigners (*metics*) and slaves being excluded.[3] So the construct of "the people" who participated in direct democracy was a limited one, which is not so different from our own day — whether considering the matter of the legally excluded or the voluntarily uninvolved.

As in other things, Athens cast its influence on Rome to some extent. But the idea of direct popular democracy pretty much died there. While an active imagination might find subsequent mass popular participation in governance in one place or another, at one time or another (the Germanic tribes, for example, or Iceland), there is no real direct line of descent from these ancient practices to modern ones.[4]

The New England town meeting of colonial days is often cited as another example of direct democracy. There, as in Athens, every adult male could participate in decision making, although at first there were religious as well as age and gender requirements. The early New England town was small, religiously and culturally unified. Popular participation in governance reflected the intertwining of church and state, and political practices followed church-based ones. Ultimately, popular democracy at the town level did survive secularization in New England, and it has persisted to some degree to the present day, particularly in the smaller towns.[5]

Even before the end of the seventeenth century, however, population growth and geographic spread made the town meeting increasingly unwieldy; representative governance began to replace it. Moreover, the idea of direct mass political participation did not exercise much influence on the rest of America, which has honored it more in rhetoric than in practice. The American experience from the colonial period on was overwhelmingly one of the development of representative political institutions. It was that practice that the founding fathers sought to perfect in the Constitution, and that their successors turned into political democracy — long qualified on gender, race, and other bases, but broader than before.

One exception to the decline of direct democracy from the early national period on had to do with the adoption and amendment of state constitutions. It became increasingly common after about 1820 for changes in these documents to be submitted to voters for approval or rejection. In some states, various other issues were occasionally put out for popular decision, as well.[6]

Equally or perhaps even more influential than the New England experience was the Swiss one. It became the model for many of the advocates of direct legislation in the American states at the end of the nineteenth century. Modern Switzerland had modeled its own constitution on the American one, but jumped ahead of the New World in developing direct democracy. Switzerland was similar to the United States in some ways, particularly in aspects of its polity, where the distribution of power between commune (*Gemeinde*), canton, and national government paralleled the American city-state-federal system.

The referendum process, where, as in Athens or early New England, the people could come together to approve or reject decisions made by government, went back in some cantons to the sixteenth century. But the expansion of that process, along with the initiative, and implementation through the ballot rather than public meeting, was a nineteenth-century development, spreading from canton to canton until it became nearly universal and was placed in the 1874 federal constitution. Direct legislation became a key feature of Swiss democracy, unique for its time, and a major and constant force behind decision making at all levels of government. In the fact that direct legislation in Switzerland was and is national as well as cantonal and communal, it reached a stage that has yet to take place in the United States (efforts in that direction are mentioned in Chapter 6).[7]

Would-be American political reformers visited and read about the Swiss experiment in the late nineteenth century and were inspired to bring it to these shores. Chief among these converts were the Populists and other western radicals and reformers of the 1890s, which is why the early statewide successes of direct democracy were almost exclusively in the West: South Dakota in 1898; eight more western states plus Maine by 1910; and then three more western states, including California, one year later.[8] At the same time, western cities had also adopted direct democracy and were implementing it frequently by the first decade of the twentieth century.

California was thus one of the first states to adopt direct democracy; more to the point, it has used these mechanisms almost constantly and with accelerating frequency throughout the twentieth century — more so than any other state. With the origination of increasingly fundamental and general, sometimes draconian, measures by voter groups (especially since the famous Proposition 13 in 1978), along with the professionalization of the entire process from signature gathering through legal challenge and defense, direct democracy has become both a major enterprise and a significant problem.[9]

Curiously, historians of California, even of its politics and government, have paid little attention to direct legislation. Study of the topic has been confined primarily to political scientists and public policy experts, where prescriptions for "reform" were often the main concern, with the historical background at best of secondary interest.[10] There has been little effort by scholars to relate what was going on in the direct legislation process to broader coinciding political, social, economic, and other developments in California society. Since most important issues in California life, from the Progressive Era to the present day, have indeed been reflected in, and often decided by, the direct legislation process, this was an omission waiting to be filled. That, along with the effects of the initiative and referendum on the structure and nature of California politics and government, required a close examination of the development of direct legislation over time.

This study investigates the origins and development of the initiative and referendum in California from the 1890s to the present day. The topic is an important one for understanding not only the development of California, but often for national insights as well. For one thing, the process is widespread. Every state but Delaware uses the initiative process for approving constitutional amendments, and most use it also for bond issues.[11] Currently, twenty-seven states have the popular initiative and/or referendum. Thus, what has happened in California has been reflected, although generally to a lesser extent, in other places. More importantly, the direct legislation process has clearly mirrored the major issues in California and national life from decade to decade. Thus, to study the California initiative and referendum is to study a microcosm of the major sociocultural, economic, political, and other issues that the people and politicians have cared about, in the state and beyond.

Direct legislation has been controversial from the very beginning. It is, after all, a denial of the basic premises of representative democracy, based on the argument that representative democracy sometimes does not work. There have always been critics who denied the validity of the direct legislative process itself, arguing that it replaces a well-established and effective system of legislation with an inferior new system that perverts the governmental process.[12]

The contrary argument, which has convinced three generations of Californians, is that rule by the people must extend beyond representation when that representation does not, in fact, do the people's bidding. At the outset, when South Dakota, California, Oregon, and other states instituted direct legislation at the turn of the century, it seemed not only a reasonable but a necessary step. Many people, led by middle-class business and professional groups, were convinced that large economic interests controlled their state legislatures, buying obeisance of the politicians, which, in turn, guaranteed those interests continued freedom to direct the economic life of their states. Thus, it was an extension of democracy to empower "the people" to act directly when their legislators were not doing their will.

These questions are addressed in Chapter 1, which seeks to explain the way in which direct legislation came to California. (My titular starting date of 1898 is somewhat arbitrary, but does reflect the political emergence of the issue at the local level.) Inevitably, an examination of the origins of direct legislation requires some reconsideration of the nature of California Progressivism, of which the initiative and referendum were definitely a part.[13] As we shall see, California Progressivism was very much a function of individual and group interest and political activity, with cooperation among individuals and interest groups resulting more from construed political need than from construed commonalty of purpose. Thus, the various issues that came to be seen as the elements of Progressivism were actually combined with some reluctance and some happenstance, and quite often represented different constituencies.[14]

Subsequent chapters are organized on a chronological basis, followed by topical divisions within. It became obvious early in the study that it would be impossible to take topics like sociocultural conflict, taxation, or the environment, and follow them one by one from 1912 to 1998. The substance of such questions changed considerably over time, and many of them were very much products of their eras (e.g., an alien land law in 1920 and the ending of affirmative action programs in 1998), sometimes with connections to other issues across topical lines. One always loses something with chronological organization, but in this case it turned out to be the best way to present and analyze the development of direct legislation.

The actual chronological divisions that separate Chapters 2 through 6 are arbitrary. There have been few distinct "natural divisions" in the development of direct legislation. Rather, the substance of initiatives and referendums, and the groups that were most active in the politics of direct legislation, shifted gradually with the major problems of the times in California and the nation. What might be a logical break point in one area of political activity, such as taxation, might not be equivalently so in another, such as governmental reform. The divisions that I ultimately decided upon were those that seemed to serve the best analytical purposes, where questions carried over from one time period to the next proved not unduly difficult to handle. The uneven length of the book's chapters reflects the increasing importance of direct legislation in recent decades.

This is a work of history, not one of policy analysis, prediction, or prescription for change, although none of the latter are entirely absent. I seek to explain here the main themes of initiatives and referendums in a series of time-determined periods. I particularly want to focus on the way in which important California and American problems and issues — and group interests — were reflected in battles over direct legislation, and what decisions were made in these matters by the people of the state. At the same time, the development over time of the institution itself will be analyzed: Who used direct legislation? What factors led to success or failure? What were the roles of money, professionalization, and political organization? Whose interests were actually served? How were the nature of California government and California politics affected by the constant use of direct legislation? Finally, I will look at the contemporary status of direct legislation, its strengths and weaknesses as seen by political professionals, outside observers, and the California public.

My focus here is on popular initiatives and referendums — those placed on the ballot by petition. I do sometimes refer to legislative propositions as well, when they are important aspects of a particular problem or trend. But I have not tried to include information about every one of the popular initiatives and referendums that have appeared on California ballots since 1912 — a number that reached 300 in 1998 (plus about 850 propositions placed on the ballot by the legislature for constitutional amendments, bond issues, or other matters). Rather, I have selected individual propositions for inclusion because they fit at least one of several criteria: (1) propositions encompassing major trends and group conflicts in a given time period, such as Prohibition in the 1920s and crime in the 1980s and 1990s; (2) propositions that were individually very important and/or divisive, such as the overthrow of open housing legislation in 1964 and Proposition 13's revolution in taxation in 1978; (3) groups of propositions that appeared repeatedly, relating to important trends in the state or the nation, like public welfare and campaign finance reform; and (4) propositions that revealed the major forces, particularly financial, operating in California politics at a particular time, such as the debate over oil exploration in the 1930s and the incredibly expensive battle in the 1980s and 1990s between insurance companies and trial lawyers.

Even with these criteria, this study ends up referring to quite a large number of initiatives and referendums. This can sometimes be daunting for the reader, particularly because, until the 1982 general election, propositions were numbered separately for each election. Thus, there is a Proposition 10 for the 1936 general election and a Proposition 10 for the 1938 general election—and a Proposition 1 in every election. In 1960, the state started including initiatives and referendums on the June primary ballots as well as the November general election ballots, with the result that there are often two propositions with the same number in the same calendar year. Hopefully, the context will avoid confusion about what is being discussed at any point. As an additional tool, I have included Appendix A, which is a chronological listing of all direct legislation measures—their numbers, dates, type, descriptive names, and whether they passed or failed. This should help the reader refresh his or her memory as propositions are mentioned in the text.

The research material for this study is quite various—from manuscript collections to newspapers, from campaign broadsides to myriad government documents. Inevitably, it includes a good deal of quantitative data—voting returns, census information, campaign spending reports, and public opinion polls. This data is a key part of both the descriptive and analytical material on direct legislation. Thus, the book includes numerous tabular presentations of data, accompanied by discussion of their significance. I believe these tables provide the reader with a clear and convenient summary of some of the study's most important findings.

The statistics have been kept straightforward and simple—only percentages and coefficients of correlation. This is for two reasons. First, all of the data except the public opinion polls was reported at the county level, and these are large and heterogeneous units that permit only gross analysis. And second, I wanted to make the book accessible to a variety of readers, including myself, resisting the ease with which modern computer programs make it possible for any scholar to generate highly sophisticated statistics which he or she neither needs nor, perhaps, understands, and which needlessly alienate readers. Appendix B provides information on the general methodology of the study and an explanation of correlation coefficients for any readers who are not clear on their interpretation.

Since many of my main sources (manuscript collections, government documents, etc.) are cited again and again, I have used abbreviations for them in my notes. The meaning of each of those abbreviations is given at the start of the Notes section following the text.

# 1  Progressivism and the Origins of Direct Legislation

Two factors account for the development and adoption of the initiative and referendum in California. The first of these was the phenomenon of "progressivism," a primarily middle- and upper-class effort to expand the role of government for political and economic reform. Since one of the tenets of Progressivism was the belief that weakening of politicians and strengthening of "the people" would result in better government, the issue of direct legislation became popular in numerous cities and states. In California, where the Progressives took power with the 1910 gubernatorial election of Hiram Johnson, the initiative, referendum, and recall were part of their reform program.

The second factor in the adoption of direct legislation in California was the leadership of John Randolph Haynes. Indeed, neither the origins of the issue, nor its ultimate incorporation in the measures advocated by the Progressives as they sought power, nor its implementation under Governor Hiram Johnson can be understood apart from Haynes, who sometimes seemed about the only person in California who really cared about the initiative, referendum, and recall. He was in many ways a unique personality, who corresponds little to the traditional picture of the Progressive. Whether that factor is idiosyncratic, or quite common in the history of Progressivism, relates directly to the question of the nature of Progressivism.[1]

John Randolph Haynes was born in rural Pennsylvania in 1853, in a middle-class family whose English ancestors had been involved in both political and religious reform. He established a successful medical practice in Philadelphia and was also involved in local politics, opposing the Philadelphia Republican machine. This influenced his lifelong interest in public affairs and his commitment to the political empowerment of the masses.[2] Haynes moved with his family to Los Angeles in the 1880s, where he became extremely wealthy through his medical practice and a variety of investments and other economic interests, at the same time becoming socially prominent and active in public life. Like others of his class, Haynes joined the Chamber of Commerce, served on the boards of several corporations, and was active in numerous social clubs and organizations. Unlike them, however, he was a Christian Socialist and a Fabian. Even at the height of his medical career, Haynes devoted a tremendous amount of time to a wide variety of public issues, including some that were quite unpopular with most middle-class Californians.[3]

Haynes had been influenced by William Dwight Porter Bliss, an Episcopal minister and founder of a Christian Socialist society. Bliss's movement was less ideological than practical, focusing on such reforms as women's suffrage, child labor, graduated taxes, public ownership, and the idea of direct legislation.[4] Bliss's influence on Haynes's thinking provides at least a partial explanation of both the range and the relative radicalism of Haynes's political and social activism. He was deeply involved, for example, in the issue of mine safety, corresponding extensively with government and private agencies, and urging federal regulation.[5] Haynes was not a Social Darwinist, and he argued for the importance of environment rather than heredity in the formation of character; thus he became an advocate for vagrants, African-Americans, child workers, and other submerged groups, and he also had good relations with organized labor. Most of his positions have not generally been seen as "typical" among Progressives.[6]

Haynes shared with other Progressives a suspicion of big business, and particularly of its political power. And he shared his generation's fascination with science and factual information: to prepare an article on sterilization, for example, he wrote 517 letters to asylums, reformatories, and other institutions to obtain data to include in his analysis.[7] Haynes devoted an impressive amount of time to each of these issues and others, but it was politics and government that became the main focus of his reform interests between about 1895 and World War I. Haynes's interest encompassed several aspects of political and governmental reform, including the short ballot, political corruption, and the direct primary. But, above all else, he focused on direct democracy, which became an article of faith as well as efficiency:

Let me confess it gentlemen, democracy is a part of my religion. . . . We find that happiness, enlightment [sic] and propserty [sic] among the people increase in precisely the same ratio as do their power, influence, and participation in government. Responsibility tends to develop the best that is in us.[8]

But if his commitment was moral, his approach was scientific. He studied the practice of direct democracy everywhere it existed, constantly, beginning in the mid-1890s, keeping copious clippings and notes, corresponding widely, and becoming a nationally recognized expert on the initiative, referendum, and recall.[9]

It is important to note in this context that Haynes, despite the great vari-

ety of his reform interests, was never a leading figure in statewide Progressivism, although he was a powerful presence locally. He supported many of the
Progressives' issues, contributed a good deal of money to them, and wrote to
Progressives, as to others, in seeking to implement direct democracy. But he
remained an outside figure, rarely spoken of by regional and statewide Progressive leaders, and he was clearly not important in their planning and
politics.[10] He appears never to have actually joined the Lincoln–Roosevelt
Republican League, the heart of California Progressivism, perhaps because
it was Republican and he never considered himself one, despite supporting
almost all of the Republican Progressives.[11]

It is also significant that none of the other leading Los Angeles Progressives, such as Meyer Lissner, E. T. Earl, Marshall Stimson, or Edward A.
Dickson ever evinced much interest in direct democracy. This was equally
true in northern California, where only Milton T. U'Ren (who was secretary-
treasurer of Haynes's Direct Legislation League) was really involved. Hiram
Johnson, for example, was still reputedly unclear on the operation of the
initiative, referendum, and recall when he ran for governor in 1910.[12]

Like many other Progressive causes, direct democracy was first introduced at the city level and later became statewide in focus. The original
political impetus came from the Populists, who had raised that issue, among
others, locally and nationally. As early efforts at Los Angeles political reform
proved unsuccessful, the time became ripe for an effort at structural reform
in the mid-1890s.[13] The date of the actual founding of the Direct Legislation
League is unclear, but it seems to have begun operation in 1898.[14] It was
in 1898 that the local chapter of Bliss's Union Reform League, of which
Haynes would become president, proposed the initiative, referendum, and
recall to the city's Board of Freeholders, which had been created for the
purpose of preparing a new city charter. The Board did support a watered-
down proposal without the recall in its proposed charter, but the advocates
of direct democracy opposed the proposal because of this weakness, and it
failed to win voter approval. Haynes then became a candidate in the 1900
Board of Freeholders election, vowing to develop a new charter that included real direct democracy. He won the support of both major parties and
received more votes than any other candidate. But the state Supreme Court
invalidated the Board of Freeholders as an institution, temporarily halting
the development of the issue.[15] California voters, however, did approve a
constitutional amendment in 1902 that permitted home rule cities to amend
their charters by initiative local action, and this was a key to implementation
of local direct democracy.[16]

When the city council refused to support charter amendments for direct
democracy, Haynes invited a group of civic leaders to a dinner in 1902,

soliciting support for a new nonpartisan "Committee on Charter Amendments." From this base, Haynes worked for additional endorsements, from the Municipal League, local labor unions, even the mighty Southern Pacific Railroad and the Los Angeles Times (which would change its position soon after). Such broad-based support persuaded the city council to act, and the initiative, referendum, and recall were proposed as charter amendments in 1902. In the campaign, the recall was the most controversial, but all three passed, making Los Angeles the first city in the United States to so act.[17] Los Angeles reformers, including Haynes and organized labor, made it also the first city to actually recall a public official — Councilman J. P. Davenport in 1904; they then mounted a recall effort in 1909 against Mayor Arthur C. Harper, who resigned before the election.[18]

A variety of Los Angeles interest groups also made quick use of the initiative and referendum. The referendum was used twice in 1909 by reform groups, on the sale of street railroad franchises and on increased telephone rates. The initiative was first used in 1904 or 1905 for similar measures, and again in 1906 by the Anti-Saloon League. Other California cities rapidly followed Los Angeles's lead: twenty-one of them had modified their charters to permit the initiative and referendum by 1910. In almost all cases, direct democracy was part of a package of political reforms, generally including the direct primary and nonpartisan local elections.[19] The inclusion of numerous issues expanded the proposals' bases of support, which would be the case, also, at the state level.

Building on the momentum of Los Angeles's success, Haynes acted immediately to move consideration of direct democracy to the state level. And until California Progressives were well organized in 1907 under the Lincoln–Roosevelt Republican League, it was Haynes and the Direct Legislation League that kept the issue alive. He first focused on the new legislature elected in 1902, that would meet in 1903, hoping for constitutional amendments to institute direct democracy. The Direct Legislation League circulated petitions statewide, seeking 100,000 signatures before the legislature met. During the campaign, Haynes wrote directly to every legislative candidate, asking for commitments on the issue. And he arranged for similar letters to be sent to them from the California State Federation of Labor and from individual unions as well as from agricultural groups. He was also able to boast of official endorsements by both the Democratic and Republican parties.[20]

Haynes's campaign intensified after the election. He appeared at a meeting of all newly elected state senators and assemblymen from south of the Tehachapis, urging full implementation of direct democracy at all levels of government. It was, he said, a "great wave" sweeping the United States. As with his operations in Los Angeles, he sought as broad a backing as possible, in this case with representatives from the Municipal League, from organized labor, and from organized farmers. There seemed to be general agreement among the neophyte legislators that the process was beneficial at the city and county level, but some feared that, statewide, it could undercut the powers of the legislature.[21]

The Direct Legislation League tried to tap every possible source of support, staying away from any issues that might be divisive. A concerted approach was made to religious leaders, resulting in distribution of a broadside signed by Congregational, Methodist, Lutheran, Presbyterian, Baptist, African Methodist, Episcopal, and other leaders. Similar efforts were made with the state Socialist Party, the state Prohibition Committee, and a wide variety of nonpolitical organizations.[22]

Once the legislature met, Haynes was personally financing a lobbyist for the direct democracy propositions, P. B. Preble of the Alameda County Federated Trades Council. And he personally appeared in February 1903 with his signed petitions and with resolutions from a wide variety of groups, primarily farmers' clubs and labor.[23] The legislative debate was not extensive, revolving primarily around the number of signatures to be required to put a measure on the ballot. But not a lot of legislators shared Haynes's enthusiasm for direct democracy; it was not a front burner issue. Interestingly, Walter F. Parker, the Southern Pacific's man in Sacramento, was on the floor of the Assembly when it voted on the measure and did not oppose it, perhaps because the railroad had not yet developed a policy on the issue. It passed in the Assembly, but lost by one vote (14–13) in the senate.[24]

The initiative, referendum, and recall continued to be introduced into subsequent sessions of the legislature, in 1905, 1907, and 1909, but with no effect. It appears that the Southern Pacific decisively turned against it, responding to the fact that the successful implementation of direct democracy in cities across the state was trumpeted by its proponents as a way to overthrow the railroad's influence. This was an important factor in legislators' actions, since the Southern Pacific did have the power to limit their advancement in the legislature.[25]

Haynes and U'Ren were nonetheless able to maintain the coalition of groups behind direct democracy and even to broaden it. Like many devotees to a cause, Haynes cared little where the support came from. He even developed a strong, albeit more or less secret association with the Anti-Saloon League, and ministers from the League worked as his assistants for a while.[26] At the same time, women's suffrage groups, socialists, the unions, and others continued to be solicited. Money, however, was harder to come by than endorsements, perhaps because to most supporters this was only one of the causes they were interested in. U'Ren constantly complained of the need for funds, and Haynes appears to have personally provided much of the financing.[27]

The key to any possible success was in broadening the basis of support. And that became possible with the inclusion of the initiative, referendum, and recall in the body of proposals advocated by the organized California Progressives.

The Lincoln–Roosevelt Republican League *was* the Progressive movement in California politics, and as such was a key vehicle for making statewide direct democracy happen. It was founded in 1907 by Chester Rowell and Edward A. Dickson, who met in Sacramento when covering the legislature for their respective newspapers, the *Fresno Republican* and the *Los Angeles Express*. Both men were offended by the incapacity and corruption of the legislature, which, they were sure, was due to the power of the "machine," meaning the Southern Pacific.[28] Two meetings, one in Los Angeles in May, and a second in Oakland in August, got the organization started.

The early meetings were agreed only on the problem of the Southern Pacific. Little thought had been given by the organizers to the development of a complete program, although some who attended were devoted to various issues. Like any political group, the Progressives, if they were to succeed, had to lead in the direction the voters wanted to go, which created an opportunity for advocates of proposals like direct democracy. Haynes worked every meeting, in person when possible, urging the initiative, referendum, and recall; others advocated the statewide primary, workmen's compensation, women's suffrage, outlawing racetrack gambling, and other issues. The result was more or less perfunctory approval of most of these measures, with direct democracy being somewhat controversial (Rowell would long be suspicious of the idea); but the real agreement was to focus on the problem of the Southern Pacific machine.[29]

The Southern Pacific did become more active in the legislature and in politics generally, fearing the possible ramifications of these new proposals. Walter Parker of the Southern Pacific told Haynes at the time that direct democracy was dangerous to the railroad's interests. The Southern Pacific also worked to undermine the effort in the legislature to get a direct primary law, which was presented by the reformers as the necessary first step for the implementation of other changes.[30]

As these issues became increasingly controversial, the breakup of the Republican Party progressed, with almost all the reform impetus becoming focused in the Lincoln–Roosevelt Republican League. The League grew rapidly, as Dickson, Rowell, and Meyer Lissner, among others, developed a statewide organization, and strived, with considerable success, to persuade potential Republican candidates that League support was crucial to their victory. The general popularity of reform issues, moving up from the cities, along with effective leadership, showed results: by the 1908 Republican state convention, the League was supported by 40 percent of the delegates.[31]

The inclusion of direct democracy among League issues met with some specific objections and opponents. Chester Rowell felt that the initiative and referendum had been misused at the local level, and that this would be even more the case at the state level; this was, he said, "the worst possible way" to deal with complex questions. Harris Weinstock, an important figure in California progressivism, had prepared an extensive study of the issue for the Commonwealth Club in 1905. While personally persuaded of its value in making "democracy possible on the largest scale," he recognized some real dangers as well. Chief among these was that of giving too much power to radicals, such as socialists, populists, or Prohibitionists. The initiative, particularly, could "promote radical legislation." Dickson, too, expressed fear of the same groups becoming too influential, and even more concern was expressed about the recall, especially the recall of judges.[32]

Debate on the issues among Progressives was not great, however. The Lincoln–Roosevelt League needed groups like the Direct Legislation League and people like Haynes and U'Ren if it had any hope of succeeding. The popular followings that such organizations and individuals had, and the money they could provide, were key sources of League strength. And the Direct Legislation League was never reluctant about flexing its muscle to achieve its own aims.[33]

By the 1909 session of the state legislature, the anti–Southern Pacific forces probably made up a majority of the representatives of both parties. They had some legislative successes, such as removing the option of a straight party choice from the ballot, and, especially, passing a direct primary bill for all statewide offices. But despite bipartisan support, efforts for legislation on more divisive issues like railroad regulation and direct democracy were unsuccessful. The Southern Pacific was still powerful, but its failure to halt the direct primary bill provided the Lincoln–Roosevelt Republican League with one of the tools it needed to take over the Republican Party in the 1910 primary.[34]

The Direct Legislation League saw 1910 as the most promising year yet for implementation of its program. Once again it sought to get commitments from candidates of both major parties in the August primary and again in the November general election. Likewise, it solicited all of its traditional allies, trying, as one supporter put it, "to line up the unions, the improvement clubs, church and temperance folds (*quietly*) and all the progressive forces."[35] The League's greatest success, perhaps, came when both parties adopted planks including the initiative, referendum, and recall.[36]

Hiram Johnson, in his 1910 campaign for the gubernatorial nomination and election, followed the Lincoln–Roosevelt tradition of speaking mainly in generalities, focusing on "a contest for freedom . . . from William F.

Herrin and the Southern Pacific Company, who have debauched, polluted and corrupted our state." He had assured Haynes of his support for direct democracy early on, and did refer to it in speeches where he listed what the Progressives planned to do once in power. But his own focus was on tactics and the Southern Pacific, trying to offend as few potential supporters as possible by not overemphasizing any issues that might be divisive.[37]

Johnson's victory in the 1910 elections was not overwhelming: he won the Republican primary with 47 percent of the vote, and the general election with 46 percent. But it was a historically high plurality, and he did carry 35 of the 58 counties. More important, Progressives of both parties did well, while conservatives did badly. For example, of the eleven state senate members up for reelection who had opposed direct election of U.S. senators, four were defeated in the primaries, two were defeated in the general election, and four did not run. Those who had opposed railroad regulation did no better. And results in assembly contests were similar. Progressivism was in control.[38]

The Progressive Republicans did organize both houses of the new 1911 legislature, with a whole raft of proposals put on the table but no certainty that they would prevail. It was possible that the conservatives — including Republicans and Democrats who had nominally endorsed direct legislation during the campaign — and the Southern Pacific still had majorities on individual issues. Lissner, as party chairman and key Johnson adviser, promoted the whole list of Progressive proposals, including direct legislation, and Dickson advised the new governor that direct legislation was probably the most important of the proposed reforms.[39]

Johnson endorsed the entire Progressive agenda, with the exception of women's suffrage, in his inaugural address.[40] This included the statement that "the first step in our design to preserve and perpetuate popular government shall be the adoption of the initiative, the referendum, and the recall." But in the first few months of his administration, while the legislature was preparing what finally emerged as twenty-three constitutional amendments, the governor spent most of his time on organizational matters. In issue terms, he seemed most interested in the railroad commission plan, which directly confronted the Southern Pacific, and in an alien land law, as a step to Asiatic exclusion, which he, like most California Progressives, favored.[41]

One key problem for the governor, and the Progressive leadership, was the fact that so many individuals and groups had pet measures that they tried to put ahead of everything else. Johnson complained about this: Fremont Older pushing the eight-hour day, Harris Weinstock employer's liability, Lieutenant Governor A. J. Wallace local option, and so on. But by June he did turn his attention to direct democracy, strongly supporting the initiative, referendum, and recall, along with the other proposed amend-

TABLE 1.1   Correlations of Vote in 1910–1911 California Elections

| | Yes on initiative and referendum | Yes on recall | Yes on railroad commission | Yes on women's suffrage | Yes on workmen's compensation | For Johnson in 1910 primary | For Johnson in 1910 general election |
|---|---|---|---|---|---|---|---|
| Yes on initiative and referendum | 1.000 | | | | | | |
| Yes on recall | .945 | 1.000 | | | | | |
| Yes on railroad commission | .358 | .369 | 1.000 | | | | |
| Yes on women's suffrage | .245 | .321 | −.360 | 1.000 | | | |
| Yes on workmen's compensation | .060 | .087 | .134 | −.039 | 1.000 | | |
| For Johnson in 1910 primary | −.257 | −.324 | −.199 | .120 | −.130 | 1.000 | |
| For Johnson in 1910 general election | −.170 | −.150 | .242 | −.557 | .051 | −.062 | 1.000 |

NOTE: Pearson product moment correlations, based on percentage voting Yes on the candidate or measure, with data aggregated by county and weighted by county population. For clarity, only one side of table is shown, since both sides are identical.

ments, and traveling the state to speak for them once they had been adopted by the legislature.[42]

In the legislature itself, given the number of measures, quite a few of which proposed significant changes, voting often revolved around one's general attitude toward Progressive reform. There were, however, some differences in the constituencies of the various measures. And there was considerably more debate over the recall than on the initiative and referendum. To foes of reform, including the Southern Pacific, the recall seemed particularly threatening. Even some proponents of other reforms, including the initiative and referendum, feared that the recall was not a good idea, and many shared the common view that recall of judges was particularly pernicious. But Haynes and the Direct Legislation League continued to insist on keeping the three measures together, and Lissner and Johnson, while realizing the danger involved, remained steadfast. Their combined forces did prevail: the initiative and referendum amendment passed the Assembly 71–0 and the Senate 35–1; the recall amendment passed 70–10 and 36–4.[43]

The proposed constitutional amendments, including direct democracy, women's suffrage, railroad regulation, and workmen's compensation constituted a fundamental change in California government and politics. Devotees of each issue worked hard to secure its passage in the October 1911 special election, and this was not least the case in terms of advocates of direct democracy. U'Ren maintained contact with Lissner, reminding him that the Southern Pacific was by no means dead and that it was using recall of the judiciary as a stalking horse for its efforts to kill both direct legislation amendments. And the Direct Legislation League continued to work its traditional sources of support, including both major parties and the Socialists (who had done well in the 1910 election).[44]

Their worries, in fact, were excessive: 22 of the proposed 23 amendments passed, and quite easily, except for women's suffrage which just squeaked through. The direct democracy measures had the highest rate of approval: 76 percent for the initiative and referendum, and 77 percent for the recall (obviously the public did not share the widely voiced fears about the latter). Workmen's Compensation received 69 percent of the vote, a Railroad Commission 64 percent, and Women's Suffrage 51 percent (women's suffrage also drew the largest number of votes cast, followed by the two direct democracy measures).

There are some interesting aspects to this vote, however, as suggested in Table 1.1, which provides coefficients of correlation for voting data. There are few strong relationships to be seen in this county-level data between votes for the various reform measures; they are much weaker than one might anticipate from the nature of the campaign, as well as from the contempo-

rary and historical literature on progressivism. Only the initiative/referen-
dum and the recall votes are strongly related to one another, demonstrating
that the voting public saw the three popular democracy devices as integral
parts of one empowering whole. Overall, the table provides potent support
to the idea that each of the Progressive measures had its own constituency.
Even if we remove women's suffrage from consideration, since it had dis-
tinctly cultural characteristics, the relationships between the direct legislation amendments and those for the railroad commission, and especially that
for workmen's compensation, are weak. Among the voters, as among the
Progressives themselves, broad-based support of the whole gamut of reform
issues was far from general.

Even more intriguing is the lack of any significance in the relationship
between Hiram Johnson's vote for governor in the 1910 primary and general elections, and the Progressive measures he had campaigned for a year
later. Moreover, for those amendments whose vote does have some modest
relationship with voting for Johnson (the direct legislation measures and
women's suffrage), that relationship is negative rather than positive: the
more likely one was to vote for the reform, the less likely he or she was to
vote for Hiram Johnson. These were issues whose time had come, it seems.
And it also seems that the Direct Legislation League (and, perhaps, other
groups behind the other measures) had in fact done a good job of building
multipartisan and nonpartisan organizational support for their measures.
The Lincoln–Roosevelt League, and the Progressive Republicans who won
control of the state in 1910, appear to have been less influential, or perhaps
just less generally important, than one has been led to think, which may also
go a long way toward explaining why they maintained power for such a
short period of time.[45] To some degree, they were supporting issues that had
broad general support and individual constituencies that preceded, or existed apart from, progressivism.[46]

Once established, the initiative and referendum were quickly used by
Californians. For example, six popular measures (plus two legislative ones)
qualified for the 1912 ballot: three referendums, two initiative constitutional amendments, and one initiative statute. Four of them dealt with governmental matters, one with horseracing, and one with taxation. The last,
Proposition 8, comprised the first appearance of the Single Tax in California, an idea that would come back again and again over the next twenty
years, always with broad opposition from both business and Progressive
groups, and always unsuccessful.[47]

All three referendums were "rejected," but just what that meant to California voters is not entirely clear, since the language of referendums and the
meaning of a Yes or No vote were not easy to understand. A Yes vote on a

referendum meant a vote in favor of the statute as passed by the legislature, whereas a No vote meant a vote to revoke that statute; in effect, then, a vote Yes meant a vote against the aim of the referendum. Just how many voters cast their ballots in a manner opposite their intentions is impossible to know. Only with time did the official voter pamphlets begin to explain more clearly what each voting choice represented.[48] All three 1912 referendums had No majorities and were classified by the Secretary of State as "Defeated," which in fact meant that the referendum's sponsors were successful in repealing the legislation. It was enough to confuse anyone.[49]

Some of the potential, and also the problems, of direct legislation became clear in 1914, when there were 48 propositions on the ballot, of which 21 were voter-proposed and 27 came from the legislature. There was also a controversial gubernatorial contest (the reelection of Hiram Johnson as a Progressive rather than Republican candidate), plus congressional, assembly, and other candidate contests. The voter had a lot of work to do.

In total, between 1912 and 1918, there were 41 citizen-initiated measures, plus an additional 58 put on the ballot by the legislature. It is important to be aware of the large number of legislature-sponsored propositions in order to get an idea of the overall number of questions that voters had to try to deal with. Of the 41 popular propositions, 11 were referendums, 15 were statutes (including bond acts), and 15 were constitutional amendments. From the start, proposition sponsors often sought to enact their interests as initiative constitutional amendments rather than statutes because constitutional amendments were more difficult to undo, even though they required more signatures to get on the ballot. Of the initiative measures, only 10 of 31 were successful; 7 of the 10 referendums were "defeated," which meant in fact that they were successful in revoking legislation.

Table 1.2 tries to distribute these measures by election year and subject. The subject categories are inevitably somewhat arbitrary, since so many specific topics were involved and some propositions had ramifications in more than one category. The table does show that many different issues and interests were involved. From the start, a diverse body of individuals and groups had concluded that this new political mechanism could be used to implement their own special interests. Significantly, voter interest and participation were greater on popular propositions than on legislative ones, a characteristic that would prevail throughout the history of direct legislation. Californians were also more likely to vote on initiatives than on referendums, perhaps because they understood them better.

Varying levels of voter participation from one subject area to another are even more significant. Measures with some social and cultural characteristics tended to draw the largest numbers of voters, another phenomenon that would persist in direct legislation voting to the present day. Just as women's

TABLE 1.2    Subjects of Direct Legislation, 1912–1918

| Election | Sociocultural | Government | Voting, direct legislation | Business, economics, taxation |
|---|---|---|---|---|
| 1912 | 1 | 4 | 0 | 1 |
| 1914 | 6 | 4 | 2 | 9 |
| 1915 | 0 | 0 | 2 | 0 |
| 1916 | 2 | 1 | 1 | 1 |
| 1918 | 2 | 0 | 0 | 5 |

suffrage had the highest voter participation in 1911, two of the three Prohibition initiatives—an eight-hour law, red-light abatement, and a mandatory day of rest—had unusually high voter participation in 1914.[50] Two more Prohibition measures had the highest voter participations in 1916, and exactly the same was true in 1918.

In 1912, for another example, 71 percent of voters did vote on the antihorseracing measure, while only about 55 percent voted on three referendums that related to government organization. In 1914, 91 percent of voters had checked their ballots on the extreme Prohibition measure (Prop. 2), 82 percent voted on the anti-saloon measure, 88 percent voted on the eight-hour law, and 77 percent voted on prize fights and on the anti-prostitution referendum. Voter participation on all the other measures was notably lower. Likewise, in 1916, over 90 percent of those who came to the polls voted on that year's Prohibition measures, whereas only 64 percent voted on the referendum that defeated the legislature's open primary law, a very controversial Progressive issue.[51]

Table 1.3 introduces another important factor associated with sociocultural issues and propositions: voter agreement and ideological consistency on many of these issues was both strong and persistent over time. The agreement over the 1914–1918 period relative to the issue of liquor regulation, particularly total Prohibition, is especially striking. Relationships among the various Prohibition measures are extraordinarily strong, including the negative relationship between pro-Prohibition measures and Proposition 47 in 1914, which sought to ban further elections on the subject of liquor control altogether. The smaller but still significant negative relationship with Proposition 1 in 1918 reflected the fact that it was an anti-saloon measure, which was less clearly defined than the more basic issue of total Prohibition.

Two other issues were strongly associated with voting on Prohibition, although at a somewhat reduced level: the successful 1914 effort to maintain a statute outlawing prostitution, and the initiative statute for an eight-hour day. Their relationship to one another was very strong, and overall voting fit into the above pattern on liquor as well. Thus, the origins of the major cultural conflicts of the 1920s were quite clear in the period through World War I. It was already possible to predict the broad effects that the Ku Klux Klan, immigration restriction, nativism, Prohibition, and other socio-cultural conflicts would have on American life and politics.

This suggests a slightly closer look at a few of these issues, particularly the regulation of alcohol. Prohibition groups and the issue of Prohibition had already played a role in the early development of direct legislation, with Haynes trying to use them for his purposes, and the Prohibitionists trying to use the Direct Legislation League for theirs. That continued in the 1914 election, when both Prohibition and anti-prostitution groups solicited Haynes for Direct Legislation League support.[52] On the other side, according to journalist Franklin Hichborn, the liquor interests worked with anti-direct legislation interests to put Proposition 47 on the 1914 ballot, an initiative constitutional amendment that would forbid any initiative measures on statewide Prohibition for eight years.[53] The voters turned down both Proposition 47 and the Dry's Proposition 2.

The anti-liquor people were well organized, but were divided into subgroups that had different specific aims, which tended to weaken the movement overall. For example, in 1916, Proposition 1 mandated a full Prohibition law for California, while Proposition 2 forbade liquor only in public places. Many Prohibition groups and leaders opposed Proposition 2, fearing it would undercut their own measure.[54] Both measures were opposed in the ballot pamphlet by the California Associated Raisin Company, representing grape growers, and both lost. The anti-Prohibition forces were quite well organized and did not lack for funding. They stressed the adverse effect liquor control would have on California's economy, and their arguments were echoed daily during the campaign by the pro-business press.[55]

Ballot proposals in 1918 virtually duplicated those of 1916: one anti-saloon proposition and another for full state Prohibition. Both sides worked hard and spent a lot of money, and once again the anti-liquor measures drew the largest number of voters. The results were two more losses for the Prohibitionists.[56] One measure of the Prohibitionists' difficulty was that in both 1916 and 1918 the full Prohibition measures received a slightly smaller vote percentage than the less drastic ones. But the issue was certainly not about to die.

The single tax issue also generated much interest, and, like the question of Prohibition, it would survive failure in these early years and return

TABLE 1.3 Relationships Among Sociocultural Propositions, 1914–1918

| Election and proposition | 1914: Prop. 2 Prohibition | 1914: Prop. 3 8-hour law | 1914: Prop. 4 Prostitution | 1914: Prop. 20 Prize fights | 1914: Prop. 45 Day of rest |
|---|---|---|---|---|---|
| 1914: Prop. 2 Prohibition | 1.000 | | | | |
| 1914: Prop. 3 8-hour law | −.588 | 1.000 | | | |
| 1914: Prop. 4 Prostitution | .883 | −.425 | 1.000 | | |
| 1914: Prop. 20 Prize fights | .833 | −.447 | .825 | 1.000 | |
| 1914: Prop. 45 Day of rest | −.387 | .844 | −1.60 | −.201 | 1.000 |
| 1914: Prop. 47 Anti-prohibition | −.945 | .673 | −.761 | −.729 | .521 |
| 1916: Prop. 1 Prohibition | .980 | −.549 | .877 | .839 | −.360 |
| 1916: Prop. 2 Prohibition | .971 | −.576 | .883 | .860 | −.379 |
| 1918: Prop. 1 Anti-saloon | −.440 | .183 | −.378 | −.301 | .152 |
| 1918: Prop. 22 Prohibition | .964 | −.526 | .892 | .848 | −.344 |

NOTE: Pearson product moment correlations, based on percentage voting Yes on the measure, with data aggregated by county and weighted by county population. For clarity, only one side of table is shown, since the two sides are identical.

| 1914: Prop. 47 Anti-prohibition | 1916: Prop. 1 Prohibition | 1916: Prop. 2 Prohibition | 1918: Prop. 1 Anti-saloon | 1918: Prop. 22 Prohibition |
|---|---|---|---|---|
| 1.000 | | | | |
| −.916 | 1.000 | | | |
| −.916 | .990 | 1.000 | | |
| .326 | −.452 | −.366 | 1.000 | |
| −.883 | .988 | .981 | −.462 | 1.000 |

repeatedly. The vaguely worded Proposition 8 in 1912 was criticized as a disingenuous effort to introduce the single tax idea; Proposition 5 in 1916 and Proposition 19 in 1918 were straightforward pleas to put a land-taxation-only policy into the state constitution. Business opposition to these measures was extreme, with talk of large-scale layoffs and declining state revenues that would impoverish government and be particularly devastating to local governments.[57]

While all three propositions were defeated decisively, opponents were so fearful of the single tax that, like Prohibition opponents, they advocated changes in the initiative process to try to impede further propositions on the measure. Calling themselves the People's Anti-Single Tax League, they worked from 1917 on to kill the single tax by making it harder to get it on the ballot. They finally created Proposition 4 of 1920, which proposed a constitutional amendment to raise from 8 percent to 25 percent the number of signatures required to qualify any taxation initiative; the proponents' argument in the *California Ballot Pamphlet* of that year specifically acknowledged that it would "curb the activities of single tax advocates." This was not, single tax opponents learned, a viable way to defeat the single tax because California voters, then as later, were firmly opposed to any changes in direct legislation policy, and the measure lost decisively.[58]

Conservative groups, especially business groups, had generally opposed adoption of the initiative and referendum, but they were among the first to use them, primarily to undo some of the Progressive legislation of Hiram Johnson's first term. Conservatives were, for example, behind two referendums in 1914 that tried to revoke 1913 statutes that regulated investment companies and established a state water commission (Propositions 5 and 6).[59] They failed in both cases.

Conservatives focused most of their political direct legislation against Johnson administration laws to weaken the political parties; in this they had broad support from a variety of groups, including leaders of both parties. In 1913 the legislature, under Progressive control, had passed two laws. The so-called "Direct Primary" bill regulated primaries and made all but the highest offices nonpartisan. The companion "Form of Ballot" law removed party designations from the ballot. This legislation was quite consistent with general Progressive ideas about the malevolent effects of political parties on their conception of democracy. And both laws were subject to referendum in a special election in October 1915.

The campaign against the laws was quite vigorous. It included national as well as state party leaders, such as Champ Clark of Missouri, U.S. Senator from California James Phelan, Republican congressman Frank P. Woods, and potential Republican presidential candidate Myron T. Herrick of Ohio.[60] Also, there was a joint conference of representatives of the Republican, Democratic, Socialist, and Prohibition parties early in October that supported the referendum. Business opposition to the laws was also intense.[61] The conservative *Los Angeles Times* conducted a long, vitriolic campaign, both on the ill-effects of the legislation, and even more, as part of its general bitterness against Johnson and the Progressive takeover of the Republican Party.[62]

The referendums were "defeated," which means that they won, invalidating the two statutes. In each case, 58 percent of those voting on the measures voted to revoke the statutes, but turnout for this special election was extremely low in general, less than one-third of that in the 1914 off-year election. Low turnout would continue to be a characteristic of special elections.

Governor Johnson immediately called a special session of the legislature to enact a somewhat different direct primary law, creating, in effect, an open primary, where voters could declare their party membership each time they went to the polls. The opposition mounted another referendum, Proposition 4 on the 1916 ballot, to invalidate the new law. The campaign was similar to that of 1915, but somewhat less intense because more attention was being focused on the presidential campaign and Governor Johnson's race for the U.S. Senate.[63] Once again the legislation was invalidated, this time with 52 percent of those voting on the measure opting to revoke it. But voting on the measure was again relatively low: 69 percent of those voting in this election did vote on Proposition 4, compared to the almost 100 percent who voted on the two Prohibition initiatives on the same ballot. Political and governmental issues, regardless of who was supporting or opposing them, just did not elicit the same level of response as sociocultural ones.

The entire direct democracy system was itself a significant issue during this period. In anticipation of much more recent times, when virtually every initiative is subject to testing in the courts, Pacific States Telephone and Telegraph in 1912 had challenged an Oregon initiative law as a violation of the Fourth Amendment's guarantee of "a republican form of government." The suit finally found its way to the U.S. Supreme Court, which upheld the law on the basis that it was a purely political question, not subject to federal political interference.[64]

Conservative newspapers like the *Los Angeles Times* and the *San Francisco Chronicle* editorialized constantly about the evils of the system. The *Times*, as early as 1912, argued that it was costing too much, and continued for some years to allege other evils, finally prompting Haynes to write publisher Harry Chandler that it would be "a sound and wise business policy to exercise scrupulous care in telling the truth, even about government measures or ideals of which you disapprove."[65] The *Chronicle*, in 1917, launched a vigorous campaign, in the name of reform, on "the abuses of the initiative and recall," not the least of which was the use of paid signature gatherers — thus raising for one of the first times an issue that would be permanently associated with the evils of direct legislation. The *Chronicle* and others also applauded the suggestion that there should be a constitutional amendment permitting a 10 percent counter-petition to keep a proposition that had been approved by the standard 8 percent of signatures off the ballot. Similarly, there were efforts to prohibit initiatives for taxation measures.[66] Such proposals would continue well into the 1920s.

There were some legitimate reform ideas as well, including the question of paid signature gatherers. Republicans wanted changes that would permit more contributions and expenditures, but also more precise reporting of the sources of money for and against each measure. And even strong defenders of direct legislation noted as early as 1914 that there was a problem with the forging of names on petitions.[67]

Not surprisingly, John R. Haynes was the main watchdog protecting his legislative children. When Senator W. F. Chandler proposed a bill to change the recall system, permitting the recall to take place but not the vote for a replacement at the same time, Haynes took immediate action. It was antidemocratic, he said, and would divide the progressive forces in California.[68] Haynes recognized that there were some abuses, particularly forgeries of signatures and some misrepresentation by petition circulators, as well as use of the mechanism by "selfish and corrupt interests." But he argued that only minor changes were needed. He opposed the banning of paid circulators, as well as various other proposals, and concluded, "I would leave the initiative, referendum, and recall provisions . . . as they are."[69] He would continue this defense well into the next decade.

## On Progressivism

Studying the origins and development of direct democracy in California has perforce involved considerable attention to the broader phenomenon of California Progressivism. The two seemed sometimes aligned, or even merged, and at other times quite separate from one another. This relationship provides some insights into the long-standing disagreements among historians about several interrelated questions: What was the nature of Progressivism, and of reform in the early twentieth century? Did some generally definable thing called Progressivism really exist? Who were the people called "Progressives," or "reformers," and whom did they actually represent?[70] And, one can add, what does this chapter contribute to the debate? Hopefully, such an inquiry provides additional insight, as well, into the ideas and forces behind the coming of direct legislation.

The fact that individual issues tended to have their own constituencies, and that general agreement was difficult to achieve, deserves restatement here. The Direct Legislation League constantly marched to its own drummer, often to the dismay of other Progressives. In the campaign for approval of the proposed amendments, for example, the League brought in Senator Moses Clapp of Minnesota to speak in favor of the two direct legislation amendments, something that Chester Rowell found disruptive: "It will do nothing, except incidentally, for any other amendment." The League, he said, was just not cooperating.[71] Similarly, Lissner had argued that there was no need for a separate short ballot organization, and he resigned from the League of Justice in Los Angeles, arguing that "there is a danger in a multiplicity of organizations."[72] This was not simply an organizational problem, but one of divergent interests as well. The Direct Primary League and the Direct Legislation League, for example, while logically parallel in focus, had only one common member on their executive or advisory committees; and Haynes, despite the variety of his interests, never devoted real effort to the former. Nor did all the direct primary people favor direct election of senators.[73]

Certain other issues of the day also intruded, not least those related to labor and radicalism. The Progressive period in California was also a time of intense labor and socialist activity, both organizationally and politically, highlighted in the former case by the 1910 bombing of the *Los Angeles Times*, and in the latter by the near-victory of socialist Job Harriman in the 1911 Los Angeles mayoral election.

Haynes was basically sympathetic toward the working class and not dismayed by radicalism. And the Direct Legislation League was probably closer to organized labor than to any other interest group. Without labor's support, in fact, it is not likely that the League would have been so influential for such a long period of time.[74] There were other California Progressives who had some sympathy for organized labor, primarily those who were interested in social issues. Their number included E. T. Earl, Francis Heney, Fremont Older, Hichborn, and Weinstock. But almost none shared Haynes's sympathy for socialism.[75]

Most Progressives were either noncommittal on labor (Lissner argued that "unionism is [not] an issue in the movement undertaken by the Lincoln–Roosevelt Republican League") or downright hostile. The latter was particularly true in the southern part of the state. And even in the north, where leaders like Johnson recognized the importance of labor's support for Progressive political success, an effort was made to keep organized labor at arm's length.[76] Given the variety of positions among Progressives on this issue, it was hard to reach consensus.

Something similar existed with the issues of temperance and Prohibition. Haynes, as seen above, made good use of an alliance with various temperance groups in promoting direct democracy, but he did so secretly, for fear of alienating important anti-temperance supporters. Lincoln–Roosevelt Republican League activists worried about the Prohibitionists becoming too powerful, in much the same way as they regarded organized labor. This was well seen in 1910, when Johnson's running mate was A. J. Wallace, a Dry, which caused other Progressive leaders no end of concern. It was a divisive issue and one for which no easy solution was available.[77] Other issues of "moral" content, such as red-light abatement and prize-fight regulation, while considerably less important, had similar effects.

Racial issues, on the other hand, were not divisive, since the Progressives tended to share the popular views of the time. Only Hichborn, of all the Progressives, was sympathetic to Asians; the rest uniformly supported Asiatic exclusion and an alien land law, as did both major parties. The Progressives were not very interested in problems associated with European immigration or African-Americans, probably because California was so far removed from the centers of their settlement. When labor or radicals were castigated, it tended to be for their positions, not their ethnicity or religion. And the *Los Angeles Times*'s efforts to encourage anti-Semitism seemed to fall upon deaf ears so far as the Progressives were concerned: Lissner, the *Times*'s target, was the organizational head of their movement, and Weinstock was seriously considered for governor in 1910 before Johnson agreed to run.[78]

With very few exceptions (Haynes being the most notable), the California Progressives were definitely Republican; it was the Lincoln–Roosevelt *Republican* League. Support by the Democrats for reform measures in the legislature was certainly welcome, but no effort was made to minimize partisanship. Progressives were, as Rowell noted, determined "to reform the Republican party, even if we had to smash it in the process." They might split over the choice of La Follette or Roosevelt as national leader in 1912, but they simply assumed that reform was innately within Republicanism, and that they were quite properly focused in that party.[79] This, at least, did not add to the centrifugal forces of the movement.

Contemporaries and later students of California Progressivism pointed, as Mowry did, to the centrality of the Southern Pacific in eliciting a reform political response by business and professional people who became the heart of the movement. But, in fact, this was only partly the case. Certainly the Southern Pacific was well organized for political purposes and had considerable power up to 1910 or so. But that may be as much because of the recency of arrival of so many Californians and their lack of organization as it was because of the railroad's innate power. Also, the Progressives exaggerated the power of the SP because it was the only clear target available to them and because it provided one issue on which they could all agree.

John Buenker's stress on the role of individual group interests, and the need of coalitions to implement those interests if such coalitions were to survive, reflects on the national level what is seen in looking at the relationship between Haynes and his Direct Legislation League, on the one hand, and the Lincoln–Roosevelt Republican League, on the other. This is echoed, also, in Robert Crunden's observation that "the private problems of gifted men became public issues."[80] In some ways, then, the Southern Pacific was as much a stalking horse as it was a real issue. Every good man could agree that it was iniquitous, as indeed it was, and be persuaded to rail against it, especially because, in so doing, he could hope to find allies to join him in what he was really interested in.

There was a strong moral tone to the beliefs and actions of many Progressives. Certainly Haynes saw life as pretty much of a moral crusade. And most of the Progressives viewed their public activities in similar terms.[81] This made them resolute and helps explain their successes. But it also made them inflexible, since compromise does not marry well with moral fervor. If moral purpose gave Progressivism elements of strength and commitment, it also served to undercut unity within the movement because such purpose was associated by many individual Progressives with their own personal agendas. The political realities discussed above suggest that this factor tends to be exaggerated as an explanation of the nature of Progressivism.

More useful as a paradigm of Progressivism is the concept of the entrepreneur. It has long been agreed by historians that the Progressives were essentially similar — in background, education, religion, wealth, socioeconomic status — to those they opposed, which argues against any class-based interpretation of Progressivism.[82] This, in turn, has led to suggestions that the Progressives were entrepreneurial in terms of being "men on the make" — seeking their own political and/or economic advantage in political and economic systems that for one reason or another were closed to them.[83] This idea gets closer to the nature of California Progressives and Progressivism, although the concept of personal advantage needs careful definition.

The California Progressives in public life were *motivationally* and *behaviorally* operating like business entrepreneurs. They were entrepreneurs in another area, that of public affairs. And like other entrepreneurs, their behavior was not reactive — to political, economic, or other systems. Studies of entrepreneurship, from Schumpeter on, have stressed the individualist motivation, "the drive to do, to win, to create, to found a dynasty, a private kingdom," where the making of money is at most only part of the equation.[84] The Progressives were entrepreneurs in the political arena, thinking and behaving quite similarly, but with a different focus. Thus, as the businessman saw opportunities in oil or retailing or whatever, the Progressive as entrepreneur saw opportunities for success in the rising public interest in issues that came to be labeled "reform." The motivation and the behavior were pretty much the same.

Why one man became the head of a large corporation or small business and another became a reformer in the public arena is not entirely clear. Certainly, chance played some role; so, too, did familial and other influences on individual attitudes and moral/ethical values. As with entrepreneurs in business, reformers were activists and strivers. Likewise, some operated in a single area and others got involved in a whole bevy of activities. They, too, were seeking primarily to make their mark. In this context, it is entirely natural that the Progressives would be leery of any entrenched interest — corporations, unions, political machines, and so on. The Progressives may indeed have believed that individuals were virtuous and organized interest groups self-seeking, as some historians have concluded.[85] But even more, they perceived such interests as impediments to their own self-assertion.

If political activity, reform or otherwise, is seen as of a piece, motivationally and behaviorally, with business activity, one need no longer search among people of such similar backgrounds for correlates of "reform" or "conservatism." That they ended up on opposite sides of public issues is not all that important. There were certain types of people who exercised leadership in turn-of-the-century America, and, as always, different individuals ended up in different endeavors for reasons of interest, opportunity, and chance.[86]

Unlike business, political reform did not usually offer material rewards. The rich and/or unusually committed, like Haynes, or those whose occupations were based on such involvement, such as newspapermen Dickson and Rowell, could stay with it for the long run; most, however, were obliged to tend to other matters as well. And even the psychic rewards were often transitory — public policy for most people does not generally lend itself to as clear and long-term a sense of accomplishment as does activity in the private sector. So a lot of Progressives got bored, or burned out, and moved on to other things, and Progressivism declined.

But the issues the Progressives raised and the solutions they proposed took on a life of their own, and in many cases went on long after Progressivism itself had disappeared. This was particularly the case with the initiative and referendum, partially because Haynes never relented from his commitment and partially because those reforms immediately and permanently won over a majority of California voters.

Direct legislation was very much a part of the ideas and interests of progressivism and became one of its most enduring legacies. It personified to many Progressives, not least Haynes, a structural improvement on the representative political system which expanded democracy and confounded "special interests." To them, it was a moral improvement as well, predicated on the assumption that the rule of "the people" was the noblest aim of democracy, and that these political devices were a path to fulfilling that ideal. The initiative and referendum, in ensuing decades, would be put to purposes their authors never anticipated, with the line between "the people" and "the interests" often unclear. But the supporters of direct legislation over those decades would continue to defend it in terms very like those of the Progressives, and a very large proportion of Californians would continue to agree with them.

# 2 Direct Legislation in Good Times and Bad, 1920–1939

Neither the relative prosperity of the 1920s nor the depths of the Depression in the 1930s diminished the enthusiasm of Californians to make use of the initiative and referendum. Between 1920 and 1939, 71 initiatives and 22 referendums qualified for the ballot (another 46 were titled but failed to garner enough signatures to qualify). From the voter's perspective, there were even more, because 152 legislative measures (bond acts and constitutional amendments) were also on these ballots, so that voters during this period actually encountered 245 different propositions. Voters did not necessarily make a distinction between legislative measures and popular ones, which were mixed together on the ballot. To the voter they were all ballot measures that had to somehow be evaluated and decided upon. And the public did require some persuasion: only 30 percent of proposed popular initiatives were successful (52 percent of the measures submitted by the legislature were approved).[1] Referendums fared better: 41 percent of referendums "passed" — which meant that the statutes were upheld; therefore, the drafters of the referendums, who wanted to undo the laws, actually prevailed 59 percent of the time. However, the percentage of voters who were confused about what a Yes or No vote on referendums actually meant continued to be a problem, albeit to an indeterminable degree.[2] This was further confused by the fact that until the 1930s, the wording of the ballot argument summaries for the Secretary of State's *Ballot Pamphlet* was done by proponents and opponents rather than by the Secretary of State's office.

In general, the popular propositions were more controversial than the legislative ones and elicited considerably more voter participation. In 1930, a typical year in this regard, none of the popular initiatives or referendums received fewer than one million votes, whereas 10 of the 21 legislative measures received well under that figure. The popular measures were increasingly likely to be supported by hefty campaign contributions and by professional management. These propositions also reflected a variety of issue concerns, which showed some change over time; for example, Prohibition remained a crucial issue through the 1920s, whereas labor and welfare issues became increasingly common starting in the years of the Depression.

Table 2.1 summarizes the popular initiatives and referendums of this period by general subject. Some measures could be put under two or more categories (the welfare propositions of the late 1930s have been listed under "Labor and welfare," but could arguably have been classed as "Socio-cultural," or as even "Taxation and bonds"), but the table nonetheless provides an introduction to the kinds of issues that groups of California voters were confronting in the 1920s and 1930s.

Social and cultural matters continued to draw the largest number of voters, reflecting the extent to which such issues dominated the national scene, as well, particularly in the 1920s. For example, the five measures in this classification in 1920 (dealing with five separate issues) received the five highest numbers of votes among fifteen initiatives and referendums in that election. This remained generally the case throughout the period, with an occasional highly controversial proposition from another category also rating among the top measures in terms of voter participation. Not surprisingly, propositions related to liquor control were among the most controversial: there were nine of them between 1920 and 1936, with an average voter participation rate of 84 percent, compared to a rate of 76 percent for all initiatives and referendums.

The liquor question refused to go away and elicited constant controversy throughout the period. Full Prohibition measures had been defeated in 1914 and 1916, and lost again in 1918 with 57 percent of the voters opposed to an initiative constitutional amendment. When the legislature then passed a state enforcement law echoing the federal Volstead Act (defining "alcoholic" as one-half of 1 percent and totally outlawing production, possession, sale, etc.), a 1920 referendum invalidated the law by a vote of 54–46 percent. But the Prohibitionists were successful in 1922 when the voters narrowly (52–48 percent) upheld the Wright Act, the state's enforcement law, which again applied the Prohibition amendment and the Volstead Act to California law. Its main argument was that it simply followed other states in upholding federal law.[3]

Voters were quite consistent in their positions relative to alcohol. From the mid-1920s to the ending of Prohibition in 1933, the relationships among votes for all of these elections tended to be strong (see below and Table 2.3). Each side was firm in its resolve over a relatively long period of time, although there were some differences between advocates of temperance (e.g., anti-saloon laws) and the larger number who would settle only for complete Prohibition.

When the Prohibition forces were well organized, such as was the case with women's organizations in their 1926 effort to defeat Proposi-

TABLE 2.1  Subjects of Direct Legislation, 1920–1939

| Election year | Sociocultural | Government and law | Initiative and referendum | Business and economics | Taxation and bonds | Labor and welfare | Education |
|---|---|---|---|---|---|---|---|
| 1920 | 5 | 2 | 1 | 3 | 3 | | 1 |
| 1922 | 2 | 3 | 1 | 6 | 2 | | |
| 1924 | 1 | | 1 | 1 | 1 | | |
| 1926 | 3 | 3 | | 2 | 1 | | |
| 1928 | 2 | 1 | | 1 | | | |
| 1930 | 1 | 2 | | 2 | ● | | |
| Special 1932 | | | | 2 | | | |
| 1932 | 3 | | | 2 | 1 | | |
| Special 1933 | | | | | 1 | | |
| 1934 | 2 | 5 | | 2 | | | 1 |
| 1936 | 2 | 1 | | 2 | 3 | | 1 |
| 1938 | | 1 | | 4 | 2 | 2 | |
| Special 1939 | | | | 3 | | 1 | |

tion 9, which would repeal the Wright Act, they could succeed, even when being considerably outspent by their foes.[4] With time, however, the anti-Prohibition forces became even better organized and financed: the Wright Act Repeal Association, supported by wine grape growers, bottle manufacturers, hotels and restaurants, and others raised $69,000 for the 1932 campaign (more than double the amount raised in 1926), and convinced more voters than ever before (69 percent, with 91 percent of voters voting on the measure, Prop. 1) that the Wright Act should be repealed regardless of what Congress might do relative to federal Prohibition.[5]

The issue continued after the federal revocation of Prohibition in 1933, but the Prohibitionists were fighting a losing battle. There was an apparent anti-saloon constitutional amendment, Proposition 2, in 1934, but in many ways it actually freed up the serving of liquor in hotels, restaurants, and other places. Its 64 percent margin of victory did not necessarily indicate an anti-liquor vote, which was clarified in the overwhelming defeat (73 percent to 27 percent) on the same ballot of Proposition 13, a local-option amendment.[6] Two similar propositions in the 1936 election suffered the same fate, being opposed by two-thirds of the voters.

These elections also illustrate the increasing role of money in proposition campaigns and the difficulty of finding the true sources of that money. The Northern and Southern Business Councils were, at least in part, fronts for the California Liquor Industries Association. Campaign Statements indicate one lobby giving money to another, with the original source not easy to find. This would become an even greater problem over time, as the amounts of money involved got greater and greater.[7]

After 1936, the anti-liquor forces continued their efforts but for years repeatedly failed to qualify their measures for the ballot. When they finally did qualify another local-option proposition, in 1948, the issue once again drew higher participation than any other measure, and was rejected by 70 percent of the voters. In the 1920s, especially, this was the single most culturally divisive issue in California and the nation, which was well reflected in the arena of direct legislation. After 1933, however, it lost any broad appeal and survived only because of a few die-hard true believers.

One of the most bitter, and prescient, of the cultural conflict propositions of the time was the alien land law, Proposition 1 of 1920. It reflected the long-term anti-Asian sentiments in California, going back to the time of the Gold Rush. Those prejudices, originally directed toward the Chinese, had been redirected primarily to Japanese immigrants in the twentieth century, and expanded as the Japanese immigration increased and as the group succeeded as small farmers and businesspeople throughout the state. Opposition was economic as well as nativistic: labor unions, farm and business groups, and leading Progressives at the time of Hiram Johnson's governorship all favored restrictions on land ownership by these "aliens ineligible to citizenship."[8] To many, in this age of racism and nativism, anything that discouraged or disempowered immigrants, especially non-white ones, was as much a reform as controlling child labor or instituting direct legislation.

The state legislature had passed an alien land bill in its 1913 session, but it had been watered down through the influence of some business groups, European investors, and the federal government.[9] The war and postwar experiences of ethnic and labor conflict only exacerbated American and California nativism, making a stronger alien land law a popular issue for direct legislation by 1920. Earlier sources of opposition, federal and state, had dried up, and, as one observer put it, the sentiment to punish the Japanese with an alien land law "reflected a very general state-wide movement, a strong sentiment."[10] There was some opposition, from religious and other sources, but it was greatly outnumbered by those who supported the proposition. And efforts by the Japanese-Americans themselves, noting that they cultivated less than 2 percent of California's farmlands and made up less than 2 percent of its population, were simply ignored.[11] As with the national Red Scare going on in the United States at the same time, facts and rational arguments had little weight.

The alien land law initiative, Proposition 1, drew more voters than any other of the fifteen direct legislation and eight legislative measures on the 1920 ballot, a voter participation rate of 90 percent of those voting in this election. It also had the highest margin of victory of any popular measure, 75–25 percent (exceeded only by a legislature-proposed alien poll tax constitutional amendment that received 82 percent approval).

Because the ideas behind Proposition 1 cast such a long shadow on California history, down to the incarceration of Japanese-American citizens in World War II, it is reasonable to look a bit more carefully at the vote for this measure, as is done in Table 2.2.

What the table suggests is the generality of anti-Japanese sentiment. If anything, the proposition was supported by the vote of the wealthier and more "enlightened." When one does the mental gymnastics required for negative statistical relationships and referendum voting (where Yes means opposition to the referendum), the upshot is that those opposing Prohibition and those opposing an increase in women's property rights both tended to somewhat disproportionately favor the alien land law. So two groups that would be expected to represent contrary sociocultural groups voted the same way on this issue. The small but positive correlations between supporting the alien land law and the two agricultural wealth variables, and the lack of any relationship with support of the single tax or percent illiterate, are additional indications that the law appealed to a large part of the middle class. This is consistent with the broad national middle-class support for

TABLE 2.2    Correlates of Voting in Favor of the Alien Land Law
(Proposition 1), 1920 General Election

| Variable | Correlation with vote on Proposition 1 |
|---|---|
| Pecentage voting Yes on prohibition (Prop. 2 of 1920) (Referendum) | −.563 |
| Percentage voting Yes on community property (Prop. 13 of 1920) (Referendum) | −.488 |
| Single tax (Prop. 20 of 1920) | −.167 |
| $ value of all crops, 1920 | .258 |
| Mean $ value per farm, 1920 | .313 |
| % illiterate, 1920 | .059 |

NOTE:  Pearson product moment correlations, based on percentage voting Yes on propositions and data from U.S. Census of 1920, with data aggregated by county and weighted by county population.

nativism and reaction during and after World War I, and reifies the depth of anti-Orientalism in 1920 California. It was supported less by special groups than by Californians in general.

The community property referendum (Proposition 13) had had a tortured history, passing the legislature several times, only to be vetoed by the governor. Finally, a version was passed that received the governor's approval and it was immediately challenged by a referendum in this election. Chester Rowell, a leading Progressive, wrote the defense of the law for the ballot pamphlet, arguing that it was not diminishing a husband's control of family affairs. The argument against the law was very traditional, saying that it was unfair to men and would weaken their control over their own earned wealth.

The No vote prevailed by 68–32 percent, invalidating the law and maintaining the status quo. It was another interesting example of how the question of women's rights never became an integral part of the California Progressive reform agenda; Rowell's was the only Progressive voice raised in defense of the community property law. Community property was not as clear-cut or controversial an issue as women's suffrage had been, however: while there had been a negative relationship between voting for women's suffrage in 1911 and support for Prohibition, there was a fairly strong positive relationship between support for Prohibition and for the community property law in the early 1920s. Moreover, there was no meaningful statistical relationship between the vote for women's suffrage in 1911 and that for community property in 1920.[12]

Other issues with strong cultural and social content also received attention — as with Prohibition, mainly in the 1920s. Horseracing with gambling had been around as an issue for quite some time. In 1914, a proposal to permit pari-mutuel betting under control of a state commission was overwhelmingly rejected by 70 percent of the voters. Another try was made in 1926 with the same result: two-thirds of the voters rejected it. When a third try was made in 1932, it, too, lost, but by only 51 percent. Such issues were losing their force as the 1920s came to an end. Additionally, this issue, like Prohibition, was by no means only cultural; there were important economic interests at play, such as horse breeders and potential racetrack owners, who raised relatively large sums in their vain effort to resurrect horseracing with betting.[13]

There was a somewhat similar history to the case of boxing and wrestling, with the question being whether or not the professionalization of such sports was ethical. In 1914, an initiative to essentially ban professional boxing had been successful, with 56 percent of the vote. But in 1924, Proposition 7 okayed professional boxing and wrestling under regulation by a state commission, with the support of a bare majority of 51 percent of those voting. Opponents, perhaps hopeful due to the closeness of the 1924 vote, mounted a counter-initiative in 1928 to specifically revoke Proposition 7. This initiative, Proposition 5, garnered more publicity than the previous two campaigns. There was widespread opposition from the press across the state, as well as from a wide variety of popular organizations. The result was the defeat of the measure by almost two-thirds of the voters.[14] This, too, was an issue of sociocultural conservatism whose time was passing.

Table 2.3 looks at the relationships among a number of these sociocultural issues, to ask if there was consistency, at the county level, in terms of a multi-dimensional conservative or liberal position on such issues in the 1920s and early 1930s. The answer is mixed. There is agreement among the various measures related to Prohibition, with the exception of the 1918 initiative, which was firmly couched in wartime needs for grain and appealed to patriotism. The other Prohibition measures do have significant positive relationships, although the correlations decline over time. This is probably explained by the considerable population growth and movement between the 1920 and 1930 censuses, and also because the anti-Prohibition vote in 1932, which drew a huge voter participation rate of 91 percent, had a landslide 69 percent vote against the state's Prohibition law.

The 1924 boxing and wrestling measure was in favor of these sports, whereas the 1928 measure sought to reverse it. Since the relationship between voting on the two measures is totally insignificant, rather than the strong negative relationship one might expect, there does not seem to have been great consistency among voters on the issue, even though they both drew about the same voter participation (76 percent and 80 percent). The 1924 vote in favor of boxing does have significant negative correlations with voting in favor of Prohibition in 1920 and 1922, which does seem culturally consistent.

There is ideological consistency within time periods, as in opposition to Prohibition, Bible reading, and regulation of professional boxing, along with support of horseracing, in the period 1926–1932. (These ideologically consistent time periods would lengthen in the 1930s and after.) Some voters did remain consistent on some issues, particularly deeply held sociocultural ones. The data also show, however, that proposition-specific and other factors overwhelmed ideological ones in many cases, particularly when studying the matter with county-level data.

As Table 2.1 indicated, the area of business and economics involved the largest number of direct legislation matters, but this included a wide variety of propositions, both in terms of private interests and of efforts to use government to regulate private interests. Not the least of these issues involved water and power resources, long a central concern in California history and an interest of the Progressives that continued into the 1930s. The Johnson administration, among its other regulatory statutes, had enacted a law creating a state water commission that had the power to adjudicate water rights. A 1914 referendum (Proposition 6) tried to invalidate the law, but the Johnson administration was upheld with a very narrow 50.7 percent of the vote (only 64 percent of voters voted on this measure, as compared to 91 percent who voted on the Prohibition measure on the same ballot).

The water issue returned and broadened to also include electrical power in the 1920s, as the remaining Progressives adopted it as their principal proposed reform of the period.[15] They put virtually identical initiatives on the ballot in 1922, 1924, and 1926. All of them proposed a state water and power commission that would have the right to issue bonds and to use the proceeds to expand public water and power facilities. All three lost by overwhelming majorities of at least 70 percent. Many of the most influential California Progressives worked hard for these measures, including John R. Haynes, Rudolf Spreckels (who was listed on the "pro" side in the 1922 and 1926 official ballot pamphlets), Franklin Hichborn, and William Kent. They also contributed most of the money, spending as much as $150,000 per campaign, which was a lot at the time (over $1 million in 1995 dollars).[16]

TABLE 2.3    Correlations for Voting on Sociocultural Issues, 1918–1932

| Proposition | 1918: Prop. 22 Favors prohibition | 1920: Prop. 2 Favors prohibition | 1922: Prop. 2 Favors prohibition | 1924: Prop. 7 Favors boxing, wrestling | 1926: Prop. 6 Favors horseracing |
|---|---|---|---|---|---|
| 1918: Prop. 22 Favors prohibition | 1.000 | | | | |
| 1920: Prop. 2 Favors prohibition | −.293 | 1.000 | | | |
| 1922: Prop. 2 Favors prohibition | −.270 | .818 | 1.000 | | |
| 1924: Prop. 7 Favors boxing, wrestling | −.038 | −.556 | −.520 | 1.000 | |
| 1926: Prop. 6 Favors horseracing | −.178 | .396 | .244 | −.170 | 1.000 |
| 1926: Prop. 9 Opposes prohibition | −.226 | .336 | .257 | −.224 | .886 |
| 1926: Prop. 17 Favors bible reading | .305 | −.147 | −.114 | .096 | −.733 |
| 1928: Prop. 5 Opposes boxing, wrestling | .124 | −.053 | .033 | .049 | −.551 |
| 1932: Prop. 1 Opposes prohibition | −.283 | .314 | .232 | −.150 | .859 |
| 1932: Prop. 5 Favors horseracing | −.168 | .162 | .068 | −.043 | .386 |

NOTE: Pearson product moment correlations, based on percentage voting Yes on propositions, with data aggregated by county and weighted by county population. For clarity, only one side of table is shown, since both sides are identical.

| 1926: Prop. 9 Opposes prohibition | 1926: Prop. 17 Favors bible reading | 1928: Prop. 5 Opposes boxing, wrestling | 1932: Prop. 1 Opposes prohibition | 1932: Prop. 5 Favors horseracing |
|---|---|---|---|---|
| 1.000 | | | | |
| −.831 | 1.000 | | | |
| −.611 | .713 | 1.000 | | |
| .939 | −.907 | −.673 | 1.000 | |
| .419 | −.113 | −.023 | .367 | 1.000 |

Opponents criticized both the public competition with private water and power companies and the $500 million in bonds that the measures permitted the commission to sell. The private power companies opposed the three propositions most vigorously (Pacific Gas and Electric conducted an extensive direct-mail campaign), as did at least 50 California Chambers of Commerce and other business organizations.[17]

Finally, in 1933, the state legislature passed its own water and power act, although a more modest one. It created a state water project authority for the Central Valley Project, to develop water and electric energy in the Sacramento and San Joaquin Valleys. The power companies were still adamantly opposed and mounted a referendum for a special election in December 1933 (Proposition 1). Once again, Haynes and some of the other aging Progressives swung into action and the legislation was barely upheld with 52 percent of the vote.[18] This was a unique victory, very probably an echo of public support for similar measures being then taken by the New Deal. Implementation of an expensive new water policy in the midst of the Depression was difficult, however, and it was only with the start of federal intervention and financing that the Central Valley Project really got under way.[19]

More general utility regulation was even less successful. For example, after the legislature passed a bill permitting cities and counties to sell bonds for the purpose of acquiring public utilities, a referendum (Proposition 13, November 1938) was mounted to kill the legislation. The private utility companies hired Clem Whitaker, a leading professional in initiative qualifying and promotion, who raised a good deal of money for a well-publicized campaign that resulted in a 74 percent vote to reject the law.[20] Overall, the water and power battle illustrated the decline of the Progressives and of public support for most of their interests.

Questions of oil and gas rights also began to emerge at this time, reflecting an increased awareness of southern California's potential riches in these minerals, and a consistent public opposition to any threat to California's beaches. Two referendums appeared in a May 1932 special election. In Proposition 1, voters overwhelmingly rejected (79 percent) a law that had created a state conservation commission; there was debate as to which interest groups were really involved and what the hidden costs might be. At the same time, voters approved, by a 59 percent vote (Proposition 2), a law that forbade the leasing of state-owned beach lands for mineral and oil production.[21] The city of Huntington Beach proposed an initiative in the fall election of the same year (Proposition 11) that would grant to it control over its tidelands, including the ability to produce minerals. It was quite clear to all that the main purpose of the measure was to permit the city to prosper from the development of oil, and it was controversial within the city, as well as more broadly: the mayor and city attorney supported the initiative and the local Chamber of Commerce opposed it.[22] The voters rejected Proposition 11 decisively.

A new initiative in 1936 (Proposition 4) would have prohibited tideland oil drilling, but permitted slant drilling into the tidelands from on shore. Supporters, including such groups as the California Federation of Women's Clubs and the Native Sons of the Golden West, argued that this would protect the beaches and raise money to maintain them. But opponents focused on the limitations on competition inherent in the measure, and it was narrowly rejected.[23] The state then passed two new laws, permitting oil drilling on state-owned lands at Huntington Beach and requiring competitive bidding for drilling leases. Both were subjected to referendums in 1938 (Propositions 10 and 24), and both laws were rejected by huge majorities.[24] The public was obviously very leery of any commercial use of beach property, although the rate of voter participation was well below that on sociocultural matters: these four measures, over a six-year period, had a rate of 76–80 percent.

A somewhat different situation ensued in 1939, when the legislature passed a law creating an oil conservation commission that could limit the production of oil and gas and otherwise regulate the industry. A referendum (Proposition 5) ensued to revoke the law, which led to a controversial campaign. The legislation was supported by Governor Culbert L. Olson, the Roosevelt administration, the Navy, the CIO, and even Standard Oil. Opposition (i.e., support for a No vote to revoke the law) came from smaller oil companies and conservatives who were generally leery of expanding government regulation in this age of the New Deal.[25] The campaign was vigorous, with much money spent on both sides, billboards all over the state, and a high level of voter interest.[26] The measure received the second highest voter participation rate among all propositions (just behind "Ham and Eggs," see below), particularly high for a special election. And the voters rejected the law decisively, by 61–39 percent. They seemed ultimately persuaded that it was a "big oil" measure that would result in higher prices.[27]

Another frequent business issue, in this age of economic modernization, was professionalization, particularly in the area of health care. There was conflict between various kinds of practitioners (medical doctors, chiropractors, etc.) and, often, within professional groups as well. There were, for example, several groups that sought to speak for California chiropractors, and they were often at loggerheads with one another. The public's response, overall, seemed to favor more stringent medical standards, but confusion was not absent.

As early as 1914 there had been an initiative statute to regulate "drugless practitioners," which would create a state regulatory board but actually leave chiropractors and others with expanded rather than contracted independence. It had been rejected by a strong 67 percent majority. In 1920 a much stronger initiative appeared, creating a new Board of Chiropractic Examiners, separate from the Board of Medical Examiners, for licensing and regulating that profession. Many chiropractors and osteopaths supported the measure because it would get them out from under the control of medical doctors. But the Federated Chiropractors of California argued against the proposition, saying that it would "make things easy for inferior chiropractic schools."[28] The measure (Proposition 2) was rejected by a tiny 50.8 percent majority. Two years later there were two more initiatives on the ballot. Proposition 16 proposed a considerably more powerful Board of Chiropractic Examiners and Proposition 20 proposed the same for osteopaths. The practitioners of these two modalities seem to have generally approved the measures because of their strong desire to get away from the control of the medical doctors.[29] This time, both measures passed with solid majorities.

All of these propositions drew fairly strong voter response for the time, with about 80 percent of the voters marking their ballots on the initiatives. Just what the voters understood they were voting for is difficult to tell, since, with similarly named organizations on each side, it was often unclear exactly who was for what.[30]

These issues continued into the 1930s, with two initiatives (Propositions 9 and 17) in 1934, one for chiropractors and one for naturopaths. In both cases, these seemed on the surface to increase professional requirements, but critics argued they actually decreased them. According to the *Los Angeles Times*, this was the continuation of a bitter dispute among chiropractors that had started with Proposition 16 in 1922, with the Board of Chiropractic Examiners, which supported the propositions, in long-term conflict with the California Chiropractic Association, which opposed them. Several other organizations, with a conflicting litany of names, could be found endorsing one side or another in the *California Ballot Pamphlet*, or raising money for the campaign.[31] The California Medical Association also vigorously opposed both 1934 measures, whether as threats to quality medical care or to its own power, and raised money to hire Clem Whitaker's Campaigns, Inc. to run its campaign.[32] All of this generated strong voter interest: the two propositions had higher voter participation than any but two Prohibition initiatives. But both were rejected, by 62 percent for the chiropractic proposition, and 69 percent for the naturopathic one.

Five years later, the drama was played out once more, in Proposition 2 of 1939. The two main players of 1934 had the same pro and con roles as before, with additional chiropractic organizations found on either side. Defenders of the proposition argued in their campaign materials that this would be the first real amendment since 1922 and that it reflected new knowledge accrued since that time. Opponents continued to argue that the proposal cheapened the profession. And the California Medical Association once again joined the opposition. But neither side raised as much money as they had in 1934; it may be that the chiropractors, as well as the public, were getting tired of the battle.[33] Seventy percent of the voters opposed the initiative.

With so many propositions on the same or similar issues, one might well hope to learn something about the consistency or inconsistency of voting behavior. Table 2.4 endeavors to discover this by looking at relationships among the votes for the various propositions.

There are stronger relationships than one might logically expect, given the difficulty the average voter must have had distinguishing the "good guys" from the "bad guys." This is particularly the case for the earlier period, through 1922, where the relationships range from strong to very strong indeed (even for an initiative which seemed to regulate dentistry, although in fact it did the opposite). The vote, in part, reflected California Progressivism, of which the ideas of business regulation and professionalization were an intimate part. Indeed, for the long 25-year period covered by Table 2.4, there is striking consistency in voting. Given that the first five propositions in the table were seen as essentially pro-regulation, and the last three anti-regulation, the direction of the correlations is consistent. Many voters, to the best of their knowledge, seem to have stuck to their feelings on the regulation of medical practice.

More and more businesses were being affected by direct legislation, either by regulations they did not welcome or by their own measures which sought to achieve some statutory or constitutional advantage. With this, money was becoming more and more important — for signature gathering, campaign management, advertising, and so on. Direct legislation was no longer an avenue for amateurs, whatever its origins may have been: big bucks and professional managers were becoming essential ingredients of success for all but a very few popular initiatives and referendums.

A good example is Proposition 22 in 1936 ("Retail Store License"), a referendum seeking to undo 1935 legislation that had established a "licensing fee" for retail stores. The fee ranged from $1 to $500, depending upon the number of stores owned. Exceptions were written into the law for certain multi-site businesses, such as filling stations, theaters, and restaurants. Thus, the proposed law's clear aim was to help small businesses that were becoming unable to compete with chain stores. Proponents argued that it would protect such businesses and promote competitive pricing; opponents saw it as threatening and patently unfair.[34] More to the point, the chain

TABLE 2.4  Correlations for Voting on Professionalization Issues,
1914–1939

| Proposition | 1914: Prop. 46 Drugless practice | 1918: Prop. 21 Dentistry | 1920: Prop. 5 Chiropractors | 1922: Prop. 16 Chiropractors |
|---|---|---|---|---|
| 1914: Prop. 46 Drugless practice | 1.000 | | | |
| 1918: Prop. 21 Dentistry | .743 | 1.000 | | |
| 1920: Prop. 5 Chiropractors | .555 | .359 | 1.000 | |
| 1922: Prop. 16 Chiropractors | .722 | .453 | .647 | 1.000 |
| 1922: Prop. 20 Osteopaths | .652 | .313 | .708 | .864 |
| 1934: Prop. 9 Chiropractors | −.267 | −.022 | −.181 | −.086 |
| 1934: Prop. 17 Naturopaths | −.570 | −.380 | −.216 | −.376 |
| 1939: Prop. 2 Chiropractors | −.288 | −.331 | −.116 | −.303 |

NOTE: Pearson product moment correlations, based on percentage voting Yes on propositions, with data aggregated by county and weighted by county population. For clarity, only one side of table is shown, since both sides are identical.

stores were well organized and raised a huge campaign chest that enabled them to mount a professional campaign that produced far greater voter participation on this measure (90 percent) than any of the other 22 propositions on the ballot, and convinced 56 percent of the voters to vote to revoke the law.

| 1922:<br>Prop. 20<br>Osteopaths | 1934:<br>Prop. 9<br>Chiropractors | 1934:<br>Prop. 17<br>Naturopaths | 1939:<br>Prop. 2<br>Chiropractors |
|---|---|---|---|
| 1.000 | | | |
| −.132 | 1.000 | | |
| −.437 | .404 | 1.000 | |
| −.260 | −.276 | .141 | 1.000 |

Campaign Statements had been required by law since 1924 (a less definitive predecessor law had passed in 1921), with somewhat less than wholehearted compliance. On the chain store issue, they were filed by seven groups, three of them against the law and four of them in favor of it. That says little, however, since the No side had 94 percent of the money: the California Chain

Store Association reported raising just over $1 million; Safeway Stores, which contributed $358,000 of that million, also filed a separate Campaign Statement for $85,000 of direct expenditure. The most successful group supporting the law, the Anti-Monopoly League of California, reported $66,000 in total expenditures. The one other No group and two other Yes groups all raised and spent less than $10,000.

Obviously, direct legislation had become big business. And, while this campaign was an unusually expensive one, that was so only to a degree. Big expenditures were becoming more and more common, but they are often difficult to trace in this period when the required reporting was not always taken too seriously. It is also sometimes difficult to tell from a Campaign Statement which side a group was on: it had to report which proposition(s) it was interested in, but not which side it was taking. Additionally, one could not always determine, from Campaign Statements, exactly where the money came from and went to; this was true particularly in the area of expenditures, where often only the name of an individual was given, rather than that of a company.

As noted already, over one-third of the California Chain Stores Association money came from one merchant, Safeway Stores. Obviously, this huge supermarket chain felt greatly threatened by the legislation. Many other chain stores contributed fairly large sums, but nothing like that: F. W. Woolworth gave $15,000; Kresge, the other major "dime store," $5,000; other grocery and drugstore chains also contributed. There were relatively few small contributions: this was a big business effort all the way. The Anti-Monopoly League, on the other hand, survived on large numbers of small pledges, the vast majority of which were in the range of $25–$50; very few were over $100.

Both sides utilized professionals. One of the Chain Stores Association's first expenditures was a bit over $15,000 to Joseph Robinson's Robinson and Co., the prime signature solicitors for California direct legislation since about 1918. Robinson claimed to have never failed to secure enough signatures for his clients and to have been involved in the vast majority of initiatives that got on California ballots.[35] The Chain Stores Association also paid at least $220,000 to Lord and Thomas, an advertising agency that organized much of the campaign. The Anti-Monopoly League obviously operated on a smaller scale, but nonetheless spent $12,000 of its total funds for commissions to solicitation firms (unnamed in the Campaign Statement), and another $12,000 for "campaign management," including a couple of advertising agencies. The direct legislation business was booming.[36] Additionally, one of the truisms of the entire history of direct legislation had become increasingly clear: while a preponderance of money could in no way guarantee that a proposition would succeed, it could almost always guarantee that one could be beaten.[37]

Taxes were another area of some controversy in the 1920s and 1930s. In the early stages of the Depression a number of groups came together to sponsor an initiative constitutional amendment proposing the first state income and sales taxes. The proceeds of these taxes were to be consigned to education, with the argument that much of the burden of financing education would thus be lifted from the counties. One of the issues most debated was whether or not any of the money would be used for increasing teacher salaries, an idea which seemed to be widely opposed.[38] Two-thirds of the voters rejected the measure (Proposition 9 of 1932).

When the legislature passed its own income tax measure in 1935, opponents sought to undo it with an initiative constitutional amendment (Proposition 2, November 1936) that not only repealed that law, but required that any further proposed income taxes on individuals be approved, first by a two-thirds vote in each house of the legislature, and second by a majority popular vote as well. The proposition was broadly opposed by educational, farm, and business groups, had a lower rate of voter participation than one might expect (71 percent, well below the chain store and local option propositions), and was rejected by two-thirds of those voting.[39] The public was not ready in the 1930s to impose the straitjackets on government that would become popular a generation or so later. Nor did measures associated with taxation attract the level of voter participation that would also come later.

Special-purpose taxes and appropriations did not fare much better than general ones. In the 1920s, when automobiles became a central interest and enthusiasm of middle-class Americans, desire for a modern road system spread throughout the state. But the question of how such roads should be financed was divisive. In 1926, voters rejected both a gasoline tax to finance road building (Proposition 4) and an initiative constitutional amendment to annually appropriate funds for highway construction (Proposition 8). The latter proposition also defined "primary" and "secondary" roads, with major financing going to the primary ones. Interestingly, this measure generated strong conflicts between northern and southern California, reflecting the rapid growth of the latter. Northern California interests supported Proposition 4 and opposed Proposition 8, whereas southern California interests took the opposite positions. The Automobile Club of Southern California, for example, was a major supporter of Proposition 8, and spent $42,000 publicizing it, while the California State Automobile Association was on the opposite side. All told, over $100,000 was spent on the campaigns for and against these two propositions.[40]

On the surface, these were two like propositions, raising money to build highways, both of which were defeated by the voters. But they clearly reflected contrary interests, and one was based on taxation while the other wasn't. The voters apparently saw the difference, since there was an almost perfect negative correlation ($-.907$) between the vote for the two measures.

A dozen years later, the two automobile associations came together to support Proposition 4 of 1938, which would have created a new Highway and Traffic Safety Commission, appointed by the governor with consent of the state senate. It would have replaced a number of other agencies, including the non-paid State Highway Commission, and, supporters argued, it would remove highway regulation from politics. The proposition had broad-based support, from the state Chamber of Commerce, California Federation of Women's Clubs, other middle-class organizations, and the California State Federation of Labor. The opposition to Proposition 4 was made up primarily of insurance companies and the California Highway Patrol (which would come under the control of the new commission). Opponents used another of the professional campaign organizations, L. L. McLary's Public Affairs, Inc., stressing the costs of the new commission as a diversion of needed gasoline tax funds from other uses. And they persuaded 60 percent of the voters to turn the initiative down.[41]

Other special interests were also reflected by tax measures in these years, not least California's burgeoning dairy industry. On two occasions, the state legislature passed special taxes on the manufacture and sale of oleomargarine. Both laws led to referendums, Proposition 3 in 1926 and Proposition 18 in 1936, which were major battles between the dairy industry and the food industry which manufactured margarine. The "Anti-Food Tax Association" spent $115,000 to defeat the law in 1926, while the California Dairy Council spent about $55,000 to support it.[42] Both laws were decisively rejected by the voters.

No taxation issue generated as much heat as that of the single tax, which frightened business, government, and all the forces of "respectability" for years. It was one of those issues with a small but committed coterie of devotees, who, despite constant failure at the polls, were able to qualify it as an initiative year after year. The idea, which traced back to the 1879 publication of Henry George's influential book, *Progress and Poverty*, had been advocated by a variety of groups ever since. Its basic argument was that a single tax, on land values, would be fair, would undercut the wealth and power of monopolies, and would obviate the need for any other type of taxation. As such, it had been a hobgoblin of the rich and comfortable ever since; to all but its advocates it seemed not only revolutionary, but economically catastrophic as well.

Chapter 1 showed that the single tax idea was introduced to direct legislation as early as the election of 1912 and reappeared in 1916, 1918, and 1920. In each case it was proposed as an initiative constitutional amendment, and in each case it failed — by greater majorities each time (58 percent, 69 percent, 75 percent, 74 percent). It never generated the voter interest of sociocultural issues like Prohibition, tending, rather, to be about in the middle in terms of voter participation rate; in 1920, in fact, the single tax initiative had the lowest rate of all twenty direct legislation propositions. In 1922 the single tax (Proposition 29) failed again, with 81 percent of the voters against it. In both 1920 and 1922, however, efforts to make the single tax go away forever by increasing the number of signatures needed to get such measures on the ballot also failed to succeed (Haynes, no particular friend of the single tax but a determined defender of the initiative process, signed the ballot argument against it as a "deadly attack on democracy").[43]

It appeared for a while that the single tax idea had died, but it was, in fact, only dormant, and was one of the many panaceas under consideration as cures for the Great Depression. It became known in the mid-1930s as the "Ralston Amendment," after "Judge" Jackson H. Ralston, a successful Washington, D.C., attorney and longtime single taxer who had retired to Palo Alto. Ralston was the key leader of the renewed single tax movement during the Depression.[44] He had started working on his initiative in 1933 with a proposal to eliminate the sales tax, avoiding mention of the controversial "single tax" idea to get broader acceptance. With the help of organized labor, he hoped to put this proposition on the 1934 ballot, but ultimately failed to get enough valid signatures, even with the use of paid solicitors.

The measure did qualify as Proposition 1 on the November 1936 ballot. But it was challenged in court by opponents who argued that its language masked the shift of taxation to land values, and it was thrown out by the California Supreme Court, with the effect that there was no Proposition 1 in that election. Earlier, a fairly strong grouping of organizations had already been formed to oppose the proposed Proposition 1, along with Proposition 2, the anti–income tax measure previously discussed.[45]

In its last gasp, the single tax appeared once more, as one almost-hidden part of a complex initiative constitutional amendment in 1938, Proposition 20. Ralston's organization was again very short of funds and had lost the support of organized labor, which was busy defending itself against the anti-labor Proposition 1 on the same ballot. The fact that the "Ham and Eggs" movement (see below) also had a proposition on this ballot further divided liberal and radical voters. Moreover, critics did see the single tax hidden inside this measure and railed against it. Opponents comprised a broad range of groups, from real estate boards (the San Francisco Real Estate Board gave Clem Whitaker's Campaigns, Inc. $25,000 to campaign against it) to Chambers of Commerce to the League of Women Voters and the California Teachers Association.[46] Much of the opposition was combined with opposition to Proposition 25, the "Ham and Eggs" measure; to many business interests, these two initiatives were a common threat, even though their supporters had no connection with one another.[47] The single tax had its worst showing ever, with 83 percent of the voters opposing the proposition.

Direct legislation tends always to reflect the major concerns of its times. Just as numerous initiatives and referendums in the 1920s mirrored the socio-cultural conflicts of that decade, the decade of the Depression and New Deal witnessed the introduction of concerns about organized labor and the welfare state. Industrialization was both growing and spreading in California, with the result that both the hardships of the Depression and conflicts between management and labor were increasingly common and widespread.[48] Union membership began to grow rapidly as a result of the National Industrial Recovery Act of 1933 and then the Wagner Act of 1935, particularly after the latter was upheld by the Supreme Court in 1937. Employers, for their part, had long been well organized, especially in San Francisco; groups like the Industrial Association and the Merchants and Manufacturers Association were committed to fighting unionization and maintaining the open shop across the state by all available means, with no great concern for the law.

The conflict had come to an early head in 1934, with the longshoremen's strike that covered the whole Pacific coast. Ultimately, twelve thousand workers went on strike, with the Teamsters Union aiding them by boycotting the docks, and the ports were gridlocked. Management refused to negotiate, violence ensued (with police support of management), conservative Governor Frank Merriam sent the National Guard into San Francisco, and the longshoremen's strike evolved into a general strike that created considerable panic in the state and gained notice across the nation. Labor made some significant gains in 1934, the same year that saw Upton Sinclair's near-miss try at the California governor's mansion — two not unrelated Depression phenomena that created more fear among business and conservative groups.[49]

The issue was far from resolved in 1934, the statewide battle in fact being in its early stages. Union organization grew rapidly in the mid-1930s, with individual unions gaining certified bargaining status and even, in some cases, what employer groups feared most — the closed shop. Employer determination to maintain the open shop never waned, however, and the initiative process provided employers the possibility of achieving at the ballot box what they had not accomplished in negotiations. Perhaps, also, the people would help them undercut the growing effects of federal labor legislation.

Proposition 1 of 1938 was an omnibus measure that touched on many of the labor issues of the day. It would limit picketing and boycotts; prohibit "seizure of private property," as in the sit-down strikes that had proved so effective in the East; and prohibit "abusive statements or threats of violence." Both sides were well organized and very active in this initiative campaign, but they were also cautious: California did not yet have as broad-based a labor-management division as states east of the Mississippi, and the general views of Californians on labor-related issues were far from clear. It would be easy for either side to lose support if it took positions that might be seen as "extreme." Thus, the pro–Proposition 1 "California Committee for Peace in Labor Relations" stressed the measure's focus on eliminating "sitdowns, coercion, intimidation" and other excessive practices, but also argued that it did not interfere with collective bargaining nor did it conflict with the Wagner Act. Similarly, one of labor's widely distributed brochures did not even mention unions at all (except for the union printing label at the bottom), but instead displayed a full-page picture of President Roosevelt, plus photos of various Hollywood figures, all of whom opposed the initiative.[50]

Many groups, from farm organizations and ill-defined others in the Yes camp, to the American Federation of Labor and public employee groups for the No forces, publicized their positions widely. Radio was used extensively. Anti-labor forces tried to connect the opposition to "radicalism," as allegedly existed in the more-extreme Congress of Industrial Organizations, and in the fearsome Harry Bridges of west coast longshoremen's union and 1934 strike fame.[51] A good deal of money was spent as well. Campaign Statements were filed by a large number of organizations, most of them with names that obfuscated any sense of whom they represented. The California Committee for Peace in Labor Relations, mentioned above, was the main sponsor of the initiative, and declared expenditures of $188,000; "Southern Californians, Inc.," another supporter of Proposition 1, spent about $120,000, with $35,000 of that going for professional petition circulators. The major donors to both of these anti-labor campaign organizations were businesses of one kind or another; for example, the McCann-Erickson advertising agency gave $6,400 to Southern Californians, Inc.[52]

Several individual unions, Labor's Non-Partisan Alliance, and state, regional, and local labor federations (both AFL and CIO) also filed Campaign Statements. A "Citizens Committee Opposing Initiative No. 1" raised $15,500, primarily in donations from 55 individual unions, ranging from less than $10 at the bottom to $864, from the Teamsters. These pro-labor organizations all received large numbers of very small donations, accumulating an overall total of perhaps $100,000.[53]

Most important, probably, was that 1938 was a liberal year in California politics and that the battle over Proposition 1 was to a considerable extent a contest between Republicans and Democrats, conservatives and liberals. There were 25 propositions on the 1938 ballot and Proposition 1 had the highest level of voter participation (94 percent); it was defeated by 58–42 percent. Republican Governor Frank Merriam, who supported the measure, lost his bid for reelection to Democratic state senator Culbert Olson, an ardent New Dealer, and other Republican candidates were hurt as well.[54] The Proposition 1 controversy introduced the question of organized labor versus management to California direct legislation; that question would become more common in the decades to come.

The second most popular proposition of 1938, in terms of voter participation, received less than a thousand fewer votes than Proposition 1. And it introduced another of the curious issues among California initiatives that, like the single tax, represented a small but devoted coterie of followers who managed to get it on the ballot again and again. This issue, "Ham and Eggs," was very much a creature of the 1930s — of the Depression and the rise of the welfare state.

The 1930s had seen a number of radical proposals gain popular support, from the single tax, to Upton Sinclair's End Poverty in California movement, to the Townsend movement that spread from Long Beach across the nation and to the halls of Congress. It was Townsend's Old Age Revolving Pensions, Inc., more than any other movement, that influenced the ideas of Ham and Eggs; Townsend had advocated pensions of $200 a month, paid in scrip, for every citizen over the age of 60, so long as the person was retired from work and spent the money within one month. This would relieve a group that was suffering greatly from the Depression, open up jobs for younger people, and provide needed inflationary pressure on the economy.[55]

Ham and Eggs was begun by Robert Noble, a radio personality, but soon taken over by Willis and Lawrence Allen, who were promoters and hustlers more than anything else (Willis had been convicted of using the mails to defraud in 1934).[56] Originally named "$30 Every Monday Morning," the "Ham and Eggs" nickname soon became more popular (the official title of the initiative, given by the Secretary of State, would be "Retirement Life Payments Act"). Proposition 25 of 1938 not only guaranteed weekly $30 payments to everyone over age 50, but also specified that the governor must select one of three named persons (chosen by the Allens) as administrator, to serve until a successor was elected in 1940. In addition, it specified that any part of the California constitution that conflicted with it was automatically repealed, and that if any section of the proposition was itself declared unconstitutional, only that specific section would be invalidated.[57]

Since it was an initiative constitutional amendment, Proposition 25 required valid signatures from a number of registered voters equal to 8 percent of the vote in the preceding gubernatorial election — about 188,000; popular enthusiasm was such that its supporters were able to submit more than four times the requirement, the highest number of signatures ever collected for a proposition to that date.[58] Another indication of its popularity was that in the 1938 Democratic primary for U.S. Senator, Sheridan Downey, a supporter of Ham and Eggs, had defeated President Roosevelt's choice, the incumbent William Gibbs McAdoo. Downey went on to defeat his Republican opponent, Philip Bancroft, in the general election.[59]

The campaign was an extremely vigorous one, getting even more attention than the battle over labor in Proposition 1. It was waged in the press, in flyers and pamphlets, and in numerous radio broadcasts. Virtually all of the press, business groups, and individual businesses of all kinds condemned the proposition, predicting economic chaos and dictatorial administration if the proposition were to succeed.[60] The Ham and Eggers responded in numerous publications, daily radio shows in at least eight cities, and hell-raising speeches and rallies, stressing the program's academic and intellectually respectable origins, its mainstream characteristics, and the ways in which it would help everyone, not just the elderly.[61]

A lot of money was spent, as well, and if everyone was obeying the law and submitting Campaign Statements specifying all their receipts and expenditures, the Ham and Eggers raised and spent by far the most. The filings for "California State Pension Plan $30 a Week for Life" amounted to about $330,000 in receipts and expenditures. The filing noted that members paid 30¢ per month dues, and that the organization had 220,304 members. This suggests real success in broadening the movement and in fund-raising, and explains how the group was able to buy so much radio time.

Ham and Eggs' leading opponents in raising funds were the northern and southern California divisions of the "Citizen's Federation to Vote No on 25." The northern division of the group raised $26,000, of which over 99 percent came from the State Chamber of Commerce. The southern division raised $49,000, of which 36 percent came from the State and Los Angeles Chambers of Commerce, the rest from a wide variety of businesses and individuals. The State Chamber of Commerce also filed for itself, for an additional $15,000 it spent in a combined opposition to Propositions 25 and 20 (the single tax). Several other organizations also combined their campaigns, but none reported more than about $1,000 in expenditures. It would not be unreasonable to conclude that there was quite a bit more money spent against Proposition 25, given its drastic nature, which simply went unreported.

Ham and Eggs had a number of successes in 1938 — in gaining members, receiving contributions, and influencing candidate elections. And it drew a voter participation rate of 94 percent. But only 45 percent of those voters supported the proposition; 55 percent decided against them.

The Allens were ready to try again, but there was considerable conflict

TABLE 2.5  Correlations for Voting on Depression-Era Socioeconomic Propositions

| Proposition and characteristic | 1938: Prop. 1 Anti-labor | 1938: Prop. 20 Single tax | 1938: Prop. 25 Ham and eggs | 1939: Prop. 1 Ham and eggs | Percentage age 21–24 in school | Percentage urban |
|---|---|---|---|---|---|---|
| 1938: Prop. 1 Anti-labor | 1.000 | | | | | |
| 1938: Prop. 20 Single tax | −.339 | 1.000 | | | | |
| 1938: Prop. 25 Ham and eggs | −.330 | .282 | 1.000 | | | |
| 1939: Prop. 1 Ham and eggs | −.300 | .267 | .916 | 1.000 | | |
| Percentage age 21–24 in school | −.044 | −.348 | −.189 | −.149 | 1.000 | |
| Percentage urban | −.311 | .733 | .079 | .088 | .689 | 1.000 |

NOTE: Pearson product moment correlations, based on percentage voting Yes on propositions and on 1940 U.S. Census data, with data aggregated by county and weighted by county population. For clarity, only one side of table is shown, since both sides are identical.

within the leadership. Some felt that the Allens' reputation had hurt Proposition 25's chances, and they also resented the money that the Allens' advertising agency had reaped through handling all of the advertising and radio time buying. However, the Allens controlled their new weekly, *National Ham and Eggs*, and the radio broadcasts, which also continued. The result was a variety of lawsuits and loss of all mainstream political support.[62]

Nonetheless, the pair put forth Proposition 1 of 1939, nearly identical to its predecessor, and again specifying two names as the only choice for administrator, to remain in office until 1944. Additionally, the Ham and Eggs group hired a professional organizer, George McLain, to create a real political organization to promote the proposition; this included perhaps 20,000 petition circulators, even more poll watchers, and thousands of telephone campaigners and drivers to take people to the polls on election day.[63]

The November 1939 election was a special one, consisting of only five direct legislation propositions (plus local measures in some places). The greatest statewide attention was paid to Ham and Eggs, and the opposition was much broader than had been the case one year before: the California PTA, the head of the American Civil Liberties Union, the whole Economics Department at UCLA, as well as myriad business groups prophesied economic disaster if Proposition 1 passed.[64] Perhaps the fact that the Depression had worsened in the past year created greater polarization and more widespread middle-class fears of what the provisions of Ham and Eggs might do.

Proposition 1 led the other four measures in voter participation: 2,926,761 people voted on this measure — more than for any proposition in the presidential election years of 1936 or 1940, or in the gubernatorial election of 1938. And it lost by a greater margin than in 1938, with two-thirds of the voters in opposition.[65] Another try in 1940 failed to garner enough signatures to make it to the ballot. Ham and Eggs, or at least the Depression version, had failed.[66] But it was very much a reflection of its times, of the suffering of the Depression. And the idea would return in the 1940s under new leadership.

Table 2.5 looks at the relationships among several of the socioeconomic propositions, and two census variables, to seek any commonalty in voting over the decade. There are notably fewer strong correlations here than there were with the sociocultural propositions studied above. That those who voted for Ham and Eggs in one year were very likely to vote for the measure a year later is no surprise. There are positive relationships for not voting against labor in Proposition 1, voting for the single tax, and voting for Ham and Eggs, which reflect a working-class overlap on these three issues. But the relationships, while statistically significant, are quite modest: these were primarily separate groups, each with its own constituency. The strong relationship between percentage urban and support for the single tax probably reflects the fact that urban counties had somewhat less opposition to this forlorn measure (defeated by 83 percent of the vote) than rural ones. Other than that, however, none of these measures is a good predictor of another; each initiative tended to generate its own particular support and opposition.

Direct legislation relating to government and elections was also quite common in the 1920s and 1930s. One of the most disputed such issues in the 1920s had to do with reapportionment of the state legislature and of seats in Congress, a reflection of important demographic changes taking place at that time. The state's population had risen by 44 percent between the censuses of 1910 and 1920, and population grew even more in the 1920s, when it increased by another 65 percent. Los Angeles County had 27 percent of the state's population in 1920 and 39 percent in 1930. San Francisco County held 15 percent of the state's population in 1920, but that decreased to 11 percent ten years later. After that, Alameda County came next with about 10 percent, and no other county had as much as 5 percent of the state's population; 48 of the 58 counties had 1 percent or less of the state's population. Regionally, the ten southern counties had 42 percent of the state's population in 1920, which rose to 54 percent in 1930; small wonder that representatives of the rest of the state were worried about the political effects of this population change.[67]

Demographic changes in California reflected national ones. Congress, for the first time, had not reapportioned House seats after the 1920 census; there was a strong reluctance among rural state representatives to see the states with big cities gain members at their expense. And the same thing happened in California: the state legislature did not reapportion congressional or state legislative districts, as required by law. The legislative impasse reflected north versus south, rural versus urban, and San Francisco versus Los Angeles animosities, since redistricting based on population would move the balance well to the south and to the cities.

This controversy led to two initiatives in the election of 1926. Proposition 20 would create a state reapportionment commission empowered to reapportion districts after each census if the legislature failed to do so for three months. It specified that the reapportionment should be by population and would have clearly favored urban areas; it was referred to as the "Los Angeles plan." Proposition 28 also directed that a commission be created if the legislature did not act; it left assembly seats to be apportioned by population, but also specified that no county could have more than one state senator, and that no senatorial district could comprise more than three counties. This would hurt the cities, especially Los Angeles (Sierra, Alpine, and Mono counties, with a combined 1920 population of 2,986 would together have the same representation in the state senate as Los Angeles county, with a 1920 population of 936,455 — and that would be even more disproportionate after the 1930 census).[68]

Neither measure got the amount of publicity its importance might have called for, nor did they attract a great deal of attention. Each had a voter participation rate of 67 percent, while several other measures on the ballot had rates of 85 percent. Proposition 20 lost, gaining only 39 percent of the vote, whereas proposition 28 won with 55 percent. The city of Los Angeles, in one of the many bizarre results in the history of initiative elections, voted overwhelmingly for Proposition 28 and against Proposition 20. It did gain seven assemblymen from the resultant legislation but lost seven state senators.[69]

Two years later, Proposition 1 of 1928 sought by referendum to revoke Proposition 28 and the 1927 Biggs Reapportionment Act that had been passed because of it. The effort to revoke had some organized support from politicians in both parties, but there was better-organized and -funded support from both business and farm groups to maintain the new law.[70] Again, voter participation was not very high — 68 percent, as opposed to 80 percent of the voters who voted on that year's boxing and wrestling measure. And the law was upheld by the same 55 percent margin that had passed Proposition 28 two years before. The redistricting issue remained somewhat unsolved and would continue to engender regional and partisan conflict.

Direct legislation was itself a significant issue during this period, and was subject to considerable discussion and several ballot propositions. Sometimes, criticism of direct legislation was really focused on particular interest groups that were using it to the chagrin of others, as was the case with the single tax, as seen above and in Chapter 1. The People's Anti-Single Tax League had first tried to kill the single tax with Proposition 4 in 1920, an initiative that would change the required number of signatures needed for qualifying tax-related initiatives from 8 percent to 25 percent of the vote in the preceding gubernatorial election.[71] This led to the creation of the League to Protect the Initiative, with Haynes as president, and Hiram Johnson and other Progressives as honorary vice-presidents. The League ran an active campaign all across the state, stressing defense of the initiative process.[72] While the single tax initiative on the same ballot was overwhelmingly defeated, Haynes and his supporters were successful in getting Proposition 4 rejected by 59 percent of the voters. Voters were clearly not voting in favor of the single tax, but in defense of direct legislation. It is interesting to note, however, that, of the twenty direct legislation propositions on the 1920 ballot, fifteen had higher rates of voter participation than did Proposition 4; a significant number of voters did not seem to care much about the issue.

Two years later, the same anti–single tax forces tried again, this time with Proposition 27, which would have increased the signature requirements to 15 percent rather than 25 percent.[73] The outcome was almost identical to that of 1920, and even fewer voters marked their ballots on the issue (64 percent, compared to 73 percent two years earlier).

The Progressive issue of water and power control, which was discussed above, also led to criticism of the initiative process. The conservative *San Francisco Chronicle* complained that the recurrence of the measure, after its being defeated two years previously, reflected the ease with which the initiative process could be abused: "No trouble what the measure is, if you have enough money you can get them [the requisite signatures] in just the bay cities and Los Angeles." It was too easy to get signatures, and it was an easy way for the solicitors to make money; if people had to go somewhere to sign up, "there would never be an initiative petition."[74] The same paper complained again in 1927 about the fact that a law on truck weight tax was being held from enforcement for two years because a referendum (Proposition 8 of 1928) was to be filed against it. This was a misuse of the referendum process, the paper argued, and did not really reflect popular sentiment.[75] Chester Rowell, a leading Progressive but never an unqualified supporter of direct legislation, echoed the *Chronicle*'s skepticism by 1928: "Ostensibly a weapon of the people, it has turned out to be the tool of individuals, to be used mostly for obstruction," as in the examples of reapportionment and road construction. But in the same column, Rowell recognized its importance "to escape the worst evil of our present state government," so he wasn't sure exactly what should be done.[76]

The same sentiments reappeared in the late 1930s when Ham and Eggs seemed, like the single tax, to be an extreme issue that a dedicated minority was bringing to the ballot again and again. The San Francisco Real Estate Board began a campaign to end the "absurd waste incurred by crackpot initiative proposals," and the *Chronicle* continued its twenty-year campaign against the process for the same reason.[77] The line between opposition to direct legislation because of the ends to which it was being put, and opposition to the process in general, was not always clear: one ran into the other. But the process had come under considerable questioning in the 1920s and 1930s.

As early as 1917, there had been criticism of the role of paid petition solicitors as a violation of the ideal of direct legislation being the result of popular enthusiasm. Associated with this was the argument that the public wasn't really all that interested in direct legislation: if not for the paid solicitors, few measures would ever make it to the ballot. Critics also contended that the process gave too much power to the cities because only they had sufficient population to make signature solicitation profitable. The increasingly large number of propositions, popular and legislative, state and local, also came in for criticism: how could one expect the average voter to make sense of it all? In this early period, also, signature validation was done under contract, with the contracts going usually to public officials, who were therefore "paid by private parties to perform a public duty."[78] And the state legislature's Jones Committee in 1923 concluded that too much money was being spent on initiatives, providing "a menace to our election system"; "of the seven important measures on the ballot in 1922, that side won which spent the most money."[79]

The League to Protect the Initiative, which meant essentially Haynes, worked hard to counter each of these criticisms.[80] Curiously, Haynes seemed little perturbed by the rise of paid solicitation, although he surely had not anticipated it while developing direct legislation. When the Jones Committee recommended a reform requiring that all petition signatures be made at a designated place before a county official, Haynes argued that this would destroy direct legislation, making it "impossible for the common people" to get any measures on the ballot. He had, as noted above, vigorously opposed the 1920 and 1922 propositions that would have raised the required number of signatures.[81] Franklin Hichborn at this time was being paid directly by Haynes to represent the League to Protect the Initiative in Sacramento. It was thus not very surprising that his journalistic articles of the time were defensive of the institution.[82]

A. J. Pillsbury's massive 1931 three-volume compilation for the Commonwealth Club of San Francisco evaluated the strengths and weaknesses of direct legislation, but provided a general business and middle-class endorsement of the process. It also provided a venue for defenders like Haynes and Hichborn to write their own essays relative to specific aspects of the initiative process.[83]

More criticism arose in the late 1930s. In 1938 the legislature was considering bills to reform the process by making initiatives more comprehensible, keeping the ballot shorter, requiring more signatures, and having signatures accepted only at a county clerk's office. It also considered the idea, clearly inspired by Ham and Eggs, of prohibiting any measure that had already been defeated at two successive elections. Some of these concerns reflected Chester Rowell's increasing criticism in his column in the *San Francisco Chronicle*. He was now arguing that initiatives and referendums "have become a means of confusion and tinkering, crackpot schemes and frequent frustration of public information." They were undermining the work of the legislature.[84]

One leader of the successful 1938 Culbert Olson campaign for governor, state senator Robert A. Kenny, said he planned to introduce legislation to "end all initiatives." The president of the state Chamber of Commerce announced a statewide conference to "correct the abuses" of the initiative, and the head of the California Farm Bureau Federation echoed Kenny's comments about the initiative undermining the legislature and said that the state would be better off without it.[85] None of these ideas came to anything at the time, but they did indicate continued questioning, particularly by some powerful and generally conservative interest groups, of the overall wisdom of the direct legislation process.

As the 1930s ended, direct legislation was, if anything, a greater force in California political life than it had been previously. Money had always been important, but was becoming increasingly so. Big money could not guarantee victory for a proposition, indeed, often failed. But big money could usually guarantee the ability to defeat a proposition, and this would become increasingly true over time. Most initiatives and referendums had their own constituencies, although individual issues and some general ideological orientations—especially on sociocultural matters—did generate consistent voting patterns over time. More and more groups, with more and more special interests, were using the direct legislation device; given that, a frequent lack of voting relationship from one measure to another is hardly surprising.

One final possible indicator of both level of voter participation and rates of proposition success or failure should be considered: ballot position. Voter participation rates varied considerably from one proposition to another within elections, as, of course, did the success or failure of individual propositions. To what extent was a "fatigue factor" involved? Did voters become more negative, or just stop marking their ballots, as they went down the often intimidating list of propositions? The 1920–1938 period is a good one for confronting these questions because it had a consistently large number of both popular and legislative propositions. Table 2.6 looks at the relationship between ballot position, on the one hand, and levels of voter participation and of proposition success, on the other.

It should be borne in mind while looking at this data that a *negative* correlation signifies a *positive* result, since the "highest" ballot position is the one with the lowest number — 1, then 2, then 3, and so on. Thus, if there is a relationship between high ballot position and, for example, voting Yes, we would expect the lowest ballot number to relate to the highest percentage voting Yes. The table includes data for both direct legislation (popular) measures alone, and for direct legislation and legislative measures combined, because both calculations are potentially significant. Given that legislative and popular measures were mixed together on the ballot, the latter is probably a better indicator of "voter fatigue," particularly in terms of rate of

TABLE 2.6   Correlations of Ballot Position with Rate of Voter
Participation and Proposition Success, 1920–1938

| Election | Voter participation: Direct legislation only | Voter participation: All propositions | Percentage voting Pro: Direct legislation only | Percentage voting Pro: All propositions |
|---|---|---|---|---|
| 1920 | −.776 | −.551 | −.079 | .080 |
| 1922 | −.374 | −.234 | −.566 | −.386 |
| 1924 | —[a] | .050 | —[a] | −.023 |
| 1926 | −.833 | −.643 | −.202 | −.015 |
| 1928 | —[a] | −.284 | —[a] | .000 |
| 1930 | .261 | −.464 | −.236 | −.044 |
| 1932 | −.892 | −.859 | −.567 | .130 |
| 1934 | .025 | −.428 | −.751 | −.263 |
| 1936 | .308 | −.239 | .627 | .332 |
| 1938 | −.121 | −.351 | .198 | −.189 |

NOTE:  Pearson product moment correlation between ballot number of proposition and
(1) total vote per proposition and (2) percentage of favorable votes per proposition ("Pro" is
based on Yes on initiatives, No on referendums). Only coefficients set in boldface are
statistically significant.
[a]Too few propositions for calculation.

participation. Also, the table uses the term "Pro" rather than "Yes," because
a Yes vote on an initiative and a No vote on a referendum each represent
success for the drafters of the proposition. We are seeking to know if a low
ballot number is at all related to the rate of voter participation and/or the
likelihood of a proposition being successful.[86]

Understanding this, Table 2.6 suggests that ballot position did have a
meaningful relationship with voter participation, sometimes a quite significant one (1920, 1926, 1932). In those strong correlation years, it matters
little whether one looks at all propositions or just the direct legislation ones:
the propositions higher on the ballot attracted more voters. There are two
elections (1930 and 1934) where ballot position has a statistically significant
but lesser relationship to participation when looking at all measures, but
is definitely not significant if one looks only at direct legislation. And there
are several elections where there is no significant relationship either way.

For this, there is no ready explanation, other than the fact that every election is distinct in the types of measures included and in voter interest and enthusiasm.

A reasonable conclusion from Table 2.6 is that ballot position was one of the factors that contributed to voter participation — that, overall, more people voted on the measures higher on the ballot than otherwise. But the variations in the numbers, as well as simple logic from studying general response to and publicity about individual ballot measures, makes it clear that this was indeed only one of several factors involved. One sees again and again, in this 86-year history, how direct legislation propositions, regardless of ballot position, had higher voter participation rates than legislative ones, and how some issues — such as those with sociocultural content — were consistently more involving than others.

Relative to the question of how ballot position might have affected the likelihood of a proposition's being successful, the table is less useful. There are few significant relationships here, whether one looks only at direct legislation or at all propositions together. Essentially, ballot position does not influence a measure's likelihood of success or failure. Voters seem to have looked for the propositions they were particularly interested in supporting or opposing.

By the end of the 1930s, direct legislation had modernized and professionalized. It was increasingly likely that the most controversial issues of the time would somehow come directly before the voters for their decision. Direct legislation was becoming a "fourth branch" of California government rather than a simple lifeboat to be used only in extreme circumstances. And that role would not diminish in the ensuing decades.

# 3   Old Issues and New, 1940–1969

The years between 1940 and the end of the 1960s witnessed considerable change in the United States and in California. Once again, in the state, direct legislation often reflected and sometimes led those changes. World War II itself did not importantly influence direct legislation, but its many consequences assuredly did. The war and postwar period brought a rapid population increase in California, with concomitant increases in industrialization and urbanization. Moreover, all of these factors were disproportionately associated with southern California, creating tensions that threatened the traditional balance between the regions and the traditional locus of financial and industrial matters in the Bay Area.

The population increase in Los Angeles and San Diego consisted not least of African-Americans seeking the new industrial jobs the war and Cold War made available. Racial discord in California, which had traditionally been focused on Asian immigrants, now became much like that in the rest of the country, with black-white conflict playing an increasingly important role in the 1950s and 1960s. Industrialization also meant that organized labor became a greater presence in California, and labor-management conflict was more frequent. Now, however, it was a somewhat more even match than in the past, with labor often able to equal management in fund-raising ability and campaigning.

Some old questions, like liquor control, no longer excited a very large part of the population, but matters related to moral values were still important, ranging from control of obscenity to the role of religious schools to the fostering of national loyalty. The general prosperity of the time made voters more supportive of expanded public services, even as they worried about the burden of increased taxes. The place of the poor in this more-prosperous California, and the obligation of the non-poor to succor them, likewise elicited considerable attention, and controversy.

Direct legislation in California during this period reflected the fact that the New Deal and war years had considerably refocused American attention

TABLE 3.1 Subjects of Direct Legislation, 1940–1968

| Election year | Sociocultural | Government and law | Business and economics | Taxation and bonds | Labor and welfare | Education |
|---|---|---|---|---|---|---|
| 1940 | | | 1 | | | |
| 1942 | | | 2 | 1 | 1 | |
| 1944 | | | | | 2 | 1 |
| 1946 | 1 | | | | 1 | 1 |
| 1948 | 2 | 1 | 2 | | 3 | |
| 1949 | | | 1 | | 1 | |
| 1950 | 1 | | | 1 | 1 | |
| 1952 | | 1 | 1 | 1 | 1 | 1 |
| 1954 | | | | | 1 | |
| 1956 | | | 1 | | | |
| 1958 | | | | 2 | 1 | |
| 1960 | | 1 | | | | |
| 1962 | 1 | 1 | | | | |
| 1964 | 2 | | 1 | | 1 | |
| 1966 | 1 | | | | | |
| 1968 | | | | 1 | | |

away from the state and local level to the national. With more questions being dealt with at the national level, it stood to reason that state-based solutions were somewhat fewer than before. Indeed, from the start of the 1940s through the end of the 1960s, the use of direct legislation did decline markedly. For example, the number of proposed initiatives in this 30-year period was only 38, compared to 71 in the much shorter 1920–1938 time span discussed in the preceding chapter. Moreover, there were only 2 referendums in this period, compared to 22 in the preceding one (the referendum process would subsequently fall into almost total disuse). Additionally, there was an increase in the rate of proposed direct legislation measures that failed to obtain enough signatures to qualify for the ballot.[1] There were also three indirect initiatives in this time period, the first and last ever proposed: the procedure was done away with in 1966.[2]

The reduced number of direct legislation propositions did not signify any decline in the institution's impact, however, because important issues arose and controversy was often intense. As before, central questions of California life were put directly to the people rather than being resolved in the legislature. Furthermore, conscientious voters did not necessarily have much less to do, since the number of legislative proposals continued at the same pace as before. There were 229 legislative constitutional amendments and bond acts in this period. There were also, for the first time, legislative initiative amendments and legislative statute amendments, eleven of the former and one of the latter. Both types are proposals initiated by the legislature to amend statutes already established either by the initiative process or by the legislature itself. As with the other measures proposed by the legislature, these had a high rate of success.[3]

As of 1960, initiatives and referendums could be included in primary elections, rather than just general and special elections. All of the measures on June primary ballots in that decade, however, continued to be legislative ones. It was not until June 1970 that a direct legislation proposition appeared on a primary election ballot, after which time the practice became common.

That the subject matter of direct legislation propositions in the period 1940–1968 varied somewhat from those of the 1920–1938 period can be seen by comparing Table 2.1 with Table 3.1. The social and cultural propositions reflected both older issues, such as Prohibition and gambling, and newer ones, particularly race and civil rights. The last was but one example of how direct legislation in this period introduced sociocultural public policy conflicts that would become permanent parts of the California political landscape. Labor and welfare measures focused on increasingly bitter battles over unions, particularly the union shop versus the closed shop, and on a continuation of welfare proposals of the Ham and Eggs type, albeit under a new name and new leadership. Taxation issues also continued to be controversial, including the first efforts to deal with the escalating property tax, which anticipated the pivotal Proposition 13 of 1978.

While fewer Californians were interested in liquor control by this time, those who did care were still extremely active, with six efforts to put initiatives on the ballot between 1940 and 1956. Only two of these actually qualified, both of them in 1948. Proposition 12 was a straightforward effort to put local option in the state constitution, whereas Proposition 2 would put a 1947 alcoholic beverage statute into the constitution and, probably, make local option impossible. It is possible that Proposition 2's main aim was to undercut Proposition 12, since it was supported financially by liquor-related unions and some liquor companies. Real anti-liquor groups, like the California Temperance Federation, raised money and campaigned to defeat Proposition 2 and support Proposition 12. Business groups like the California and Los Angeles Chambers of Commerce opposed both of them.[4] The issue still aroused popular interest, as evidenced by voter participation rates of 89 percent and 90 percent, respectively. But 69 percent of the voters opposed Proposition 2, and 71 percent opposed Proposition 12, signifying that liquor regulation no longer had a chance in California. All subsequent efforts did not even make it to the ballot.

This "modern" thinking relative to alcohol did not extend to gambling, however. A 1946 effort to legalize dog racing had the highest voter participation rate in that election, and was turned down by 77 percent of the voters (a similar effort in 1976 would be defeated by 74 percent of the vote).[5] An even more controversial gambling measure, Proposition 6, was on the 1950 ballot. It would have legalized off-track betting on horseraces and other forms of gambling. Moreover, it was proposed by Willis Allen and Roy Owens, of Ham and Eggs fame, who once again tried to use the initiative process to give themselves public positions: the initiative specified that they would be two of the original five state commissioners. They had tried to label the initiative the "Pensions and Welfare Funding Act," but the Secretary of State insisted on "Legalizing and Licensing Gambling." All of this made the measure even more controversial, and its defenders' argument that legalized gambling would help cut taxes won few converts. The opposition, comprised of businesses and various other organizations, raised over $200,000 for their anti-Proposition 6 campaign, using some of the money to hire Campaigns, Inc. to direct it. In the balloting, 77 percent of the voters rejected off-track betting.[6]

This anti-gambling sentiment prevailed as late as 1964, when the first effort at a state lottery (Proposition 16) had a 93 percent voter participation rate and was defeated 69 percent to 31 percent. Like the Allen and Owens initiative in 1950, this proposition also tried to control who would be appointed to the new State Lottery Commission, which was one of the criticisms made by its opponents.[7]

Two other sociocultural issues during this period merit mention because they reflected the changing focus of cultural conflict in the 1960s. In 1962, Proposition 24 represented extreme Cold War anti-communist sentiment. It was known as the "Francis Amendment," after assemblyman Louis Francis, one of its key supporters. Among other things, it would have denied political party status to communist and "subversive" organizations, denied public employment to members of such organizations, and required all employees of public educational institutions to respond to congressional committee inquiries about their affiliations. Some influential extreme conservatives, like Henry Salvatori and Patrick Frawley, supported the measure. But both incumbent Governor Edmund G. "Pat" Brown and his 1962 opponent Richard Nixon openly opposed it, as did conservative newspapers like the *San Francisco Chronicle* and the *Los Angeles Times*. All critics denounced the excessive nature of the measure and its questionable constitutionality.[8]

Proposition 24 lost by a vote of 60–40 percent, a striking statistic given public opinion polls that suggested steadily increasing support for the measure. For example, in a Field Institute (California) Poll in July, of those saying they favored Nixon for governor, 52 percent also said they favored Proposition 24 and 28 percent opposed it, whereas of those supporting Governor Brown, only 39 percent favored Proposition 24 and 42 percent were opposed. In the September poll, the difference was significantly less: 59 percent of Nixon's supporters and 52 percent of Governor Brown's supporters said they would vote in favor of Proposition 24.[9]

Similarly, 52 percent of those who had voted for John F. Kennedy in 1960, and 57 percent of Nixon voters in that election, indicated they would support Proposition 24, as did 53 percent of registered Democrats and 56 percent of registered Republicans. Neither age, level of education, nor employment status had much effect on support levels for Proposition 24; a few groups (the unemployed, people over 60) supported the measure by a bit under 50 percent, but in each case they had more Undecideds rather than more opponents. The only clear distinction in the poll was that based on religion: 55 percent of Protestants and 57 percent of Catholics favored Proposition 24, whereas 61 percent of Jews opposed it — the only identifiable group with a strong majority against this harsh anti-leftist initiative.[10]

Obviously, some people changed their minds by election day, or, more likely, did not vote on the proposition. There were 25 propositions on the 1962 ballot, but 23 of them were legislative. The two popular initiatives were last on the ballot, numbers 23 and 24 (there was a Prop. 1A, as well as a Prop. 1). Proposition 24 had the second highest voter participation rate

TABLE 3.2 Correlations for Voting on Sociocultural Issues, 1962–1966, and Census Characteristics

| Variable | 1962: Prop. 24 Subversives | 1964: Prop. 14 Fair housing | 1966: Prop. 16 Obscenity | Percentage born in different state | Percentage age 20–21 in school | Percentage urban |
|---|---|---|---|---|---|---|
| 1962: Prop. 24 Subversives | 1.000 | | | | | |
| 1964: Prop. 14 Fair housing | .764 | 1.000 | | | | |
| 1966: Prop. 16 Obscenity | .839 | .812 | 1.000 | | | |
| Percentage born in different state | .772 | .682 | .700 | 1.000 | | |
| Percentage age 20–21 in school | −.195 | −.472 | −.340 | −.290 | 1.000 | |
| Percentage urban | .330 | .026 | .016 | .386 | .403 | 1.000 |

NOTE: Pearson product moment correlations, based on percentage voting Yes on propositions and data from 1960 U.S. Census, with data aggregated by county and weighted by county population. For clarity, only one side of table is shown, since both sides are identical.

among all measures on the ballot, but still that was only 82 percent—considerably lower than was usual for socioculturally divisive direct legislation. Some of the early supporters of Proposition 24 apparently changed their minds, and some just didn't bother to vote.

Another controversial sociocultural measure appeared in Proposition 16 of 1966, a draconian anti-obscenity initiative statute. It would have redefined obscenity and tightened the rules for state intervention in the issue; conspiring to violate the obscenity laws was to be a felony. Opposition was broad, including most newspapers and many religious organizations. When Los Angeles's Town Hall organization polled its middle-class business and professional members, they voted 234–77 against the measure.[11]

Proposition 16 was the only non-legislative proposition on the November 1966 ballot, and it drew the largest number of voters by a considerable margin. Its defeat was not as decisive as that of Proposition 24 four years earlier, but it was still unambiguous: 56 percent against to 44 percent in favor (there would be another controversial anti-obscenity measure in 1972 — see Chapter 4). All the same, there seems to have been a fairly strong conservative voting bloc on sociocultural issues in the 1960s, which is explored a bit further in Table 3.2.

The table shows strikingly strong relationships among three conservative measures in the 1960s: opposition to alleged subversives, opposition to open housing (discussed below), and opposition to obscenity. The votes on these issues reflect the strong conservative-liberal division in the United States generally during this period, the time of the civil rights movement, the Johnson–Goldwater presidential contest, the John Birch Society and other extremist conservative organizations, and the rising controversiality of the war in Vietnam. A large number of the same people saw these three propositions in the same light.

In terms of background variables that might help explain what distinguished these socioculturally "conservative" and "liberal" voters, one is once again confined to the questions asked on the census. There was a strong relationship between being a comparative newcomer to California and supporting a conservative position on these propositions. Newcomers brought relatively more conservative ideas with them to California and/or became more socially conservative as a result of their own marginality in California society at that time. It is then quite logical that the percentage of those aged 20–21 who were still in school, a characteristic that reflects both level of education and relative wealth, had a negative relationship with these socioculturally conservative propositions. The negative relationships are not very strong, but they are statistically significant for fair housing and obscenity. These were ideas that made relatively more elite Californians uncomfortable. On the other hand, the insignificant relationship between this variable and the vote on Proposition 24 reflects the broader base of fear of subversion at the height of the Cold War. Similarly, even urban residence has a modestly significant relationship with voting for Proposition 24, whereas it has none with the other two measures.

The anti-subversives and anti-obscenity campaigns showed that, while the specifics of sociocultural propositions may have changed since the 1920s and 1930s, such propositions remained among the most engrossing and most controversial of the measures that Californians were dealing with a generation later. And this was nowhere clearer than in the "new" issue of race, which began to play an important role in initiative politics at this time. Proposition 14 of 1964 was only the most striking of a series of initiatives that reflected the rising tide of racial division in post–World War II California.

The issue was introduced in 1946, with Proposition 11, an initiative statute for fair employment practices that would forbid discrimination in employment on the basis of "color, national origin, or ancestry" and would create a state commission to enforce the law. The initiative was prompted by the fact that a similar proposal had been debated by two sessions of the legislature but had not been acted upon; moreover, Governor Earl Warren had never endorsed the idea or tried to move it through the legislature.[12] Thus, Proposition 11 was a good example of the original idea behind direct democracy, that is, offering the people a chance to act when the legislature refused to do so. In this case, however, "the people" were by no means united on what the proper solution should be.

Opposition to Proposition 11 was widespread and included a large part of the organized California middle class. Town Hall (Los Angeles), for example, issued an extensive report on the proposition that generally supported its ends but decried its means. Morality could not be legislated, the report said; an individual had the right to control his own business; the law could be misused by "militant individuals or groups"; members of different races could be forced to work together when they did not want to; and "minority group members would be attracted to California from the South . . . in ever-increasing numbers." The Los Angeles Chamber of Commerce made many of the same arguments.[13] The *San Francisco Chronicle* offered up a common complaint, that the measure would punish employers but not workers, and argued that such an issue should be handled by the legislature rather than the initiative process.[14] Farm interests also joined the anti-Proposition 11 campaign, since they believed their own use of minority workers would be threatened by the law. Not surprisingly, opponents of the proposition raised considerably more funds than did supporters.[15]

Support for the measure came primarily from liberal Democrats, and from civil rights and African-American leaders. However, even some of the latter questioned the proposition, fearing that allowing the people to vote on such a basic right suggested that its legality was debatable. They preferred to leave the issue in the legislature. Some also felt that fair employment practices should be combined with fair housing, as basic civil rights.[16]

The public was definitely not ready for fair employment: Proposition 11 had one of the highest voter participation rates (85 percent) of this off-year election and was defeated by 71 percent to 29 percent. It would take another thirteen years and action by the legislature to finally get fair employment practices implemented.[17]

The issue of fair employment was replaced by that of public housing in the next two elections. The question of public housing involved more than just race, but racial attitudes were definitely an important part of the issue. As early as 1948, Proposition 14 had raised the question in an initiative constitutional amendment that would have committed the state to raise up to $100 million as part of a multifaceted effort to provide public housing to the poor.[18] And Proposition 10, two years later, another initiative constitutional amendment, was an effort by many of those who had successfully opposed Proposition 14 to pound a long nail into the coffin of open housing: it would require a popular vote before any public housing project could be undertaken by the state.

Antagonism to Proposition 14 was probably more economic than racial. Its most open opposition came from the building trades, which spent at least $110,000 against it. But other business groups joined the effort, stressing the competition with private business, the likely tax increase, and the reduction of local agency power that would result.[19] Liberal, labor, and African-American groups and spokespersons were the main defenders of the proposition, but they found little public support. They could not overcome broad opposition to the initiative, which lost by 69 percent to 31 percent.

Two years later, the more extreme anti–public housing Proposition 10 showed less unanimity of opinion, barely passing by a vote of 51 percent to 49 percent. The building trades groups supported this measure, as did both the Los Angeles and the California Chambers of Commerce. The Chambers argued that the long-term debt and taxes associated with public housing were real economic dangers, and that workers in the private sector would lose their jobs because private industry could not compete with government. The "bureaucrats" and "radicals" were the opponents that this measure would strike down.[20]

Opposition to Proposition 10 was broader than support for Proposition 14 had been. The conservative *San Francisco Chronicle*, always leery of direct legislation, argued that putting this measure into the constitution and requiring an "obligatory referendum on every low-rent housing project" was a bad idea. There was also opposition from the Los Angeles Housing Authority, from organized labor (including both the AFL and the CIO), from the NAACP, and from such mainstream groups as the Veterans of Foreign Wars and the American Legion.[21] Still, the opponents of fair housing managed to eke out another victory.

Race was not the only important issue for Propositions 14 and 10 in 1948 and 1950, as it had been for the fair employment Proposition 11 in 1946. But both of the later measures included rising racial tension and conflict as part of their equations.

The culmination of these developments came in the civil rights era of the 1960s, specifically in the effort to use the initiative to invalidate the legislature's fair housing Rumford Act. In this case, race and racial conflict were at the heart of the struggle. Both pro– and anti–civil rights groups were emboldened and embittered by the battle over Proposition 14 of 1964, which clearly exacerbated racial relations in California. In the minds of many, it played no small role in the black alienation that culminated in the Watts riots in Los Angeles less than one year later.[22]

Byron Rumford, an African-American from the East Bay area, had been first elected to the California Assembly in 1948. Since then, he had consistently sought both fair housing and fair employment legislation. With Democrat Edmund G. "Pat" Brown as governor, a fair employment practices bill had been passed in 1959, as had the Unruh Civil Rights Act. Rumford's fair housing bill was submitted to the legislature in its 1963 session with the blessing of Governor Brown, Assembly Speaker Jess Unruh, and the state Democratic Party. Conservatives in the legislature fought adamantly against it, but Unruh, an extraordinarily effective legislative leader, got it passed in September 1963.[23] Opponents immediately countered with Proposition 14, which would invalidate the new law by guaranteeing every citizen the right to refuse to sell, rent, or lease their property to anyone they chose.

From the start, real estate interests were bitterly opposed to the new law. The California Real Estate Association and the Apartment House Owners Association, particularly, led the battle to undo it. They could additionally bank on the broad unpopularity of open housing among Californians in general. But the proposition, as a constitutional amendment, went well beyond simple real estate regulation: it would invalidate aspects of the Unruh Civil Rights Act as well as the Rumford Act.[24] Moreover, the year 1964 was a presidential election year wherein liberal-versus-conservative issues and candidacies made news all across the country, and events surrounding the civil rights movement were daily headline fare. Considerable national attention was paid to the Proposition 14 battle, with outside money from national real estate and other interests coming in to help both sides.

Proposition 14 supporters were very well organized, with centralized fund-raising and campaign direction. By late August, the main pro-14 interest group, the "Committee for Home Protection," had already raised

$340,000.[25] The defenders of open housing were also numerous, representing the Democratic Party leadership, organized labor, churches, the League of Women Voters, and a variety of liberal groups. There was strong Hollywood involvement, with a big anti-Proposition 14 rally at the Hollywood Bowl. But much less money came in for their cause, and, most important, the majority of Californians were just not ready for open housing.[26] Ninety-six percent of those voting marked their ballots on Proposition 14, a higher level of voter participation than for any other of the seventeen measures in that election. And two-thirds of them supported the initiative, opting to kill fair housing in California.

Certainly, there were some purely economic forces at work here, but the focus of the campaign had been on fair housing for "Negroes." The broader issue of race relations in general was the major spoken and unspoken theme of the campaign, and the racial factor was determinative in how many voters marked their ballots. California was not Alabama in 1964, but neither was a majority of its population ready for full racial equality. The following summer Watts would erupt with fires that illuminated the depth of this problem in California.[27]

Ultimately, the Rumford Act survived, because Proposition 14 was ruled unconstitutional by both the California and U.S. Supreme Courts as a violation of the Fourteenth Amendment. The Supreme Court's ruling ensured that California would have a fair housing law, but it did not erase the antagonism that the battle over fair housing had generated.

Closely related to sociocultural issues were those dealing with social welfare and organized labor, both of which struck at deeply held values as well as purely social and economic interests. Chapter 2 traced the rise of propositions on these topics in the 1930s; they definitely did not disappear with the ending of the Depression. Labor conflict expanded in the war and postwar years as California became more and more industrial and had to confront the labor-management conflicts that other industrial states had experienced. And, despite federal relief programs and Social Security, the drive for a state pension system continued. Indeed, the legacy of Ham and Eggs was very much evident throughout the 1940s and into the 1950s.

Ham and Eggs had lost in the elections of 1938 and 1939, but the national Townsend movement, which had inspired Ham and Eggs, continued to exist. Its California branch tried to qualify an initiative in 1940, but failed to collect enough signatures; it was able, however, to use those same signatures four years later to get Proposition 11 on the 1944 ballot.[28] (The Townsend Clubs had similar initiatives in that year in Arizona, Oregon, and Washington.) The measure proposed $60 per month pension for persons over age 60, who, in typical Townsend Plan fashion, could not work and had to spend the money within each given month. The initiative had financing features similar to those of the 1938 Ham and Eggs proposition, and included repeal of the sales tax and creation of a gross income tax. Dr. Townsend himself, then living in Chicago, signed the ballot argument in favor of Proposition 11, and the Townsend Clubs managed to raise about $100,000 for the California campaign. But they garnered precious little outside support: the press, the state PTA, the California State Employees Association, and a wide variety of business and commercial groups outspokenly opposed the proposition.[29] Interestingly, one of the signers of the anti–Proposition 11 argument in the *California Ballot Pamphlet* was George H. McLain, who represented himself as "Chairman, Citizen's Committee for Old Age Pensions." This was the same George McLain who had been hired to help run the 1939 Ham and Eggs campaign, and who had his own ambitions that were very much in conflict with Proposition 11.

Proposition 11 had an 87 percent voter participation rate, second highest after right-to-work (see below), among twelve measures on the ballot. Slightly more than two-thirds of those voting rejected the proposal. As with Ham and Eggs, a majority of Californians were unpersuaded that the measure's multifaceted provisions made for an acceptable package.

There then followed ten years of propositions and counter-propositions, with mixed fates, and in which George McLain was the foremost advocate or opponent. There were almost two old-age pension propositions on the November 1948 ballot. Former Ham and Eggs leaders introduced one that combined a pension scheme, reapportionment of the state senate, a state board of naturopathic examiners, and other features, including the appointment of Willis Allen as commissioner of pensions at a salary of $15,000 per year. The proposition did get enough signatures, but it was invalidated by the state Supreme Court on two grounds: it contained too many different subjects, and it was a "revision of" rather than an "amendment to" the state constitution.[30]

McLain's group did qualify Proposition 4, called the "Aged and Blind Act," in 1948. It was a constitutional amendment that would change California's law relative to old-age and blind relief, raising the amount of pensions and easing age and income requirements. It also would centralize aid in a state office, under an elected Director of Social Welfare. Critics focused on the inflationary aspects of the proposition, the freezing of benefits regardless of need, and the increased bureaucracy being created. But there was also some self-serving concern of agencies like the California Council for the Blind, which would lose power to the new state agency and director.[31] Various business interests also opposed the measure, but McLain had a genius for organization and also the support of numerous liberals, such as James Roosevelt.[32]

Proposition 4 garnered an 89 percent voter participation rate, just behind the two measures dealing with liquor regulation, and squeaked to victory with 50.5 percent versus 49.5 percent of the vote. That led to immediate criticism from a variety of sources. The California Council for the Blind said that "pension politicians [had] hoodwinked the voters of California" into passing an initiative with many bad parts only because the aged and blind did need higher pensions. The Council was joined by the California Taxpayers Association in its call for revocation of the new Article XXV of the constitution. The Taxpayers Association, an old, established anti-tax group, criticized the new program's cost, its centralization, and other specifics as well.[33]

The immediate result was easy qualification for Proposition 2 in the 1949 special election. This initiative constitutional amendment would simply undo Proposition 4, reinstating the previous welfare system. It would remove those under 65 from the old-age pension rolls, restore family responsibility, and definitely lower the costs to the state. The campaign was quite fierce, with a broad-based coalition favoring the new measure. Conservative newspapers like the *Los Angeles Times* and *San Francisco Chronicle* waged long pro-2 campaigns, but so, too, did Governor Warren, the League of Women Voters, the state PTA and Federation of Women's Clubs, and numerous other state, regional, and local middle-class organizations.[34] Big money was also spent by both sides, particularly by Proposition 2's proponents, who hired Robinson and Co. for signature solicitation and Campaigns, Inc. to help organize and run the campaign. Overall, these groups collected and spent over $600,000 (about $4 million in 1995 dollars).[35] McLain had really scared them.

Sensing defeat, McLain tried dissimulation, having his workers call voters in San Francisco and Los Angeles to tell them that the way to get rid of the McLain organization was to vote No on Proposition 2.[36] But McLain's forces failed this time. Proposition 2 drew more voters than any other of the twelve measures on the ballot, and it won by a more decisive vote than had Proposition 4 the previous year: 57.5 percent to 42.5 percent. On the whole, there were voting publics who opted consistently for or against McLain's efforts, but there were also voters who made few distinctions among welfare propositions (or didn't understand their specifics) and supported every welfare measure they found on the ballot.

This became clearer, or perhaps more muddled, with the election of 1952, when the McLain organization once again had an initiative on the ballot, in this case, Proposition 11. McLain used the indirect initiative process in 1952 because it required only the same number of signatures as for a statutory initiative, rather than the larger number required for a constitutional amendment, even though Proposition 11 would undo the constitutional changes instituted by Proposition 2 three years earlier.[37] McLain's proposal would once again move administration of old-age pensions from the counties to the state, repeal the relatives' responsibility requirement, change the property requirements for eligibility, and replace the maximum $75 payment with a more flexible cost-of-living one. In their ballot pamphlet argument, the McLain forces quoted the Bible, "as God said to Honor thy Father and thy Mother." The three signers were: "Mrs. Amelia Mayberry, Pioneer Organizer of California P.T.A., Age 88; Mrs. Eva Warring, 79-year-old Gold Star Mother; George McLain, Chairman, California Institute of Social Welfare."[38]

Interest-group response was pretty much the same as it had been to McLain's 1948 effort, with a broad coalition of middle-class business and professional groups advocating defeat. Also, McLain's own organization seems to have been smaller and less well organized than before.[39] McLain lost again: the voters rejected Proposition 11 by 56 percent to 44 percent, almost the same as the margin by which they had beaten him by approving Proposition 2 in 1949.

McLain lost yet again, two years later, by the same margin, on Proposition 4 in the 1954 general election. That initiative constitutional amendment focused mainly on old-age pensions, raising the maximum pension to $100 a month and empowering the legislature only to raise, not lower, the amount. It was the only direct legislation measure on that year's ballot, along with nineteen propositions from the legislature, and it had the highest voter participation rate (90 percent) of them all. McLain had some union support, but business, government, and professional groups argued strongly against the rigidity of the proposal, its cost in taxes, and its threat to bring large numbers of old people to California in search of higher pensions.[40]

Thus, McLain had a mixed history on the pension issue. He played a role in successfully defeating the Townsend proposal in 1944, won with his own measure in 1948, had that victory overturned in 1949, and failed in both 1952 and 1954 to undo what had happened in 1949. In the process, whatever his controversial motives may have been, he showed real organizational wizardry in his ability to garner signatures, popular support, and enough money to run his campaigns. But in the final analysis, the business and professional middle class, established charitable organizations and government agencies, and a large part of the public in general saw his proposals as too drastic and too expensive.

Table 3.3 looks at the relationships in the voting on all of the welfare measures, from the first Ham and Eggs vote in 1938 through McLain's last initiative in 1954. Some of them stand out. For example, the correlation between the two Ham and Eggs propositions, in 1938 and 1939, is extremely strong, as one might expect. But there are no significant correlations between those two and any of the others, except for the final McLain vote in 1954, for reasons that are not entirely clear. The 1948–1949–1952 votes have very strong relationships with one another: those who voted for McLain's program in 1948 did so again in 1952, and also voted against the 1949 proposition (negative correlation) that undid the 1948 vote. But the table also shows that McLain lost his traditional support in 1954; that election does not correlate significantly with the others. It may be that the 1954 Proposition 4's narrower focus, on old-age pensions only, lost him some of his earlier support. By the same token, the significant correlation between that initiative and the earlier Ham and Eggs measures makes sense — many former Ham and Eggers could see in it a proposal very much like those they had supported in 1938–1939.

The 1949 vote stands alone. It related, as above, very strongly and negatively to the two McLain measures just before and after it. But it had no significant correlation with any other elections. Its voters were a one-time coalition brought together by opposition to McLain and his program. The two census variables have few significant relationships. There is a moderately significant negative correlation between both education/class and percentage of urban voters, on the one hand, and 1944 voting for the Townsend Plan on the other. This is to be expected, because the Townsend Plan nationally had its greatest appeal among the elderly, the poor, and small town Americans.

This battle over welfare is an example of the difficulty of resolving complex issues through the initiative process. The welfare program involved major financing and other economic questions. It required a large administrative apparatus and, as seen, a balancing of federal, state, and county power and programs. Because there were so many technical factors involved, and such a wide variety of interests, it was perhaps simply not an issue to be resolved by the "no compromise" nature of direct legislation.

Social welfare, particularly for the aged, was a significant issue in California in this period, reflecting a new awareness of the possibilities and problems that had emerged with the passage of Social Security by the New Deal in 1935. There was obviously much concern about the way California should fit into this new system and considerable disagreement about the specifics.

Labor issues were also important in direct legislation at this time. The increased industrialization and unionization of southern California during the war continued to expand in the postwar era; the state was now a major urban and industrial center, and it could not escape the management-labor conflict that ensued. Chapter 2 looked at the most significant anti-labor initiative of the 1930s (Proposition 1 of 1938), which had been rejected by the voters. The period from 1940 to 1970 witnessed five more direct legisla-

TABLE 3.3  Correlations for Voting on Welfare Issues, 1938–1954, and Census Characteristics

| Proposition | 1938: Prop. 25 Ham and eggs | 1939: Prop. 1 Ham and eggs | 1944: Prop. 11 Townsend Plan | 1948: Prop. 4 McLain | 1949: Prop. 2 Anti-McLain | 1952: Prop. 11 McLain | 1954: Prop. 4 McLain | Percentage age 20–24 in school | Percentage urban |
|---|---|---|---|---|---|---|---|---|---|
| 1938: Prop. 25 Ham and eggs | 1.000 | | | | | | | | |
| 1939: Prop. 1 Ham and eggs | .910 | 1.000 | | | | | | | |
| 1944: Prop. 11 Townsend Plan | .222 | .147 | 1.000 | | | | | | |
| 1948: Prop. 4 McLain | −.294 | −.182 | −.229 | 1.000 | | | | | |

| | | | | | | | | | |
|---|---|---|---|---|---|---|---|---|---|
| 1949:<br>Prop. 2<br>Anti-McLain | .225 | .079 | .196 | −.775 | 1.000 | | | | |
| 1952:<br>Prop. 11<br>McLain | −.105 | .010 | −.141 | .785 | −.840 | 1.000 | | | |
| 1954:<br>Prop. 4<br>McLain | .458 | .537 | .085 | .088 | −.251 | .286 | 1.000 | | |
| Percentage<br>age 20–24<br>in school | −.136 | −.058 | −.352 | −.027 | −.054 | .014 | −.269 | 1.000 | |
| Percentage<br>urban | .115 | .107 | −.384 | −.212 | −.020 | −.094 | −.023 | .645 | 1.000 |

NOTE: Pearson product moment correlations, based on percentage voting Yes on propositions and data from 1950 U.S. Census, with data aggregated by county and weighted by county population. For clarity, only one side of table is shown, since both sides are identical.

tion measures dealing with organized labor, with overall mixed results for both sides. Like sociocultural and welfare propositions, those involving organized labor also drew very high voter participation rates — they were issues of real practical and emotional power for many Californians.

In 1942, Proposition 1 was a referendum that sought to undo a recent act of the legislature outlawing "hot cargo" and "secondary boycott" actions by workers for the duration of the war. The official ballot pamphlet sought to explain each of these practices, in which workers take action against an employer, not for their own labor relations but because of labor disputes in other companies with which this employer is doing business. The ballot pamphlet also explained the peculiar wording of referendums, wherein a Yes vote was actually a vote against the referendum and in favor of maintaining the law passed by the legislature. This explanation was not very clear if one relied only on the official summary; but if voters also read the pro and con arguments, the meaning of Yes and No votes became clearer.[41] The new language was an improvement over earlier ballot pamphlets so far as referendums were concerned, but how carefully most voters read the pamphlet is conjectural.

Probably the most important factor in the ultimate upholding of this legislation was that it was wartime and the law was designed to last only as long as the war continued. Moreover, it was easy to represent the law as a moderate measure, and the campaign for upholding the legislation was relatively low key and localized.[42] California labor was well organized by this time, and did conduct a major fund-raising and publicity campaign against the law. But it was difficult to persuade a majority of Californians that the legislation was "Slave Bill 877."[43] Proposition 1 drew a voter participation rate of 90 percent, the highest among eighteen measures on the ballot, and the state law was upheld by 55 percent of those voting.

That the California public had not become anti-labor in wartime became clearer two years later, when a right-to-work initiative was decisively defeated. Proposition 12 in the 1944 general election was a constitutional amendment that would have guaranteed the right of workers to be hired without joining a union and would forbid unions from interfering with such hiring activities.

The campaign over Proposition 12 was intense. Organizations in favor of it were formed in both northern and southern California. Numerous businesses, conservative newspapers like the *Los Angeles Times*, the Los Angeles Chamber of Commerce, and the majority of members of Town Hall, Los Angeles, all supported Proposition 12.[44] Interestingly, the California State Chamber of Commerce opposed the proposition "in the interest of national unity," possibly as a considered response to labor's wartime no-strike pledge.[45] Organized labor, moreover, ran a stronger and better organized campaign than its opponents, raising much more money and gathering a wider variety of supporters, from the Roman Catholic Bishop of San Diego to the California Teachers Association and the League of Women Voters.[46]

As with Proposition 1 two years earlier, Proposition 12 drew a 90 percent voter participation rate, higher even than the Townsend Plan Proposition 11 on the same ballot. And it was easily defeated: 59 percent of the voters said No.

In 1948, however, labor suffered a setback. Proposition 3 was an initiative statute to modify a Progressive Era railroad regulation that had established a minimum number of brakemen per train as a safety measure. This initiative would remove that law and instead authorize the Public Utilities Commission to set the number of brakemen. While the measure applied only to one union, it was seen as important both to railroad companies and to the leaders of organized labor in general, both for its specifics and as a symbol of the battle between management and labor. The postwar period was experiencing a great deal of labor strife nationally, and the 1947 passage of the anti-labor Taft–Hartley Act by Congress, over President Truman's veto, emboldened employers to try to reverse the gains that organized labor had achieved in the preceding dozen years. Both sides ran active campaigns on Proposition 3. The "California Committee Against Featherbedding" raised $625,000, over half of it from the Southern Pacific Railroad; it used Robinson and Co. to collect signatures, and the increasingly important Whitaker and Baxter law firm to help organize the campaign. The unions, stressing the "safety" factor in larger brakemen crews, raised about $114,000, a good deal less than in the right-to-work campaign four years earlier; not as many individual unions were persuaded of the importance of this initiative.[47]

Proposition 3 attracted a voter participation rate of 85 percent and just barely squeaked through, with 50.9 percent of the vote. Despite the "logical" argument of modern trains needing smaller crews, there was a residual suspicion of railroads, especially the Southern Pacific, in California, plus an expanding working class that just generally supported organized labor, resulting in its almost defeating the proposition.

In 1958 another right-to-work measure became very much entangled in contemporary California politics. The main sponsor of Proposition 18, an initiative constitutional amendment, was the "Citizens Committee for Democracy in Labor Unions," an employers group. But it also had the highly publicized support of Senator William F. Knowland, who was then running a very controversial, right-wing campaign as the Republican candidate for governor.[48] This was one of the first instances of a candidate linking his campaign to a specific initiative in hope of getting the support of those favoring the proposition; such maneuvering would become increasingly popular in the future.[49] The still very conservative Los Angeles Times also supported the proposition, in a front-page editorial criticizing the "multimillion dollar argument" of its opponents.[50]

However, opposition to Proposition 18 was quite overwhelming. The Republican governor, Goodwin Knight, then running for the Senate, and Republican Senator Thomas Kuchel, as well as Democratic Attorney General Edmund G. "Pat" Brown (who was running against Knowland for governor) all opposed it. All of them were listed as opponents in the official *California Ballot Pamphlet* for that election, along with President Eisenhower, Vice President Nixon, two-time Democratic presidential candidate Adlai Stevenson, and Chief Justice Earl Warren. Such influential supporters, joined by groups ranging from the NAACP to the California Board of Rabbis, plus the entire labor movement, made for a very powerful coalition.[51]

Proposition 18 had an impressive 95 percent voter participation rate, the highest among eighteen measures on the ballot. And 60 percent of the voters rejected it, as they did Knowland's candidacy for the governorship.

Because Proposition 18 was on several Field polls between July and October of 1958, one can see how public perception of the issue changed over time. In July, for example, 46 percent of respondents said they thought they would vote No, 34 percent would vote Yes, and 18 percent were Undecided. By September, mid-campaign, the No voters had risen to 51 percent, with matching small declines in both Yes and Undecided voters. And in the early October poll, 55 percent said they would oppose Proposition 18, whereas the Yes choice had remained at 31 percent and Undecided had declined to 13 percent. Thus, there had been very little change over time in those who supported right-to-work, but the number who had made up their minds to oppose it had steadily risen. Several groups showed marked change between the earliest poll and the latest one. The percentage of self-defined Republicans who planned to vote No rose from 25 percent to 33 percent, and that of Democrats rose from 58 percent to 71 percent. Only 41 percent of women planned to vote No in the first poll, but this number rose to 53 percent in the last. And the percentage of big-city residents (places of 500,000 or more) who would vote No increased from 51 percent to 64 percent. The overwhelming critical opposition to the measure by national leaders, including President Eisenhower, clearly had a cumulative effect.[52]

The final labor measure during this period was Proposition 17 in 1964, an initiative statute very similar to Proposition 3 of 1948 in that it also related to the size of train crews. Its main aim was to remove firemen from trains, since their jobs had been made superfluous with the arrival of diesel engines. The railroad unions were nonetheless determined to preserve these jobs. Proposition 17 would also repeal earlier initiative provisions that specified train crew size and would bring state policy into line with decisions of a federal arbitration board. Once again, as in 1948, the voters were presented with a clear management-versus-labor issue, which both sides interpreted in terms both of its specifics and its long-term implications.

However straightforward the issues may have seemed, the stakes were high to both sides, with large amounts of money involved. Millions of dollars were spent on the campaign.[53] The supporters of the proposition were particularly well heeled and well organized. In addition to the railroads, they included many Chambers of Commerce, the California Association of Manufacturers, numerous newspapers, and so on.[54] Proposition 17 won easily, with 61 percent of those voting in favor.

During this period, then, narrowly constructed anti-labor measures such as outlawing the secondary boycott in wartime and limiting train crew size succeeded, persuading a majority of voters that the restrictions were both logical and ethical. But major anti-labor programs like right-to-work did not engender the same levels of support, and failed. The state had become sufficiently urban and industrial that, in this period of strong national and state labor organizations, labor was generally able to defend its broad and central interests.

These propositions affecting labor were spread over a rather long period, from 1942 to 1964, with large time gaps between them. Not surprisingly, there are few meaningful statistical relationships among the elections. The 1942 and 1944 propositions were strongly related (Pearson .635), as were the 1958 and 1964 propositions (.583), which shows consistency in voting. There were no really strong relationships between voting on any of these measures and 1950 or 1960 census data; with data aggregated at the county level, class phenomena are difficult to see.

Table 3.1 showed a fairly large number of direct legislation measures related to business and business regulation during this 1940–1968 period. Unlike earlier and later periods, however, there were no topics that appeared repeatedly. Rather, different concerns arose, generally just once, and then disappeared. But some of these garnered a great deal of public concern and reflected important divisions in California society at that time.

One such issue, as much an aspect of contemporary popular culture as of economics, related to television, an important part of American life by the 1960s. Proposition 15 in 1964 was an initiative statute that would prohibit pay television, a new and controversial idea at the time. Its only defenders seemed to be those who wanted to enter this potentially profitable enterprise, such as Sylvester ("Pat") Weaver, a former head of the National Broadcasting Company.[55] On the other side was a huge constituency that abhorred the idea of television that was not "free." Some of this opposition, to be sure, was from businesses that felt threatened by what pay-TV might offer, not least movie theater owners (who had felt threatened by television in general when it first appeared in the late 1940s).[56] Organized labor, too, felt economically threatened and took a strong stand in favor of the proposition.[57] The restriction against pay-TV was very popular with ordinary Californians as well, with much expression of fear for the disappearance of "free baseball" and who knew what else.[58]

Despite the great emotion of the Johnson–Goldwater presidential campaign, and the bitter conflict over Propositions 14 (open housing) and 17 (railroad train crews) in this election, Proposition 15 drew the second highest level of voter participation (94 percent, just behind the 96 percent for Prop. 14). Television, in 1964, was a major part of California's economic and cultural life. Two-thirds of the voters approved the proposition to bar pay-TV.

Another controversial initiative in the same 1964 election drew a 93 percent level of voter participation, the same percentage as voted on the railroad train crew issue. This was Proposition 16, the first lottery proposal to make it to a California ballot. The initiative would have created a state lottery, with 74 percent of its funds earmarked for education and 26 percent for prizes and administrative expenses for a new Lottery Commission. The initiative also named the American Sweepstakes Corporation of Pasadena as the administrator of the lottery for its first ten years. In addition to the controversiality of a lottery per se, and the question of whether or not it would really lower taxes and benefit education, there was much criticism of the naming of the administering company in the initiative itself, without any procedure for competitive bidding. This was reminiscent of the failed strategies of George McLain, Willis Allen, and others, particularly in the old-age pension initiatives, who had tried to control who would administer their programs. Not surprisingly, American Sweepstakes was the major contributor to the campaign: of the $550,000 raised by proponents, it contributed at least $350,000.[59]

Opponents of the measure raised much less money, but they really didn't need it, given the level of popular opposition. Sixty-nine percent of the voters turned the lottery down, and by the same majority voters approved a legislative constitutional amendment (Proposition 13) that forbade such naming of specific corporations in direct legislation.

Daylight-saving time was a somewhat similar issue: there were significant economic interests associated with it, but also emotional ones ("God's time," and so on). It had first been broached in 1930, where it led the 26 measures in voter participation rate at 91 percent (second place went to a Sunday closing law, and the rest were far behind), and was defeated 76 percent to 24 percent. Daylight-saving time was considered by the legislature at least five times after that, but never passed. In 1940, it was the only direct legislation measure (Proposition 5) among seventeen propositions on the ballot. Supporters stressed advantages like expanded leisure time, benefits to working people, and reduced traffic — none of which proved to be particularly persuasive to the voters. Opposition was strong. Movie theater owners, for example, were convinced that expanded daylight hours would mean declining attendance. The California Federation of Labor, the State Federation of Women's Clubs, religious leaders, and agricultural groups all railed against it, for a variety of reasons.[60] As ten years earlier, this proposition had the highest voter participation rate (80 percent; it was the only direct legislation measure in 1940) and lost overwhelmingly, 70 percent to 30 percent.

By 1949, the opposition to daylight-saving time had declined and consisted primarily of drive-in movie theater chains and a few other businesses.[61] The *Los Angeles Times*, which had opposed the 1930 and 1940 propositions, supported Proposition 12 of 1949. The issue had become one of essentially urban-versus-rural values, the paper said, and now in urbanized California more people would be helped than hurt.[62] That was part of the explanation, but it was also the case that the level of Yes votes in 1949 compared to 1940 increased considerably more in northern than in southern California. Voter participation was almost as high as for the anti-McLain vote in that special election, and daylight-saving time was finally accepted, with 55 percent of the vote.

Another business-related initiative that engendered much interest during this period reflected concern with the world oil supply in 1956, the year of the Suez crisis. Proposition 4 was the only direct legislation measure among nineteen propositions on that year's presidential ballot. It would have created a new state Oil and Gas Conservation Commission, taking control away from the Division of Natural Resources, to regulate drilling and other oil operations in order to eliminate waste. Some of the Commission's actions, however, would require the agreement of the oil companies.[63] The initiative's proponents, primarily business and industry in general, and the oil companies in particular, succeeded in giving it the title "Oil and Gas Conservation." Given the oil crisis of that year, advocates could argue that it was a step toward American energy independence that would not only eliminate waste but also maximize production. They mounted a huge campaign for the proposition, deluging the public with advertising and publicizing the support of such military leaders as Admiral Chester Nimitz and General Omar Bradley.[64]

The Proposition 4 campaign was, in fact, a good example of the power of the "military-industrial complex" that President Eisenhower would warn against four years later. Opponents countered with the argument that this was a "big oil" measure, deceptive and misleading, and one that again threatened state-owned tidelands and the public interest. Organized labor stressed the likelihood that the measure would result in more imported oil and the loss of American jobs.[65]

Total expenditures in this campaign came to almost $5 million, by far the highest in this period, and in constant dollars the single most expensive campaign between 1958 and 1978.[66] Even though the anti-Proposition 4 argument was far less well funded and organized, the focus on tidelands and the power of "big oil" was persuasive: the proposition led all others in the 1956 election, by over 600,000 votes, with 93 percent voter participation; 77 percent of the voters said No. This campaign was a classic example of the truism that money alone cannot guarantee the success of an initiative or referendum.

Taxation of one sort or another had been a ballot issue from the inception of direct legislation, and proposals had ranged from the frequent efforts of the single taxers to a variety of attempts to use taxes for regulating various aspects of business activity. But the pace picked up in this period, with proposals focusing particularly on the income tax, and in 1968, the first major proposition for property tax reform, which anticipated the cataclysm of the 1970s.

As early as 1932, Proposition 9 had proposed an income tax to help pay for schools. Two-thirds of the voters turned it down, but in 1935 the state legislature did pass an income tax law. Opponents of that tax mounted Proposition 2 in 1936, an initiative constitutional amendment that would undo the legislature's action and additionally would require that there be no state income tax unless it was approved in a popular initiative and also by a two-thirds majority in each house of the legislature. In a reversal of the 1932 vote, 62 percent of the voters refused to undo the income tax statute. And when exactly the same proposal was made again, by Proposition 4 in 1942, it garnered the same result, albeit with a somewhat lesser majority vote of 54 percent. The initiative had some business support, but it also had fairly broad opposition—from farm groups, liberals, and the California Teachers Association.[67] Interestingly, although these tax measures drew fairly strong voter participation rates, they were still significantly lower than rates for sociocultural, labor, and welfare propositions.

In 1950, questions of excessive property taxation were raised, although only in terms of personal property, not real estate. Proposition 1 would ban personal property taxation by any government agency in California. Opposition was widespread. Von T. Ellsworth, who was Director of Research and Legislative Representative of the California Farm Bureau Federation, and who had played a leading role in defending the income tax in the 1936 and 1942 elections, led the battle against Proposition 1. The State and Los Angeles Chambers of Commerce, as well as the California Teachers Association, also opposed it. The *San Francisco Chronicle* argued that the state would lose $200 million per year if Proposition 1 passed. Fund-raising, however, did not reflect those kinds of sums, perhaps because few individuals stood to gain or lose a great deal. Proponents raised about $100,000, mostly from small businesses, and the opponents gathered the same amount, which was more than they needed.[68] Eighty-one percent of the voters rejected the initiative.

In 1951, the legislature passed a bill that granted property tax exemption to nonprofit private schools, which meant primarily religious schools. This led to a 1952 referendum, Proposition 3, that sought to undo the legislation. Defenders of the law argued that it would help alleviate the shortage of schools that had developed as a result of rapid wartime and postwar population growth. They also stressed that the tax relief would go to schools for the handicapped as well as religious schools. Opponents of the law argued that it was nothing more than a state subsidy for religious education and that the state would suffer a serious tax revenue loss. Both sides claimed that their positions defended the separation of church and state. Perhaps the endorsements of the law by the chairs of both political party state committees provided the edge that supporters of the law needed.[69]

Proposition 3 drew the highest voter participation rate (92 percent) among the 24 propositions on the 1952 ballot, even outdrawing McLain's pension Proposition 11. The legislature was upheld, just barely, in this referendum, with 50.8 percent of the voters approving the law.

Six years later, opponents of this tax exemption tried again, this time with an initiative constitutional amendment rather than a referendum. Proposition 16 in 1958 would permit continuing tax exemption for schools for the physically handicapped, but specifically remove that exemption for "religious or private schools." Protestant and Roman Catholic church leaders were the main opponents of the proposed change, and the campaign was highly charged.[70] It was also one of the most expensive of the era, with the two sides raising and spending almost $2 million.[71]

Strong religious support for the status quo had its effect: in a September Field poll, 48 percent of respondents said they would vote No on Proposition 16 and 34 percent planned to vote Yes; one month later, the No voters had risen to 56 percent and the Yes voters had declined to 30 percent. Among population groups, there were no significant attitude variations based on political party identification, level of education, urban-versus-rural residence, or gender. Age did make some difference — the older the respondent, the less likely he or she was to oppose the initiative (62 percent opposition for those age 21–29 versus 51 percent opposition for those age 60 and over). Religion also was significant: an overwhelming 80 percent of Roman Catholics opposed removing the tax-free status of parochial schools, whereas only 51 percent of Protestants shared that view, and Jews favored the initiative by 48 percent Yes to 40 percent No.[72] By election day, the negative argument had become even more persuasive, with a 95 percent voter participation rate on Proposition 16, and a 67 percent No vote.

The same 1958 ballot contained another effort to implement progressive taxation. Proposition 17 would have reduced the sales and use tax and increased the progressive income tax on a sliding scale up to a 46 percent maximum (from the then-current 6 percent). It also required that any further changes in income tax rates be approved by popular vote. The proposition's main support came from organized labor. The California State Federation of Labor argued that the regressive sales and use tax provided 63 percent of the general fund, at serious cost to the non-rich, whereas the proposed change would be fairer, more economically sound, and would result in dramatic rate increases only among the very rich. Moreover, labor argued, the overall effect would be an increase rather than a diminution of state revenues.[73]

Business and conservative anti-tax groups were outraged at the proposal. The California Taxpayers Association, for example, said that this was "the first time it had ever opposed a tax reduction measure," but that Proposition 17 was "a serious threat not only to state activities, but to public schools and to the aid to the needy programs."[74] Business and professional groups were equally opposed. Members of Town Hall of Los Angeles voted 387–18 against it. Chambers of Commerce and numerous ad hoc organizations distributed lots of campaign materials; leaders of both the Democratic and Republican parties in California denounced it; and both the PTA and the California Teachers Association, fearing a loss of financing for schools, voiced their opposition.[75]

As with Proposition 16, the public perception of Proposition 17 developed over time. In a September poll, 38 percent of voters were planning to vote No and 40 percent to vote Yes, with 20 percent Undecided. By early October there had been a significant switch: the No response had risen to 48 percent and the Yes had dropped to 31 percent, with the Undecideds remaining at 20 percent. Republicans, not surprisingly, leaned more strongly against Proposition 17 (57 percent, to 44 percent for Democrats), and a higher level of education (which correlates strongly with wealth) also predicted increasing opposition (41 percent No for those with less than a grade school education to 67 percent for college graduates). Men were more opposed (53 percent) than women (44 percent), but the latter were not actually more in favor of the proposition, just more undecided.[76]

One month later, on election day, 91 percent of voters took a stand on this proposition (not quite as many as those voting on the religious school tax measure or on right-to-work Prop. 18), with 82 percent of them opposing the proposed change in the tax structure. The public had been scared off by an effective opposition campaign that portrayed the initiative as an extreme measure, one that could result in inadequate funding for schools and other government programs.

Thus, in the 1950s, voters had chosen not to end personal property taxation, had twice voted to uphold the law providing property tax exemption for religious and other nonprofit schools, and had overwhelmingly rejected a proposal to replace part of the sales tax with a more steeply graduated income tax. Table 3.4 shows the relationships among the votes for these elections and some additional variables.

The table indicates few significant relationships, which is itself of some importance. Most of these propositions had their own constituencies, and the voting public appears not to have made the same connection among them that it did with sociocultural and other subjects of direct legislation. Some of the relationships, however, do merit observation. The overwhelming vote against the 1950 effort to halt personal property taxation stands alone — it has no significant correlation with any other elections or background variables. But there is a positive correlation between the two votes against granting a tax exemption to religious schools, Proposition 3 in 1952 and Proposition 16 in 1958. This involved voting No on the 1952 referendum and Yes on the 1958 initiative. (Since the anti-tax exemption forces lost by a tiny margin in 1952 and a huge one in 1958, it is likely that some voters in 1952 were confused by the complexities of referendum voting.) The fact that these two elections are strongly negatively correlated with support for the 1968 property tax initiative (see below) suggests that opposition to tax exemptions for religious schools was based at least in part on cultural principles rather than on general attitudes toward taxation. This conclusion is supported, also, by the negative relationships with the two background census variables, especially percentage urban. Proposition 9 in the 1968 general election (see below) has insignificant or negative correlations with all the other elections, but strong ones with background variables. People who had migrated to California and residents of urban areas — two groupings that often overlapped — were definitely more likely to vote for this proposed reform.

Proposition 9 emerged out of rapid changes taking place in the California real estate market in the 1960s. People were moving in and prospered, and the rising demand for housing drove prices upwards — and with them, property taxes. By the mid-1960s the demand for property tax relief, especially for homeowners in southern California, had become a powerful popular force that inevitably entered politics. Several initiatives to deal with the property tax problem were proposed starting in 1960, but none of them qualified for the ballot until 1968. More and more, blame for rapidly in-

TABLE 3.4   Correlations for Voting on Taxation Issues, 1950–1968, and Census Characteristics

| Proposition | 1950: Prop. 1 Personal property | 1952: Prop. 3 Against tax exemption | 1958: Prop. 16 Against tax exemption | 1958: Prop. 17 Income tax | 1968: Prop. 9 Property tax | 1960: Percentage born in another state | 1960: Percentage urban |
|---|---|---|---|---|---|---|---|
| 1950: Prop. 1 Personal property | 1.000 | | | | | | |
| 1952: Prop. 3 Against tax exemption | -.024 | 1.000 | | | | | |
| 1958: Prop. 16 Against tax exemption | -.129 | .415 | 1.000 | | | | |

|  | | | | | | |
|---|---|---|---|---|---|---|
| 1958:<br>Prop. 17<br>Income tax | −.123 | .204 | .102 | 1.000 | | |
| 1968:<br>Prop. 9<br>Property tax | .265 | −.726 | −.550 | −.073 | 1.000 | |
| 1960:<br>Percentage born in<br>another state | −.159 | −.457 | −.207 | .242 | .530 | 1.000 |
| 1960:<br>Percentage urban | .060 | −.393 | −.414 | −.332 | .569 | .386 | 1.000 |

NOTE: Pearson product moment correlations, based on percentage voting Yes on propositions (percentage voting No on 1952 referendum) and data from 1960 U.S. Census, with data aggregated by county and weighted by county population. For clarity, only one side of table is shown, since both sides are identical.

TABLE 3.5   Percentage Responding Yes, No, or Undecided to Questions on How They Planned to
Vote on Propositions 1A and 9, 1968 General Election

| Voter subgroups | Prop. 1A: Yes | Prop. 1A: No | Prop. 1A: Undecided | Prop. 9: Yes | Prop. 9: No | Prop. 9: Undecided |
|---|---|---|---|---|---|---|
| Republicans | 34 | 19 | 47 | 31 | 38 | 29 |
| Democrats | 41 | 22 | 36 | 33 | 44 | 28 |
| Age 21–29 | 40 | 20 | 39 | 36 | 35 | 26 |
| Age 40–49 | 37 | 23 | 40 | 29 | 39 | 32 |
| Age 60–69 | 36 | 23 | 40 | 26 | 48 | 26 |
| Income $5,000–$7,000 | 42 | 17 | 40 | 25 | 41 | 32 |
| Income $7,000–$10,000 | 36 | 26 | 39 | 33 | 38 | 28 |
| Income $10,000–$15,000 | 37 | 23 | 40 | 30 | 49 | 22 |
| Income above $15,000 | 37 | 23 | 38 | 33 | 47 | 21 |
| California resident 3–5 years | 28 | 33 | 39 | 24 | 40 | 36 |
| California resident 5–8 years | 42 | 18 | 39 | 39 | 26 | 35 |
| California resident over 15 years | 37 | 21 | 41 | 31 | 43 | 26 |
| Southern California resident | 31 | 23 | 47 | 39 | 39 | 21 |
| Bay Area resident | 48 | 16 | 37 | 24 | 49 | 27 |

SOURCE:   Responses to Field Institute poll fi6806 (18–21 Oct. 1968); only selected subgroups are shown.

creasing tax rates was focused on Los Angeles County Assessor Philip E. Watson, even though it was not the assessor but the county supervisors and other agencies that actually set the rates. The assessor's job was to take the rates and work out the assessments, but Watson's name appeared on the property tax bill. Mindful of the criticism, and with political ambitions of his own, Watson sponsored what would be Proposition 9 on the November 1968 ballot, generally called the "Watson Amendment," the first major initiative dealing directly with property tax rates.[77]

Proposition 9 proposed a property tax cap of 1 percent of full market value rather than the 20–25 percent tax on assessed value that was then current.[78] According to its supporters, Proposition 9 would decrease property taxes "an average of 50 percent." It also mandated that property taxes be used only for "property related" services, with "people related" ones, such as education, health, and welfare being financed by the state.[79] The proposal generated a heated reaction from several quarters in government and business and among public interest groups seeking other avenues to property tax reform. The state legislature panicked, fearing chaos as a result of its own failure to act on the problem; leaders of both parties and Governor Ronald Reagan joined in opposing the initiative. Critics on the right feared an increased income tax and those on the left argued that far more relief would go to landowners and businesses than to the average homeowner. Schools and other essential services would suffer grievously, according to groups like the California PTA and the California Teachers Association. Large companies such as Standard Oil fulminated against it as well, with similar arguments. All of these divergent groups, especially businesses and the California Teachers Association, contributed big money, raising about $1 million for the campaign.[80]

At the last minute, the legislature came up with its own alternative, Proposition 1A, which ultimately received support from Governor Reagan. This measure was a considerably less ambitious proposal that was designed, more than anything else, to undercut and defeat Proposition 9.[81] Proposition 1A offered homeowners a tax exemption of $750 of the assessed value of owner-occupied dwellings, and required the state to reimburse local governments and administrative agencies for any tax revenues lost by this exemption. It also authorized a one-time payment of $70 to every homeowner for the 1968–1969 assessment year, since the new exemption would not take effect until the following year.[82]

Table 3.5 shows public attitudes toward these two propositions based on a Field Institute poll about two weeks before the election. Probably the most striking feature of the table is the percentage of Undecideds so late in the campaign. That fact is consistent with answers to another question asked about the two propositions, that is, whether or not respondents had heard of them. For each group listed in the table and for each of the two propositions, generally between 40 percent and 60 percent had *not* heard of either measure that late in the campaign. Given the level of concern about property taxes, and the considerable publicity surrounding the two measures, these responses are a good illustration of voter ignorance, something not at all confined to this election. Ignorance did not necessarily lead to apathy: 91 percent of 1968 general election voters voted on Proposition 9 and 89 percent on Proposition 1A.

More Democrats than Republicans tended to favor Proposition 1A, despite its advocacy by a Republican governor; both Democrats and Republicans strongly opposed Proposition 9. Age made little difference on 1A, but increasing age did correlate with stronger opposition to 9 — older people seemed to be more impressed by anti-Proposition 9 propaganda. Somewhat the same was true of income: there was little difference across income relative to the more modest Proposition 1A, but there was an increase in opposition to Proposition 9 as income went up. Wealthier people were more likely to see the "radical" aspects of Proposition 9 and its alleged dangers for the overall economy. Length of residence in California had a less clear effect on voting patterns (although the data in Table 3.4, above, suggest that newcomers were relatively more likely to support Prop. 9), but there was some variation by region: Bay Area residents were clearly more in favor of 1A and against 9, whereas southern California residents were undecided on 1A and evenly split on 9. This might be explained by the fact that Proposition 9 had originated with the Los Angeles County Assessor, who was responding to a serious local problem.[83] Finally, looking back at Table 3.4 once again, residents of urban areas tended to support Proposition 9, which is logical enough, given that urban area property values had increased the most rapidly.

The election results were much more decisive than the October poll suggested. Proposition 9 was overwhelmingly defeated, garnering only 32 percent of the vote, whereas Proposition 1A squeaked by with a 53 percent majority. The property tax problem was by no means solved, however, as Chapter 4 will demonstrate.

Education was another issue much involved with taxes, but it existed in a separate context in the 1940s and 1950s. Education issues arose with the rapid population growth of wartime and postwar California and found a public that was generally supportive of expansion and improvement of the state's public schools. One example was Proposition 9 of 1944, an initiative constitutional amendment that would raise per-pupil funding from $60 to $80, and increase the share of school expenses paid by the state rather than the individual counties. It did involve a tax increase, but supporters pointed to the "1.5 million new residents" in California and the need to serve their children.[84]

The proposition's main support came from the California Teachers Association and the California Council of Education. The former turned the campaign over to professionals and raised about $122,000. Numerous other organizations also championed the initiative, ranging from service clubs to the PTA, from the California State Federation of Labor to the American Legion Auxiliary.[85] Opposition came primarily from conservative newspapers and business groups such as the Los Angeles Chamber of Commerce and Town Hall of Los Angeles, which argued that California already spent enough on education and that the increased taxation would damage the economy.[86] But the public, perhaps influenced by the war, was in a positive mood toward education at the time, and the measure passed easily with 64 percent of the vote.

Two years later, another initiative constitutional amendment, Proposition 3, proposed further raising per-pupil expenditures to $120, of which $90 would be given to local school districts; it also established a minimum $2,400 salary for teachers. Moreover, it granted authority to local school districts to make their own determination of how much money was to be raised by school district taxes. Once again, it was primarily the California Teachers Association that organized and funded the drive for the initiative, stressing continued population growth and inadequate facilities. And despite the measure's being more substantial than its immediate predecessor, there was less opposition. As with the 1944 measure, the Los Angeles Chamber of Commerce opposed Proposition 3, but Town Hall Los Angeles was divided, and even the Los Angeles Times, perhaps reflecting postwar confidence, endorsed the measure.[87]

Of the seventeen measures on the ballot in 1946, Proposition 3 had the second highest voter participation rate (86 percent, just behind the 90 percent rate for a proposition for greyhound racing), and it won easily with 74 percent of the vote. It symbolized, among other things, that the California Teachers Association had become one of the real powerhouse interest groups on the left in California, with enough influence and cash to rival the big forces on the right, such as the state Chamber of Commerce.

The same scenario played out again in 1952, when Proposition 2 aimed to change the constitution once more to raise per-pupil spending to $180 per year, with at least $120 of that going to the local school districts. The old tax-fearing foes were still around, including the Los Angeles Chamber of Commerce, Town Hall Los Angeles, and the California Farm Bureau Federation. But the State Chamber of Commerce, both political parties, and the California Federation of Business and Professional Women's Clubs joined the Teachers Association, the PTA and the California AFL in supporting it. The proponents' fund-raising, driven by the California Teachers Association, raised almost $350,000, while the opponents, led by the Farm Bureau and real estate interests, were able to raise less than 10 percent of that sum.[88]

Another interesting aspect of this campaign was a rising recognition of the ethnic diversity of California. Proposition 2's supporters placed ads in a variety of foreign and ethnic newspapers, drawing newer Californians into their battle for better schools.[89] And it all worked: 88 percent of voters marked their ballots on Proposition 2, 65 percent of them in approval. The next decade would see serious voter concern about taxation, as discussed above, but in the immediate postwar and early Cold War years Californians were optimistic about growth and not fearful of modest increases in taxation, at least where education was concerned.

A number of issues associated with government and elections were also involved in direct legislation during this period. One of them, another legacy of California Progressivism, was cross-filing, the process whereby a candidate could enter the primaries of multiple parties. By the era of Governor Earl Warren, who won both parties' nominations in 1946, the practice had become associated with continued Republican domination of California politics.[90] So Democratic activists decided to try to undo cross-filing by initiative in 1952. Like George McLain in the same year, they used the indirect initiative route and rushed their collection of signatures in 1950 so the number required would be based on the 1946 gubernatorial election, when turnout had been low. The entire qualifying effort was conducted by a small number of people, based on a $40,000 donation from John B. Elliott, a longtime Democratic activist.[91]

Proposition 13 of 1952 was supported mainly by Democrats and organized labor, for whom, by this time, Democratic success was crucial for its own well-being; they argued that in 80 percent of statewide races the same person had won both primaries, leaving voters without a choice. A few other groups, including the League of Women Voters, also saw the end of cross-filing as a needed reform. Republicans believed they would lose state and congressional seats if cross-filing were ended, and argued to the public that Proposition 13 would bring "big city political machines" back to California. Their opposition was joined by business groups across the state, for whom Republican success was as important as that of the Democrats was to labor. But neither side was well funded and the campaign was relatively modest on both sides.[92]

The issue was further confused by the fact that the legislature, in an effort to quash Proposition 13, put its own Legislative Statute amendment on the ballot.[93] Its Proposition 7 specified that candidates' party affiliations should be placed next to their names on the ballot, but it did not end cross-filing. Proponents of Proposition 7 hoped that it would undercut support for the more drastic Proposition 13, which is exactly what happened. The Democratic Party, in some confusion, supported both propositions, with some worrying about what would eventuate if both happened to pass.[94]

Proposition 7 had a 78 percent voter participation rate, compared to the 89 percent who voted on cross-filing. But in the column that counted, Proposition 7 received a 73 percent Yes vote, whereas Proposition 13 just barely lost with a 49.96 percent Yes vote. Cross-filing would live on for another seven years, until Governor Edmund G. "Pat" Brown and the Democrats took control and removed it by legislation.

Another political issue reflected the growing conflict between southern California, especially Los Angeles County, and northern California, in terms of the disparity in their representation in the state senate. This had been a controversial issue as early as the 1920s, as described in Chapter 2. The assembly imbalance was corrected after the 1930 census, but the senate continued to be apportioned on a non-population basis. In the meantime, the disparity increased. Los Angeles County's population rose from 2.2 million in 1930 to 6 million in 1960, while that of San Francisco rose from only 634,000 to 740,000. Indeed, in 1960 only one other California county had as many as 1 million people — and that was San Diego County, another part of southern California. Moreover, Orange County, situated between these two, was already the fifth most populous in the state. Those three counties alone comprised 49 percent of the state's population in 1960. And the County of Los Angeles had only one state senator.

Small wonder, then, that the maldistribution of the state senate had become such an issue, not only between southern and northern California, but also between rural areas and urban ones. To some degree, that made it also an argument of Democrats versus Republicans and liberals versus conservatives. Three times during this period efforts were made to change the districting of the state senate to a more population-based system.

Proposition 13 in 1948 proposed redistricting on the basis of population but with the condition that no county could have more than ten senators. The campaign was quite intense, with a great deal of publicity. Most of the vocal opposition came from business groups that feared the increased power of organized labor that would come with greater urban representation.[95] The campaign did not, however, excite the electorate, since only 81 percent of voters marked their ballots on the proposition, the lowest total of any of the direct legislation measures in that election. And it was easily defeated, 68 percent to 32 percent.

Supporters of redistricting waited a dozen years before trying again, with Proposition 15 of 1960, which sought to establish forty senatorial districts, with apportionment based on "population, area, and economic affinity." It was a complicated measure, providing that twenty senators must be from thirteen southern counties, based on the same formula used for apportioning highway funds; no county could have more than seven senators. This proposition differed from that of 1948 in that it emanated almost entirely from Los Angeles interests. But its confusing nature resulted in even Los Angeles Mayor Norris Poulson and Governor "Pat" Brown opposing it, along with the usual business and conservative groups. The conservatives provided the major financing.[96] The outcome was very similar to that of 1948, with a participation rate of 80 percent and 65 percent voting No.

Two years later, Proposition 23 of 1962 would have created 50 senatorial districts, once again apportioned on "population, area, and economic affinity." No county was to have more than six senators, and no district was to encompass more than three counties — an effort to assuage more rural and conservative interests. Once again, business groups were the proposal's primary opponents, but they managed to raise only about $250,000 for this campaign. The least populated counties offered strong bipartisan support because Proposition 23 offered them greater guarantees than its predecessor. Moreover, the initiative was publicly supported by President Kennedy, Governor Brown, former Vice President Nixon, and a host of others, including many of the state's major newspapers.[97]

The Field organization asked voters their opinions of Proposition 23 at several points in the campaign. When asked how they would vote on this issue, 45 percent responded Yes in March, 59 percent in September, and 47 percent in October. Just why there was such a drop-off between mid-September and mid-October is at least partially explained by some of the responses. Support among Democrats declined from 59 percent in September to just under 51 percent in October, and among Republicans from 59 percent to 42 percent. Obviously, despite Nixon's nominal endorsement, the Republicans on the whole were working against Proposition 23. There was a similarly dramatic drop among the college-educated, from 64 percent Yes to 46 percent; but the decline was actually quite broadly based since groups with less education also declined in their support, although not at such a dramatic level. Union members were one group that remained supportive of Proposition 23, but even their support declined in the one-month period from September to October, going from 65 percent to 58 percent.[98]

The campaign had started out strong but faded in its last month. Californians were not persuaded that the proposed change was a good one and feared giving too much power to the big cities, especially Los Angeles. Once again, voter participation was modest, at 79 percent, and while advocates of redistricting did better than in 1948 and 1960, they once again failed, 53 percent to 47 percent.

Although the total number of direct legislation measures declined in the period 1940–1968, they were nevertheless frequent, and important. They dealt with the most significant cultural, social, economic, and political issues of the time. Not all of those issues achieved their ultimate resolution by 1968, to be sure. But the questions had been raised and debated, and the development of direct legislation in this period set the stage for the tremendous upsurge in initiative activity that would emerge in the ensuing decades.

# 4 Howard and Paul to the Rescue, 1970–1982

The 1970s were a time of continued prosperity in California. The Cold War kept the defense industry humming; middle-class employment rose, and with it wealth. But taxes were rising, too, keeping alive the concern with excess taxation that had developed in the late 1960s. This was particularly true of property taxes; for example, assessments rose 29 percent per year in San Bernardino County and 30 percent per year in Orange County in the period 1973–1976. Moreover, given the "single roll" assessment principle for commercial and residential property established by the legislature in 1967, the property tax burden was rising fastest for single-family dwellings.[1] By the mid-1970s income tax revenue was also increasing, with the effect that there was a rapidly growing budget surplus. Thus, one reality behind the tax reform movement of the decade was that the state government could afford to cut taxes and/or to assume more of the burden of education and welfare from local government.[2]

If proposals for tax reform did not develop as rapidly as one might have expected, it should be remembered that the number of direct legislation measures had slowed in preceding decades. It was not easy to rouse enough people to qualify direct legislation propositions: twenty of them dealing with property or income taxation failed to qualify between 1970 and 1978 (seven in 1976 alone), although their increasing number did reflect the problem. The number of initiatives in general did pick up in the 1970s, in part because of new and divisive issues, including taxation, and in part because the popular sense of strong government leadership, which had existed under Governors Pat Brown (1959–1967) and Ronald Reagan (1967–1975), began to decline. Doubts about the legislature seemed to lead to some hesitancy within the legislature, which only made the doubts greater and the need for direct legislation more persuasive.[3]

Following Los Angeles County Assessor Philip Watson's failure to lower property taxes with Proposition 9 in 1968, the next reform effort came from the California Teachers Association. Its Proposition 8 in June 1970 was titled, "Taxation for Schools and Social Welfare." It tried to ease the property tax burden in two ways: (1) by requiring that 50 percent of public school costs and 90 percent of social welfare costs be funded by sources other than property taxes; and (2) by increasing the homeowners property-tax exemption from $750 to $1,000. The CTA spent more than $1 million on the campaign, first hiring Robinson and Co. to solicit signatures, and then Whitaker and Baxter (Clem Whitaker was campaign manager for Prop. 8) to run the campaign. Opponents, who ranged from Governor Reagan and the business community to the League of Women Voters, focused on the proposal's rigidity, the increase in non–property taxes, and the undercutting of local government power.[4] Ninety-three percent of the voters cast their ballots on this proposition, but 72 percent of them were unpersuaded and the measure was trounced.

This led Assessor Watson to try again, with Proposition 14 of November 1972. This initiative constitutional amendment was very like his Proposition 9 of four years earlier: it put a ceiling on property taxes, moved all welfare spending and most school spending to the state, and increased sales, liquor, and other taxes to compensate for the property tax decrease. Additionally, it cut per-pupil spending from $995 to $825, to strike a note of economy.[5]

Once again, no tax reform proposal seemed able to please very many groups in California. Both Governor Reagan and former Governor Brown opposed Proposition 14, as did the League of Women Voters, the California Federation of Labor, the California State Chamber of Commerce, the NAACP, the California Teachers Association, and, it seemed, just about everybody else.[6]

To make things worse for Watson, the legislature once again undercut him, as it had in 1968, and even got its measure on the earlier June primary ballot. Proposition 7 would simply raise the homeowner's exemption to $1,570, a very moderate approach to the problem. Proposition 7 had a relatively modest 86 percent voter participation rate, sixth highest among ten propositions on the ballot; but if the increased homeowner's exemption was not particularly exciting, it was nonetheless successful, supported by two-thirds of those voting.

Thus, by the time Watson's measure appeared on the November 1972 general election ballot, voters perceived that they had already implemented some "reform" five months earlier.[7] Watson's Proposition 14 attracted a lot of attention nonetheless, and 92 percent of the voters participated (a number of other propositions drew even more votes in a large and extremely controversial set of initiatives). But it fared even less well than his Proposition 9 four years earlier: it lost by the same two-thirds margin as Proposition 7 had won by in the spring.

Governor Reagan then stepped into the taxation dispute with an initiative of his own. Proposition 1 was the only measure in the November 1973 special election, and it reflected Reagan's position that taxes and government spending should be lowered at the same time. It was an initiative constitutional amendment with numerous provisions, including limitations on state expenditures, dedication of surplus revenue to tax reduction, elimination of the personal income tax for low-income persons, a one-time 20 percent tax credit in 1973 to all taxpayers, automatic further tax reductions, and a two-thirds legislative vote requirement for new or changed state taxes.[8]

Proposition 1 was a hodgepodge proposal, basically conservative in ideology and unrealistically sanguine in its expectation that lower spending would balance the tax cuts. According to the legislature's nonpartisan legislative analyst, A. Alan Post, local tax increases would be inevitable in the face of decreased state expenditures of $620 million in the first year, which would worsen to a $1.366 billion decrease in the fourth.[9] Proposition 1 had support from conservative groups and tax cutters, but strong opposition from the majority Democrats and almost all liberal groups.[10]

One thing the popular governor could not do was get many voters to turn out for a special election, despite the fact that almost $2 million was spent by the two sides: the total vote was the lowest in twenty years, and the measure lost 54 percent to 46 percent. But much of Proposition 1 comprised the message Reagan would use to become a national Republican figure by 1976 and that he would carry with him to electoral victory and the White House four years later.

While numerous attempts were made to mount new property tax reform initiatives in the next few years (including 1976 efforts by Paul Gann, Philip Watson, and Howard Jarvis[11]), none of them qualified until June 1978, when Howard Jarvis and Paul Gann rocked California and, soon after, a good bit of the United States.[12]

Howard Jarvis had a fairly lengthy political history before 1978, all of it unsuccessful. It included a run for the Republican nomination for the Senate in 1962, a non-qualifying property tax reform initiative as early as 1972, a campaign for the state Board of Equalization also in 1972, and entry into the Los Angeles mayoral primary in 1977. He became chairman of the United Taxpayers Organization, originally a small group that was mainly composed of the elderly, but one that became the basis of a grassroots movement that expanded with the increasing restiveness at rising property taxes.[13] Paul Gann had had an even longer political career, dating from the 1950s. He was involved in local politics in Sacramento, organizing, running for office, and gaining experience in trying to qualify initiatives. He was always closely allied to and active in the Republican Party, and his contacts and associations were with Republicans, although his partisanship did not seem to directly influence his choice of direct legislation projects. One of his first

statewide activities (through lobbying rather than dire
been in support of legislation to regulate the retirement
tors — an example of the suspicion of government and p
vaded his entire career.[14] In 1974 he created People's Ad
was originally a local group and focused on the problem (
later recall that by 1975 "many thousands" of people v
lead a battle against the property tax, and that he and Jarvis had both tried
unsuccessfully to qualify initiatives to that effect in that year. The two men
finally met in 1977 and agreed to work together on a common measure in
1978.[15] Los Angeles Assessor Philip Watson had also been in communica-
tion with them, but he had to pull out of politics for a while because of heart
surgery; what Jarvis and Gann ultimately created, he believed, was a radical
reworking of his draft proposition.[16]

What they came up with was indeed drastic. Proposition 13 was an initiative constitutional amendment for the June 1978 primary election. It proposed setting the value of real property at its 1975–1976 market value, and
limiting property tax to 1 percent of that value. It would also limit the assessed increase in a property's value to 2 percent per year if the property was
retained by the same owner, with property to be fully reassessed if ownership
changed. Any revenue increase would require a two-thirds vote of the legislature, and local government taxes could be increased only with a two-thirds
vote of the voters.[17] This amounted to an extraordinary cut in tax revenue of
about $7 billion for 1978–1979, which would particularly affect the educa-
tional and welfare support the property tax gave to local government. The
two-thirds vote provisions would also make it extremely difficult for tax
rates to change, and the fact that Proposition 13 was a constitutional amendment meant that it could be changed only by another constitutional amendment, requiring a relatively large number of signatures.[18] Equally important,
the proposition and its campaign stressed the general anti-government crusade that both Jarvis and Gann would pursue for the rest of their lives.[19]

Both Jarvis and Gann led grassroots organizations with primarily volun-
teer but highly motivated workers. The two men actually maintained their
distance from one another; they shared no particular liking for one another,
and in fact each was quite jealous of the other's success. They maintained
separate organizations that coordinated signature gathering and some campaigning. Beyond that, as Gann put it, "We just each went our own way."[20]
But the system worked nicely enough, as their grassroots groups, well coordinated between state and county organizations, gathered 1,263,000 signatures, of which just over 1,000,000 were valid (more than double the number needed to qualify an initiative constitutional amendment). This was the
first time ever that more than 1,000,000 signatures had been solicited, as
well as the first time for such a high rate (81 percent) of valid signatures.[21]

Another example of the mass nature of Proposition 13's support can be in the source of campaign funds. There were a number of organizations involved, some state and some local, and following the trail of the money is quite difficult. But "Yes on 13," the main fund-raising group, received more than eleven thousand contributions, with just under 50 percent of them less than $50. This was very much a grassroots effort, although real estate and other business interests were also involved. "Yes on 13" collected $1.5 million of the total $2.2 million raised by all pro-13 groups, as opposed to an even $2 million for their opponents.[22]

As with the Watson measures, the qualifying of Proposition 13 prompted the legislature to act, albeit ultimately with too little, too late. It passed the "Behr" bill, known officially as the Property Tax Relief Act of 1978, and also put Proposition 8 on the June ballot. This measure proposed to amend the constitution to allow for the split tax roll provision in the Behr law. The effect of the measure would be to establish separate property tax rates for residential and commercial property and to place some revenue limits on state and local government. Proposition 8 also provided for about $1.2 billion in tax relief for 1978–1979 through a 30 percent reduction in homeowner's property taxes (as compared to the approximately 50 percent reduction offered by Prop. 13).[23] Thus, the ensuing campaign largely involved supporting one initiative and opposing another.

The campaign was bitter. Defenders of Proposition 13 had to counter charges that police, fire, and other services would be shut down, that contingency plans in government offices were preparing for 35,000 layoffs in Los Angeles County alone, and that Moody's had suspended ratings on new California bonds until after the election.[24] But the Jarvis and Gann forces were able to build on the general popularity of what they were doing. They accused their opponents of concocting a "political snow job." The 1 percent tax rate, they said, would provide more than adequate revenue for the state. And they constantly stressed the idea of wasteful spending by government, noting specifics like "phony sick leave grants," too-generous pension plans, and the costs of "prevailing wage" schedules for state employees.[25]

Proposition 13 backers, most particularly Jarvis, were outstanding at publicizing their cause. Jarvis became somewhat of a media darling; he was feisty, colorful, and always provided a good story for print media or television, much to the chagrin of his opponents.[26] He and Gann defined the issue, leaving their opponents on the defensive. Moreover, behind them stood the benevolent image of former Governor Reagan—weren't Jarvis and Gann, after all, only echoing what Reagan was saying all over the country?[27]

Their opponents were numerous and were nearly able to match Jarvis and Gann in dollars. The state PTA endorsed Proposition 8, arguing that the tax cuts of Proposition 13 would hurt the state's schools. The California Federation of Teachers, with AFL–CIO support, was equally critical, as was the

California State Employees Association. Los Angeles Mayor Tom Bradley and Governor Jerry Brown, along with most liberal and Democratic leaders, joined them, although John Fitzrandolph, one of the anti-Proposition 13 leaders, feared the effect of too much involvement by politicians, given the public's anti-government mood: "Taxes weren't what that thing [Prop. 13] was all about. Politicians were what that was all about."[28] There were many predictions of doom, from the closing of the L.A. County Museum of Art and libraries to the total loss of paramedic units, but little of this seemed to register with the public.[29] On the contrary, the news, late in the campaign, that the state was projecting a $3.6 billion surplus in 1978 and $5 billion by 1979 only seemed to confirm Jarvis's argument that the taxes weren't needed and the government was not to be trusted.

The campaign was definitely successful in making the public aware of and involved in the issues. Pre-election polls showed an unprecedentedly high Yes response when voters were asked if they had "heard of" Propositions 13 and 8.[30] Turnout of registered voters on June 6 was unusually high — at 69 percent, the highest of any off-year election at least since 1916, and probably ever. (Turnout for most presidential primaries was not as high and had never been higher than 73 percent.) Of those who voted, 97 percent cast ballots on Proposition 13, and 92 percent on Proposition 8, far ahead of any of the other ten propositions. Proposition 13 received a 65 percent Yes vote, while Proposition 8 was defeated 53 percent to 47 percent. Jarvis and Gann had pulled off a real grassroots-based political triumph.[31]

The Field Institute California Poll questioned Californians about their attitudes toward both Proposition 13 and Proposition 8 over the course of the campaign. Table 4.1 analyzes some of the more salient results from the final poll one week before the election.[32]

What is most striking is the breadth of support shown for Proposition 13. Also, data for a number of often significant variables, such as education, religion, and region of state, are not given in the table because there were few meaningful differences within those statistical categories for them. Republicans were clearly more committed to Proposition 13 than Democrats; the latter showed about the same majorities for both propositions. Self-defined "political philosophy" was perhaps the strongest indicator, with a clear increase in support of Proposition 13 and decrease in support of Proposition 8 as one moved right on the liberal-to-conservative continuum. Quite similar, and not unexpected, is the cross-tabulation between responses on a question about the state government's "tax efficiency" and the respondent's positions on the two propositions; obviously, those who were satisfied with the status quo would opt for Proposition 8 over Proposition 13.

Union members professed support for Proposition 13 in almost the same proportion as non-union members, despite the very strong anti-13 cam-

TABLE 4.1    Percentage Responding Yes to Questions on How They
Planned to Vote on Propositions 13 and 8, 1978 Primary Election

|  | Will vote Yes on Prop. 13 | Will vote Yes on Prop. 8 |
|---|---|---|
| Party registration | | |
| Democrat | 55 | 53 |
| Republican | 75 | 38 |
| Other | 65 | 46 |
| Political philosophy | | |
| Strong conservative | 82 | 27 |
| Moderate conservative | 71 | 42 |
| Middle-of-the-road | 61 | 46 |
| Moderate liberal | 48 | 60 |
| Strong liberal | 27 | 70 |
| Rate state government's tax efficiency | | |
| Very Inefficient | 78 | 31 |
| Somewhat inefficient | 56 | 55 |
| Somewhat efficient | 43 | 66 |
| Very efficient | 44 | 65 |
| Labor union membership | | |
| Union member | 60 | 48 |
| Not union member | 64 | 47 |
| Age | | |
| 18–29 | 51 | 56 |
| 30–39 | 56 | 51 |

paign mounted by the leaders of organized labor; their desire for lower
property taxes made such appeals unsuccessful. Age, at least up until retirement age, was strongly correlated to support for Proposition 13; older and
more established voters were also more likely to be homeowners, those most
affected by skyrocketing taxes. The same conclusion emerges from examin-
ing the income distribution category; everybody liked Proposition 13, but
those who were wealthier liked it more.

The racial line is also very clear. Overall, whites, Asians, and those of
"Spanish descent" (the poll's terminology) were pretty much in agreement,
despite the fact that Hispanics tended to be poorer. But blacks were overwhelmingly opposed to Proposition 13 and by far the strongest supporters,
along with "Strong liberals," of Proposition 8. The slight difference between
male and female responses reflects the somewhat more politically liberal

TABLE 4.1 *Continued*

| | Will vote Yes on Prop. 13 | Will vote Yes on Prop. 8 |
|---|---|---|
| Age | | |
| 40–49 | 68 | 45 |
| 50–64 | 71 | 42 |
| 65 and older | 66 | 41 |
| Race/ethnicity | | |
| White | 66 | 45 |
| Black | 18 | 74 |
| Asian | 63 | 64 |
| "Spanish descent" | 60 | 52 |
| Annual income[a] | | |
| Under $10,000 | 53 | 55 |
| $10,000–$20,000 | 58 | 51 |
| $20,000–$30,000 | 67 | 42 |
| $30,000 and over | 69 | 45 |
| Gender | | |
| Male | 66 | 45 |
| Female | 59 | 50 |

SOURCE: Based on responses to Field Institute poll fi7806 (29–31 May 1978).
NOTE: Selected subgroups only. Includes only those who answered Yes or No to the question.
[a]Because this question was open-ended, there is minor overlap of categories.

position that women have maintained in general in recent times. Correlates of this vote are considered below.

One can conclude from the poll data responses on Proposition 8 that if the legislature had acted earlier, even with a more modest tax cut, it might well have undercut Jarvis and Gann. But its inaction for so long, followed by timid response, reinforced the public's scorn for the legislature and government in general and created a vacuum that made the passage of Proposition 13 possible, even likely. All the strengths and weaknesses of legislation by popular ballot were applied to California's tax problem in 1978, and the success of Proposition 13 provided a precedent for additional measures in the future.

Proposition 13 was not an end in California, but a beginning. This was so for several reasons: (1) the public continued to be amenable to arguments about excessive government spending and taxation; (2) Jarvis and Gann continued to be ambitious for additional initiative experiments, whether for reasons of principle or demagoguery; and (3) various interest groups saw how they could use Jarvis or Gann as fronts for initiatives seeking their own particular aims.

These factors, especially the first and third, also help explain the national ramifications of Proposition 13. Its message of excessive taxation and government waste engendered popular enthusiasm across the country and led to numerous initiative-driven efforts to cut property and other taxes and to limit the powers of government in general.[33] Along with the complementary presidency of Ronald Reagan in the 1980s, Proposition 13 launched the role of California's initiatives as national models. Other, related ideas, like limitations on government spending and term limits (see Chapters 5 and 6) would follow, all inspired by the California example. From being almost unique in the nature of its political life, Jarvis and Gann had turned the state into a national bellwether.

Jarvis and Gann moved apart after 1978, pursuing their interests separately. Gann struck almost immediately, sure of his own wisdom and rectitude and of the nature of the enemy:

For the first time in 6,000 years of recorded history, Proposition 13 brought together capital, labor, management, education and politics — bureaucracy. All goose-stepping down life's highway together to defeat Proposition 13 and we still beat the hell out of them.[34]

With that sense of unique personal mission, Gann could hardly not continue his activism.[35] Logically enough, he segued from the issue of excessive government taxation to that of excessive government spending. In November 1979, Proposition 4 appeared on the ballot for a special election that had been called particularly because of this measure and an even more controversial legislative one on busing for racial integration. The proposal was quite similar to former Governor Reagan's 1973 proposition, in that it tried to keep state and local government spending from rising, in real dollars, above 1978–1979 levels. It would amend the constitution so that the state, counties, cities, school districts, and special districts could only increase their spending above 1978–1979 levels relative to increases in population and the consumer price index. Any excess of revenues over expenses was to be returned to the public by lowering tax rates.[36]

Gann argued that the measure was necessary in order to protect Proposition 13, which government bodies were trying to undermine by raising other taxes and fees.[37] He also used the popularity of Proposition 13: the new campaign was titled "Spirit of 13" and that was its theme. The idea was popular and signatures were readily gathered, some by volunteers and some by paid solicitors. Gann had originally hoped to qualify the proposition for the 1980 primary, but the signatures came in fast enough that it made the November 1979 ballot. One reason for this, certainly, was the strong business support behind the measure. The treasurer of the Spirit of 13 organization was John T. Hay, executive vice-president of the California Chamber of Commerce, and both the Chamber and the California Association of Realtors were deeply involved in both soliciting signatures and financing the campaign. Quotas for both signatures and contributions were assigned to a variety of business groups, a reflection of the careful organization throughout the Proposition 4 campaign.[38]

The general popularity of the idea was such that few groups would speak out against it. Howard Jarvis considered opposing the proposition, but ultimately thought better of it and provided an endorsement.[39] The polls in June showed strong approval from both Republicans and Democrats. Such bipartisan support from the voters had to play some role in Proposition 4's support by liberal Democratic House Speaker Leo McCarthy, as well as Republican Minority Leader Carol Hallett and many others. There was some vocal opposition, from such groups as the League of Women Voters and the California Labor Federation, but their voices were clearly overwhelmed by the chorus of support.[40]

Gann and his supporters had the money, the organization, and contemporary public sentiment behind them. Even though this proposition and the one on school busing were controversial, turnout was extremely low in 1979 — only 37 percent of registered voters showed up, even fewer than for Reagan's Proposition 1 in the 1973 special election. Of those who did come to the polls, 94 percent voted on Proposition 4 and 74 percent of them endorsed the measure. Gann was riding high.

Meanwhile, Howard Jarvis was no less ambitious than Paul Gann; while Gann got involved in cutting government spending, Jarvis stayed with the issue of taxation. His Proposition 9 on the June 1980 primary ballot was a constitutional amendment that aimed to write into the constitution two statutes already enacted by the legislature (the indexing of rates for the personal income tax and the repeal of the business inventory tax). In addition, an entirely new provision proposed to reduce personal income tax rates to 50 percent of those of 1978. This was a draconian measure, but Jarvis now had a powerful organization in his California Tax Reduction Movement. He was able to raise very large sums of money, hire professional signature solicitors and campaign managers, and mount a sophisticated, large-scale campaign — the grassroots were not so important any more.[41]

This time, however, the opposition was broader and better organized. Opponents stressed the drastic effects that would result from Proposition 9; tax cuts and controls created by Proposition 13 were one thing, they argued, but to cut taxes so greatly now would definitely eliminate needed govern-ment services. The measure would also clearly benefit the rich far more than anyone else: 30 percent of the cuts would go to the top 3 percent of earners; a family with $75,000 in income would save almost $2,000, whereas a family with an income of $17,500 would save $131.[42] This theme was adumbrated by many representatives of the University of California and California State University, not least including David S. Saxon, the president of the Univer-sity of California, who argued that all levels of education in the state were threatened by the proposal.[43] The state's legislative analyst, William Hamm, said that the surplus that had existed at the time of Proposition 13 was now largely gone, and that the state could not afford Proposition 9. These argu-ments seemed to be reinforced by Standard and Poor's lowering of the state's bond rating from AAA to AA+. The *Los Angeles Times* agreed that the state could not afford the measure, and the *Sacramento Bee* noted that Jarvis was attacking the "least onerous and most progressive" of the state's taxes. The Los Angeles City Council went on record 10–1 against the measure. And when conservative economist Arthur Laffer of the University of Southern California signed the ballot argument in favor of Proposition 9, he was countered by the more prestigious conservative economist, Nobel Laureate Milton Friedman, who opposed it.[44]

The negative message got through, even though the initiative's opponents spent only half as much as the Jarvis forces. In the May Field poll, 82 percent of the respondents had heard about Proposition 9, but of them, only 51 percent felt they knew enough to make a decision and 47 percent said they would wait to hear more about it. That was not too promising, coming the month before the election. Jarvis had not made the kind of impression on voters that he had two years previously. Moreover, of those who felt they knew enough to make a decision, 69 percent said they would vote No.[45]

The ballot box reflected those responses. Ninety-six percent of voters did vote on Proposition 9, the highest voter participation rate on any of the eleven measures on the June 1980 ballot, but this time 61 percent voted against Howard Jarvis.

Jarvis, however, was not easily discouraged. If the measure he wanted could not be passed, he would rework it so that it would succeed. That entailed dropping the massive tax cut section of Proposition 9, focusing instead on the indexing of rates for the personal income tax. In addition, Jarvis now sought to introduce the measure as a statute rather than a consti-tutional amendment, which would require fewer signatures to qualify. By early 1981, Jarvis was engaged in an extensive letter-writing campaign to drum up support for another try.[46] Proposition 7 in the June 1982 primary provided for "full indexing" of the state income tax beginning with the 1982 tax year; this differed from the 1978 initiative, which had proposed an index based on the California consumer price index less 3 percent. The difference was not major. More important was the idea of not letting taxes rise because of inflation: that was an issue easy to understand, and popular.

Opponents of Proposition 7 once again stressed the danger to the state of declining revenues, and also the idea that the income tax would become even less progressive given the low rates to be paid by the wealthiest Californians.[47] But the measure did not get too much attention in a campaign with eight other direct legislation propositions; indeed, two rival initiatives that sought to do away with gift and inheritance taxes got more attention and more voters, as did a referendum on legislation related to the Central Valley water project. Jarvis's Proposition 7 nevertheless passed with 54 percent of the vote. It was a less extreme measure than the 1980 proposal, but it represented a victory all the same.

Tables 4.2 and 4.3 show the relationships among the anti-tax and anti-spending initiatives from Watson's first try in 1968 through Jarvis's modest victory in 1982, and between these elections and some background census variables.

In terms of the elections themselves, the vote on the 1970 effort by the California Teachers Association to switch the burden of school and welfare support to the state has a strong relationship with the vote on Watson's first try at reform just seven months previously, and has modest relationships with the other tax-cutting initiatives. Indeed, all of the anti-tax and anti-spending propositions between 1972 and 1982 have positive relationships with one another, with the strongest correlations being among Jarvis and Gann's Proposition 13 of 1978, Gann's Proposition 4 of 1979, and Jarvis's Proposition 9 of 1980. These initiatives clearly represent the heart of the anti-tax and anti-spending movement, with a solid block of voters committed to the Jarvis–Gann ideas in the late 1970s. The commitment extended, a little less powerfully, to Jarvis's 1982 income tax indexing proposition as well, and was also significantly related to Reagan's 1973 effort to cut both taxes and spending.

In terms of background variables, once again the fact that the data are aggregated at the county level masks some of what one might expect. For example, the poll data in Table 4.1 show a stronger relationship between wealth and support for Proposition 13 than is seen here—a statistically significant but not particularly strong one. Wealth does seem more supportive of tax cutting than of limiting spending. Family income's strongest relationship is with the Jarvis income tax cut in 1980; this is not surprising, since that measure more directly benefited the wealthy than any other group.

Looked at from the other direction, the negative correlations between voting for these propositions and unemployment are as logical as are the positive ones with family income. The unemployed were generally less likely

TABLE 4.2    Correlations for Voting on Tax-Related Propositions, 1968–1982

| Date[a] and proposition | 1968g: Prop. 9 Property tax (Watson) | 1970p: Prop. 8 Taxation for schools and welfare | 1972g: Prop. 14 Property tax (Watson) | 1973s: Prop. 1 Tax and spending (Reagan) |
|---|---|---|---|---|
| 1968g: Prop. 9 Property tax (Watson) | 1.000 | | | |
| 1970p: Prop. 8 Taxation for schools and welfare | .728 | 1.000 | | |
| 1972g: Prop. 14 Property tax (Watson) | .234 | −.070 | 1.000 | |
| 1973s: Prop. 1 Tax and spending (Reagan) | .404 | −.124 | .486 | 1.000 |
| 1978p: Prop. 13 Property tax (Jarvis–Gann) | .475 | −.008 | .325 | .536 |
| 1979g: Prop. 4 Limit spending (Gann) | .312 | −.234 | .491 | .732 |
| 1980p: Prop. 9 Income tax (Jarvis) | .415 | −.061 | .410 | .907 |
| 1982p: Prop. 7 Income tax (Jarvis) | .044 | −.246 | .205 | .315 |

NOTE: Pearson product moment correlations, based on percentage voting Yes on propositions, with data aggregated by county and weighted by county population. For clarity, only one side of table is shown, since both sides are identical.

[a]After date, "p" stands for primary, "g" for general, and "s" for special election.

| 1978p: Prop. 13 Property tax (Jarvis–Gann) | 1979g: Prop. 4 Limit spending (Gann) | 1980p: Prop. 9 Income tax (Jarvis) | 1982p: Prop. 7 Income tax (Jarvis) |
|---|---|---|---|
| 1.000 | | | |
| .776 | 1.000 | | |
| .653 | .788 | 1.000 | |
| .495 | .443 | .439 | 1.000 |

TABLE 4.3 Correlations of Voting on Tax-Related Propositions, 1968–1982, with 1980 Census Characteristics

| Proposition[a] and census characteristic | Mean family income | Percentage of families below poverty level | Percentage of labor force unemployed | Percentage of high school graduates (males over age 25) | Percentage urban | Percentage foreign born | Percentage born outside California |
|---|---|---|---|---|---|---|---|
| 1968g: Prop. 9 Property tax (Watson) | .255 | .383 | -.499 | -.170 | .446 | .720 | -.143 |
| 1970p: Prop. 8 Taxation for schools and welfare | .084 | .593 | -.242 | -.343 | .369 | .747 | -.443 |
| 1972p: Prop. 9 Property tax (Watson) | -.100 | .157 | -.048 | -.252 | -.027 | .163 | .162 |
| 1973s: Prop. 1 Tax and spending (Reagan) | .393 | -.239 | -.527 | .173 | .240 | .212 | .382 |

| | | | | | | | |
|---|---|---|---|---|---|---|---|
| **1978p:**<br>**Prop. 13**<br>**Property tax**<br>**(Jarvis–Gann)** | .304 | −.210 | −.277 | .144 | .029 | .062 | .069 |
| **1979g:**<br>**Prop. 4**<br>**Limit spending**<br>**(Gann)** | .121 | −.195 | −.208 | .133 | .004 | −.135 | .463 |
| **1980p:**<br>**Prop. 9**<br>**Income tax**<br>**(Jarvis)** | .441 | −.306 | −.553 | .261 | .279 | .207 | .433 |
| **1982p:**<br>**Prop. 7**<br>**Income tax**<br>**(Jarvis)** | .285 | −.436 | −.250 | .488 | .053 | −.108 | .366 |

NOTE: Pearson product moment correlations, based on percentage voting Yes on propositions and data from 1980 U.S. Census, with data aggregated by county and weighted by county population.

*a* After date, "p" stands for primary, "g" for general, and "s" for special election.

to be homeowners who would benefit from lower property taxes, and they recognized the fact that the Reagan and Jarvis income tax cuts really bene-fited the wealthy more than themselves. The general threat to welfare pro-grams posited by all of these propositions was an additional caution to the unemployed, who were also likely to need a variety of welfare services. The same arguments hold for the percentage of families below the poverty level, although in this instance there are fewer strongly significant correlations. That correlations of the vote with both categories, the percentage unem-ployed and the percentage of families below the poverty level, moved in the same direction makes sense.

Whether voters were of foreign or native birth, urban or rural residence, or high school graduates had no determinable effect on voting patterns for these propositions. The last category had more significance earlier in the century, when graduation from high school was a mark of middle-class status; by the 1970s, that was no longer true, and the 1980 census did not ask about college graduation. There is no significant correlation between the percentage of voters born in the United States but outside of California with voting for these propositions, although toward the end of the period the relationships were more positive. Perhaps this shows that in-migrants of the 1940s–1960s slowly rose in status and had more to lose over time, but that conclusion is entirely speculative.

The tax and spending revolt was real and very important in California from that time to the present. It did not stop in 1982 and it did not stop in California. Its effects on other states were immediate: at least six states had some sort of major tax-cutting proposals placed on their ballots in Novem-ber of 1978, and Idaho's proposition was a near-duplicate of Proposition 13.[48] Nationally, the radical Kemp–Roth income tax reduction proposal had been sitting in Congress since 1977 with little interest or support. But with the passage of Proposition 13 it suddenly became popular, picking up 179 congressional supporters, and came to a vote. It was defeated in the House, to be replaced by a less drastic tax bill. But the impulse for tax reduction had become national.[49] And when Ronald Reagan entered the White House in 1981, the "Spirit of 13" gained a very important champion.

The question of the effects of these anti-tax and anti-spending measures on California was and still is subject to dispute. Part of the reason was the size of the state budget surplus at the time of Proposition 13. For a while, the state was able to pick up the burden of school and welfare costs that had previously been financed from property taxes. But that turned out to be only a temporary solution. In part, the effects of Proposition 13 and its successors have varied over time along with the state of the California economy, and this has provided sufficient data for both supporters and opponents of these initiatives to "prove" their case.

Howard Jarvis himself acknowledged that at least 100,000 public jobs were lost in the first year after Proposition 13's passage (" . . . which some people think is a disaster, and I think is a blessing"), but he countered that "562,000 new jobs in private industry" more than compensated for those losses. Others agreed with him.[50] In fact, the loss of public jobs was real, but, in the short run, slower than many had feared because of a bailout from state funds. Los Angeles County received $580 million from the state in 1978, and in 1979 Governor Brown and the legislature proposed a bailout for that year of $4.5 billion. Thus, the effects of Proposition 13 were buffered in such a way that many perceived Jarvis and Gann to have been correct.[51]

To others, the public job loss, however moderate, was itself a significant indication of Proposition 13's deleterious effects. Los Angeles Mayor Tom Bradley bemoaned the loss in the first year after Proposition 13, and his office's inability to "maintain the momentum" on programs like affirmative action. And the Los Angeles County Grand Jury reported after a five-month study of the effects of Proposition 13 that the county's 70,000 employees were "uncertain and depressed," that productivity had suffered along with morale, that there was a "brain drain" of highly skilled workers leaving public employment, and that job turnover had increased by 50 percent.[52]

That was only one area of the effects of the anti-tax and anti-spending initiatives of that time and later. Across the state, renters, angry at not receiving any aid while homeowners were saving a bundle, began rent freeze and rollback efforts, with some cities, like Santa Monica, enacting rigid rent-control laws.[53] With the passage of a few more years, cities began to be hit seriously by the decline in both state aid and federal revenue sharing, and tried to compensate by raising "fees" that did not come under the two-thirds vote provisions of Proposition 13 (this procedure itself would be confounded by later initiatives; see Chapter 5). And the state, trying to keep up its new obligations while also receiving less tax revenue, began to float larger and larger bond issues that considerably increased its indebtedness and questioned its creditworthiness.[54] By the late 1980s city infrastructure and services were in major decline, the state's once-proud public school system ranked among the lowest in the United States in per-student spending, and signs of decline were everywhere to be seen. But the public seemed to have been permanently converted by Paul Gann and Howard Jarvis — higher taxes and increased government spending remained unacceptable solutions.

The anti-tax and anti-spending sentiment of this period also played a significant role in the most important effort at political reform of the 1970s, the June 1974 Political Reform Initiative (Proposition 9). Jarvis and Gann had constantly justified tax cuts by pointing to government waste and the ineptness or nefariousness of politicians. Ronald Reagan, likewise, had made criticism of the size and intrusiveness of government a keystone of his political career. More and more, the public read in their papers and saw on television accounts of corruption and influence peddling in public life, and of the increasing power of big money and "special interests" in California and national politics. Then, in 1973–1974, the Watergate scandal was constantly in the public's eye, providing an immediate example of the need for control of the political process.[55]

Two groups were the prime developers and movers of Proposition 9 — Common Cause and People's Lobby. The former was the more "mainstream," having originated in opposition to the Vietnam War, which led to study of the governmental process, and then to concern with campaign financing and public disclosure; it also had a large membership base. People's Lobby was a very small group, run by Ed and Joyce Koupal, who had made it a successful signature solicitation company; it shared many of the same concerns about the nature of the contemporary political process. The two groups were brought together by a third force, California Attorney General Edmund G. "Jerry" Brown, son of the former governor who was himself planning to run for governor in 1974.[56]

The specifics of the initiative were worked out carefully, with a good deal of popular involvement. Common Cause, for example, held 60 open public hearings across the state for input from any interested persons or groups. People's Lobby engaged in a careful study of past initiatives and potential competitors in order to maximize the likelihood of success. There followed serious negotiations between the two groups, which were by no means entirely in accord. Common Cause opposed putting spending limits into the proposition without also including contribution limits and public financing, while People's Lobby strongly advocated spending limits, which it saw as a very popular issue with the masses.[57]

What came out of these negotiations was a complex and comprehensive initiative statute, with input and support from Ralph Nader's California Citizen Action Group as well as the two parent organizations. Among its more important clauses: (1) creation of a new Fair Political Practices Commission, with power to hold hearings, investigate, issue orders, and impose fines; (2) tightening of the law regulating Campaign Statements, requiring much greater specificity about contributors; (3) new limits on campaign expenditures for statewide candidates and ballot propositions; (4) new requirements for lobbyist registration and limits on gifts by lobbyists; (5) tightened conflict-of-interest rules; and (6) some changes in the rules for the ballot pamphlet, including public examination of its text.[58]

The two organizations had little trouble collecting more than the 330,000 signatures required for an initiative statute. People's Lobby had ten thousand volunteers who gathered 325,000 signatures in 53 of California's 58 counties. Common Cause got another 195,000 signatures, so together they had a huge margin to guarantee enough valid signatures.[59]

The campaign was fairly intense, but behind it was the sense that the public overwhelmingly supported the idea of campaign reform. Most politicians of both parties were frightened by it, and while the initiative was in the developmental stage in 1973, the legislature tried to undercut it by passing two bills, the Moscone conflict-of-interest law and the Waxman–Dymally campaign reporting law.[60] Once again, however, the legislators had avoided an issue until it was thrust upon them, and responded with too little, too late. Fans of the initiative process had another example of legislative bankruptcy to cite in defense of their efforts.

The main opposition to Proposition 9 came from politicians, organized labor, and business groups. Labor, particularly, was scared by the initiative, since it would be classified as a lobby under the new law's terms, and it would be harder for labor to skirt around the rules than would be the case for private business. The California Labor Federation voted unanimously against the measure, and the AFL–CIO Committee on Political Education (COPE) withdrew its earlier support for Jerry Brown and Jerome Waldie for the Democratic gubernatorial nomination because both men supported Proposition 9.[61] Business opposition was also quite strong: the California Taxpayers Association called it a "flagrant intrusion on the right of free speech and petition," an idea echoed by such opponents as the State Chamber of Commerce, the California Medical Association, and other business groups. Much of the press and many city and county governments argued that while the general idea was good, the specifics of Proposition 9 had too many flaws. Thus, the opposition was widespread.[62]

Some political candidates and officeholders were scared out of support for Proposition 9 by this opposition, but others, like Jerry Brown, who won the Democratic gubernatorial nomination that year, Mayor Tom Bradley of Los Angeles, Mayor Pete Wilson of San Diego, and popular California Secretary of State March Fong Eu were open supporters. Indeed, Brown made it an important part of his campaign image of being someone from the outside, an independent and reform candidate.[63]

Proposition 9 was the only direct legislation initiative among the nine propositions on the June 1974 ballot. It had the highest voter participation rate, 90 percent, and an overwhelming 70 percent to 30 percent victory. The public, at least, was ready for campaign reform.

Interestingly, huge sums of money were not raised for this campaign, probably because to most groups the threat was indirect. Moreover, there was real question as to whether or not the proposed law would survive court tests, and it was not entirely clear whether lobbyists would actually be hurt or helped.[64] Supporters, mainly Common Cause, spent about $600,000, while labor raised about $115,000 in opposition (business group expenditures were not trackable).

In fact, the spending limits on campaigns for public office were ruled unconstitutional by the U.S. Supreme Court in 1976, and the spending limits on initiatives were invalidated by the California Supreme Court in the same year. Moreover, there was a great escalation of campaign spending after 1974, as lobbyists and legislators found ways to work around the new system, aided, of course, by these court decisions. The disclosure provisions did survive court test and became the basis for further efforts at campaign reform in the next decade.[65]

Another significant and unexpected effect of Proposition 9 was the rapid development of political law firms. Vigo Nielsen, a member of Common Cause and supporter of Proposition 9 in 1974, as well as a partner in a Sacramento law firm, said that the passage of the initiative was "the foundation of what this law practice is now all about." The new rules and FPPC regulations resulted in an increased need for sponsors of initiatives and referendums to have informed legal advice for every stage of the process, from proposition drafting through fund-raising and post-election defense or attack. A large and profitable legal industry was created, without whose skills successful initiative campaigns became almost impossible.[66]

Sociocultural issues were as divisive in the 1970s as they had been earlier, although their specific nature reflected new ideas and new conflicts. In the 1972 general election, for example, there were nine direct legislation measures, of which several had strong sociocultural content. One of them, Proposition 18, was an anti-obscenity initiative statute, very similar to Proposition 16 of 1966. It would have given broad powers to state and local governments to regulate obscenity, replaced the concept of "redeeming social importance" with one of "contemporary community standards," and increased penalties for misdemeanor infractions. The measure had some mainstream leadership, including endorsements from the popular singer Pat Boone and from Governor Reagan and the California Chamber of Commerce. But the mainstream press condemned it as extreme and unconstitutional. Opponents, especially in the entertainment industry, raised a lot of money for a well-organized professional campaign against Proposition 18.[67] It fared even less well than the 1966 one, with a 68 percent vote against it.

There was also a marijuana decriminalization proposition in this election, which drew the highest number of voters of any of the 22 measures on the ballot (95 percent). It would have removed criminal penalties for growing, possessing, or using marijuana and had support from a wide variety of respectable organizations.[68] But the public at large still saw the use of marijuana as a moral, even criminal issue, and Proposition 19 was rejected by two-thirds of those voting. The combination of the huge voter participation rate and the landslide rejection of the measure offers some insight into public sentiment about "drugs" in general.

Racial relations entered the 1972 general election with some vigor, in an anti-busing initiative that proposed to override the "Bagley Act" that had made school districts responsible for developing integration plans. Proposition 21 was an initiative statute that guaranteed that no student could be forced to attend a particular school (i.e., be bused) for reasons of his or her "race, creed, or color." Despite the prescient argument of opponents that the initiative was unconstitutional and would be invalidated by the courts, it met with great enthusiasm. Busing was an inflammatory issue in the 1970s, deeply opposed by the white middle class.[69] Sixty-three percent of those voting approved the measure. And seven years later a very similar legislative constitutional amendment was approved by a 69 percent majority (Prop. 1, 1979 general election). Race continued to be very divisive in California in this decade. And race also played a role in the vote on Proposition 22, which dealt with agricultural labor relations (see the discussion below).

The 1972 general election also introduced one of the most divisive and long lasting of all contemporary sociocultural issues — crime. It seemed to Californians that wherever they turned, there was evidence of crime and violence; lawlessness seemed rampant. The Watts riots of 1965 had affected Los Angeles deeply and in many ways, and had resonated throughout the state. In 1969 Californians were shocked by the brutal murders carried out by Charles Manson and his bizarre cult of followers; that crime remained before the public for a year and a half, as the press followed Manson's arraignment and trial, until he was finally convicted in January 1971. This era was also the time of the spectacular kidnapping of Patricia Hearst by the radical black Symbionese Liberation Army, and then of her apparent conversion to their cause and participation in a bank robbery. She was not caught until the summer of 1975. One month later, Lynette "Squeaky" Fromme, one of Manson's followers, tried to shoot President Ford. And a few weeks after that, Sara Jane Moore also took a shot at Ford but missed. All of these events took place in California, and they were only the more outrageous and sensational signs of crime out of control. Small wonder that crime and punishment played such a frequent role in the direct legislation of the 1970s and after.

Like the marijuana and obscenity initiatives, Proposition 17 on the death penalty had an extremely high voter participation rate in the 1972 general election (94 percent, which equaled the vote for the three major presidential candidates). The California Supreme Court, interpreting U.S. Supreme Court guidelines, had ruled the state's death penalty unconstitutional in February 1972, and this initiative was a rapid response that aimed to modify the constitution so as to legally reestablish it. The ensuing debate pretty much rehashed long-held conservative-versus-liberal views on the subject, but the public clearly wanted capital punishment back, and 68 percent of those voting approved Proposition 17.[70] The state Supreme Court, however, dealing with specifics of the new law, struck it down in 1976. The legislature, led by future Governor George Deukmejian, responded with a new capital punishment law the following year. Governor Jerry Brown, a firm opponent of the death penalty, vetoed the bill, but the legislature passed it over his veto, a rare occurrence in California government.[71]

Supporters of harsh sentencing for violent crime wanted to expand, beyond the legislature's guidelines, the application of the death penalty and of minimum sentencing. So, in 1978, led by state senator John V. Briggs, they proposed an initiative statute for the general election (Proposition 7) that would tighten the language of the law in order to guarantee the possibility of the death penalty and defined "special circumstances" under which the only acceptable penalties were death or life imprisonment without the possibility of parole.[72] The issue continued to draw an emotional response from the voting public. In the California Poll of mid-August 1978, only 50 percent of respondents had heard of Proposition 7; nonetheless, 84 percent of those polled said they would vote for it. By mid-September, 59 percent had heard of it (whereas 95 percent had heard of the anti-smoking Proposition 5), but still 80 percent were in favor; and in the final pre-election poll, 76 percent of respondents said they would support Proposition 7.[73] The poll was a pretty good predictor: 71 percent of voters did vote Yes. Interestingly, voter participation on this measure, at 89 percent, was considerably lower than on the initiatives dealing with smoking and with school employee homosexuality (97 percent and 96 percent, respectively). The death penalty issue did not always arouse quite the emotion of some others, but Californians clearly favored it.[74]

Four years later, Paul Gann returned to his early interest in crime. He said that he had been more and more impressed with the prevalence of crime, unsafe streets, and laxity of enforcement by the courts. In conjunction with some Republican politicians, he threatened Governor Brown and the Democratic legislature that unless they passed a "Victims' Bill of Rights" (with ten specific points), he would see that it was done by initiative the following year.[75]

So, while Howard Jarvis had his second income tax indexing initiative on the 1982 primary ballot, Paul Gann had his Proposition 8, called the "Victims' Bill of Rights," an omnibus anti-crime measure. At the same time, Gann was also involved in an unsuccessful effort to mount a recall of Chief Justice Rose Bird, primarily on the basis of her "softness" on crime and the death penalty. In his mind, the two actions were complementary parts of the same crusade.[76]

Proposition 8 was both a statute and a constitutional amendment. It included numerous provisions: new procedures relative to treatment, sentencing, release, and other matters for those accused and convicted of crime; restitution to victims; the right of safe schools; changed rules regarding exclusion of relevant evidence and bail, plus use of prior felony convictions; severe diminution of the mental/emotional illness defense; restrictions on plea bargaining; and others.[77] In addition to Gann, key support came from Attorney General George Deukmejian, who was running for governor and planned to make crime the keystone of his campaign, and Republican Lieutenant Governor Mike Curb.[78] Gann's Citizens Committee to Stop Crime was definitely in charge, and very well coordinated; it had a large number of private citizens and officeholders to help with signature solicitation. The Gann people kept careful track of politicians at all levels who supported Proposition 8 and sent frequent form-letter solicitations to politicians, and especially, law enforcement personnel, enclosing an "Endorsement Card" to be returned. This permitted them to announce the names of police chiefs, sheriffs, district attorneys, and others who were committed to their crusade.[79]

Proposition 8 was opposed on several fronts and was in and out of the courts. The California trial lawyers, leading opponents of the measure, went to court to try to keep it off the ballot by challenging the number of signatures. Questions were also raised about its alleged coverage of more than one subject, which was not legal. Secretary of State March Fong Eu at one point was instructed by the courts not to qualify the initiative. Finally, the Supreme Court ruled 4–3 (with Chief Justice Bird on the losing side) in favor of the initiative's legality, and instructed Eu to put it on the June ballot.[80] Several of the state's leading newspapers were also against Proposition 8, arguing that it tried to do too much, was too involved and confusing, and could cost the state up to $50 million per year.[81]

This breadth of criticism had some effect, but not enough to defeat the measure, which won with 54 percent of the vote. That was not the end of the story, however, because over the next two and one-half years, the California Court of Appeals handed down more than 50 opinions on various aspects of the measure, but still numerous questions were unanswered. The court did rule that Proposition 8 did not violate the single-subject rule and could not be applied retroactively — the former pleased Gann, the latter disappointed him. But other components of the measure, including the use of prior convictions at trial and the denial of legal insanity as a defense would have to wait for a ruling from the Supreme Court. Ironically, the plea bargaining restrictions and victim's rights provisions of the measure were little implemented.[82]

Five months after the Proposition 8 battle, in the 1982 general election, another crime-related initiative was on the ballot. Proposition 15 required the registration of all concealable weapons (handguns). As is always the case with gun control, it was an emotional issue. The initiative had strong law enforcement support, but much popular and organizational opposition, which focused on how easily criminals could evade the regulations while the rights of law-abiding citizens would be infringed. There was also really big money on both sides. Supporters of Proposition 15 raised $2.3 million, but opponents raised $5.3 million, with about half of that coming from the National Rifle Association.[83] The infusion of so much money into the campaigns created a high level of awareness of the measure: in early October, already 90 percent of registered voter respondents to a California Poll had heard of the initiative, an extraordinarily high percentage at that stage of any campaign.[84] Similarly, the initiative had a high 94 percent voter participation rate. It was ultimately defeated with 63 percent of the vote. This was a case where big money did win, but the victory was aided by the strong pro-gun and anti-crime sentiment in California.

Another issue with some sociocultural content, where money perhaps played an even more significant role, was Proposition 5 of November 1978, the first anti-smoking measure to make it to a California ballot. It would have prohibited smoking in most public places and in most workplaces, educational institutions, and health facilities. And it would require restaurants to provide non-smoking areas. What is notable about the initiative is the total amount of money spent on it, $7.1 million, which set a record for spending up to that time. Of that amount, opponents raised and spent 90 percent, or $6.4 million.[85] The spending had some effect over time: in the September Field poll, 47 percent of respondents said they would support the proposition, compared to 49 percent who said they would not; one month later, support had declined to 42 percent and opponents had risen to 56 percent.[86] And that was about how it came out on election day: 97 percent of voters participated in voting on this proposition, an extremely high rate, and 54 percent of them voted against the regulation of smoking. Given that one-third of the respondents to the California Poll identified themselves as "smokers," that may have been equally as important in the defeat of the measure as the amount of money spent against it.

Two years later another anti-smoking proposition emerged. Proposition 10 in November 1980 was a milder proposal. It simply would have required that there be smoking and non-smoking sections in enclosed public places, places of employment, and health and educational facilities. Restaurants were not mentioned at all. It was, however, the first time that the matter of "second-hand smoke" was mentioned, with the pro-10 argument in the ballot pamphlet mentioning how nonsmokers were being affected by smokers.[87] The principal support organization, Californians for Smoking and Non-Smoking Sections, for some reason decided on a "light-hearted approach" in their advertisements. Political consultant Larry Levine defended the approach by saying, "It is an issue that is not life or death. We think lightness and a sense of humor are appropriate."[88] In retrospect, this was a bizarre idea, and not a very productive one.

Opposition came not only from the tobacco companies, but from a large section of the California business community as well. Spokespersons for the California Manufacturers Association and the California Chamber of Commerce criticized the costs to businesspeople; members of the Commonwealth Club stressed the level of government interference in private affairs and violation of individual rights.[89]

The proposition excited less interest and less money than its predecessor: supporters spent $1 million, including qualification costs, while opponents spent $2.7 million just on the campaign.[90] Voter participation on this measure was nonetheless 90 percent, highest among the eleven propositions on the November 1980 ballot, and the outcome was almost identical to that of two years before: 53 percent of voters said No.

Table 4.4 looks at the relationships among the votes on sociocultural issues between 1972 and 1982. In addition to the propositions previously discussed, it also includes Proposition 22 of 1972, on agricultural labor relations (discussed below) and Proposition 6 of 1978, which sought to punish homosexual public school teachers.

The table shows a striking consistency in relationships on a "liberal"-versus-"conservative" basis on these sociocultural issues. Correlations among conservative and liberal positions (which are distinguished in the table by the use of regular and boldface type, respectively) are almost always strongly positive, whereas correlations between conservative and liberal positions are almost always strongly negative. For example, in 1972 voters in favor of the death penalty were also very likely to strongly favor controlling obscenity and limiting the rights of agricultural labor, and to oppose legalizing marijuana and school busing. They were very much in favor of tightened criminal sentencing and the death penalty, and of prosecuting homosexuals, in 1978, and were strongly opposed to gun control in 1982. For reasons that are unclear, the correlations do not extend to Paul Gann's criminal justice Proposition 8 of June 1982, but that vote has few strong correlations with any other propositions.

By the same token, "liberal" voting on decriminalizing marijuana in 1972 had strong negative relationships with such conservative positions as opposing busing and the United Farm Workers union, or supporting the death penalty and the control of obscenity.

There are some exceptions to this general conservative-liberal dichotomy, but overall it is impressive. Only the two measures for limiting smoking do not fit this model, and they probably should not be classed as ideologically based issues. There were apparently too many smokers among all ideologi-

TABLE 4.4 Correlations for Voting on Sociocultural Propositions, 1972–1982

| Date[a] and Proposition | 1972g: Prop. 17 Death penalty | 1972g: Prop. 18 Obscenity | **1972g: Prop. 19 Marijuana** | 1972g: Prop. 21 Anti-busing | 1972g: Prop. 22 Agricultural Labor |
|---|---|---|---|---|---|
| 1972g: Prop. 17 Death penalty | 1.000 | | | | |
| 1972g: Prop. 18 Obscenity | .728 | 1.000 | | | |
| **1972g: Prop. 19 Marijuana** | −.826 | −.821 | 1.000 | | |
| 1972g: Prop. 21 Anti-busing | .561 | .560 | −.614 | 1.000 | |
| 1972g: Prop. 22 Agricultural labor | .533 | .564 | −.708 | .239 | 1.000 |
| **1978g: Prop. 5 Smoking** | −.261 | −.313 | .430 | .010 | −.400 |
| 1978g: Prop. 6 Homosexuals | .743 | .779 | −.906 | .623 | .548 |
| 1978g: Prop. 7 Death penalty | .752 | .733 | −.843 | .797 | .433 |
| **1980g: Prop. 10 Smoking** | −.339 | .519 | .502 | −.399 | −.282 |
| 1982p: Prop. 8 Criminal justice | .257 | .372 | −.335 | .540 | .143 |
| **1982g: Prop. 15 Gun control** | −.724 | −.819 | .898 | −.460 | −.702 |

NOTE: Pearson product moment correlations, based on percentage voting Yes on propositions, with data aggregated by county and weighted by county population. For clarity, only one side of table is shown, since both sides are identical. Variables in **bold type** are basically "liberal" and those in ordinary type are basically "conservative."

[a]After date, "p" stands for primary and "g" for general election.

| 1978g: Prop. 5 Smoking | 1978g: Prop. 6 Homo-sexuals | 1978g: Prop. 7 Death penalty | 1980g: Prop. 10 Smoking | 1982p: Prop. 8 Criminal justice | 1982g: Prop. 15 Gun control |
|---|---|---|---|---|---|
| 1.000 | | | | | |
| −.288 | 1.000 | | | | |
| −.231 | .872 | 1.000 | | | |
| .653 | −.512 | −.520 | 1.000 | | |
| .118 | .542 | .469 | −.474 | 1.000 | |
| .558 | −.890 | −.773 | .553 | −.352 | 1.000 |

cal and partisan groups for this idea to clearly fit within either a "liberal" or "conservative" parameter.

Table 4.5 looks at the relationships between the vote for these propositions and some background variables from the 1980 U.S. Census. The results are not as clear as those in Table 4.4, with the relationships being generally less significant. The data does, however, support some valid generalizations. Most notably, higher family income, higher education levels, and a higher percentage of voters from urban areas all correlate positively with "liberal" positions on these sociocultural issues. These characteristics tended to predict a relatively greater opposition to harsh criminal penalties, controls on obscenity, discrimination against homosexuals, and limiting the rights of agricultural workers; and a relatively greater support for gun control, legalization of marijuana, and regulation of smoking (school busing is an exception). There are some variations on individual issues among these three population groups, but even these are consistent in their similarity.[91] Foreign-born voters took similarly "liberal" positions on these sociocultural issues. However, membership in either of two other population groups was a poor predictor of voting on these propositions: the percentage of the population that was unemployed and, especially, the percentage of families below the poverty level. This was largely true, also, for those born in states other than California, although that variable does show some relationship with support for harsher criminal justice and is also the only variable with a significant correlation — a positive one — with opposition to school busing.

Looking at voter participation rates and at the emotional reaction elicited by many of these propositions, as well as the data in Table 4.5, one sees that while the content may have changed from one decade to another, sociocultural issues remained frequent and powerful in California politics. Individually and collectively, these were issues that citizens cared about very deeply.

The conflict over agricultural labor relations during this period can be classified both as a management-labor dispute and a sociocultural question of minority rights, particularly the rights of Mexican and Mexican-American laborers in California's huge agricultural enterprises. Not surprisingly, the issue was reflected in direct legislation, as well as in the fields and in the legislature.

The rise of the United Farm Workers (UFW) under César Chávez, particularly during the great grape boycott that lasted from 1968 until the early 1970s, finally resulted in a union contract in this sector of agriculture. But the owners of California's farms and other business groups were not reconciled to the change, and hoped to both undercut the contracts that had been signed and to avoid any new ones. To achieve their goals, they used a variety of tactics, both legal and political, including making deals with the Teamsters Union in hope of undercutting the ethnically based and more insistent UFW. From the start, this was an ethnic conflict as well as an economic one.[92]

Although the growers had a sympathetic governor until 1975 in Ronald Reagan, the Democratic legislature was less obliging. Since the National Labor Relations Act excluded agricultural workers, and the California legislature had been unable to agree on state legislation to deal with the problem, efforts to resolve the dispute by means of direct legislation were almost inevitable. Proposition 22 — another of the numerous and controversial measures on the November 1972 ballot — represented the growers' effort to impose their own solution. The proposition aimed to specify both permissible and prohibited labor tactics; it would forbid certain types of strikes, picketing, and boycotts; and it would have created an Agricultural Labor Relations Board that would have considerable power over both the process of union certification and enforcement of this statute. The measure was designed to undercut the legal structure under which Chávez's UFW had established itself, and to make agricultural worker unions weaker and more subject to management dictates.[93] The proposition also reflected an inter-union conflict, with the Teamster's Union essentially allied with management in hope of displacing the UFW as the major union in California agriculture.[94]

The growers mounted a vigorous campaign, arguing, among other things, that the lettuce boycott was nothing more than a jurisdictional dispute between the two unions and that Proposition 22 would simply level the playing field between the two unions, since without the measure the UFW would continue to hold an unfair advantage over the Teamsters. The proponents also raised a good deal of money, a total of $705,000 compared to the opponents' $210,000, virtually all of it from various grower groups.[95]

Finding themselves on the defensive against what seemed broad general sympathy for the farm workers, the growers conducted a highly misleading campaign that suggested that their proposition was in fact pro-worker: "For Farmworkers Rights — Yes on 22."[96] There had apparently been even earlier chicanery on the proponents' part. The California Farm Bureau Federation had not only spent a quarter of a million dollars to qualify Proposition 22, but it had also allegedly used illegal means to solicit signatures, both by misleading people about the measure and by using minors to do much of the solicitation. This led the Democratic secretary of state, Jerry Brown, to file suit to have the proposition removed from the ballot, arguing that at least 63,000 of the signatures were invalid. The state Assembly began an investigation shortly before the election, which produced a lot of bad publicity for the promoters of the initiative, even though the proposition was not removed.[97]

All of this hurt the growers' cause, as did the fact that the campaign, seen

TABLE 4.5 Correlations of Voting on Sociocultural Propositions, 1972–1982, with 1980 Census Characteristics

| Date[a] and proposition | Mean family income | Percentage of high school graduates (males over age 25) | Percentage of foreign born | Percentage of families below poverty level | Percentage of unemployed | Percentage born in different state | Percentage urban |
|---|---|---|---|---|---|---|---|
| 1972g: Prop. 17 Death penalty | −.390 | −.337 | −.273 | .063 | .218 | .114 | −.284 |
| 1972g: Prop. 18 Obscenity | −.556 | −.376 | −.379 | .156 | .390 | .254 | −.512 |
| **1972g: Prop. 19 Marijuana** | .443 | .431 | .437 | −.085 | −.328 | −.171 | .432 |
| 1972g: Prop. 21 Anti-busing | .119 | .187 | −.213 | −.308 | −.197 | .532 | .040 |
| 1972g: Prop. 22 Agricultural labor | −.453 | −.523 | −.404 | .129 | .512 | −.163 | −.584 |

| | | | | | | | |
|---|---|---|---|---|---|---|---|
| **1978g:**<br>**Prop. 5**<br>**Smoking** | .428 | .399 | .184 | −.289 | −.571 | .290 | .564 |
| 1978g:<br>Prop. 6<br>Homosexuals | −.448 | −.266 | −.566 | −.040 | .310 | .366 | −.391 |
| 1978g:<br>Prop. 7<br>Death penalty | −.323 | −.163 | −.394 | −.008 | .173 | .433 | −.218 |
| **1980g:**<br>**Prop. 10**<br>**Smoking** | .359 | .118 | .201 | −.061 | −.295 | −.342 | .392 |
| 1982p:<br>Prop. 8<br>Criminal justice | −.034 | .388 | −.540 | −.525 | −.058 | .661 | −.168 |
| **1982g:**<br>**Prop. 15**<br>**Gun control** | .633 | .385 | .655 | −.080 | −.603 | −.168 | .654 |

NOTE: Pearson product moment correlations, based on percentage voting Yes on propositions and 1980 U.S. Census data, with data aggregated by county and weighted by county population. Variables in **bold type** are basically "liberal" and those in ordinary type are basically "conservative."

[a]After date, "p" stands for primary, "g" for general election.

TABLE 4.6    Support for Proposition 14 (1976 General
Election: Agricultural Labor Relations) Among Those Who
Were Aware of It

|  | Percentage responding favorably[a] |
|---|---|
| Party identification | |
| Republican | 27 |
| Democratic | 76 |
| Independent | 59 |
| Political philosophy | |
| Strong conservative | 21 |
| Moderate conservative | 44 |
| Moderate liberal | 76 |
| Strong liberal | 93 |
| Labor union membership | |
| Respondent | 76 |
| Neither respondent nor other member of household | 53 |

SOURCE: Based on Field Institute poll fi7605 (24 July–2 Aug. 1976).
[a]Percentage responding that they "definitely will favor" or "probably will favor" Proposition 14.

in the context of the national boycotts of grapes and lettuce, became national in scope. Pro-labor and pro–minority rights groups across the country spoke out against Proposition 22. Unions, Democratic officeholders, the clergy of major faiths, and numerous others, both locally and nationally, criticized the proposed statute.[98]

The end result was that the growers' wealth was unavailing. Ninety-three percent of the voters cast ballots on Proposition 22 (just a point or two lower than the numbers voting on the marijuana, death penalty, and obscenity propositions discussed above), and 58 percent of them voted No.

When Jerry Brown replaced Ronald Reagan as governor in 1975, the farm workers and Chávez had friends in both the executive and legislative branches of government (and also in the judiciary, where California Chief Justice Rose Bird oversaw a liberal majority on the state's highest court). This led to pro-UFW legislation in 1975, including a guarantee of worker's rights to vote in certification elections and an impartial Agricultural Labor

Relations Board. When the growers, who were losing certification elections, began working for a change in the law, the UFW responded with an initiative of its own. Proposition 14 of November 1976 was an initiative statute whose main aim was to protect the 1975 legislation.[99]

This measure was less sensational than Proposition 22 had been four years earlier, but the sides were the same and the spending was three times as heavy — a total of $3,257,000 by the two sides. A California Poll in 1976 asked a sample of Californians about their attitude toward Proposition 14. This was fairly early in the campaign — late July to early August. At that time, 38 percent of those polled had either heard of or "may have heard" of Proposition 14, whereas 62 percent had not yet heard of it. Eighty-four percent had an opinion about the proposition, even if they had not heard of it previously; of those who had an opinion, 52 percent "definitely" or "probably" expected to favor it, while 48 percent "probably" or "definitely" thought they would oppose it.[100] Table 4.6 summarizes the responses among those who had heard of Proposition 14 in this summer poll. The few variables that showed significant differences were party identification, political ideology, and union membership.

Responses reconfirm the correlation data in Table 4.5, showing that the measure reflected yet again the strong liberal–conservative split of the 1970s. Proposition 14, with the UFW essentially trying to preserve its protected position, did not elicit the broad sympathy of Proposition 22 four years earlier. The union no longer operated under the image of an exploited underdog. Also, the lack of voter awareness of the issue and, possibly, disproportionate spending produced a different result than in 1972. There was a 94 percent voter participation rate on Proposition 14, the highest in the 1976 general election, but the UFW's proposition lost, receiving only 32 percent of the vote.

Environmental issues, especially those related to water, beaches, and oil and gas exploitation, had played a role in direct legislation from the 1920s. This was no less the case in the 1970s and early 1980s. The state's water supply continued to be a major problem for California; likewise, the conflict between environmental protection and economic interests in underground resources and the state's forests remained controversial. There were eight environmentally related initiatives before California voters between 1970 and 1982, not including the two anti-smoking measures that were, in the minds of many, also environmental. These issues related to all of the themes just mentioned, as well as new ones like nuclear power and recycling. On the surface, it appears that the "environmentalists" won three times and lost five, but that is not necessarily true if one looks more deeply into the issues. In some cases, it was business and involved unions on one side, defending jobs and economic growth, and environmental organizations on the other, defending the woods and waters. But in other cases, the sides were a good deal less clear. And in no case were there just "good guys" against "bad guys." Always on these issues, there existed a congeries of interests, selfish and selfless. They were complicated issues, not easy for the voters to handle.

One reason for the number of initiatives on environmental issues at this time was that the legislature had proved incapable of handling them. Proponents of the first of these, Proposition 9 in the June 1972 primary, argued that over one thousand environmental measures had been submitted to the legislature in 1970, and almost none of them had been resolved.[101] This initiative statute dealt with a wide variety of issues: composition of motor fuels; shutting down of plants that violated air quality standards; restrictions on leasing and extraction of oil and gas from tidelands or submerged lands or onshore slant drilling; a five-year ban on construction of nuclear powered electric generating plants; pesticide restrictions; conflict of interest regulations; and more.[102] This was stretching the "one subject" rule for direct legislation probably beyond the breaking point.

The issue drew a lot of attention, and a total of $1.6 million spent by the two sides, but its large number of provisions made it more likely to offend more people.[103] It was the only direct legislation initiative among the ten propositions on the 1972 primary ballot and drew the highest voter participation rate (93 percent), but was decisively defeated 65–35 percent.

Considerably more popular attention was paid to another conservation measure five months later, when Proposition 20, the "Coastal Zone Protection Act," was one of the nine controversial popular initiatives in the 1972 general election. The proposition was almost identical to a measure that had been submitted to legislature and passed in the Assembly, but had failed to survive opposition by the senate and Governor Reagan.[104] Its aim was to control a newly defined coastal zone that extended one thousand yards inland from the mean high tide line. It created a new State Coastal Zone Conservation Commission and six Regional Commissions, whose permission was required for any new development in that zone. Its stated charge was the "protection, preservation, restoration, and enhancement of the environment and ecology" of the coastal zone. The initiative also appropriated $1.25 million per year for administration of the law for five years, after which time the law would expire (and could then be reconsidered).[105]

About 100 organizations had loosely combined into a "Coastal Alliance," with the Sierra Club playing the main role, in order to solicit signatures and push the initiative through. They managed to generate broad-based support, including both of California's United States Senators and ten congressmen, numerous Los Angeles city officials, and organizations ranging from the American Association of University Women and the PTA to the

League of Women Voters and the United Auto Workers. Their defense of the initiative focused on the idea that coastal land was special and thus merited a special kind of protection.[106]

The opposition was even more organized, raising $1.2 million to the proponents' total of about $250,000 (the disproportion in spending was so great that the Federal Communications Commission ordered Bay area television stations to provide free time for the proponents[107]). They hired the Whitaker and Baxter organization to run their campaign, focusing on statewide advertising on television and billboards.[108] Shell Oil placed advertisements in major newspapers, the Los Angeles Building and Trades Council emphasized the loss of jobs that would ensue, and numerous other business and labor organizations, as well as coastal cities, joined the battle to defeat the initiative.[109]

Like other initiatives in this election, Proposition 20 drew a high (92 percent) level of voter participation, and despite the wealth and organization of the opposition, the measure passed with 55 percent of the vote. This was also an unusually successful initiative in that when it expired in 1976, at the start of Jerry Brown's governorship, it was replaced by legislature's own Coastal Act that extended the protected area to five miles from the coast and tightened up other regulations as well.[110]

A "Wild and Scenic Rivers" initiative (Prop. 17), which endeavored to halt construction of a dam on the Stanislaus River, appeared on the June 1974 primary ballot. Environmentalists had first tried to halt the dam project in the courts, and then with a petition to President Nixon. When both of these failed, they resorted to the initiative. The contest was largely between environmental groups, such as the Sierra Club and the Environmental Defense Fund, which supported the initiative, and many business groups and potential dam contractors on the other side. The latter raised and spent a great deal more money. Outgoing Governor Reagan also opposed the proposition, while Democratic gubernatorial candidate Jerry Brown endorsed it.[111] Opponents prevailed, narrowly: Proposition 17 lost 53 percent to 47 percent.

A more controversial initiative proposing to ultimately eliminate nuclear power plants from the state appeared on the 1976 primary ballot. At the time, California had only 3 operating nuclear plants, but there were 4 more under construction and plans for 31 more over the next twenty years. Proposition 15 would have halted new nuclear plant construction and restricted currently operating plants to operation at only 60 percent of their licensed capacity. After five years, existing plants would be derated 19 percent per year unless the legislature certified that they were safe.[112] It was a confusingly written proposition and also confusingly presented as a "Nuclear Safety Initiative." Also, the wording was such that a Yes vote would be a vote against nuclear power and a No vote would be a vote for it. One of the proposition's Sierra Club backers concluded that they would have done better to be more straightforward and say they were trying to end nuclear power completely.[113]

Environmentalists were split on the measure; to some of them, the decline of nuclear power would mean increased use of coal, which could be environmentally worse. Business opponents took advantage of this lack of unified support, since they were unified in opposition, and really took control of the issue with their stress on job loss.[114] The stakes were high, and a lot of money was involved. The supporters of Proposition 15, organized into nine separate major campaign committees, spent $1.25 million.[115] The opponents were more richly endowed; their $4 million in spending included over $400,000 by Bechtel Corp., more than $250,000 by General Atomic Company, and $453,000 by Pacific Gas and Electric.[116]

One week before the election, the Field California Poll asked a representative sample of Californians about Proposition 15. Most interesting, perhaps, is that, so close to the election, 60 percent of respondents felt they "know enough" about the issue, whereas 39 percent said they would wait before making up their minds. Table 4.7 looks at the relationship of selected variables with position on Proposition 15 among those respondents who had "definite" feelings about how they would vote (1,441 out of 2,085 respondents).

It is not surprising that the more one believed nuclear power was important and safe and that nuclear plants should continue to be built, the more one was likely to be opposed to the anti-nuclear proposition. It is more surprising that only a small majority of those who felt nuclear power should be cut back definitely supported Proposition 15, and of those who believed nuclear plants should no longer be built, only 50 percent definitely supported the proposition. Perhaps some of the inconsistency may be explained by confusion over just what a Yes or No vote meant, as noted above. That may also explain why 35 percent of those who said nuclear power was "somewhat important" said they were definitely or probably going to vote for the proposition.

There was some difference between Democrats and Republicans on the issue, although 59 percent of Democrats were nonetheless on the No side. The difference was somewhat greater between those who identified themselves as "conservative" or "liberal," but, still, exactly one-half of the latter were definitely or probably going to vote No. Union membership or non-membership did not make a significant difference, either — some unions were supportive of the environmental measure but others were bitterly against it. Neither did age make much difference in voting preference. There is little variation among groups from their twenties through their fifties. People above sixty,

TABLE 4.7    Position on Proposition 15 (1976 Primary Election: Nuclear Power Plants) Among Those Who Had Definite Feelings

|  | Definite Yes | Probable Yes | Definite No | Probable No |
|---|---|---|---|---|
| Importance of nuclear power | | | | |
| Extreme importance | 11 | 4 | 13 | 72 |
| Somewhat important | 19 | 16 | 21 | 44 |
| Not too important | 57 | 17 | 14 | 12 |
| Not at all important | 79 | 6 | 5 | 11 |
| Is nuclear power safe enough? | | | | |
| Safe enough | 8 | 5 | 15 | 73 |
| Cut back | 55 | 15 | 12 | 18 |
| Continue to build nuclear plants? | | | | |
| Continue to build | 8 | 4 | 14 | 74 |
| Stop building | 50 | 16 | 15 | 19 |
| Party registration | | | | |
| Democrat | 29 | 12 | 15 | 44 |
| Republican | 14 | 5 | 16 | 66 |
| Other | 37 | 7 | 15 | 37 |
| Ideology | | | | |
| Conservative | 14 | 7 | 15 | 64 |
| Middle-of-the-road | 21 | 8 | 15 | 56 |
| Liberal | 38 | 13 | 15 | 35 |
| Labor union member? | | | | |
| Respondent is | 25 | 9 | 11 | 56 |
| Neither respondent nor spouse | 23 | 9 | 16 | 52 |

SOURCE: Field Institute poll fi7604 (31 May–5 June 1976).
NOTE: Numbers reflect percentage responding in each category.

somewhat surprisingly, were the most strongly opposed to Proposition 15: 68 percent of those age 60–64 and 71 percent of those age 65–69 were "definitely no" in their responses.[117]

Ultimately, the negative campaign prevailed easily. Ninety-five percent of voters cast their ballots on the issue, and 68 percent of them voted No. Among other things, this campaign supports the truism that money can't guarantee a win in initiative campaigns, but it often is able to defeat them.

The year 1982 witnessed four initiatives related to the environment, one in the primary and three in the general election. Proposition 9 in the primary was a referendum against a 1980 statute that had added a peripheral canal to the Central Valley Project as part of an expanded water facilities program to bring more water from northern to southern California. The law also included environmental regulations and fish and wildlife protection; it was a complex piece of legislation with many parts.[118] The legislation had fairly broad-based support from some business groups, labor, the Urban League, and other liberal groups.[119] But supporters were greatly outspent by backers of the referendum, who aimed to undo the law. The main campaign organization, Californians for a Fair Water Policy, spent over $2 million on the campaign, and a number of smaller groups added to that sum.[120] Of the twelve measures on the June ballot, Proposition 9 had the highest voter participation rate (94 percent) by a good margin, and the legislature's new law was rejected by 63 percent of the voters. Strong northern California opposition to the statute was a key element in the outcome.[121]

In the fall of 1982, Proposition 11 proposed requiring a five-cent refund value for all refillable beverage containers. It had strong support from consumer and environmental groups, the state PTA, and labor and other liberal organizations, and $900,000 was raised for the campaign.[122] The opposition consisted of business groups like the California Chamber of Commerce and the California Grocers Association, which disparaged the costs of the program. They were joined by some rival environmental groups that insisted that the program would increase the use of fuel and water and therefore was not really environmentally sound. Opponents had already raised $5.3 million by mid-October, much of it from bottle and can makers and from beverage companies; they were thus able to spread their message throughout the state.[123] Proposition 11 tied with the handgun registration initiative for highest voter participation rate (94 percent), but the opponents were just too strong and it lost by 56 percent to 44 percent. This was, at least in part, another example of the power of money to defeat, if not to win, initiative campaigns.

Proposition 12 in the same fall 1982 election was a curious measure and related to the environment only tangentially, since its main aim was nuclear peace. The initiative would simply require the governor to write a letter to the President to request that the United States and the Soviet Union stop all testing, production, and deployment of nuclear weapons. In large part, the proposition was a reaction to President Reagan's aggressive foreign policy, and to similar developments in Washington: a measure very much like Proposition 12 had come to the floor of Congress in August and had been just barely defeated by the administration.[124]

The main organization behind the initiative was "Californians for a Bilateral Nuclear Freeze." The group made a striking effort and raised over $3 million from a huge number of contributors: its official Campaign Statement filings of contributions received ran about 1,000 pages.[125] The initiative carried in the November election, with 52 percent of the vote; its effect on American defense policy in the 1980s appears to have been insignificant.

The final environmental measure in November 1982 was Proposition 13, dealing with water resources. In part, it was an effort to resuscitate parts of the law that had been annulled by the Proposition 9 referendum five months earlier. It was smaller and more narrowly focused, however, dealing with water conservation, river use, and water storage. It elicited relatively little attention — in the early October California Poll, only 47 percent of respondents were aware of this initiative, compared to 87 percent for the beverage container measure and 67 percent for the anti-nuclear one.[126] Proposition 13's opponents raised lots of money against it, and it was easily defeated by 65 percent of those voting on the measure.[127]

Table 4.8 looks at the relationships in the vote for these eight propositions to see if there was any consistency in voting on environmental issues. Given the specifics of the propositions, and the fact that the "environmental side" of any issue was not always entirely clear (Prop. 9 on the peripheral canal was at least as much about northern versus southern California as it was about environmental issues), there is still a relatively high level of agreement on most of them. The more clearly environmental the propositions were, the more likely they were to correlate strongly, as in the case of air quality, coastal zone protection, wild rivers, and water resources. Interestingly, support for the nuclear weapons freeze was quite significantly related to these four issues as well; whether that was due to the somewhat logical relation between the environment and nuclear weapons, or to the fact that both issues appealed to the same people, is moot. The nuclear power initiative stands to some degree apart from the others, in that it had no significant relationship to the vote on air quality or that on wild rivers. But it did relate strongly to support for beverage container control, and fairly strongly to coastal zone protection and the nuclear weapons initiative. There is also some logical effect of time, in that the peripheral canal vote related significantly to other 1982 measures but not to the earlier ones. One must remember that Proposition 9 in the 1982 primary was a referendum, so that a No vote on that measure is comparable to a Yes on other pro-environment issues, and that negative correlations are therefore logical.

Given the variety of factors that enter into elections, the change in specifics from one proposition to another, and the varying amounts of money from one campaign to another, there is a relatively impressive consistency in voting on the environment that is comparable to the consistency for voting on sociocultural issues (see Table 4.4).

In the hectic twelve years between 1970 and 1982, California voters were called on to decide 39 popular initiatives and referendums. This was not a

TABLE 4.8    Correlations of Voting on Environmentally Related
Propositions, 1972–1982

| Date[a] and proposition | 1972p: Prop. 9 Air quality | 1972g: Prop. 20 Coastal zone | 1974g: Prop. 17 Wild rivers | 1976p: Prop. 15 Nuclear power |
|---|---|---|---|---|
| 1972p: Prop. 9 Air quality | 1.000 | | | |
| 1972g: Prop. 20 Coastal zone | .577 | 1.000 | | |
| 1974g: Prop. 17 Wild rivers | .661 | .550 | 1.000 | |
| 1976p: Prop. 15 Nuclear power | .168 | .507 | .246 | 1.000 |
| 1982p: Prop. 9 Peripheral canal | .171 | −.353 | −.107 | −.803 |
| 1982g: Prop. 11 Beverage containers | .258 | .527 | .420 | .858 |
| 1982g: Prop. 12 Nuclear weapons | .626 | .597 | .501 | .666 |
| 1982g: Prop. 13 Water resources | .798 | .607 | .689 | .424 |

NOTE:  Pearson product moment correlations, based on percentage voting Yes on propositions, with data aggregated by county and weighted by county population. For clarity, only one side of table is shown, since both sides are identical.

[a]After date, "p" stands for primary and "g" for general election.

huge number, spread out over sixteen elections, but it was not evenly distributed: most elections in this time period had one or two direct legislation measures, whereas the 1972 general election had nine and the 1982 primary had eight. Indeed, the two 1982 elections together had thirteen — one-third of the total for the period. The rate had definitely picked up after Proposition 13 of 1978. Additionally, conscientious voters also had to deal with 152

| 1982p: Prop. 9 Peripheral canal | 1982g: Prop. 11 Beverage containers | 1982g: Prop. 12 Nuclear weapons | 1982g: Prop. 13 Water resources |
|---|---|---|---|
| 1.000 | | | |
| −.743 | 1.000 | | |
| −.403 | .656 | 1.000 | |
| −.100 | .515 | .755 | 1.000 |

legislative measures mixed in with the popular ones on these ballots, for a grand total of 191 propositions, or an average of 12 each time voters went to the polls.

Of the 39 direct legislation measures, 15 (38 percent) were successful — that is, a majority Yes vote on initiatives and a majority No vote on referendums. (For the legislature's propositions, 73 percent were successful). Thus, voters seemed to be quite discriminative; additionally, as was seen in Tables 4.2, 4.4, and 4.8, voters also tended to be consistent on broad issue categories over time.

This was not an easy process for voters, starting with their confrontation with signature solicitors. In 1982, for example, qualification of an initiative constitutional amendment required 512,000 signatures and that of a statute, 320,000 — plus, always, a considerable excess of 20–30 percent to compensate for invalid signatures. The signature solicitation business had become well organized and very profitable. Most voters then and now do not really stop to analyze carefully what they are signing; circulators just ask them to sign, or to sign for a simplified idea ("Do you want your taxes cut?" "Do you want to save the beaches?"). Well under half of signatories actually read the petition or even discuss it with the solicitors. The process has been described by one practitioner:

Generally, people who are out getting signatures are too god-damned interested in their ideology to get the required number in the required time. We use the hoopla process. First, you set up a table with six petitions taped to it and a sign in front that says SIGN HERE. One person sits at the table. Another stands in front. That's all you need — two people. . . .

We operate on the old maxim that two yesses make a sale. First we ask if they are a registered voter. If they say yes, we ask them if they are registered in that county. If they say yes to that, we immediately push them up to the table where the person sitting points to a petition and says "Sign this." . . . If a table doesn't get 80 signatures an hour using this method, it's moved the next day.[128]

Not surprisingly, the costs of successful initiatives were rising during this period. For everything from signature solicitation to television and direct mail advertising to legal advice and defense, money was crucial. In the 1970s alone, fourteen initiative elections involved more than $1 million in spending (and $1 million in 1975 was equivalent to three times that amount in the mid-1990s). The spending ranged from highs of $7 million in the first anti-smoking initiative of 1978 (Prop. 5) and $6.5 million on the anti-nuclear power plants issue in 1976 (Prop. 15), down through several of the tax, labor relations, and environmental propositions, and such cultural issues as obscenity and homosexuality.[129] But money did not necessarily mean success. One study of just the one-sided spending campaigns from 1968 to 1980 found that the big-money side prevailed in eleven of seventeen initiative campaigns; however, in nine of those eleven, big money was successful only in defeating a measure, and only in two of the campaigns did disproportionate spending get an initiative passed.[130] In any event, the era of big bucks spending had begun and voters needed to exercise more discrimination than ever before.

Understanding any initiative itself, of course, was far more important and

TABLE 4.9 Measures of Political Participation, 1982
(percentages)

| | Registered to vote, 1982 | Voted in 1982 primary election |
|---|---|---|
| Family Income | | |
| Under $10,000 | 79 | 56 |
| $10,000–$20,000 | 77 | 70 |
| $20,000–$30,000 | 80 | 67 |
| $30,000–$40,000 | 87 | 74 |
| Over $40,000 | 87 | 77 |
| Highest grade completed | | |
| 8th grade or less | 77 | 71 |
| High school graduate | 73 | 68 |
| 1–2 years college | 83 | 67 |
| College graduate | 87 | 70 |
| Master's degree | 84 | 75 |
| Master's degree plus | 94 | 80 |

SOURCE: Based on Field Institute poll fi8206 (1–4 Oct. 1982); some small educational categories eliminated.

complex than how it had qualified; it called for some education and sophistication. But the voting public tended to be quite representative of the population at large. Table 4.9 looks at just two background variables and two measures of political participation in 1982. The fact that the 1982 primary had eight direct legislation measures makes it ideal for such an inquiry. The data suggest a modest but real effect of education and family income on one's likelihood to be a registered voter and to go to the polls. This is particularly clear for both background variables with voting registration, and for income with voting in the 1982 primary election. The figures for education and primary turnout are somewhat more clouded.[131]

In the fall of 1982, the Field Institute included a large number of questions about direct legislation on its California Poll. Some of these are summarized in Table 4.10, which compares all respondents, those who were and were not registered to vote, and those who had or had not voted in the 1982 primary. Differences between these groups are small. Indeed, they occur only on those questions where one would logically expect them — expressions of interest in propositions and in the amount of care the respondent devotes to studying them.

TABLE 4.10  Public Opinion on Direct Legislation, 1982 (percentages)

| | All respondents | Registered voters | Not registered to vote | Voted in 1982 primary | Did not vote in 1982 primary |
|---|---|---|---|---|---|
| Propositions elections are a "good thing" | 80 | 85 | 79 | 85 | 84 |
| A. Can trust the public to "do what is right" on propositions "most of the time" | 39 | 40 | 37 | 41 | 38 |
| B. Can trust the public to "do what is right" on propositions "some of the time" | 42 | 41 | 46 | 41 | 40 |
| Have a "great deal of interest" in propositions | 42 | 46 | 26 | 52 | 32 |
| Give propositions a "great deal of review" | 38 | 41 | 26 | 46 | 29 |
| Disproportionate spending has "a great deal of effect" on which side wins | 61 | 64 | 52 | 63 | 65 |
| A. Legislature enacts "more coherent" policies | 47 | 54 | 47 | 55 | 49 |
| B. Public enacts "more coherent" policies | 43 | 46 | 53 | 45 | 51 |

| | | | | | |
|---|---|---|---|---|---|
| A. Legislature better to decide "large scale government programs or projects" | 41 | 45 | 37 | 44 | 46 |
| B. Public better to decide "large scale government programs or projects" | 53 | 55 | 63 | 56 | 54 |
| Legislature more influenced than public by "large interest groups"[a] | 63 | 69 | 60 | 72 | 62 |
| Many important issues are "too complicated" for simple Yes or No proposition[a] | 78 | 79 | 79 | 78 | 80 |
| Job of making laws should be left to elected representatives[a] | 60 | 61 | 61 | 62 | 58 |
| Where only one side has big money, result reflects the interests, not the will of people[a] | 83 | 84 | 86 | 84 | 82 |

SOURCE: Based on Field Institute poll f18206 (1–4 Oct. 1982); selected data and categories.

NOTE: Percentage responding as described. Where two items are from the same question, they are labeled "A" and "B".

[a]Includes "agree strongly" and "agree somewhat."

In general, the respondents supported the idea of direct legislation, but at the same time were ambivalent about the question of whether the public or the legislature was best equipped to enact laws. They overwhelmingly agreed with the basic idea that elected representatives should make the laws, and the idea that many issues do not readily lend themselves to the simple Yes or No of direct legislation. Other questions on the poll reflected the same ambivalence. For example, 84 percent of respondents agreed "strongly" or "somewhat" that initiatives and referendums allow the public to decide matters that politicians avoid for fear of offending certain groups, but 84 percent also agreed "strongly" or "somewhat" that since many people don't follow politics regularly they may not be able to make informed decisions.[132]

These respondents, like the Progressives before them, felt that the legislature was too prone to be influenced by interest groups, even though on two of the questions they recognized that disproportionate spending could control the outcome of initiatives as well. Most basically, this sample of Californians reflected well the by-then traditional idea that direct legislation is imperfect but nonetheless necessary because politicians are not to be trusted. And they were in the process of persuading other Americans toward the same conclusion.

The period 1970–1982, prompted in no small way by the coming of Howard Jarvis and Paul Gann, set the stage for significant changes in the nature and effects of direct legislation in California. More issues and more divisive ones, bigger and bigger money behind bigger and bigger stakes, and expanded questioning of the validity of the initiative and referendum were on the horizon.

# 5   Initiatives All Over
the Place, 1984–1994

The pace of direct legislation picked up in the 1980s. Californians voted on 62 direct legislation propositions, an average of over 5 per election. (The legislature added 114 of its own propositions in these elections, for a grand total of 176.) Even more indicative of this trend, there were also 224 initiative drives that were titled by the secretary of state but failed to gain sufficient signatures to qualify for the ballot. Everybody, it seemed, had a law they wanted to pass.[1] All of the qualifying measures were initiatives; there have been no referendums since 1982.[2] Twenty-seven of the initiatives were successful (43 percent), while 36 were defeated.

As in earlier periods, the initiatives were not evenly distributed in the twelve elections of these years. Some ballots had only one or a few, while the 1988 general election had twelve and the 1990 general election thirteen. The *California Ballot Pamphlet* for the 1990 general election ran 142 pages in length, plus 79 more in a *Supplemental Ballot Pamphlet* of late-qualifying measures. It would be safe to say that, for quite a few California voters, this was somewhat more heavy reading than they were accustomed to.

Indeed, the period saw an avalanche of information, with particularly large increases in television advertising and direct mail. Given that, and the increasingly high stakes involved for major California interests, the amounts of money thrown into initiative campaigns also rose to unprecedented heights. The $10 million mark was broken in 1984, and from that time on the sums just grew greater and greater.[3]

Some categorization of this flood of direct legislation measures can be helpful, and that is done in Table 5.1. As before, the categories are somewhat arbitrary: the three initiatives dealing with AIDS, for example, as well as the one for legalizing marijuana, are listed under Health and Welfare, even though they also could have been included under sociocultural issues. Indeed, six of the propositions are included in more than one category because, from an analytical perspective, they clearly dealt with two or more distinct areas of activity.[4]

TABLE 5.1 Subjects of Direct Legislation, 1984–1994

| Date[a] of election | Sociocultural, including crime | Environment | Government and elections | Health and welfare | Auto insurance and litigation | Taxation and spending |
|---|---|---|---|---|---|---|
| 1984p | | | 1 | | | |
| 1984g | 2 | | 2 | 1 | | 1 |
| 1986p | | | | | 1 | |
| 1986g | 1 | 1 | 1 | 1 | | 1 |
| 1988p | | 1 | 2 | 1 | | 2 |
| 1988g | | 2 | | 3 | 5 | 1 |
| 1990p | 1 | 2 | 2 | | | |
| 1990g | 4 | 5 | 3 | 2 | | 3 |
| 1992g | 1 | | 3 | 3 | 1 | 2 |
| 1993s | 1 | | | | | |
| 1994p | | 1 | | | | |
| 1994p | 4 | 1 | | 3 | | 2 |

[a]After date, "p" stands for primary, "g" for general election, and "s" for special election.

The distribution of propositions in these categories is not greatly different than in earlier years, except for an increased number of health and welfare measures and the need to create a new category to encompass the intense battle between insurance companies and trial lawyers in this period. The contents of most of the propositions do vary from previous years, with the exception of a strong continuation of the opposition to taxes and government spending that had arisen in response to Jarvis and Gann's Proposition 13 of 1978 and Paul Gann's attempt to limit government appropriations (Prop. 4 of 1979). Indeed, Californians continued to feel, overall, that taxes were too high and that government could function with smaller size and less revenue. This sentiment well reflected the very popular iteration of these ideas by President Reagan (1981–1989) and, to a lesser degree, Republican Governor George Deukmejian (1983–1991).

Given the centrality of these taxation and expenditure measures during this period, it will be helpful to summarize them, as has been done in Table 5.2. A few things stand out. For one, Howard Jarvis and Paul Gann, and their successors, were very active in this period — both of them on taxation and Gann also on limiting government expenditures. (Others were also involved in some of these measures, but it seems worthwhile to follow the careers of Jarvis and Gann because of their importance in this period.) Between them, they won five and lost five, not a bad average compared to the overall track record for initiatives, but Jarvis and Gann were somewhat more successful at defeating propositions than at passing them. The table also makes obvious that money was by no means triumphant: in the cases of Propositions 36, 71, 72, and 185, proponents outspent their opponents, sometimes by as much as ten to one, but nonetheless lost. On the other hand, as was the case for Propositions 61, 134, and 167, disproportionate spending to defeat propositions often continued to be successful.

The "Gann initiative" of 1984 was a comprehensive measure that was possibly more designed and financed by assembly Republicans than by Gann himself.[5] Proposition 24 not only would cut the legislature's appropriations by 30 percent, but also would change the composition of assembly and senate committees to make them more proportionate to party representation, and it would require a two-thirds vote for a variety of legislative actions. As such, it would decrease the power of the Democratic majority and of Speaker Willie Brown, of whom Gann was very critical.[6]

There is no doubt that Gann was sincerely committed to reducing the power and costs of government, even if he did see it from a Republican perspective. He had a huge correspondence in 1983 soliciting support for the proposition, and received hundreds of letters asking for petitions and other materials to support the campaign. An equally large number of letters came to him, both before and after the primary, criticizing Willie Brown and

TABLE 5.2  Taxation and Government Spending Initiatives, 1984–1994

| Date[a] of election | Prop. No. | Subject[b] | Spending For (thousands of dollars) | Spending Against (thousands of dollars) | Voter participation rate (percent of those voting) | Outcome |
|---|---|---|---|---|---|---|
| 1984p | 24 | Decreases appropriations for legislature (Proponent: Gann) | $ 874 | $ 330 | 82 | Approved |
| 1984g | 36 | Property tax restrictions, two-thirds vote for tax increases (Proponents: Jarvis and Gann) | 8,771 | 1,663 | 91 | Rejected |
| 1986g | 61 | Compensation of public officials (Proponent: Gann) | 1,137 | 6,643 | 91 | Rejected |
| 1986g | 62 | Local government and district taxation (Proponent: Jarvis) | 3,611 | 14 | 88 | Approved |
| 1988p | 71 | Appropriations limit adjustment (Opponents: Jarvis and Gann) | 2,520 | 245 | 86 | Rejected |
| 1988p | 72 | Emergency reserve, taxes reserved to transportation (Proponents: Gann and Jarvis) | 2,833 | 172 | 88 | Rejected |

| | | | | | | |
|---|---|---|---|---|---|---|
| 1988g | 98 | Minimum level of school funding (Opponents: Jarvis and Gann) | 5,807 | 491 | 89 | Approved |
| 1990g | 129 and 133 | State sales tax increase for drug prevention and prisons (Opponent: Gann) | 1,937 | 12 | 89 / 90 | Rejected / Rejected |
| 1990g | 134 | Alcohol surtax | 2,053 | 41,191 | 93 | Rejected |
| 1990g | 136 | Property taxes and two-thirds vote for initiative-created taxes (Proponents: Jarvis and Gann) | 8,236 | 93 | 90 | Rejected |
| 1992g | 163 | Ends taxation on certain food products | 2,130 | 0 | 92 | Adopted |
| 1992g | 167 | Increases tax rates on upper-income taxpayer; minimum rates for corporations; lowers sales tax | 942 | 9,843 | 92 | Rejected |
| 1994g | 185 | Increases gasoline tax, funds to be used for highway and mass transit only | 910 | 778 | 84 | Rejected |

SOURCE: *California Ballot Pamphlet* and Campaign Statement Summaries for the respective elections.

[a]After date, "p" stands for primary and "g" for general election.

[b]The listing of Gann and Jarvis parenthetically does not mean they were the only proponents or opponents of a proposition. For propositions dating from 1988, Jarvis's name is used for the "Howard Jarvis Tax Reduction Movement," led by Joel Fox; as of 1990, Gann's name is used for the "Paul Gann Citizens Committee," which is led by his son Richard.

the Democrats for their resistance to change, and then their failure to implement the initiative.[7] So this was another truly popular initiative, but, at the same time, it was turned by the Republican assemblymen involved into a highly professional one. The law firm of Nielsen, Hodgson, Parrinello and Mueller was hired to help select a campaign firm, and Grubbs and Grubbs Political Action was hired for fund-raising. A twenty-page "Information Package" was sent to all major newspapers, and extensive media coverage marked the campaign. The proposition's political ramifications were too great for too many people to leave the campaign to chance.[8]

Despite Gann's efforts and his effect on true believers, few Californians seemed aware of Proposition 24. In the February 1984 Field poll only 28 percent of respondents had heard of it; that figure had decreased an additional 1 percent in April before rising to only 37 percent in May. Of those who had heard of the proposition in May, 45 percent were "strongly" or "somewhat" in favor, but 38 percent had "no opinion." Even in the June poll, only days before the election, 51 percent of respondents had not heard of Proposition 24. Moreover, of those who had heard of it, those in favor had dropped to 29 percent, those opposed had risen to 41 percent, and there were still 29 percent with no opinion.[9] That was reflected in the relatively low 82 percent voter participation rate for this initiative; five of the eight legislative propositions on the same ballot drew more voters, a rare occurrence.

Despite extensive press criticism of the measure, particularly in terms of its constitutionality, and probably because supporters were the most likely to vote, it won. One day after the election the legislature filed a lawsuit against it, and it was declared unconstitutional by a Superior Court by the end of 1984, with further litigation continuing into the following year.[10]

Gann was a gadfly. At the same time as he was working on Proposition 24 for the 1984 primary and Proposition 36 for the 1984 general election, he was also trying to develop a national movement to get Congress to repeal the law that required waiters and waitresses to pay income tax on their tips.[11] Perhaps he was spreading himself too thin, since the Proposition 36 campaign, despite being extremely well funded, failed. This measure, sometimes referred to as "Jarvis 4," would have prohibited any new taxes based on real property; it also would have required a two-thirds vote of the legislature for other new state taxes and a two-thirds vote of the electorate for local taxes. Jarvis was trying to hamstring all taxing entities from increases of any kind.

The relationship between Jarvis and Gann on Proposition 36 was interesting. As early as April 1983 Gann had complained about his name being used on Jarvis's California Tax Reduction Movement materials for qualifying the proposition. He seems to have been very ambivalent about it, apparently agreeing with the president of the California Chamber of Commerce that Jarvis had gone too far "on his own" with this proposition.[12] Gann did ultimately agree to co-sign the *California Ballot Pamphlet* argument in favor of the measure, but he also tried to clarify "the relationship between Paul Gann and Howard Jarvis," noting that they were both supporting Proposition 36 but that their organizations were entirely separate and that supporters should make contributions to his People's Advocate rather than Jarvis's California Tax Reduction Movement.[13]

Jarvis stressed throughout that Proposition 36 was a "Save Proposition 13" initiative, especially important because the California Supreme Court had ruled that "a new tax is not a tax increase" and that local governments could raise taxes without voter approval if the revenues went to a general fund. Jarvis tried also to associate himself with the Reagan administration, using a supportive letter from conservative economist Arthur B. Laffer, "Economic Advisor to the President of the U.S.A." At the same time, he perpetuated his image as a leader of the common man, noting that all the big corporations in the state were fighting against his initiative.[14]

The opposition stressed the unequal effect Proposition 36 would have on new businesses as opposed to old ones, its effects on the state's educational system, and the idea that the measure called for more "tax redistribution" than tax reform. An unusual combination of groups, including the Chamber of Commerce, state Superintendent of Public Instruction, state PTA, and American Association of Retired Persons (AARP) signed the ballot argument against Proposition 36.[15]

While Jarvis had won his most recent outing — his second try at income tax indexing in June 1982 (Prop. 7) — this time he lost, with 55 percent of the voters opting against him. Part of the reason can be found in the polls. Proposition 36 impressed voters more than had Proposition 24: 54 percent had heard of it in early September, and that figure rose to 78 percent by early October. In both polls, those who favored and opposed the measure were nearly equal, although the Yes group increased over time and led the No group 43 percent to 38 percent in October. However, when respondents were pressed about how they would vote "today" (whether they had heard of the proposition or not), self-identified conservatives were only 44 percent to 42 percent on the Yes side, while liberals were 71 percent to 21 percent No, and "Middle-of-the-road" voters were 48 percent to 39 percent Yes. Moreover, in terms of party identification, while 53 percent of Republicans said they would vote Yes and 50 percent of Democrats said they would vote No, self-defined Independents were 51 percent No. Jarvis had failed to sufficiently motivate the groups that generally supported him and thus did not get the votes.[16]

But Howard Jarvis was a bulldog; he brought up a similar measure one year later. Proposition 62 in the 1986 general election would restrict additional taxation by local governments and districts in two ways: (1) any special tax would have to be approved by two-thirds of the voters; and (2) any general tax would have to be approved by a two-thirds majority of the taxing body as well as by a majority of the voters. Additionally, any local general taxes that had been enacted between August 1985 and November 1986 would have to be submitted to the voters and approved within two years.[17]

The financing discrepancy between the two sides on Proposition 62 was awesome, as can be seen in Table 5.2. About half of the $3.6 million on Jarvis's side was spent on qualifying the measure, but this still left proponents with more than one hundred times the funds of the opposition (mainly public-employee groups) for the campaign itself.[18] A great deal of this money came from small contributions. Jarvis's California Tax Reduction Movement still had real popular appeal: in a Field poll that summer, 51 percent of respondents had a "favorable" opinion of Howard Jarvis, and 31 percent an "unfavorable" one.[19]

In that summer poll, only 17 percent of the respondents who were registered to vote had heard of Proposition 62, but when told that it was sponsored by Jarvis and would make it more difficult for local governments to raise taxes, 64 percent said they would vote Yes. In another poll at the end of September, also of registered voters, only 11 percent said they had heard of Proposition 62, and the Yes respondents had declined while the Undecideds had increased. Even at the end of October, only 47 percent had heard of Proposition 62 (as compared to 78 percent who had heard of Gann's Proposition 61 to cap government salaries, and 85 percent who had heard of the English-only Prop. 63), and of those who had heard of it, 34 percent said they would vote Yes, 29 percent said they would vote No, and 37 percent were Undecided.[20]

Thus, most voting decisions were not made much in advance of the election. But last-minute advertising and the *California Ballot Pamphlet*, both of which associated the measure with Jarvis (who died before the election), or possibly just the language on the ballot, obviously had an effect. Fewer people voted on Proposition 62 (88 percent) than on any of the four other direct legislation measures on the ballot (four of eight legislative measures also had higher voter participation rates), but 58 percent of them gave Jarvis the victory he had been denied one year earlier, a fitting capstone to his career. Unlike his first victory with Proposition 13, this was not built on a high level of voter awareness, but Californians wanted lower taxes, from all levels of government, even in the face of predictions of disastrous consequences. Proposition 62 was immediately challenged in the courts and was not finally ruled constitutional until 1995.[21]

Paul Gann experienced a major failure in the same 1986 election. His Proposition 61 would have set a salary cap of $80,000 for the governor and limited salaries of other officials and public contractors to no more than 80 percent of the governor's salary. It also would have required a public vote for

salary increases, and would forbid accrual of sick leave and vacation benefits. Although it was the first initiative to qualify for the 1986 ballot, it had
few defenders and Gann spent 79 percent of his organization's funds on just
getting the measure qualified, leaving little for the actual campaign.[22] On the
other side, groups from court reporters to deputy district attorneys to police
and numerous other government employees worked very hard to raise their
huge war chest. Additional woes for Gann came from a court decision in
August that struck down two parts of his ballot argument as untrue. And the
legislative analyst, in his analysis in the *California Ballot Pamphlet,* said it
was possible that the proposition could cost the state up to $7 billion in
buyouts of unused vacation and sick-leave time. Gann then tried but failed
to have his name removed from the ballot pamphlet.[23] It was Gann's greatest
defeat, with 66 percent of the voters going against him.

Showing striking determination, Gann and the Jarvis organization were
together again in the very next election, the June 1988 primary. Propositions
71 and 72 in that election had in common the fact that both sought to modify the "Gann spending limit" of Proposition 4 of 1979. But Gann and the
Jarvis group, now led by Joel Fox, were bitterly opposed to 71, whereas they
were the leading forces behind 72. Proposition 71 was called the "Honig
initiative," after Bill Honig, the State Superintendent of Public Instruction
(an elected position). It argued that spending limits, while a good thing,
should reflect changes in the cost of living and the growth of California's
population, and would modify the state constitution to that effect. Proposition 72 was quite different: it, too, would modify the constitution and the
Gann spending limit, but only so as to create an emergency reserve of 3
percent of the budget. The money would come from the sales tax and motor
vehicle fuels taxes, after a two-thirds vote of the legislature or a majority
vote of the public. Additionally, fuel tax revenues would be exempt from the
appropriation limit and would be restricted to transportation purposes, to
keep the legislature from using them for other programs. Proponents had
wanted to title it the "Paul Gann Spending Limit Improvement and Enforcement Act of 1998," but this was not accepted by the secretary of state.[24]

Proposition 71 had broad-based support from business, advocates of
public education, public employees, and groups like the League of Women
Voters and the American Association of Retired Persons. Even after spending about $800,000 on qualifying the measure, they still had well over a
million dollars for the campaign, while opponents had only a fraction of
that amount (see Table 5.2; the largest single contributor was the California
Teachers Association, at $597,000). Interestingly, while Gann was the point
man in the campaign against Proposition 71, almost all of the money for the
opposition was raised by the late Howard Jarvis's California Tax Reduction
Movement.[25]

The situation was virtually reversed for Proposition 72, not only in terms of who was for and who against, but also in terms of which side had the most money. In fact, there seems to have been some movement of funds between the pro-71 and anti-72 people, and between the anti-71 and pro-72 people as well. Most of the organizations and newspapers that supported Proposition 71 were opposed to Proposition 72. There was, however, considerably more business support for 72 than there had been business opposition to 71, since Proposition 72 would have permitted increased highway construction and other transportation-related activity.[26]

Not surprisingly, given the intermixing of the campaigns, the public was confused. A *San Francisco Examiner* poll ten days before the election found that 79 percent of the respondents said "Don't know" when asked how they would vote on Proposition 71, and 71 percent had the same response relative to Proposition 72.[27] In good part this was once again a case of voter ignorance: a Field poll one week earlier found that about 70 percent of the registered voters polled had not heard of either proposition. When told that Proposition 72 had to do with an emergency reserve and transportation, and that it was sponsored by Paul Gann, and when then asked how they would vote "today," 52 percent said they would vote Yes. But on the very next question, when the 1979 Gann limit was explained to them, as well as the argument for modifying the limit, the respondents divided equally on "Favor Keeping" and "Favor Amending" the Gann limit.[28] This provides strong support to the idea that voters, in dealing with propositions, often need considerable simplification to make up their minds. "Cutting taxes" or "sponsored by Howard Jarvis" or "increasing support for schools" were the kinds of concepts that led to easy decisions. The complexity and confused interrelationship between measures like Propositions 71 and 72 in 1988 did not.

Propositions 71 and 72 had slightly lower voter participation rates (86 percent and 88 percent, respectively) than most other measures on the June 1988 ballot. The Jarvis–Gann forces were successful in just barely defeating Proposition 71 (49 percent Yes to 51 percent No), but failed decisively in their effort to pass Proposition 72 (61 percent No). Uncertainty and confusion played a role in the voters' decisions to oppose both measures.

In the fall 1988 election, Bill Honig got his revenge. Since his main aim in proposing Proposition 71 had been to increase school funding, he approached the matter more directly with Proposition 98. It proposed to amend the constitution to establish a minimum level of 40 percent of the state's general fund for financing public schools and community colleges (rather like the successful Proposition 9 of 1944 and Proposition 2 of 1952). With an almost $6 million campaign chest, and $4.5 million of that left to spend after qualifying the proposition, plus an ability to focus publicity on the idea of school improvement, the pro-98 forces were able to run a very powerful campaign indeed.[29]

The main opponents were the California Taxpayers Association, a business-funded group, and the Jarvis California Tax Reduction Movement, which raised almost one-half of the anti-98 war chest. The latter group argued that the measure "could raise taxes 23 billion over the next ten years." Paul Gann also criticized it for nullifying the "Gann limit" and precluding the rebate of excess funds to the taxpayers.[30]

The results were a mirror image of the Proposition 71 vote five months earlier: this time 51 percent voted Yes and 49 percent voted No.[31] The element of voter confusion may have played a role in this vote, as in all the others, given that voters had to deal with 29 propositions, 12 of them direct legislation and 17 from the legislature. Interestingly, all 17 of the legislative measures and 7 of the 12 popular ones did pass. Proposition 98 did help the schools avoid some further effects of Proposition 13, but at the same time it magnified the effects of Proposition 13 by taking state money away from other programs, including higher education and social welfare.

The 1990 general election was not much easier on the voters, with thirteen popular initiatives and fifteen legislative propositions. It is no wonder that when a sample of registered voters was asked if initiatives were understandable to the "average voter," only 21 percent answered "All" or "Most," while 34 percent said "Some" and the largest group, 43 percent, answered "Only a few."[32]

Proposition 133 was one of the fall 1990 initiatives dealing with taxation, sponsored by Democratic Lieutenant Governor Leo McCarthy, who was running for reelection. It proposed to raise the sales tax by one-half percent for four years, the funds to be used for drug education, treatment, and enforcement, and also for prisons and jails. In keeping with the contemporary concern about crime, it also had provisions against early release of persons convicted of certain crimes.[33] It was in some competition with Proposition 129 on the same ballot, which sought the same ends, but via allocation of general tax funds rather than a specific tax increase. This measure was sponsored by Attorney General John Van de Kamp, who was running for the Democratic nomination for governor (unsuccessfully) when the measure was drafted. Both propositions had strong law enforcement support, and both were opposed by Richard Gann of "Paul Gann's Citizens Committee."

Both measures also had disproportionate financial support. Proposition 133 backers raised $820,000, while there were no reported funds of any kind against it. The Proposition 129 people did even better, raising $1.1 million ($277,000 of it from Van de Kamp personally), to only $12,000 for their opponents.[34] But neither measure really registered with the voters. One week before the election, in a Field poll of registered voters, only 39 percent were aware of Proposition 129 and just 28 percent had heard of Proposition 133.[35] Both measures were overwhelmed at the polls, Proposition 129 by a 72 percent No vote and Proposition 133 by 68 percent No.

There were also two propositions on the same 1990 ballot that sought to raise revenue with special taxes on alcohol. Proposition 134 was a "Nickel a Drink" proposal whose revenues were earmarked for alcohol and drug treatment and prevention programs, with some funds also earmarked for law enforcement. (Punishing crime continued to be very popular in California.) A rival measure from the legislature, Proposition 126, would have lower tax increases and send revenues to the state general fund.[36] The liquor industry supported Proposition 126 and financed a good deal of the combined pro-126/anti-134 publicity of the campaign; indeed, it appeared that more of its extensive publicity effort was geared against Proposition 134 than in favor of its own measure. That was not unreasonable, given a long-awaited California Supreme Court ruling just a few days before the election. The court ruled that when voters approved fundamentally conflicting measures, no part of the one receiving fewer votes would take effect. The decision did not, however, clarify what might happen if two approved propositions clashed on one issue but had other parts that were not in conflict. Thus, opposing Proposition 134 was at least as important to the liquor industry as promoting 126.[37]

Proposition 126 proponents had a $4 million war chest, with no reported money against it. Half of that actually came from Taxpayers for Common Sense, which was the chief money-raising entity for opposing Proposition 134. Another $800,000 came from the Beer Institute, and $600,000 from the Wine Institute. Conversely, the supporters of Proposition 134 raised $1.5 million, but that paled in comparison to the $30 million spent by their opponents. The opponents had actually raised $40 million, of which $10 million was in "transfers," including what was spent in favor of Proposition 126. The list of contributors against "Nickel a Drink" is informative. Between them, Anheuser Busch, Coors, and Miller Brewing donated $13 million, a striking example of public spiritedness. Anheuser Busch contributed yet another $415,000 to a different campaign committee, and the Beer Institute added $8 million. There were another half-dozen or so million-dollar-plus donations from beer, wine, and hard liquor groups, and many more contributions at the six-figure level. This level of fund-raising was an impressive accomplishment, unprecedented at the time in the history of California direct legislation campaigns.[38]

As one student of the election noted, the "$27 million" the alcohol industry spent on defeating Proposition 134 meant that it avoided increased alcohol taxes of $760 million per year, a 28–1 return on the industry's investment.[39] It was something to consider, not anticipated by John Randolph Haynes in 1911.

These two propositions, dealing with the price of a drink, made a considerable impression on the public. The pre-election Field poll cited above found that 73 percent had heard of Proposition 126 and 79 percent had heard of Proposition 134. Interestingly, of those who had heard of these measures, their pre-election propensities were almost identical: 49 percent Yes on Proposition 126, 50 percent Yes on Proposition 134, and 39 percent No on both. That kind of closeness is rare and suggests that both measures were perceived more in terms of their effect on the cost of alcoholic beverages than anything else. Both propositions drew almost identical voter participations (92 percent and 93 percent), and, assuming the Field sample was accurate, quite a few voters changed their minds in the days before the election: 59 percent voted against the legislative measure and 69 percent against the popular initiative. Money can defeat initiatives.

Also on the busy fall 1990 ballot was what the Gann and Jarvis organizations chose to call the "Taxpayer's Right to Vote Amendment," although its official title was considerably more pedestrian. It was an initiative constitutional amendment, Proposition 136, that would have limited in somewhat unclear ways new taxes on personal property and, more importantly, would have increased the requirements for enacting tax legislation. At the state level, it would have required that any new or increased taxes by the legislature be passed by a two-thirds majority, and that any state "special" taxes created by initiative have a two-thirds majority of those voting. "General" taxes created by initiative would continue to require only a majority vote.[40] Further, all local increases, by charter cities or any others, would require approval by a majority of the voters.

The Jarvis and Gann organizations expected that by putting this language in the constitution it would be much less subject to obstruction. Moreover, the initiative was so worded that it would take effect immediately and would even apply to other propositions on the current ballot. This meant that Propositions 129, 133, and 134, and possibly others, if they passed by less than a two-thirds majority, could nonetheless be invalid.[41] The fact that all of those measures failed, as we have seen, probably cost political lawyers millions of dollars in fees.

The campaign was vigorous, led by the Gann and Jarvis forces, although the *Los Angeles Times* charged that it was an "unholy alliance" between them and the liquor industry because it virtually guaranteed that Proposition 134 would fail.[42] The Jarvis and Gann organizations were still able to raise money—a total of $8 million, of which $3 million was spent on qualifying and the rest was available for the campaign, with some of the funds also going to another Jarvis–Gann proposition on the same ballot (Prop. 137, see below). Opponents of Proposition 136 had only $90,000. And the *Times* was correct in that a good deal of the money did come from the alcoholic beverage and related industries: $300,000 from American National Can, $1 million from the Beer Institute, almost $500,000 from Joseph Seagram and Sons, $254,000 from Brown Forman (distillers), and big donations also from Guiness, Heublein, the Wine Institute, and various others.[43] The liquor industry was working hard against taxation in 1990.

However, the Jarvis and Gann people were less successful in mobilizing the public in this campaign than in some others. In August, only 9 percent had heard of the proposition, and of those slightly more than half thought they would vote No. When the measure was explained to all respondents, 37 percent thought they would vote Yes and 43 percent No. A week before the election, little had changed: only 35 percent had heard of the proposition, and those respondents were evenly divided between pro and con, whereas all respondents were divided 34 percent Yes and 41 percent No. On election day, the ballot box reflected those responses: 52 percent of the voters turned down the latest Jarvis–Gann effort to save and expand their anti-tax position.

There were three more tax-related initiatives in the period under study, two of them in the 1992 general election. Proposition 163 was an initiative constitutional amendment and statute to undo legislation of the previous year that made the sales tax apply to snack foods, candy, and bottled water. Opponents, led by a Democratic assemblyman, had immediately called for an initiative and easily obtained over one million signatures by early 1992. Even Governor Wilson, who had supported the legislation, recognized its unpopularity and declared that he would not oppose its revocation.[44]

Proponents of the measure raised $2 million, using 40 percent of that for qualifying. Almost all of the money came in large donations from concerned interests, ranging from $86,000 from See's Famous Old Time Candies and $185,000 from Nabisco Brands to $380,000 from the Bottled Water Association PAC and $462,000 from the California Grocers Association. There was no organized opposition, and exactly two-thirds of the voters supported the proposition.

Proposition 167 was considerably more controversial, a liberal measure, led by Lenny Goldberg of the California Tax Reform Association. It was an initiative statute that would have revoked a legislative sales tax increase of the preceding year, increased personal income tax rates for the richest individuals, increased the corporate tax rate, and increased specific tax rates for insurance companies and oil companies. While the increases were small, the initiative was nonetheless derided by opponents as a "tax-the-rich" measure. It was supported by major union groups, such as the California Labor Federation, the California State Employees Association, and the California Teachers Association, and also by the state PTA, the Democratic Party, and a wide variety of social-service agencies.[45]

The State Chamber of Commerce and most large and small businesses were strongly opposed to Proposition 167, and their position was reflected in a *Sacramento Union* editorial that called the measure "ill-conceived and dangerous." One hundred thousand jobs would be lost, opponents alleged, and 100,000 more people would go on welfare. They launched a very ambitious campaign on television, in the press, and with lots of direct mail, stressing these points plus the idea that the initiative would drive businesses out of the state.[46]

While proponents raised about $900,000, about half of which went to qualifying the measure, opponents raised ten times that much, almost all in large donations: $567,000 from Bank of America, $300,000 from American Savings Bank, $538,000 from Chevron Corp., almost as much from Rockwell International, and even $459,000 from the Walt Disney Company. Mickey Mouse and big bucks prevailed, not for the last time persuading Californians against increased progressive taxation, with 59 percent voting against the initiative.

Finally, in the 1994 general election, there was Proposition 185, which proposed an additional 4 percent sales tax on gasoline. The revenue would be used for rail and other "clean" public transportation systems, and for improvements to streets and highways.[47] To proponents, who called themselves "Californians for Transportation Solutions," it was a conservation measure as well as a way to modernize highways and promote non-automobile transport. The environmental part of the argument gained the support of groups like the Sierra Club, the League of Women Voters, and the American Association of Retired Persons. Opponents called it a "$700 million tax increase" that would serve primarily the aims of special interests like the Southern Pacific Railroad.[48]

Given the rhetoric, one would have expected much more money in the campaign. Apparently, both sides were less concerned than they let on. Of the $900,000 spent by proponents, 72 percent was for qualifying the measure. More than one-half of their total revenues came from the Southern Pacific. Of the $778,000 spent by opponents, 80 percent came from five big oil companies; indeed, over 99 percent of the total came from oil companies. Thus, the major involvement on both sides was from rival big businesses; the public exhibited much less enthusiasm, particularly on the Yes side: only 84 percent of the voters participated in the Proposition 185 vote, and 81 percent of them said No.

Table 5.3 seeks to discover the level of consistency in voting on taxation and anti-government spending measures by providing correlation coefficients for some of these elections, starting with Proposition 13 in 1978 and ending with Proposition 167 in 1992. Once again, the strength of the relationships is impressive, particularly given the long time period involved and the fact that the data is aggregated by such large units as counties.

There was a strong relationship between voting for tax cuts or limitations, on the one hand, and voting to limit government appropriations and spending on the other. Thus, it is reasonable to deal with these two popular

TABLE 5.3    Correlations of Voting on Taxation and Government Spending Propositions, 1978–1992

| Date[a] and proposition | 1978p: Prop. 13 | 1979s: Prop. 4 | 1980p: Prop. 9 | 1982p: Prop. 7 | 1984p: Prop. 24 | 1984g: Prop. 36 |
|---|---|---|---|---|---|---|
| 1978p: Prop. 13 Property tax | 1.000 | | | | | |
| 1979s: Prop. 4 Government appropriations | .776 | 1.000 | | | | |
| 1980p: Prop. 9 Income tax indexing | .653 | .788 | 1.000 | | | |
| 1982p: Prop. 7 Income tax indexing | .495 | .443 | .439 | 1.000 | | |
| 1984p: Prop. 24 Government appropriations | .427 | .470 | .367 | .461 | 1.000 | |
| 1984g: Prop. 36 Tax limitations | .730 | .763 | .815 | .494 | .360 | 1.000 |
| 1986g: Prop. 61 Public officials compensation | .569 | .751 | .650 | .487 | .681 | .658 |
| 1986g: Prop. 62 Tax limitations | .720 | .830 | .768 | .478 | .588 | .822 |
| 1988p: Prop. 71 Government appropriations | −.175 | −.461 | −.302 | −.336 | −.714 | −.254 |
| 1988p: Prop. 72 Reserve, tax limitation | .456 | .650 | .549 | .444 | .556 | .725 |
| 1990g: Prop. 136 Tax limitations | .446 | .750 | .585 | .359 | .626 | .658 |
| 1992g: Prop. 167 Tax limitations | −.395 | −.707 | −.597 | −.082 | −.354 | −.595 |

NOTE:  Pearson product moment correlations, based on percentage voting Yes on propositions, with data aggregated by county and weighted by county population. For clarity, only one-half of table is shown since the two halves are identical.

[a]After date, "p" stands for primary, "g" for general, and "s" for special election.

| 1986g: Prop. 61 | 1986g: Prop. 62 | 1988p: Prop. 71 | 1988p: Prop. 72 | 1990g: Prop. 136 | 1992g: Prop. 167 |
| --- | --- | --- | --- | --- | --- |
| 1.000 | | | | | |
| .820 | 1.000 | | | | |
| −.757 | −.499 | 1.000 | | | |
| .715 | .681 | −.587 | 1.000 | | |
| .855 | .783 | −.770 | .835 | 1.000 | |
| −.682 | −.648 | .610 | −.676 | −.822 | 1.000 |

ideas as reflecting the same voter sentiments. There is also, over a twelve-year period, a striking relationship among measures that the Jarvis and Gann organizations were involved in, whether as initiators or simply as supporters or opponents. Looking down the first column of the table — correlations with the vote on Proposition 13 of 1978 — Jarvis or Gann or both favored the first eight propositions, opposed the ninth, and favored the tenth and eleventh (neither organization took a position on 1992's Prop. 167). There are significant positive relationships among all of the measures they supported, even after Jarvis's death in 1986 and Gann's in 1989. And there are negative relationships, not always but usually statistically significant, between all of those and Proposition 71 of 1988, which would have relaxed the "Gann limit" and which Gann bitterly opposed. The negative relationships between these Jarvis/Gann measures and Proposition 167 of 1992 are also logical because that was the liberal proposal to raise taxes on wealthy people and corporations.

The same conclusions emerge if one studies the data from the vantage point of any of these measures, even though the strength of the relationships varies a bit from one pair to another and there are the inevitable idiosyncratic cells. On the whole, there was a solid body of voters over this fourteen-year period who were convinced, as were Jarvis and Gann and Reagan, among others, that society could fare quite nicely with lower taxes and with smaller and lower-cost government. It is no understatement to suggest that this was one of the strongest themes of California political life in the 1980s, and one that moved to the national stage as well.

These same elections were also correlated with social and economic variables from the 1990 census, but the results did not merit another complicated table. By and large, the correlation coefficients were not high, which reflects the fact that the appeal of tax and government-spending limitation cut across class and other lines. Mean family income did correlate positively with support for most of these propositions (at the .300–.400 level, which is significant but not really strong). A similar but slightly less strong relationship existed for percent born in the United States outside of California — migrants to the state shared these popular views. In the other direction, the percent of families below the poverty level and percent unemployed tended to consistently correlate negatively with these propositions; the poor were logically unsympathetic to cutting taxes and weakening the government on which they relied. Other variables, such as urban residence and education, did not have significant relationships in either direction.[49]

The effort to control state government appropriations and spending was the most powerful direct legislation issue of the 1984–1994 period, but there were others that also generated considerable activity and had long-term ramifications. One of them was the issue of reapportionment of the state legislature, a topic that we have seen frequently in dispute and in direct legislation since the 1920s. There were, for example, three referendums on reapportionment in the 1982 primary election, all of them by Republicans and all of them trying to undo the redistricting (of the state Assembly, the state senate, and congressional districts) done by the Democratic legislature in 1981. Leading Democrats like former governor "Pat" Brown, unions, and liberal organizations worked to uphold these laws, whereas Republican leaders like former president Gerald Ford backed the referendums.[50] All three referendums were successful with votes of over 60 percent for rejecting the legislation.

In 1984 the issue was raised again, to the same purpose: Governor Deukmejian and the Republicans were trying to undercut the longtime Democratic state legislature's control of the reapportionment process. This time, Proposition 39, an initiative constitutional amendment, would have put reapportionment of the Assembly, the state senate, and congressional seats in the hands of a redistricting commission consisting of former appellate court justices, subject to review by referendum or by the state Supreme Court. This was clearly a partisan issue, although Deukmejian and his allies tried to focus the dispute on the idea of taking control of redistricting away from "the politicians." Opponents argued that removing control from elected officials would make the process of redistricting less democratic. Ethnic factors also played a role, as when UFW leader César Chávez argued that "Hispanic lawmakers would be thrown out of office."[51] Despite much publicity, the campaign did not really catch fire and the proposition was rejected by 55 percent of the voters. For the public at large, reapportionment lacked the political "sex appeal" of sociocultural or tax measures.

There were a half dozen additional efforts at reapportionment initiatives in the 1980s that failed to qualify for the ballot, until 1989, when two new proposals did qualify for the 1990 primary election.[52] Proposition 118 would have kept control of redistricting in the legislature, but would have required that any reapportionment plan have a two-thirds vote in each house and that it then be approved by a popular referendum. Proposition 119 was similar to 1984's Proposition 39 in that it would have moved the responsibility for reapportionment to a commission, in this case of "citizens," who would themselves be nominated by a panel of retired judges.[53]

Proposition 118 was supported primarily by conservative and business interests, led by television and radio commentator Bruce Herschensohn. It was criticized by the League of Women Voters, which did not believe control of reapportionment should be kept in the legislature. The League, instead, supported Proposition 119, which was less ideological and had both support and opposition from liberal groups and leaders. The California Federa-

tion of Labor opposed both initiatives for giving "control of our state legislature and Congress to big business interests and right-wing Republicans."
And the Sierra Club agreed, but for somewhat different reasons: under the
measures, the number of coastal legislators would have declined and anti-
environmental interests would have been in control.[54]

All of this exemplifies the controversiality and difficulty of passing legislation or initiatives for reapportionment. The fact that these years generally
witnessed Republican governors and Democratic legislatures goes a long
way toward explaining why the legislature failed to agree on reapportionment. And, in terms of initiatives, there were always too many interests opposed to any proposal, making it apparently impossible to get one through.
Both of these 1990 proposals lost overwhelmingly, Proposition 118 by 67
percent to 33 percent, and Proposition 119 by 64 percent to 36 percent. The
total score at that point for the twentieth century was seven out of eight reapportionment initiatives lost (the sole exception was in 1926), and all three
legislative redistrictings that were subject to referendums being undone.

In 1998 Gray Davis was elected as the first Democratic governor since
Jerry Brown; with both houses of the legislature also Democratic, the possibility arose that the logjam on redistricting would finally be broken, and in
the Democrats' favor. If the past is any judge, that, in turn, would be likely to
produce counterattacks in the courts and on the direct legislation front,
since redistricting won't cease to be a key to political power in California.

It is not surprising, in this atmosphere of general suspicion of government
and politicians, that Californians were ready for the idea of political reform.
Indeed, the Gann effort to cut the size and scope of government was seen by
many as a reform proposition, as was, for that matter, the idea of taking
reapportionment out of the hands of the legislature. Two additional ideas
also gained popularity in this period: term limits for public officeholders and
controls on campaign spending.

It was predictable that Californians, with their traditional suspicion of
party politics and politicians, would jump enthusiastically on the term-
limits bandwagon. This was consistent with the whole political tradition
descending from California Progressivism, which had stressed the virtue of
"the people" as opposed to selfish politicians and entrenched interests. What
could make more sense in this context than a system that seemed to guarantee that ordinary people would represent Californians because no one would
have the opportunity to become entrenched in office? Thus, in the 1990
general election, among 31 popular and legislative propositions, were two
initiative constitutional amendments for term limits.

Oklahoma had been the first state to legislate term limits, in September
1990, so California (along with Oregon, which also had a term-limit proposition on its fall 1990 ballot) was in position to be second. The two pro-

posed initiatives were similar, although Proposition 131 was less drastic than Proposition 140. The former, like Proposition 129 on drugs, was part of the effort by Attorney General John Van de Kamp to get to the governor's office in 1990. It would have limited statewide officials to eight successive years in office and legislators to twelve successive years. It would not have precluded the same people from running for the same office after having sat out a term. And, most controversially, it also included a number of campaign-finance reforms, plus some public financing for political campaigns. Proposition 140, led by Los Angeles County Supervisor Peter F. Schabarum, would limit statewide officers and members of the state senate to two terms, and members of the Assembly to three; unlike Proposition 131, this would be a lifetime ban for that person for that office.[55]

The campaign was vigorous and bitter — not only between those who favored term limits and those who did not, but also between backers of the two propositions. Proposition 131 had a lot of liberal support, from Ralph Nader, Common Cause, and similar groups, in good part for the campaign-reform aspects even more than for term limits. Schabarum's Proposition 140 had more conservative support, and reflected the Supervisor's own controversiality and charges against him of Voting Rights Act violations. Opposition to both measures came from a variety of special interests, ranging from organized labor on the left to business groups on the right — all fearing the loss of their influence in a newly constituted legislature.[56]

There was a considerable amount of money involved in this campaign, and it provides a good example of the complexity of following the money trail, even with rigid reporting requirements. The spending on these campaigns also showed how the accumulated funds raised by individual political figures could be used as a primary source of funding for initiatives. Supporters of Proposition 131 raised $1.3 million, the greater part of which ($870,000) was expended for qualifying expenses. Of the total, $560,000 came from Van de Kamp's political war chest. Proposition 140 raised somewhat more money, $2 million, of which only about 10 percent was used for qualifying expenses. And about $550,000 of that total came from Schabarum's political funds.[57]

Opposition spending is more difficult to follow. For one thing, there was considerable overlap in the use of funds against the two initiatives. For example, the group No on 131 and 140 filed its report under Proposition 131, but was involved in both. It raised $4.4 million of the total $6.8 million reported against Proposition 131. And the summary Campaign Statement filed for Proposition 131 shows that $2.1 million of that total $6.8 million went to "Transfers." Following the trail, one finds that No on 131 and 140 gave $550,000 to A Committee Against 140. No on 131 and 140 also gave $464,000 to A Committee Against 131, that is, another entity fighting the

TABLE 5.4    Public Opinion on Term-Limits Propositions 131 and
140, 1990 General Election (percentages)

|  | Prop. 131 | Prop. 140 |
|---|---|---|
| Late August 1990 | | |
| Have you heard of the proposition? | 23 | 21 |
| If yes, would you vote for it today? | 66 | 61 |
| All respondents, with propositions explained: Would you vote for it?[a] | 60 | 57 |
| Late October 1990 | | |
| Have you heard of the proposition? | 65 | 67 |
| If yes, would you vote for it today? | 55 | 58 |
| All respondents, with propositions explained: Would you vote for it?[a] | 45 | 62 |

SOURCE: Based on Field Institute polls of registered voters, fi9004 (17–27 August 1990) and fi9006 (26–30 October 1990).

[a]Proposition 131 described as having to do with term limits and various other reforms, including public funding of election campaigns; Proposition 140 described as only involving term limits.

same proposition. There was also A Committee Against Propositions 131 and 140 that got $2.3 million from Assembly Speaker Willie Brown's personal committee, and another $1.6 million from an entity called Californians to Protect Our Constitution, $600,000 of whose money originated from political funds controlled by state senate President Pro Tem David Roberti.[58] Such financing legerdemain helps explain why investigations of proposition funding cannot always discover just how much is spent, by whom, and for what.

To summarize, opponents of term limits raised about $7.7 million, spread over the two initiatives they wanted to defeat, and the largest part of these funds came from California state officeholders who did not want to lose their jobs.

The differences in public perception of the two measures are illustrated in Table 5.4, based on polling responses of registered voters. The level of public awareness of both propositions was about the same, and rose significantly between late August and one week before the election. Similarly, among respondents who said they had heard of the propositions, differences in support for one or the other did not vary much, although the trend of support slightly favored Proposition 140. What is most notable is the response to the question Would you vote for it? after all respondents were offered an explanation of the proposals. Proposition 131 was described as having to do with term limits and various other reforms, including public funding, whereas Proposition 140 was described only as involving term limits. The explanations did not make a big difference in how people said they would vote early in the campaign, but as voters became more informed and were then reminded by the pollster of the differences between the two propositions, the preference for Proposition 140 was striking.

These differences were reflected in the voting. Both propositions had voter participation rates of about 90 percent, but Proposition 140 squeaked through with 52 percent of the vote, whereas Proposition 131 got only 38 percent. The popularity of term limits was greater than the vote suggests; it is very likely that these initiatives suffered as a result of being confused in voters' minds with the 26 other propositions in the 1990 general election.

Controversy dogged the issue of term limits, however, in complex court proceedings that reflected the strong interests arrayed against it. In April 1997 a federal district judge struck down Proposition 140 because of the provision that barred officeholders from the same position for life: "California's extreme version of term limits imposes a severe burden on the right of its citizens to vote for candidates of their choice." The case then went to the federal appeals court, which decided on a different logic five months later. In a 2–1 vote, that court also ruled against Proposition 140, not on the question of constitutionality but on the separate question of clarity: the justices said that the proposition did not clearly inform voters that legislators would be barred from office for life. The wording applied, the court said, only to members of the legislature, not to other state officeholders. The issue then went to the U.S. Supreme Court, which issued a one-line decision against reinstatement of the suit, but offered no opinion on the merits of the case, leaving the matter open to further litigation. Two months later, to keep the drama (or the comedy) going, another federal appeals court, this time a special eleven-judge panel, voted 9–2 to uphold the law, and there was a general assumption that the Supreme Court would not intervene.[59] As was the case with other direct legislation of the 1980s and later, lawyers and the courts kept matters unresolved for years. In this case the final result was that the popular decision for term limits for California state officeholders would stand. There would be a great hustle of office-switching in 1998, as California politicians sought to find other ways to stay on the public payroll.

Peter Schabarum was intoxicated with his 1990 success and began working on three more term-limits constitutional amendments for 1992, to apply to members of county boards of supervisors and members of both the U.S. House and Senate. All three proposals originally failed to qualify, but then Schabarum was able to qualify an initiative statute for the 1992 general election.[60] Proposition 164 would bar congressional candidacy to anyone who had served in the House of Representatives for six or more of the previous eleven years; it would likewise bar Senate candidacy for anyone who had served twelve or more of the previous seventeen years.

By this time, the idea of term limits had become considerably more popular than had been the case only two years before. For example, a Field poll shortly before the election found that 71 percent of respondents who had heard of the proposition, and 59 percent of all respondents, said they would vote Yes.[61] Schabarum nonetheless ran a very active campaign all across the state, stressing, among other things, the salary raises Congress had given itself. Moreover, the Proposition 164 forces were able to raise over $1 million while the discouraged opposition raised only $73,000.[62] Proposition 164 won easily, with 64 percent of the vote. Unlike Proposition 140, however, this measure did not make it through the legal system: the U.S. Supreme Court struck down all state term limits on members of Congress on the basis that neither the states nor Congress can change requirements for federal office that were specified in the Constitution.[63]

The issue was not dead, however, because Californians were more than ever committed to the idea of mandatory rotation of office. Congressional term limits would reappear in 1998 (see Chapter 6). Moreover, as was the case with Proposition 13, California became the bellwether of a national movement (it is extremely unlikely that Oklahoma's previous action would have had much effect without California's later success). California-style efforts to limit the terms of both state and national legislators became extremely popular across the United States in the 1990s. Despite the fact that congressional term-limit legislation had been stymied by the courts, a total of eighteen states had implemented such limits for their legislatures by mid-1998. An estimated two hundred legislators were forced to retire due to such limits in 1998, with the number to increase markedly in subsequent years. And talk of a constitutional amendment to allow term limits for members of the U.S. Congress was widespread. Once again, California direct legislation resonated across the country.[64]

By no means unrelated to term limits, the issue of campaign-finance reform also heated up in the 1980s. All over the country there was increasing concern about the costs of political campaigns at all levels of government, and the resultant influence of those who were able to finance them. With television and direct mail both becoming more and more important, and costly, it seemed that honest people of modest means were being forced out of politics: one had to be either beholden to wealthy special interests or able to invest millions of one's own dollars (protected by court "freedom of speech" decisions) to run a campaign. The dilemma was deciding what aspect of campaign financing should be regulated — contributions, lobbying, spending — and how.

Californians had demonstrated concern with this issue as early as 1974, when they overwhelmingly passed Proposition 9, which provided for some regulation of campaign expenditures, required registration and contribution limits for lobbyists, and created the Fair Political Practices Commission. But a decade later the problem did not seem anywhere near solution. Nor, in fact, would it be solved in the subsequent decade, as was shown by the $30 million spent to defeat the "Nickel a Drink" Proposition 134 in 1990.

In the general election of 1984, while California voters were finally voting in favor of a state lottery, they also voted by 64 percent against an initiative statute that would have limited campaign contributions. Proposition 40, promoted by Republican assemblyman Ross Johnson, dealt with campaign contributions to candidates for state offices and was a draconian measure for its time. It would have limited donations by individuals to $1,000 per candidate and $250 per party or Political Action Committee (PAC), with a total maximum expenditure of $10,000. Political parties and PACs would also be limited to donations of $1,000 per candidate. Candidates could spend as much of their own money as they wished, and limited public funding would be provided to candidates to help match their opponent's personal funds.

No one except Johnson signed the ballot pamphlet in favor of his measure. The listed opponents included leaders of the California Farm Bureau Federation, the State Chamber of Commerce, and the California Taxpayers Association. They argued, somewhat disingenuously, that the proposition did not really limit spending, and also that it made the raising of money more difficult. Proposition 40 favored wealthy candidates, these critics said, and would spend tax money on political campaigns. These arguments were echoed by a variety of business groups, while labor unions and other liberal groups were notable in their silence.[65] Johnson was also outspent: supporters had only $300,000 for the campaign, while the opposition spent $1.2 million.[66]

The negative publicity took its toll on public support. In an early October Field poll, only 27 percent were aware of Proposition 40, but when it was described to them, 47 percent thought they would vote Yes compared to 32 percent who would vote No. By the last week of October, however, awareness had risen to 48 percent, but of those who were aware of the measure, only 21 percent were prepared to vote Yes compared to 39 percent who would vote No and 39 percent who were Undecided.[67] Most of those Undecideds apparently moved to the No column, because 64 percent of the voters opposed the proposition.

In the 1988 primary election there were two campaign-finance reform proposals, Propositions 68 and 73, fighting it out against one another (the same thing would happen in the 1996 general election; see below). In part, the measures seemed nearly identical. Both would limit political contributions, Proposition 68 for state legislative candidates and Proposition 73 for all candidates. The limit for contributions in both initiatives was $1,000 by individuals; for PACs and other organizations, the limits varied slightly, ranging from $2,500 to $5,000. But Proposition 68 permitted a kind of voluntary public financing: Californians could contribute up to $3 per year to a Campaign Reform Fund, from which candidates who met certain requirements would receive limited matching funds. Proposition 73 differed on this point, and appeared stronger: it would permit localities to set lower contribution limits, had a $1,000 annual cap on gifts and honoraria, and forbade the transfer of funds between candidates. It also prohibited any use of public funds for political campaigns — which seems to have been a lesson learned from the negative response to the public funding aspect of Proposition 40 four years earlier.[68] Moreover, on the controversial question of spending limits, Proposition 68 did have some, whereas 73 did not.[69]

The forces behind the two measures differed. Proposition 68 was supported by much of the "liberal reform establishment" of the state: leaders of the League of Women Voters, California Federation of Teachers, Common Cause, Southern Christian Leadership Conference, Consumers Union, Mexican American Legal Defense and Educational Fund, Urban League, former governor "Pat" Brown, Attorney General Van de Kamp, and Bill Honig. Proposition 73, on the other hand, was led by Joel Fox of the Jarvis California Tax Reduction Movement, and a mix of relatively minor Democratic, Republican, and Independent politicians, including Ross Johnson. Thus, the two reform groups battled one another, each accusing the other of promoting a weaker bill to undercut "true" campaign reform; the Proposition 68 people, for example, strongly criticized Proposition 73's lack of spending limits.[70]

Much of the organized opposition was to both propositions, particularly among politicians. But Republican leaders like Governor Deukmejian focused especially on Proposition 68, whereas Democratic leaders like Assembly Speaker Willie Brown and senate President Pro Tem David Roberti reserved their greatest scorn for 73.[71]

The two major opposition fund-raising groups were formally against both measures, and spent about $1.1 million.[72] The pro sides, on the other hand, were entirely separate. Supporters of Proposition 68, named Taxpayers to Limit Campaign Spending to stress their difference from the Proposition 73 people, raised just over $1 million, while Proposition 73 supporters, despite their Jarvis heritage, raised only $335,000. Because of the breadth of its support from large organizations, the Proposition 68 side had to use only 10 percent of its funds to qualify its initiative, whereas the Proposition 73 people had to spend almost 90 percent of theirs.[73] As it turned out, this campaign was another demonstration of the fact that there is always more than money involved in direct legislation.

The greater funding for Proposition 68 seemed to have some effect on public awareness. There were two California Polls that asked about these propositions, the first in early April and the second in mid-May. In the first, only 26 percent of the respondents had heard of Proposition 68, and a minuscule 5 percent had heard of Proposition 73; this figure rose to 36 percent and 22 percent, respectively, in May. When the measures were explained to the voters, the explanations mentioned spending limits for Proposition 68, although whether or not respondents picked up on the nuances of the oral questions is not clear. In any event, in April, 68 percent said they would vote Yes for Proposition 68, and 57 percent for Proposition 73; in May the figures were virtually identical.[74] Voters were generally sympathetic to the idea of reform, but it is likely that few recognized significant differences between the two propositions. Nonetheless, it was the less-well-funded Proposition 73 that won out, with a 58 percent Yes vote compared to 53 percent for Proposition 68, a difference of about 60,000 votes.

The matter was hardly resolved by the vote, however, not least because both measures passed. Direct conflicts between the two propositions were supposed to be automatically resolved in Proposition 73's favor because it had more votes, but it was not easy to sort out the conflicting passages, and Proposition 68 backers would fight in the courts to retain the provisions they said were not in conflict with 73. Within one year of the election, ten lawsuits had been filed challenging parts of both propositions, while the Fair Political Practices Commission was still trying to figure out how to interpret and apply the Proposition 73 regulations. Candidates, fund-raisers, and potential contributors for the fall 1988 election were confused about what they could and could not do in terms of fund-raising and spending. And the overall effect on campaign finance was minor.[75] Perhaps the greatest effect of these initiatives was on the attorneys; there was so much work to do that the California Political Attorneys Association was founded. Their role in the initiative process was becoming ever more crucial.[76]

One related governmental matter, dealing with the initiative process itself, took place in the 1990 general election. Both the Jarvis and Gann organizations promoted Proposition 137 to, as they saw it, protect the sanctity of direct legislation. It was an initiative constitutional amendment (these groups could still get out the signatures) requiring that any legislative changes in the laws regulating the initiative or referendum petition or voting process be approved by the voters. To its supporters this proposition was important, especially to avoid such changes as increasing the number of signatures required to qualify a proposition. Opponents believed the measure would inhibit needed reforms to the process, such as mandating disclosure of the source of funds for proposition qualification.[77]

A good deal of the liberal establishment opposed the proposition, but not very vigorously: they raised no funds at all. The Jarvis–Gann forces, on the other hand, raised and spent almost $3 million.[78] The public's interest was modest, however, in this year of so many initiatives. The 88 percent voter participation rate on Proposition 137 was the lowest for any of the thirteen direct legislation measures, and even lower than the rate for eleven of the fifteen legislative measures. The proposition lost, gaining only 45 percent of the vote. It was just too busy a year for a "mechanical" proposition of this type.

Among the powerful sociocultural issues of the 1984–1994 period, one of the most emotional was that of crime and punishment. Chapter 4 analyzed the rise of this issue from the early 1970s, involving several initiatives and culminating in the draconian Proposition 8 (the "Victims Bill of Rights") of Paul Gann and gubernatorial candidate George Deukmejian in 1982. These public concerns did not decline in ensuing years. Crime was raised as an issue in the successful 1984 campaign to establish a state lottery: opponents argued that wherever lotteries went, crime followed.[79] More important was what might be called the "quasi-initiative" of 1986, the mandatory ballot approval or rejection of continuation in office of Chief Justice Rose Bird and other members of the California Supreme Court. While the recall had not been used statewide, there was a rough equivalent in the fact that Supreme Court justices had to stand for reelection the year after their appointment and then every eight years. Bird was Governor Jerry Brown's most liberal appointee and was criticized for many decisions, chief among them her alleged "softness" on crime and especially on capital punishment. She had been narrowly approved by a 52 percent majority in 1978, but conservative criticism had grown considerably since then. She had, for example, been among the losing minority on the Court that tried to keep Paul Gann's "Victims Bill of Rights" (Proposition 8, 1982) off the ballot by ruling it unconstitutional. At the time, Gann's organization had issued a press release noting the "renewed interest in launching a re-call [sic] campaign against Rose Bird."[80]

By 1986, anti-Bird sentiment had become even stronger and better organized. Along with Howard Jarvis, former Los Angeles Police Chief Ed Davis, and assemblyman Ross Johnson, Paul Gann was on the Executive Committee of "Californians to Defeat Rose Bird." Their aim was to get rid of the Supreme Court's "super-liberal 'Gang of Four'," which included Bird, Cruz Reynoso, Joseph Grodin, and Stanley Mosk.[81] But the focus in the campaign definitely was on Rose Bird, and it met with considerable success. As early as late July, 58 percent of a Field poll sample said they would vote against her, while only 32 percent planned to support her. A slightly larger number, 62 percent, agreed with the statement that she let her personal feelings about the death penalty affect her decisions. Exactly the same percentage said they would vote against her in a late October poll, and again in a post-election poll on voting day.[82] Bird and Reynoso were decisively defeated, and Grodin lost more narrowly; Mosk, who had long-established popularity in California despite his liberalism, and Justices Malcolm Lucas and Edward Panelli, who were not targets of the conservatives, were retained in office. While these contests did not qualify as direct legislation per se, they nonetheless exhibited many of the process's characteristics, and certainly reflected popular support for a harsher criminal justice system.

In the 1990 primary election, Pete Wilson, running for the Republican nomination for governor, adopted the first of a number of strong anti-crime positions that would please right-wing Republicans who had long doubted his conservatism. Proposition 115 was a complex initiative constitutional amendment and statute that proposed removal from the California constitution and statutes any rights of defendants that did not exist under the federal Constitution.[83] It did not get a great deal of publicity but was passed by a 57 percent majority; Wilson got the nomination and, in November, the governorship.[84]

In that same primary, the legislature also had two successful anti-crime measures of its own. Proposition 114 broadened the constitutional meaning of "peace officer" to put more law enforcement personnel under the protection of the death-penalty provisions of Proposition 7 of 1978 (see Chapter 4). It was overwhelmingly approved by 71 percent of the voters. And Proposition 120 was a $450 million prison construction bond act endorsed by 56 percent of the voters.

Three taxation initiatives on the fall 1990 ballot also related to criminal justice. Propositions 129 and 133 focused on drugs, while Proposition 134 was the "Nickel a Drink" tax. None of these measures passed, for the reasons previously noted, but it was not by chance that each included a pledge to use some of their funds for prisons or law enforcement (the Prop. 133 people liked to call theirs the "safe streets" initiative). Had the public perceived any of these complex propositions more in terms of their anti-crime aspects, they might well have done better.

This was confirmed by another initiative in the fall 1990 election, Proposition 139, a constitutional amendment and statute that would permit state prison and county jail officials to contract with public and private enterprises for inmate labor. Led by Governor Deukmejian, on a "no more free ride for felons" approach, the proposition was passed with a 54 percent vote.

The question of crime control really came to a head in the 1994 general election with Proposition 184, another California initiative statute that would have strong national repercussions. This was the "3 Strikes" initiative, whose main component mandated a minimum 25-years-to-life sentence for offenders convicted of a felony who had two or more previous "serious" or "violent" felony convictions. What was most controversial was that the third conviction could be for any type of felony, even a minor and nonviolent one, so long as the two previous felonies were classed as "serious" or "violent." There were several other controversial aspects to the initiative, including the provision that crimes committed as a minor would count toward the offenders' "3 strikes," and another provision that would have removed all possibility of non-incarceration alternatives that had previously been available.[85] One curious aspect of Proposition 184 was that it was identical to a statute that had been signed into law the previous March, making the initiative essentially superfluous. Defenders argued that some legislators were trying to weaken that law, and the initiative would make sure that didn't happen.

The campaign for the proposition was presented in very emotional terms, with advertising that showed how innocent people had been killed by felons on parole, and so on. Promoters insisted that the "3 Strikes" law passed by the legislature was working and had to be defended. Attorney General Dan Lungren reported that crime was declining in California and noted that "prisoners are often seen" carrying "outlines of the '3 Strikes' and You're Out law," an unusual example of inmate reading matter. Supporters contended that the measure would save taxpayers $23 billion over the next five years.[86] Opponents focused on the fact that minor infractions, and crimes committed as a youth, could result in one's going to prison for life. And they concluded that the measure would "cost billions [of dollars] annually."[87] One side or the other, one assumes, was wrong about the money.

But the proposers of Proposition 184 had the public on their side. They had obtained 815,000 petition signatures for this initiative, more than double the number required. In a late October poll of registered voters, 92 percent were aware of the initiative, an extraordinarily high figure. Of those respondents, 61 percent favored it, 27 percent were opposed, and 12 percent were undecided. And when all respondents were pushed about how they would vote "today," the Yes figure rose to 64 percent. The fact that Marc Klaas, the father of a young girl whose brutal murder had played no small role in the rise of harsh sentencing sentiment, was a leader among those opposing Proposition 184, was not having much effect.

Supporters also had money on their side. They spent $1.3 million, which was 29 times greater than the $45,000 their opponents raised and spent. Actually, the "3 Strikes" forces raised almost $250,000 more than they spent. Of the total amount raised, over $400,000 came from the Republican Party, about $100,000 each came from the California Correctional Peace Officers PAC and the National Rifle Association, and $350,000 came from Michael Huffington, who was simultaneously spending about $28 million of his own money as the unsuccessful Republican candidate for the U.S. Senate.[88]

Despite the publicity, voter participation in the vote on Proposition 184 was only 85 percent. No proposition in this election had a participation rate higher than 89 percent, but, still, three direct legislation measures had higher rates than Proposition 184. None of them, however, had such a lopsided victory: 72 percent of those voting supported "3 Strikes." (One legislative proposition won by an even higher margin, 79 percent, and it also related to crime. Proposition 189 was a legislative constitutional amendment that added violent sexual assault to the list of crimes excepted from the right to bail.)

Table 5.5 looks at some characteristics of support for Proposition 184. It was a Republican issue, to some degree, with Governor Pete Wilson and Huffington among its most outspoken supporters, and, as seen above, the Republican Party as a key financial backer. Thus, it is not surprising that Republicans favored the initiative by a considerably higher margin than Democrats. Nonetheless, opposition to crime was very broad, and can be seen by the strong support for the proposition among Democrats as well. Ideological self-perception was an even stronger indicator, ranging from 86 percent support by conservatives to 69 percent support by moderates to 42 percent support among liberals. Indeed, self-defined liberals were the only group in this table with a majority planning to vote against Proposition 184.

Religion was also a significant factor in public attitudes toward Proposition 184 — not surprising in a decade marked by a strong resurgence of a socially conservative evangelical Protestantism. The differences between those to whom religion was very important or moderately important are insignificant, but there was notably lower enthusiasm for "3 Strikes" among those for whom religion was not very important. This was echoed by the differences in responses between those who considered themselves "born-again" and those who did not.

It is hard to generalize about the effect of income on voting behavior because support for the initiative did not increase or decrease in a straight line with income. The very high level of support in the $60,000–$80,000 income group undermines an otherwise seeming decline of support as one went up the income ladder. The pattern is a little clearer with education (which is not included in the table). Support for Proposition 184 was voiced by about 80 percent of those who had gone to or completed high school or trade/vocational school, then dropped to 74 percent for those with 1–2 years of college, 69 percent for 3–4 years of college, 65 percent for college graduates, and 50 percent for those with Master's degrees or above.[89] Thus, the income, education, and religious belief variables do suggest some relationship between sophistication and lack of enthusiasm for "3 Strikes," but that is a generalization that could easily be overstated. There were no differences in response between men and women.

The response of Hispanics is noteworthy. California Hispanics are a rela-

TABLE 5.5    Public Opinion on Proposition 184
("3 Strikes"), 1984 General Election

|  | Percentage who would vote Yes on Prop. 184 |
|---|---|
| Political party identification | |
| Republican | 85 |
| Democrat | 61 |
| Ideological self-perception | |
| Conservative | 86 |
| Liberal | 42 |
| Middle-of-the-road | 69 |
| Importance of religion to respondent | |
| Very important | 73 |
| Fairly important | 75 |
| Not very important | 58 |
| Religious belief | |
| Born-again Christian | 77 |
| Not-born-again Christian | 67 |
| Annual income | |
| Under $20,000 | 73 |
| $20,000–$40,000 | 71 |
| $40,000–$60,000 | 67 |
| $60,000–$80,000 | 77 |
| Over $80,000 | 64 |
| Race/ethnicity | |
| White | 69 |
| African-American | 62 |
| Asian | 82 |
| Hispanic | 77 |

SOURCE:  Based on responses to Field Institute poll fi9407 (21–30 October 1994) on question of how respondents would vote "today."
NOTE:  Registered voters only; 89 of 1,023 respondents who were Undecided are excluded from the calculations.

tively poor, largely immigrant group, and a relatively high number of its youth tend to get in trouble with the law. But California Hispanics are also one of the hardworking poor groups most victimized by crime, and it was on this basis that they responded to "3 Strikes." They obviously wanted felons out of their neighborhoods. African-Americans were in many ways similar, but their experiences with law enforcement and the judicial system were even more negative, which helps to explain their relatively low support for "3 Strikes." However, one should stress the word "relative," since their 62 percent support for the proposition was still a strong majority. Conversely, Asians were among the strongest supporters of the proposition, although it is impossible to know, with such a small sample, whether they represented newer or older immigrants, or native-born of Asian background.

The final area of sociocultural issues in this period revolves around ethnic conflict, a problem in California throughout the twentieth century, and one which had frequently entered the initiative process. In good part, the new propositions were driven by reaction to the increasing heterogeneity of California's population, and particularly the large numbers of legal and illegal immigrants from Mexico and Central America that were making their way to the California's cities and fields. To many Californians these immigrants posed an economic, political, and, especially, cultural threat to their own way of life; the state, in many ways, was ripe for neo-nativism.

The first evocation of these sentiments came with Proposition 38 in the 1984 general election. Like the curious Proposition 12 regarding nuclear weapons two years earlier, it was simply an opinion measure, in this case one that would require the governor to write to the President, the Attorney General, and the Congress expressing the wish that voting materials be printed only in English.[90] Its chief backer was S. I. Hayakawa, former president of San Francisco State University, who had earlier gained fame for his battle against student radicals and who was now a U.S. Senator. The Proposition 38 forces tried to get Paul Gann involved in "U.S. English," which was the name of their group, and he did meet with them but was never officially associated.[91]

It was an active issue. The state legislature had debated a bill in February 1984 calling for a constitutional amendment to make English the official language of the state, but it had been killed in a senate committee.[92] It was also an emotional issue: supporters argued that since one had to be a citizen to vote, and should know English to become a citizen, it was only right that ballot materials be in the one common language. They contended also that printing materials in other languages was both expensive and divisive. Opponents of the proposition (the opposition argument in the ballot pamphlet was signed by three California congressmen) argued that it was discriminatory and a violation of the Voting Rights Act; moreover, they said, bilingual ballots helped immigrants become better citizens and increased the number of people who actually voted.[93]

There was extensive discussion of Proposition 38 in the press, and coverage reflected the above arguments, particularly the question of whether bilingual ballots were a disincentive to learning English or a way to bring people into the political process. There was no doubt that, to some members of ethnic minorities, it was an attack.[94] It was not a big-money campaign. Supporters spent only $54,000 for qualifying the measure, and had another $75,000 for the campaign. Opponents were not organized and filed no Campaign Statement of receipts and expenses. But the voters participated in large numbers and gave the proposition an overwhelming 71 percent endorsement.

This led directly to the more threatening Proposition 63 two years later, an initiative constitutional amendment to make English the official state language. Its precise meaning was somewhat unclear, since the measure simply instructed the state legislature to enforce the official state language provision by "appropriate legislation." Once again, Hayakawa was a chief spokesman and U.S. English the main organizing body. While their campaign stressed the idea of facilitating assimilation and uniting people, there were some nasty aspects as well.[95] The opposition was led by powerful politicians of both parties, including Governor Deukmejian, Assembly Speaker Willie Brown, and Attorney General Van de Kamp. Even Daryl F. Gates, the conservative and combative chief of the Los Angeles police department, signed the ballot pamphlet's opposition argument.[96]

The Proposition 63 forces raised and spent quite a bit more than they had in 1984; however, of the $800,000 they managed to collect, almost $700,000 of that was used up for qualifying expenses. This did not leave much for the campaign. Opponents spent a total of only $114,000 on their campaign, a meager effort given the overwhelming success of Proposition 38 just two years earlier.[97] Free press coverage provided the main publicity for both sides. The issue excited great interest, and Proposition 63 was the most widely recognized of all the propositions on the ballot.[98] Moreover, this 1986 general election was driven by conservative interests, including the effort to unseat Rose Bird, Paul Gann's attack on government salaries (Prop. 61), and an anti-AIDS proposition (see below) by right-wing extremist Lyndon Larouche, as well as Official English.[99] Voter participation (93 percent) and voter approval for Proposition 63 (73 percent) were both two points higher than they had been in 1984. While numerous factors played a role in this vote, general animosity to and fear of the state's increasing cultural heterogeneity were key.

Public opinion poll results on these two "pro-English" initiatives are instructive. Both are Field Institute polls taken shortly before each of the elections. In the 1984 poll, 72 percent of respondents were aware of Proposition 38, a very high figure; in 1986 that figure was even higher for Proposition 63, at 85 percent. In 1986, 61 percent of those who had heard of Proposition 38 were in favor of it; two years later, 66 percent of those who had heard of Proposition 63 were in favor of it. Table 5.6 shows some additional characteristics of public opinion on these two propositions.

Given the nearly identical vote for the two propositions, the differences in support by several groups from one to the other is striking. This is especially the case because Proposition 63 was broader and more divisive than Proposition 38. That might explain why conservatives favored the 1986 measure more than they had the 1984 one, but it certainly would not explain the even greater jump among those who considered themselves liberals, or that among African-Americans and families earning under $10,000. Perhaps there were a notable number of last-minute mind changes in 1984 (a presidential election year with over two million more voters than in 1986), which upped the vote for Proposition 38 beyond what one might have expected from the final poll.

As might be expected, there were notable differences in support based on party identification and ideology across both elections, even if all groups were more supportive of 63 than of 38. Income level did not have much effect, except in the idiosyncratic case of the poorest voters in 1984 only. And education seems to correlate roughly with income, but neither variable stands out as a confident measure of support or rejection of either of these measures.

Hispanics were the least enthusiastic supporters of these English-language proposals, which reflected their sentiments that discrimination played a role in the initiatives' genesis. But overall, Hispanics were not so different from other Californians; indeed, in the 1986 poll, the number of Hispanics favoring Proposition 63 edged out those opposing it by a tiny margin. Similarly, a *Los Angeles Times* poll found that most Hispanics favored Proposition 63, even though their leaders did not.[100] This is consistent with the many observations about the determination of Hispanic immigrants to see that their children became proficient in English.

Proposition 63 had no real teeth, and thus not much practical effect in California, although it did demonstrate an important contemporary sociocultural division in the state. More broadly, however, it was another California initiative that resonated around the country. In the next general election, three states — Colorado, Arizona, and Florida — emulated California in passing similar laws, and by the end of the 1990s, twenty-two states had done so. In some cases, such as in Arizona, the laws passed were considerably stronger than California's. And in all cases, one sees again the influence

TABLE 5.6   Public Opinion on English Language Propositions 38 and 63, 1984 and 1986 General Elections

| | Percentage who would vote Yes on Prop. 38 | Percentage who would vote Yes on Prop. 63 |
|---|---|---|
| Party identification | | |
| Republican | 72 | 85 |
| Democrat | 54 | 61 |
| Political ideology[a] | | |
| Conservative | 71 | 83 |
| Liberal | 36 | 54 |
| Middle-of-the-road | 62 | 70 |
| Race/ethnicity | | |
| White | 64 | 76 |
| African-American | 31 | 75 |
| Hispanic | 49 | 49 |
| Annual income | | |
| Under $10,000 | 43 | 81 |
| $10,000–$20,000 | 65 | 78 |
| $20,000–$30,000 | 65 | 75 |
| $30,000–$40,000 | 62 | 62 |
| Over $40,000 | 67 | 77 |
| Education | | |
| Less than high school graduate | 51 | 74 |
| High school graduate | 63 | 86 |
| Some college | 61 | 70 |
| College graduate | 68 | 70 |
| Post-bachelor's degree | 60 | 60 |

SOURCE: Based on responses to Field Institute polls fi8407 (27–30 October 1984) and fi8606 (27–30 October 1986) to question concerning who "had heard" about the proposition and how they would vote "today." The number of "Asian" respondents was too low to be included.

[a]This question was not asked on poll fi8407, so 1984 figures are taken from poll fi8406 (8–12 October 1984).

of California as the bellwether state for its efforts to resolve major contemporary issues through the initiative process.[101]

Conservatism was riding high in the United States and California. Ethnic fears and animosities both fueled that conservatism and were exacerbated by it. This phenomenon can be seen again in debates over public schools. In the special election of November 1993, the single direct legislation measure was for a voucher system for schools that would permit students to use the vouchers at either public or "qualifying" private elementary and high schools (schools that discriminated on the basis of race, ethnicity, or national origin could not qualify, but those that discriminated on the basis of religion or gender could). Proposition 174 raised religious, racial, and other cultural animosities, as well as economic ones, and reflected a general disenchantment with the perceived failures of the public schools, especially in California cities. Additionally, there had been growing criticism among Republicans and conservatives of the power of the California Teachers Association in the Democratic legislature. Proponents of this initiative constitutional amendment argued that only competition would force the public schools to improve. They had tried to put their measure on the 1992 ballot, but had been blocked by a group of teachers, parents, and others who picketed the places where signatures were being gathered; the result was that the measure never made it to the ballot. That year, the state Legislative Counsel had also issued an opinion that the measure violated the First Amendment to the Constitution regarding separation of church and state, and the Fourteenth Amendment because it would permit gender discrimination. Thus, there was considerable controversy about Proposition 174 well before it made it to the 1993 ballot.[102]

The most vocal support of the measure came from the religious right. Pat Robertson's Christian Coalition was active in the campaign and tried to lobby among Hispanics and blacks, arguing that they could only profit from the voucher system.[103] But this was a case where the liberals were much better organized and funded. The opposition included not only all the teachers' groups in the state, but the state Democratic Party, President Clinton, the League of Women Voters, both of California's Democratic senators, the California Association of University Women, the National Council of Jewish Women, the Mexican American Legal Defense Fund, and numerous others. They argued against it in terms of principle, cost, and its alleged deleterious effect on the public schools.[104]

Supporters of Proposition 174 were seriously outspent. They did raise $3.7 million, most of it from wealthy individuals, as well as $420,000 from the California Republican Party. After spending about $1 million for qualifying the initiative, they still had a considerable campaign chest, which they used for extensive advertising. The opposition, however, raised $24 million, of which just over half came from the California Teachers Association. Many local teacher groups launched their own fund-raising efforts, raising, usually, $2,000 to $10,000 from parent and teacher contributions. The state's teachers obviously saw the idea as a threat to both their livelihoods and their convictions. Five separate organizations had filed Campaign Statements in support of Proposition 174, but twenty-nine organizations filed in opposition.[105]

In the one public opinion poll on the election, there were few demographic groups with majority support for Proposition 174. Self-identified conservatives were among the highest, but still less than a majority with 47 percent support. Republicans supported the measure at the 39 percent level, as opposed to Democrats and Independents at 25 percent. Protestants and Roman Catholics, who had the most to benefit in terms of private schooling, both were 65 percent or higher on the No side, as were 84 percent of Jews. Despite the Christian Right's direct appeal to minorities, Hispanics were 71 percent against the initiative, and blacks were close behind at 68 percent. There was almost no variation among income groups.[106]

People did care: 98 percent of the voters who turned out for this election cast ballots on Proposition 174. And 70 percent of them voted No. Sociocultural conflicts were only part of the complex of factors involved in this election. A general popular commitment to public education and the overwhelming scope of the opposition also led to the initiative's defeat.

The final initiative dealing with sociocultural issues in this period became one of the most divisive in California history: this was Proposition 187 in the 1994 general election, which dealt with illegal aliens. It would deny public social and health services, and public education, to illegal aliens; require state and local agencies to report suspected illegal aliens to both state and federal authorities; and make it a felony to manufacture, sell, or use false citizenship or residence documents. In some ways it represented the same kind of sentiment as were associated with the alien land law initiative of 1920.

The genesis of the measure was in no way mysterious. California's population included an estimated 1.6 million illegal immigrants in 1994, and that number was growing at about 125,000 per year.[107] For years, there had been constant back-and-forth debate about illegal aliens: they took jobs away from others or took jobs no one else wanted; they cost the state money or contributed to its wealth; they were totally alienated from American culture or they were, like other immigrants, anxious to become part of American culture; and so on. These were all important questions. With Proposition 187, the "Save our State" initiative, the issue came to a head.

To supporters, Proposition 187 was in the spirit of Proposition 13 and would save the state $5 billion per year. It was also argued that the reduction of public services would discourage illegal immigration, leaving more room in the state's schools and better public benefits for deserving Californians. Opponents believed that the measure could cost at least $10 billion, would not stop illegal immigration, and would throw 400,000 innocent children out of school and onto the streets.[108]

There were serious constitutional questions involved in the proposition. The denial of public education seemed to be in direct conflict with a 1982 Supreme Court decision. Also, under the rules of the federal Aid to Families with Dependent Children program, any child living in California was eligible. It seemed possible that California would lose very large sums in federal funding for other welfare programs if Proposition 187 passed.[109]

Proposition 187 was another of the measures that Governor Pete Wilson adopted to expand his conservative credentials in preparation for reelection and a hoped-for 1996 run for the presidency. He had filed suit earlier in 1988 to try to get the federal government to reimburse California for the costs of providing public services to illegal aliens, so Proposition 187 was an extension of a commitment he had already made. He was joined by many other Republican leaders, including Harold Ezell, the western region director of the Immigration and Naturalization Service under President Reagan. There was no little cultural animosity expressed in all this.[110]

The opposition was impressive. It included not only Democratic and liberal leaders, but the *Los Angeles Times, Sacramento Bee, Wall Street Journal, San Diego Union Tribune*, Cardinal Roger Mahoney of Los Angeles, Los Angeles Sheriff Sherman Block, and the League of Women Voters.[111]

Opponents also outspent supporters, $3.4 million to $1 million (of which half was needed for qualifying). Forty percent of the supporters' money came directly from the California Republican Party, with another $100,000 or so coming from the coffers of individual Republican politicians. Opposition money came from numerous local entities, plus a number of ethnic, union, and business organizations. The California Teachers Association Issues PAC, which had an obvious vested interest in not losing so many students, gave $660,000, and the California State Council of Service Employees, $350,000.[112]

A couple of weeks before the election, the outcome was not at all clear. In a poll of registered voters, 91 percent said they "had heard" about Proposition 187. Among all respondents, when asked how they would vote if the election were "today," 47 percent said they would vote Yes and 46 percent said they would vote No. Quite similarly, 51 percent thought Proposition 187 would deter illegal immigration, while 49 percent thought it would not.[113]

Some demographic characteristics made a difference in attitudes toward Proposition 187, as seen in Table 5.7. As has generally been the case, political party membership and self-defined ideology made a difference: a majority of Democrats opposed this effort to punish illegal immigrants, while

TABLE 5.7    Public Opinion on Illegal Aliens
Proposition 187, 1994 General Election

|  | Percentage who would vote Yes on Prop. 187 |
| --- | --- |
| Party identification | |
| Republican | 72 |
| Democrat | 44 |
| Political ideology | |
| Conservative | 68 |
| Liberal | 26 |
| Middle-of-the-road | 53 |
| Race/ethnicity | |
| White | 59 |
| African-American | 53 |
| Hispanic | 30 |
| Language of interview | |
| Spanish | 4 |
| Religion | |
| Protestant | 63 |
| Roman Catholic | 39 |
| Jewish | 24 |
| Annual income | |
| Under $20,000 | 45 |
| $20,000–$40,000 | 53 |
| $40,000–$60,000 | 56 |
| $60,000–$80,000 | 57 |
| Over $80,000 | 49.7 |

SOURCE:  Based on responses to Field Institute poll
fi9407 (21–30 October 1994) to question of how respondents
would vote "today."

Republicans had a larger majority in its favor. The difference between liberals and conservatives was even greater, and the small Yes majority of self-
defined "middle-of-the-road" voters helps explain the proposition's victory
at the polls.

This was also an initiative election where racial/ethnic and religious factors made a clear difference. African-Americans shared the view of whites relative to illegal immigration; indeed, they were a group, it could be argued, whose economic opportunities were most affected by illegal immigration. So their positive position is understandable; perhaps it is more significant that it wasn't larger than 53 percent—but blacks were generally also Democrats and liberals, which played a role in their reactions. Since Hispanics were the primary focus of the punitive Proposition 187, their 70 percent No is logical, as is the even stronger 96 percent No response of Hispanics who chose to be interviewed in Spanish.

Variations in poll responses by religion are consistent with attitudes in these communities. Many California Roman Catholics are also Hispanic; moreover, the Church was on record against this initiative. And Jews were traditionally opposed to regulation of immigration and other conservative social policies. Catholics and Jews were also more likely than Protestants to be Democrats and/or liberals, so their break here with Protestants reflects all of these differences. Income differences were slight, with the poorest and wealthiest having small majorities against the proposition, while modest majorities of the middle class saw it as beneficial. Education, not shown in the table, also had relatively little effect.

Voter participation on this measure, at 89 percent, was well behind that on school vouchers (Proposition 174) twelve months earlier, but was nonetheless higher than that for any of the other nine propositions on the November 1994 ballot. And Proposition 187 passed with 59 percent of the vote, a strong but not overwhelming majority.

The history of Proposition 187 was not over, however. Like most controversial initiatives in the 1980s and 1990s, it was taken immediately to court and hung in limbo for several years. In the fall of 1996 Federal District Judge Mariana R. Pfaelzer (a Democrat appointed to the bench by President Carter) halted enforcement of the new law, ruling that the denial of services to illegal immigrants was unconstitutional.[114] Other courts, in the meantime, had issued injunctions against various parts of the law. Then, in early 1998, Judge Pfaelzer issued her final ruling, a permanent injunction. She cited, among other things, the federal overhaul of the nation's welfare laws in 1996 that itself had some restrictions on benefits to non-citizens. That, she ruled, reinforced the conclusion that only the federal government could legislate on immigration; thus, all major parts of the law (excepting minor provisions like penalties for false documents) were dead. Governor Wilson and some others announced their intention to take the issue to the U.S. Supreme Court, but experts believed they had little chance of success.[115] Beyond the ill feelings it created, Proposition 187's main positive legacy appears to have been the large number of immigrants who responded by becoming citizens and voters. The lawyers, of course, also did well.

In summary of these modern sociocultural issues, Table 5.8 provides correlations for the voting on seven propositions. Once again, the results are striking: despite often being ignorant of the content of initiatives shortly before going to the polls, many voters nonetheless ended up taking consistent positions on general issue areas, whether it be taxation or government or sociocultural conflict. The table covers, over a twelve-year period, three initiatives dealing with crime, two with language intolerance, one with education (and, perhaps, race), and one with immigrants in California society. They are different from one another in many ways, but have in common a socioculturally conservative attitude toward California society. And the voting relationships between them are strong.

There are some exceptions to the general pattern, most notably the relatively low relationship between Deukmejian and Gann's 1982 Victims Bill of Rights (Proposition 8) and the other two anti-crime initiatives. But for a set of elections where the Yes percentage ranged from a low of 30 to a high of 73, to have the Yes votes nonetheless correlate so strongly suggests once again a great deal of voter ideological consistency on matters of social and cultural content.

Some of the health and welfare issues that appeared on initiatives during this period carried strong sociocultural baggage as well. This is nowhere more true than with the propositions relating to Acquired Immune Deficiency Syndrome (AIDS), which was a matter of much fear and controversy in the 1980s. Since the disease was associated in the public's mind with homosexuality, and particularly with sexual relations between males, questions of "lifestyle" and religious morality were intertwined with those of public health. This was certainly the case with Proposition 64 of November 1986 and Proposition 69 in the June 1988 primary. The measures were quite similar; they were both heavy-handed and emotionally charged. Both would have declared AIDS "an infectious disease," and labeled a carrier of the Human Immunodeficiency Virus (HIV) as someone with "an infectious condition." The names of carriers were to be placed on the list of those with reportable diseases kept by the state Department of Health Services, and they were to be subject to quarantine.[116]

The leaders of these proposition campaigns were primarily political rather than medical figures, and none of them was more controversial than Lyndon H. Larouche, Jr. Larouche was an extreme right-wing activist and would-be presidential candidate with a small but devoted national following. He came to California for the sole purpose of financing and directing these two AIDS campaigns. He was joined, among others, by Congressman William B. Dannemeyer, an arch-conservative California Republican.[117]

The propositions were controversial from the start: California Secretary of State March Fong Eu challenged the original wording of Proposition 64 in court, and the court ruled that there were three false statements in the proposed initiative (that AIDS was easily contracted, that numerous studies proved insect and respiratory transmission, and that "casual contact" also transmitted it) that must be removed from the ballot argument.[118] A three-month investigation by the state Attorney General's office also substantiated charges that the out-of-state Larouche people had broken the law by circulating petitions in California to get Proposition 64 on the ballot.[119]

Both initiatives were condemned by virtually the entire California medical community, led by the California Medical Association, as well as U.S. Surgeon General C. Everett Koop. They were joined by many California political leaders, including Republican Governor Deukmejian and Democratic Los Angeles Mayor Tom Bradley. All agreed that the proposed laws were medically unnecessary, excessive, and unenforceable.[120] This unanimity of leaders was reflected in the money each side collected. Proponents of the 1986 Proposition 64 raised only $360,000, about two-thirds of which was used to qualify the measure. Opponents had $2.8 million to publicize their message. In 1988, there was less interest on both sides: supporters of Proposition 69 raised half of what they had two years earlier, almost all of which was used for the qualification process, and opponents raised only $256,000, but that was all they needed.[121]

Public awareness of Proposition 64 was quite high in 1986: 76 percent of respondents to a California Poll were aware of the initiative one week before the election, and of those, 58 percent had already made up their minds to vote No. The comparable levels for Proposition 69 seventeen months later were 45 percent awareness and 43 percent planning to vote No — the Yes side was not larger, but more voters had yet to make up their minds.[122] In both cases, voter participation was high, and almost all of the Undecides seem to have been persuaded against the initiatives: 71 percent of those voting were against Proposition 64, and 68 percent were against Proposition 69.

Just six months after Proposition 69 there were two more initiatives dealing with AIDS; they differed from one another, and one passed while the other failed. Proposition 96 was presented as another "victim's rights" measure and dealt with sex offenses and assaults on peace officers, firefighters, or medical personnel. It stated that if the courts found there was reason to believe that bodily fluids had been transmitted during such an assault, they must order a blood test for AIDS and inform "specified persons." Proposition 102 was closer to the earlier measures, requiring physicians, blood banks, and other agencies to report patients whom they believe to be infected with AIDS to local health officers, who were required in turn to inform persons who might have been exposed. It also would have made blood donation by persons who knew they had AIDS a felony.[123] A notable

TABLE 5.8  Correlations of Voting on Sociocultural Propositions, 1982–1994

| Date[a] and Proposition | 1982p: Prop. 8 "Victims Bill of Rights" | 1984g: Prop. 38 Voting materials in English | 1986g: Prop. 63 English official language | 1990p: Prop. 115 Criminal law | 1993s: Prop. 174 Education vouchers | 1994g: Prop. 184 "3 Strikes" | 1994g: Prop. 187 Illegal immigrants |
|---|---|---|---|---|---|---|---|
| 1982p: Prop. 8 Criminal justice | 1.000 | | | | | | |
| 1984g: Prop. 38 Voting materials in English | .594 | 1.000 | | | | | |
| 1986g: Prop. 63 English official language | .585 | .904 | 1.000 | | | | |

| | | | | | | | |
|---|---|---|---|---|---|---|---|
| 1990p:<br>Prop. 115<br>Criminal law | .339 | .564 | .676 | 1.000 | | | |
| 1993s:<br>Prop. 174<br>Education vouchers | .414 | .558 | .643 | .811 | 1.000 | | |
| 1994g:<br>Prop. 184<br>"3 Strikes" | .287 | .606 | .753 | .888 | .803 | 1.000 | |
| 1994g:<br>Prop. 187<br>Illegal immigrants | .447 | .717 | .832 | .793 | .787 | .933 | 1.000 |

NOTE: Pearson product moment correlations, based on percentage voting Yes on propositions, with data aggregated by county and weighted by county population. For clarity, only one-half of table is shown, since the two halves are identical.

[a]After date, "p" stands for primary, "g" for general election, and "s" for special election.

aspect of Proposition 102 was that Paul Gann, who had contracted AIDS, was an author and sponsor of the initiative, along with Dannemeyer and other conservatives, plus some medical personnel. Proposition 96 was supported primarily by law enforcement personnel, such as Los Angeles County Sheriff Sherman Block and former Los Angeles Police Chief Ed Davis, now a member of the state senate.

Response to the two measures reflected their differences, with Proposition 102 being seen as the more radical. Proposition 96 was opposed by the American Civil Liberties Union, the American Medical Association, and various organized homosexual groups, while the opposition to 102 was much broader, including a large variety of politicians and business leaders, as well as most medical groups. Dr. Laurence White, head of the California Medical Association, was quoted as saying, "I'll burn my medical records if Prop. 102 passes."[124]

Neither of these were big-money campaigns. The supporters of Proposition 96 raised about $480,000, most of which was used for qualifying; the Gann organization raised even less for Proposition 102. Some of the opposition fund-raising groups were registered against both propositions, but they raised only about $125,000, while a separate "Californians Against Prop 102/Stop Dannemeyer" group raised $846,000 just for that campaign.[125] Given that there were 41 propositions on the fall 1988 ballot, and a number of them were even more controversial, it is not surprising that the two AIDS initiatives got relatively little money and not much attention in the press.

The voting public was influenced by campaign publicity to discriminate between the two initiatives. A poll of registered voters one week before the election found 70 percent favoring Proposition 96, but only 51 percent favoring Proposition 102.[126] That difference was reflected in the final vote, although voters were less enthusiastic for either measure than those polled a few days earlier. Proposition 96 passed with 62 percent of the vote, while Proposition 102 was defeated, with only 34 percent support.[127] It was the idea of punishing only criminals that gave Proposition 96 its margin of victory; throughout all four propositions on this issue, the public was not stampeded by the emotions surrounding AIDS.

A variety of other health and welfare initiatives appeared during this period, influenced, in part, by the downturn in the California economy that came with the decline of the Cold War. They also reflected the broader national problems of rising health care costs and a Reagan-inspired reaction against welfare spending in general. An early example was Proposition 41 of November 1984, sponsored by assemblyman Ross Johnson, who was heading "Californians to Halt Excessive Welfare Spending." This initiative statute would have created a new Public Assistance Commission to monitor medical assistance programs and limit benefits paid to no more than the national average. Proponents argued that California had the most expensive welfare system in the nation, and that the cuts would apply only to the young and healthy.[128]

Proposition 41 was, in fact, an extreme proposal, whose language was immediately challenged in court. Opponents called it "the most radical initiative ever placed on the ballot"; they argued that it would cut Medi-Cal aid to the poor by as much as a third and affect hundreds of thousands of elderly and disabled, among others. Opposition came not only from welfare-oriented groups like the American Association of Retired Persons and the California Council of Churches, but also the state Chamber of Commerce and the American Medical Association.[129] Johnson and his supporters did raise a bit more than $1 million, but had to spend about 75 percent of it just to qualify the proposition. Their opponents had $3 million and used their funds to mount an extensive campaign that highlighted the extreme nature of the proposal and the wide variety of groups in opposition.[130] They were successful: 67 percent of the voters opposed the initiative.

In 1988 liberals tried to move the state in the other direction, with a proposal to create a public corporation to disburse funds to local government and nonprofit agencies for emergency aid to combat hunger and homelessness. Funding would come from fines for violation of existing laws related to housing and food preparation, thus theoretically not costing anything to the taxpayers. A state senate study concluded that $50–$90 million per year could be raised in this fashion, to assist California's two million people unable to feed themselves and 150,000 homeless. Los Angeles Mayor Tom Bradley and various political and welfare leaders were at the forefront of Proposition 95, whereas a variety of interests, including restaurants, grocers, and real estate groups led the opposition.[131] Supporters spent about $1 million on the campaign, two-thirds of it for qualifying the proposition; opponents spent about twice as much.[132]

Californians were generally leery of relief, and Proposition 95 was always something of a long shot. In mid-October, when told by pollsters that the proposed program would be financed by fines and bonds, 48 percent of a sample of all California adults said they would vote Yes; this figure rose by only a few points in a poll of registered voters on the eve of the election, while the percentage of No voters was rising more rapidly.[133] Proposition 95 was hurt both by the success of adverse publicity and by its getting somewhat lost among the huge number of initiatives on the 1988 ballot, many of which drew a higher voter participation rate than its 89 percent. It was defeated 55 percent to 45 percent. Welfare continued to be a controversial and divisive subject in the California of the late 1980s.

The issue was raised again in a curious, multifaceted initiative constitutional amendment and statute in 1992. Proposition 165 was another effort by Governor Pete Wilson, both to expand his gubernatorial powers and to cement his reputation as a political conservative in his quest for the presidency. The measure gave the governor powers to declare a "fiscal emergency" when a budget had not been adopted (California budgets were almost always not approved until after their constitutional deadline) and to unilaterally cut expenditures in order to balance expected spending and revenues. It sought, also, to appeal to voters by holding back payment of the governor's and legislators' salaries and expenses until a budget had been signed. Additionally, the initiative would have reduced Aid to Families with Dependent Children by up to 15 percent, limited public aid to new California residents, and cut other welfare programs as well.[134]

Not surprisingly, opponents, led by Common Cause and the League of Women Voters, went to court, trying to invalidate the initiative on the basis of its dealing with more than one subject. They were unsuccessful.[135] The opposition included a wide variety of groups, some focused on the political changes and others concerned with the initiative's effects on the state's welfare system. Thus, the Democratic Party and California Council of Churches, labor unions and the California Catholic Conference, were all against Proposition 165. Republicans, a wide variety of business groups, and even President Bush supported the governor.[136]

Fairly large campaign funds were involved as well. The Wilson forces spent $1.5 million just to qualify the initiative, and another $2.5 million on the campaign (spending almost a half million more than they raised). Opponents raised $3.3 million but spent only $2.7 million. The big contributions in support were primarily from Wilson himself ($1.7 million) and the California Republican Party ($338,000). Other large contributions came from corporations. The Democrats more than matched the Republicans in opposition ($580,000), and opponents also benefited from almost $1 million from the California State Employees Association and another $312,000 from the California Teachers Association. Other public employee groups also gave major donations.[137] Funding, as in most initiative campaigns by this time, was primarily a battle of large interest groups.

Despite the intensive publicity, a late October poll found that only 56 percent of registered voters had heard of Proposition 165. When it was described to them, they divided evenly between support and opposition.[138] The final vote reflected that division: Governor Wilson lost, 54 percent to 46 percent. The combination of those who opposed the proposition's political provisions and those who opposed its welfare provisions created a coalition that the governor could not beat.

The same November 1992 ballot also had a health care initiative, proposed and financed by the California Medical Association, which provides a good example of how difficult it often was to determine who would be helped and who hurt by directly legislated statutes and constitutional amendments. Proposition 166, the "Basic Health Care Initiative," would have required employers to provide health insurance to all employees and their families, if the employee worked a minimum number of hours, with the greatest part of the cost paid by the employer. It specified a "basic benefit package," which would be legally protected by a requirement of a four-fifths vote of the legislature for any changes. Employer tax credits were included, and insurance companies would be required to offer coverage, with some controls on rates.[139] The difficulty of evaluating the costs of such a program was noted in the state legislative analyst's summary in the official ballot pamphlet: there could be state "revenue losses in the hundreds of millions of dollars annually" due to the tax credits; and there could be "state and local expenditure savings in the hundreds of millions of dollars annually" due to less need for public health programs. The net impact was "unknown," as were the general economic effects of the program.[140] The difficulty for the average citizen to analyze such information is an example of another of the problems associated with direct legislation.

An alliance of health insurance companies and small business groups had been active since 1991 in trying to dissuade the California Medical Association from mounting a universal health care initiative.[141] They had been only partially successful. Such groups were part of a very broad opposition coalition. Fast-food restaurants and other employers of large numbers of low-paid workers were united against Proposition 166, as were a large number of insurance companies — both groups because of the potential costs. On the other side of the ideological spectrum, Consumers Union opposed the measure because, it said, the benefits were inadequate and it would primarily enrich physicians, and organized labor opposed it because it feared employers' cutting workers' hours in order to avoid the program. The San Francisco Board of Supervisors, California Nurses Association, and numerous homosexual groups were opposed because the proposed statute would "not provide the health care coverage the gay, lesbian, and bisexual communities need."[142]

While opposition to Proposition 166 was ideologically diverse, its financing came almost entirely from the right. They raised $5.6 million, almost exclusively from the business groups mentioned above. Insurance companies were particularly generous, providing about 85 percent of the funds, with companies like Aetna and Prudential contributing over $200,000 each, and the Health Insurance Association of America leading the way with $1.8 million. Supporters raised "only" $1.7 million, almost all of it from the California Medical Association.[143] With such broad-based opposition and so much money, the opposition easily prevailed: 69 percent of the voters rejected Proposition 166.

The coalition opposed to Proposition 166 split apart in 1994, however, when liberal groups proposed a "single payer" health care system for the state. This measure arrived in part because of the defeat of Proposition 166 and of alternative proposals in the legislature, and it reflected the national debate on the same subject, including an unsuccessful effort by President Clinton to get a national health care system adopted by Congress. This initiative constitutional amendment and statute, Proposition 186, would have provided a broad package of standard and long-term health care benefits, including prescription drugs, mental health care, and dental coverage. It would have cost as much as $75 million per year, according to the legislative analyst. It was to be financed by new taxes on employers, individuals, and cigarettes and tobacco.[144]

Supporters included some physician groups, Consumers Union, the American Association of Retired Persons and other retiree groups, nurses organizations, and labor unions. Opponents were pretty much the same business groups that had opposed Proposition 166, particularly the insurance companies. They stressed the loss of "physician choice," the involvement of a government bureaucracy, economic danger to small business, and alleged huge new taxes. And they raised $9.3 million to get their message across. Supporters were not poor, with $3.6 million, of which about $1 million was used for qualifying the measure.[145] But they were greatly outpublicized on an issue that was very controversial from the start. California, it turned out, was no more able than other states or the nation as a whole to solve the crisis in health insurance: 73 percent of the voters opposed Proposition 186.

There were also two anti-smoking initiatives during this period, following the two that had lost in 1978 and 1980. Proposition 99 in the 1988 general election would apply a tax on cigarette and other tobacco distributors, amounting to a 25-cent tax on a pack of cigarettes, with the proceeds going to tobacco research and treatment programs, as well as health education. The measure was sponsored by the American Cancer Society, the American Heart Association, and the American Lung Association. Opponents of the initiative argued that it would increase crime, penalize the poor, and make "millions" for the "medical industry." They were led by the tobacco companies, but at the forefront of their ballot argument and their publicity was Paul Gann. The opponents spent over $21 million, compared to the supporters' $1.8 million, and blanketed the state with all kinds of publicity, including a phony senior citizens' newspaper wherein Paul Gann argued that Proposition 99 was "just another plan to raise taxes" and that it would particularly hurt older Californians in a variety of ways.[146]

This was one time when overwhelming monetary and publicity advantage did not work. Both the public opinion polls before the election, and the ballot box, handed the tobacco companies a major defeat. Proposition 99 had a higher rate of voter participation (94 percent) than any of the other 40 propositions on the 1988 fall ballot, and won with a decisive 58 percent of the vote.[147]

Six years later the tobacco industry tried another tack — their own "anti-smoking" initiative. Proposition 188 in the 1994 general election was an initiative statute for standardized smoking regulations, which proposed to override current state and local laws; it would have banned public smoking except in specific types of locations, and regulated billboard advertising and the sale of tobacco to minors. It was, according to the *San Francisco Chronicle*, a "Smokescreen of Lies" that would have replaced more stringent controls with a law that left ample room for smoking almost everywhere. It was also designed to confuse, since a Yes vote for a ballot measure titled "Statewide Regulation" was in fact a vote to weaken tobacco controls almost everywhere in the state. The Philip Morris Company was the chief villain in the piece, which did not go unremarked.[148]

The funding discrepancy was much more skewed than six years before. Supporters of Proposition 188 raised $19.5 million, to $1.4 million for the opponents. While the tobacco forces had some public support from hotel and restaurant groups, and even some labor organizations, the money was all tobacco: an extraordinary $13 million from Philip Morris, $3.3 million from R. J. Reynolds, $1.3 million from Brown and Williamson, and hefty contributions from American Tobacco Co. and Lorillard as well.[149]

Voter participation in initiative voting was down generally in 1994, but 88 percent of the voters did vote on Proposition 188, only one percentage point lower than participation on the extremely divisive Proposition 187 on illegal aliens. And despite the tobacco industry's being on the "in favor" rather than the "against" side this time, and its effort to confuse the voters, it fared much less well than four years earlier: 70 percent of the vote was No.

Equally contentious, if somewhat more even-sided, was the furious battle between insurance companies and trial lawyers, which extended over several elections but took its clearest focus in 1988. Rising auto insurance rates were a real problem for California consumers, particularly those living in urban areas, in the 1980s. This was not quite as serious as the property tax crisis ten years earlier, but it nonetheless became a popular issue, with strong economic interests involved. It was taken up by a wide variety of "reform" groups that could not, unfortunately, agree on the specifics of their reforms. Consumers Union was involved, as was Common Cause, the Center for Public Interest Law (San Diego), the Center for Law and Poverty, Ralph Nader, California Rural Legal Assistance, and environmental groups like the Sierra Club. Many of these groups had strong-minded leaders, who all too often were sure of the unique value of their own solutions.[150] The end result was four different auto insurance propositions on the November 1988 ballot, plus another by the insurance companies designed to punish the trial lawyers whom they saw as their foremost enemies.[151] Moreover, each of the four proposed insurance reforms contained numerous provisions, which pushed the single topic rule for all it was worth — and virtually guaranteed that whichever won would probably have a long history in the courts.[152]

Table 5.9 provides information on each of these initiatives, including major supporters and opponents and the dollars involved. Just what sense the public could make of all this is questionable. What was clear was that Propositions 100, 101, and 103 included some reductions in insurance rates and that, among them, 100 and 103 were supported by reform groups of one kind or another, while 101 was not. And Proposition 104 was seen, from the start, as an insurance company measure. There were real fears that more than one of the initiatives would win, leading to years of court battles. There were also some regional differences, for example, in the argument that Propositions 100 or 103 would result in higher insurance rates in northern California, with benefits only for Los Angeles.[153]

The polls reflected the public's confusion. In a September Field poll of a sample of all California adults, nearly identical majorities of between 56 and 60 percent favored 100 and 103, while 36 percent favored 101 (and almost as many opposed it); Proposition 104 was the only measure with a plurality against it (40 percent, with 31 percent favor). By the week before the election, a poll of registered voters found that the campaign had really filtered reactions. Almost all respondents had heard of the insurance propositions in general, but considerably fewer were aware of the individual initiatives. Of those who said they had heard of each measure, only 27 percent were now planning to vote for Proposition 100, a measly 10 percent would vote for 101, 42 percent planned to vote for Proposition 103 (but nearly as many, 39 percent were opposed), and 56 percent were opposed to Proposition 104. Animosity toward the insurance companies was sufficiently strong that the trial lawyers didn't look so bad. Support in the polls for Proposition 106 steadily declined, from 78 percent in July to 48 percent on the eve of the election.[154]

As the dollar figures in Table 5.9 suggest, this was a campaign with a great deal of coverage. Television and radio were saturated, billboards were posted across the state, and direct mail advertising was extensive.[155] The spending patterns and results are noteworthy. The attorneys were very much in favor of Proposition 100 because it would not affect tort lawsuits; indeed, they raised more money to support Proposition 100 than they did to fight Proposition 106. However, as the table indicates, there was a lot of "crossover" spending in this campaign, with fund-raising entities using their money for or against more than one proposition, albeit not always officially. The insurance companies were more than active, raising large sums against Propositions 100 and 103, and in favor 104 and 106. The $56 million figure for spending in favor of Proposition 104 is not a misprint.

Curiously, the one measure that passed was the least well funded. Harvey Rosenfield was the John R. Haynes or Howard Jarvis of Proposition 103, and he put together an impressive grassroots coalition that brought success.[156] The supporters of Proposition 103 spent about 62¢ per vote, whereas the insurance companies spent almost $24 per vote for Proposition 104, plus another $15 million to oppose Propositions 100 and 103. For the insurance industry, it was not a particularly good year, which demonstrates yet again that money often fails to achieve victory in initiative campaigns.

An almost equally confusing situation emerged two years later, when there were five environmental measures on the 1990 general election ballot. Once again, there were several crossover situations with committees supporting or opposing more than one of the measures. And a couple of the contests involved big money, especially the so-called "Big Green" (Proposition 128), a multifaceted environmental measure, whose proponents spent $7 million and opponents $22 million.[157] All of them lost, except for Proposition 132, a modest and modestly funded marine resources measure that banned gill nets.

The Fair Political Practices Commission published specific expenditure data for the 1988 general election, which can be analyzed to see how campaign money was being distributed by campaign committees. Table 5.10 provides percentage data for a number of the campaign committees in this election. Several things stand out. First, not all committees chose to spend their money in the same way; there are interesting variations in the approaches taken. Second, one can nonetheless see the importance that broadcast media (especially television) had come to play by this time. All but the smallest committee spent considerable parts, sometimes the lion's share, of their budgets on broadcast media (Citizens for No Fault spent $2.6 million on radio and television in Los Angeles alone). And third, professional management continued to be critical to campaign committees.[158]

This was a period when direct legislation became, if anything, more central than ever before in making or breaking basic law for the state of California. The number of initiatives was rising; the money involved rivaled and sometimes exceeded the excessive sums being applied to candidate nominations and elections; and the power of organized money, particularly in defeating propositions, was clearly felt. Yet, the voting public still could not be taken for granted, and the auto insurance propositions of 1988 are but one striking example of that fact. Often, it seems, the voters were not entirely

TABLE 5.9 1988 General Election Battle Between Insurance Companies and Trial Attorneys

| Prop. No. and Topic | Content | Supporters | Opponents | Total spending For | Total spending Against | Percentage Voting Yes |
|---|---|---|---|---|---|---|
| Prop. 100 Auto insurance | 20 percent decrease in rates for good drivers; must insure all good drivers; minimum 20 percent good-driver differential | Attorneys, Mothers Against Drunk Driving, Atty. Gen. John Van de Kamp, Congress of California Seniors | California Farm Federation, state senator Ed Davis; insurance companies | $16.5 million (California Trial Lawyers PAC — $3.8 million; Bankers for Responsible Government — $776,000; Chiropractors PACs — $836,000; hundreds of law firms) | $15 million[a] (Citizens for No Fault Sponsored by California Insurers — $13.3 million; several dozen individual insurance companies and agencies) | 41 |
| Prop. 101 Auto insurance | Bodily injury and uninsured motorist rates cut 50 percent; recovery for non-economic losses limited to 25 percent of economic loss; attorney's contingency fees limited to 25 percent of economic losses | Members of state legislature, insurance companies | Common Cause, Atty. Gen. John Van de Kamp, Consumers Union | $5.5 million (Advent Co. — $4 million; Coastal Insurance Management — $1.1 million) | $50,000[b] | 13 |

| Proposition | Provisions | Proponents | Opponents | Money for | Money against | % Yes |
|---|---|---|---|---|---|---|
| Prop. 103 Auto insurance | 20 percent decrease in auto and property/casualty insurance; new elected Insurance Commissioner who must approve rate changes; premiums to be based primarily on driving record | Ralph Nader, Voter Revolt to Cut Insurance Rates (Harvey Rosenfield, Chair) | Calif. Chamber of Commerce, state sen. Ed Davis, insurance companies | $3 million | Same as Prop. 100 | 51 |
| Prop. 104 Auto insurance | No-fault insurance for injuries; no recovery for noneconomic injuries; rates for some coverages decreased 20 percent; cancels Propositions 100, 101, and 103 | Presidents of California and southern California Auto Clubs, Diane Feinstein, insurance companies | Ralph Nader, Harvey Rosenfield, Common Cause | $55.9 million[c] (Aetna — $1.3 million; Allstate — $4.3 million; State Farm — $7.3 million; Wells Fargo & Co. — $9.4 million, etc.) | $27,000[d] | 25 |
| Prop. 106 Attorney fees | Limits contingency fees in tort claims; 25 percent for first $50,000, then declining | Insurance companies | Ralph Nader, Tom Bradley, Common Cause, attorney groups | $3.69 million (all from insurance industry) | $1.19 million (hundreds of law firms) | 47 |

SOURCE: *California Ballot Pamphlet* and Campaign Statement Summaries, 1988 General Election.

[a] This money was used against both Propositions 100 and 103.

[b] One-half of this amount was combined with a donation in support of Proposition 100.

[c] Some of this money was used in the campaigns against Propositions 100, 101, and 103.

[d] $6,000 is also part of support of Proposition 100; $20,000 is part of opposition to Proposition 101.

TABLE 5.10  Percentage Distributions of Campaign Expenditures by Selected Campaign Committees, 1988 General Election (percentage of total expenditures)

| Campaign Committee/ Total expenditure | Broadcast advertising | General operations | Newspaper and periodical | Outdoor advertising | Literature | Professional management |
|---|---|---|---|---|---|---|
| All propositions, 78–106 $124 million[a] | 35 | 4.0 | 1 | 3 | 9 | 21 |
| "Good Driver" Initiative [Yes on 100] $12.8 million | 44 | 18.0 | <1 | 8 | 18 | 12 |
| Californians Against Unfair Tax Increases [No on 99] $17 million | 49 | 0.8 | <1 | <1 | <4 | 37 |
| Citizens for No Fault [No on 100, Yes on 104] $36 million | 27 | 4.0 | 1 | 3 | 2 | 40 |

| | | | | | | |
|---|---|---|---|---|---|---|
| Californians Working Together . . . [Yes on 95] $261,000 | 1 | 50.0 | 0 | 10 | 0 | 6 | 65 |
| Citizens Against 95 $1.4 million | 84 | 1.0 | 9 | <1 | 9 | 8 | 0 |
| School Funding for Instructional Improvement [Yes on 98] $3.7 million | 56 | 3.5 | <1 | 2 | <1 | 30 | 3 |
| Consumers for Lower Auto Insurance Rates [Yes on 101] $43.6 million | 72 | 3.7 | 0 | 6 | 0 | 10 | 5 |

SOURCE: Campaign Statement Summaries, 1988 general election.

NOTE: For committees supporting propositions, this table includes only the money spent after the qualification period. Not all possible expenditure categories are included.

[a]Includes funds for both legislative and popular measures.

clear on what they were voting for, but many of them nonetheless remained consistent in their positions on general areas of California's political life.

More and more of the key issues of the time — taxation, crime, California's future as a multiethnic society — were being decided by this quasi-legislative process. Whether the law being created was good or bad was very much in the eye of the beholder.

# 6   Not Quite History, but More of the Same, 1996 and Beyond

The 1996 election year was almost an ideal type so far as modern direct legislation in California is concerned. There were many initiatives, five in the June primary and twelve in the November general election. The legislature contributed ten more propositions, four of which were modifications of earlier popular initiatives. There were initiatives rivaling one another, in the cases of healthcare, campaign reform, and, of course, attorneys and insurance companies, which meant that old issues were being revisited. Real sociocultural conflict was involved, as was the "spirit of Proposition 13." Once again, then — old questions and new ones, lots of big dollars being spent, voter confusion until late in the campaign, and then large-scale voter participation.

Looking at these proposition campaigns in detail can serve as a guide to the present and likely future status of direct legislation in California. And that status can be made even clearer with a close look at how Californians view the direct legislation process after almost a century of experience.

The 1996 elections accelerated a recent trend in initiative campaigns: the creation of campaign committees to support and/or oppose a number of ballot propositions rather than just one. One impressive example in 1996 was the clumsily named "Taxpayers Against Frivolous Lawsuits, No on Proposition 211, A Coalition of Seniors, Small Business, Taxpayers, High Technology, and Financial Services Companies and Associates (and oppose Propositions 207, 208, 210, 212, 214, 216, 217 and support Propositions 192, 200, 201, 202, 203 and 204)." The propositions involved spanned both the primary and general elections, included both popular initiatives and legislative propositions, and covered topics as varied as bonds for seismic retrofitting, auto insurance, attorney's fees, public education, healthcare, and the minimum wage. The campaign committee's bankroll was almost as large as its name — $40 million. There may in fact have been some sense of common interest for campaign committees involving themselves in such a panoply of propositions, but it was also a way for individuals or groups to disguise exactly what they were contributing to. Moreover, despite the official report title, such a combined effort can mask the fact that almost all of the money might actually be used for only one or two propositions.[1]

The 1996 elections witnessed the highest spending in California initiative history. The total $141 million spent on the 27 propositions in 1996 was more than three times the $47 million spent on 19 measures in 1994, and well above the $97 million spent on 31 propositions in 1990.[2] On a comparative basis, that comes to $5.2 million per proposition in 1996, $2.4 million per proposition in 1994, and $3.1 million per proposition in 1990. Because of these multi-proposition committees, supporting some measures and opposing others, it is difficult, and for some propositions impossible, to reach any conclusions about the extent to which money was successful in passing or defeating individual measures, although this will be analyzed below.

Another interesting innovation in 1996, albeit less important, was the first use of the Internet by campaign committees. The *California Ballot Pamphlet* for both the primary and the general election contained summaries of the measures, accompanied by information about "Whom to Contact for More Information" for and against each proposition. In addition to mailing addresses and telephone numbers, World Wide Web sites (URLs) were given for sixteen groups; these sites were also listed by the press shortly before the election.[3] It appears that the sites were primarily accessed by campaign workers and others who were already committed to each site's position, rather than serving as important sources of information for the general public.[4] But the use of the Internet opened a potentially powerful new avenue for political campaigns.

As usual, initiatives representing sociocultural conflict were among the most controversial, and none more so than Proposition 209 in the 1996 general election, an initiative constitutional amendment to end affirmative action programs in the state.[5] This measure reflected a growing national debate of the 1990s, with numerous groups, particularly conservative Republicans, demanding the eradication of affirmative action programs at all levels of government. Ward Connerly, a conservative African-American businessman on the University of California Board of Regents, had been railing against affirmative action for years. He was joined in writing the "pro" argument for the *California Ballot Pamphlet* by Governor Pete Wilson, who continued his use of propositions to improve his position among Republican conservatives, and by Attorney General Dan Lungren, a long-time leader of conservative Republicans who was aiming for the governorship in 1998.

Acrimonious argument and legal battle surrounded the proposition from the start. Proponents had originally tried to title the measure the "Civil

Rights Initiative," but when that was disallowed, they settled for "Prohibition Against Discrimination or Preferential Treatment by State and Other Public Entities." Opponents went to court to try to force use of the words "affirmative action" into the ballot language; they won at first, but the state Appeals Court overturned a lower court decision and those words did not appear. This ruling definitely helped the opponents of affirmative action; it also epitomized the legal wrangling that has become such an integral part of the direct legislation process.[6]

There was considerable money involved in the campaign, and this was one proposition whose financing was not mixed with that of other initiatives. Supporters raised over $5 million, with 20 percent of that coming from the California Republican Party. Other large contributions came from conservative individuals such as Richard M. Scaife ($100,000), publisher of the Tribune-Review Publishing Co. and one of the leading national contributors to conservative causes. Opponents were also well funded, with about the same amount of money in their campaign chest, which came from twenty separate campaign committees, large and small. Major support came from the California Teachers Association ($560,000), the Democratic Party ($375,000), and the Feminist Majority Foundation ($185,000).[7] In financing, as in other kinds of support, it was very much a conservative-versus-liberal campaign.

Governor Wilson and other leaders of the Proposition 209 campaign were surprised by the lack of big business support. But the fact was that major California employers had implemented their own affirmative action programs, many of which had worked reasonably well, and they were not interested in the possibility of violating federal government regulations. As a result, business groups did not play a significant pro-209 role, but they did respond to pressure from Wilson and Connerly not to oppose the initiative.[8] State Republican leaders were also disappointed in the silence of Republican presidential and vice-presidential candidates Robert Dole and Jack Kemp, who at first avoided taking a stand on the issue in a state where the decision on the presidential vote could be very close. Toward the end of the campaign, however, watching the polls and determining that he needed California to win the presidency, candidate Dole spent some extra days in the state and spoke out very forcefully for Proposition 209. This was a reversal of his historic position on affirmative action, but he had concluded it was essential to his carrying the state, and so he echoed proponents' ideas that the initiative would "reject racial prejudice" and was representative of "America's best principles." For good measure, he also endorsed the desire to "secure our borders" against illegal immigration.[9] The main publicity in the campaign for Proposition 209, in fact, came from political candidates who continued the tradition of using an initiative as a campaign issue.

Opponents of Proposition 209 stressed the "racism" angle. Students at California State University, Northridge, for example, set up a debate on the initiative, getting David Duke, the ex–Ku Klux Klansman and frequent political candidate from Louisiana, to appear as speaker on the Yes side. This led to a considerable hue and cry, with Proposition 209 backers decrying the association of their side with prejudice, but the anti-209 forces continued to portray David Duke as a symbol of the proposition.[10]

Throughout the campaign, public opinion polls showed a fairly consistent majority in favor of Proposition 209.[11] Table 6.1 looks at some characteristics of the support and opposition to the measure. The data are not particularly surprising but nonetheless significant. Among voters, as among politicians and activists, there was a conservative–liberal split. Clinton supporters, Democrats, and liberals all wanted to preserve affirmative action, with ideology the strongest of these three interconnected variables. Protestants were decisively in favor of Proposition 209, with Roman Catholics in the middle, and Jews slightly on the other side. Among African-Americans and Hispanics, the two groups who would be most affected by this issue, there were strong majorities, almost two-thirds, against Proposition 209, which meant, however, that one-third of each group was willing to see affirmative action end. Interestingly, income (not shown in the table) had no significant effect on respondents' attitudes toward affirmative action, but general economic outlook did. The less optimistic one's view of the economy, the more one was prone to support ending affirmative action programs, presumably because these were working-class people who felt their jobs most directly threatened by affirmative action.

Proposition 209 tied for the highest voter participation rate (94 percent) of all 27 measures on the March and September ballots, continuing the long tradition of sociocultural issues being consistently the most involving of all direct legislation. In the pre-election Field poll, 86 percent of respondents said they were aware of the issue, another strong indication of the public's interest. The 55–45 percent outcome was decisive but not overwhelming; some Californians were not sure what was right or wrong in an issue so often portrayed in strong moral terms, and in ambivalent economic terms. But the coefficient of correlation between the vote on this proposition and that on 1994's Proposition 187 (denial of social services to illegal aliens) was an extremely strong .889. This suggests, once again, that Californians tended to vote quite consistently in matters where general ideology and sociocultural content were involved.

Not surprisingly, Proposition 209 was immediately embroiled in litigation. A federal civil rights suit was filed one day after the election on behalf of female and minority contractors, labor unions, and students. Shortly thereafter, Governor Wilson filed papers asking that the suit be put on hold

TABLE 6.1    Public Opinion on Proposition 209 (Affirmative Action), 1996 General Election

| | Percentage that would vote Yes on Prop. 209 | Percentage that would vote No on Prop. 209 |
|---|---|---|
| Presidential choice: | | |
| Clinton | 37 | 63 |
| Dole | 84 | 16 |
| Perot | 66 | 34 |
| Party identification | | |
| Democrat | 37 | 63 |
| Republican | 80 | 20 |
| Independent | 59 | 41 |
| Political ideology | | |
| Conservative | 80 | 21 |
| Liberal | 23 | 77 |
| Middle-of-the-road | 53 | 47 |
| Religion | | |
| Protestant | 64 | 36 |
| Roman Catholic | 55 | 45 |
| Jewish | 47 | 54 |
| Race/ethnicity | | |
| White | 64 | 36 |
| African-American | 37 | 63 |
| Hispanic | 35 | 65 |
| Opinion — condition of California economy | | |
| Good | 50 | 50 |
| Not so good | 62 | 38 |
| Poor | 65 | 35 |

SOURCE:  Based on Field Institute poll fi9607 (29 October–3 November 1996). One hundred forty-five of the 1,082 responses that were neither Yes nor No on Prop. 209 are not included. Not all possible answers on background variables are included.

so that the state courts could rule on it first. But a federal district court judge did issue a temporary restraining order against Wilson and Lungren in late November, blocking enforcement because of the "strong probability" that the initiative was unconstitutional. By the end of 1996, the restraining order had been replaced by a preliminary injunction, and the Clinton administration had joined the case against Proposition 209. While this dispute continued into 1997, the initiative was not enforced. But in April 1997 a federal appeals court overturned the lower-court decision, ruling that Proposition 209 was constitutional, and in November 1997 the Supreme Court refused to reverse that decision.[12] Thus, Proposition 209 became valid law one year after its passage. Its effects began to be felt in 1998, most notably in a drastic decline in the number of minority students accepted by the University of California for the 1998–1999 academic year.

If the success of Proposition 209 can be interpreted as evidence of conservative success in 1996, the success of Proposition 215, for the legalization of marijuana, is possibly its opposite. That issue had been raised before, in Proposition 19 of 1972, when the public overwhelmingly rejected such legalization. The issue rose again for classic initiative reasons: the state legislature had twice passed legislation for the legalization of marijuana for strictly medical uses for seriously ill people, but Governor Wilson had vetoed both bills. And, as in other cases, unsuccessful moderate legislation was replaced on the ballot by an anything-but-moderate initiative solution. Proposition 215 would permit the growing or possession of marijuana by an individual or his or her "caregiver," if recommended by a physician, for a number of specified illnesses and "any other illness for which marijuana provides relief." The physician's "recommendation" was just that—not a prescription, and it could be "oral or written."[13]

Proposition 215 was, in fact, a radical legalization of marijuana in terms so broad that a headache or anything else might justify its use. It was also quite clearly a violation of federal law. But the public simply did not see it in those terms, partially because there were some legitimate medical personnel favoring it, and also because the pro-215 forces conducted a media blitz with expenditures of $2.2 million, while their opponents raised only $34,000.[14] Television commercials showing "medical marijuana" places shutting down to the dismay of cancer and other sufferers seem to have worked.[15]

Public awareness of the initiative, if not of its specifics, definitely grew as the campaign progressed, and from the start it appeared that a majority favored it.[16] This measure drew a voter participation rate of 92 percent, of whom 56 percent voted Yes. It was immediately plunged into litigation, and in early 1998 the U.S. Supreme Court upheld a lower-court decision that pared away much of the initiative's breadth.[17] It was an example of a proposition that had no real chance of implementation because it was so obviously in violation of federal law; such realities have often failed to deter enthusiasts in the area of direct legislation.

It is interesting to note that the coefficient of correlation between voting for Proposition 209 and voting for Proposition 215 was negative and very strong (-.771). Affirmative action and marijuana legalization appealed to quite different ideological constituencies, each of which managed to eke out virtually identical winning majorities.[18]

The great profits conflict between insurance companies and other business groups, on the one hand, and trial lawyers on the other, that began with the conflicting measures in the 1988 general election, exploded again in 1996. There were six propositions on the ballot, three in the March primary (California had switched from its regular June primary to a March primary in 1996, in order to increase its influence in the presidential selection process) and three in the November general election. Table 6.2 presents summary data on each, in order to make some sense out of this mass of initiatives that presented voters with difficult and confusing choices. In one way, at least, these measures have a certain symmetry: Propositions 200, 201, and 202 were in the spring primary, and were all efforts by the insurance industry and numerous other businesses to stifle the lawyers. All of them failed. Propositions 207 and 211, in the fall general election, represented the attorneys seeking revenge and a defense of their traditional practices. They failed, too. And Proposition 213 was different — an insurance company measure that appealed to the public's disdain for drunks and felons; it passed.

After the acrimonious election of 1988, a truce of sorts had been worked out between organized business groups and the trial lawyers. But it had broken down in 1992, leading to new "tort reform" bills in the state Assembly, and now to the rival initiatives of 1996.[19] Beyond that, however, was the increasing role of consultants. They had slowly moved from serving as advisers on initiatives to becoming actual instigators, creating initiative or initiative-opposition organizations, and then searching out sponsors, to get business for themselves. This played some part in the new activism of Silicon Valley's high-tech firms in the anti-lawyer Propositions 200, 201, and 202 in this campaign.[20]

The money trail, as noted above, was as difficult to follow as it was wide and deep, with the major campaign organizations officially devoted to numerous measures, some of which were of only tangential interest to them. There was also some passing of money back and forth between campaign committees, which confused the issue even more. One group of attorneys did specifically focus on opposing Proposition 200, to the tune of $800,000. Likewise, one independent business and insurance committee raised $917,000 against Proposition 207, and a group comprised solely of

TABLE 6.2 Insurance and Attorney Fee Propositions, 1996 Primary and General Elections

| Proposition | Main supporters | | Main opponents | | Outcome |
|---|---|---|---|---|---|
| | | Arguments | | Arguments | |
| Prop. 200: Statute. No fault auto insurance for personal injury. No lawsuits for personal injuries except in case of drunk driver or person committing or fleeing a felony. | Insurance companies, securities firms, high tech and other corporations | Along with Props. 201 and 202, will bring "unscrupulous lawyers" and runaway lawsuits under control | Attorneys, Consumers Union, Harvey Rosenfield | Will cheat consumers; insurance companies will decide on rates, penalize good drivers | Defeated (65% No) |
| Prop. 201: Statute. Limits attorneys' fees, loser pays winner's attorney fees and expenses in shareholder actions and class actions on securities law; court can require losing attorneys to pay. | Insurance companies, securities firms, high tech and other corporations | End frivolous lawsuits by unscrupulous attorneys | Attorneys, Consumers Union | Protects "stock swindlers"; makes lawsuits against companies that defraud almost impossible; financed by high tech firms to protect selves | Defeated (59% No) |
| Prop. 202: Statute. Limits attorneys' contingent fees in personal injury and other tort actions to no more than 15 percent if settled out of court; if litigated, fees for amount up to opponents' offer also limited to 15 percent. | Insurance companies, securities firms, high tech and other corporations | Eliminates "phony" and frivolous lawsuits; more cases will be settled out of court; attorney fees are excessive | Attorneys, Harvey Rosenfield | Combined with Prop. 201 to threaten pension and retirement savings; makes it harder for ordinary people to sue when cheated | Defeated (51% No) |

| Proposition | Supporters / Argument | Opponents / Argument | Result |
|---|---|---|---|
| Prop. 207: Statute. Defends attorney contingency fees and negotiation of fees; no "excessive or unconscionable" fees. | Attorneys<br>. . . . . . . . . . . .<br>Contingency fees let ordinary people fight corporations and insurance companies | Many business groups—high tech, banks, business services, securities, insurance companies<br>. . . . . . . . . . . .<br>This is a smokescreen to defend excessive attorney fees. | Defeated (66% No) |
| Prop. 211: Statute. No new restrictions on attorney-client fee arrangements; new regulations and penalties for bad conduct in securities transactions, including authorization of class actions, punitive damages. This initiative should be considered in conflict with others that may be on the same ballot dealing with similar issues. | Attorneys<br>. . . . . . . . . . . .<br>Defends senior citizens, young families, and others from securities fraud; prevents frivolous lawsuits | California Chamber of Commerce, California Taxpayers Association, securities dealers<br>. . . . . . . . . . . .<br>Californians are already protected against securities fraud; this measure is not needed; exists only to enrich "opportunistic" lawyers | Defeated (74% No) |
| Prop. 213: Statute. Denies recovery in automobile accidents to a felon in process of committing a felony or fleeing therefrom; denies noneconomic damage recovery to drunk drivers and uninsured motorists. | Insurance companies; Chuck Quackenbush, California Insurance Commissioner<br>. . . . . . . . . . . .<br>Law-abiding citizens are paying while criminals are being rewarded | Harvey Rosenfield<br>. . . . . . . . . . . .<br>This is another part of insurance industry effort to get no-fault insurance; it protects insured reckless drivers and saves money for insurance companies; Quackenbush's campaign for Insurance Commissioner was financed by insurance companies | Approved (77% Yes) |

SOURCE: Information based on *California Ballot Pamphlet*, 1996 primary and general elections; Campaign Statement Summaries, 1996 primary and general elections.

TABLE 6.3  Correlations of Voting on Insurance and Attorney Fee Propositions, 1996 Primary and General Elections

| | Prop. 200: No-fault | Prop 201: Limit attorney fees | Prop. 202: Limit attorney fees | Prop. 207: Maintain attorney fees | Prop. 211: Maintain attorney fees | Prop. 213: Felonious and drunk drivers |
|---|---|---|---|---|---|---|
| Prop. 200: No-fault | 1.000 | | | | | |
| Prop 201: Limit attorney fees | .921 | 1.000 | | | | |
| Prop. 202: Limit Attorney fees | .916 | .976 | 1.000 | | | |
| Prop. 207 Maintain attorney fees | −.248 | −.247 | −.211 | 1.000 | | |
| Prop. 211: Maintain attorney fees | −.170 | −.194 | −.247 | .255 | 1.000 | |
| Prop. 213: Felonious and drunk drivers | .803 | .903 | .937 | −.238 | −.268 | 1.000 |

NOTE: Pearson product moment correlations, based on percentage voting Yes on proposition, with data aggregated by county and weighted by county population. For clarity, only one-half of table is shown, since the two halves are identical.

securities dealers raised $2.8 million just to defeat Proposition 211. But there is no question that the big money was in the combination groups that supported Propositions 200/201/202 and opposed Propositions 207/211, or vice versa. This included about $62 million raised for the Pro-200/201/202 and Anti-207/211 group, and about $26 million for their opponents.[21]

Proposition 211 was the most threatening to its opponents, and also had the most opponents. A *Los Angeles Times* editorial railed against it as license for frivolous lawsuits because of the breadth and generality of its language. The advertising campaign against it was also huge, boasting, among other things, the support of both Robert Dole and Bill Clinton. A *Times* reporter concluded that over $40 million had been spent by the two sides on this proposition alone.[22] This could be considered organized business's greatest success, since Proposition 211 lost by a larger margin than any of the five unsuccessful measures.

Taking the largest vote on any of these measures (9.4 million) and the total of about $91 million spent on these campaigns, one ends up with approximately $9.67 per vote for five initiatives that failed at the polls. It was an expensive draw.

Voter confusion was inevitable with measures like these, and responses to one public opinion poll are illustrative. In early September, registered voters who said they had heard of Proposition 207 "having to do with attorneys fees and the right to negotiate frivolous lawsuits" were twice as likely to say they planned to vote No than Yes. But when the pollster went on with an explanation (" . . . it would prohibit restrictions on the right to negotiate the amount of attorneys' fees. It prohibits attorneys from charging excessive fees and authorizes courts to impose sanctions for filing frivolous lawsuits or pleading."), the response was reversed, with almost twice as many Yes as No responses. A reversal almost as great occurred when the same was done with Proposition 211. As the campaign went on, however, the publicity on all of these measures had its effect, and the No votes became much more definite.[23] What all the money ended up doing for each side was to expand voter interest (the voter participation rate on each of them was above 90 percent) and to virtually guarantee that the proponents did not win.

Proposition 213 was somewhat different, as noted, despite the fact that it was entirely created and backed by insurance companies (to the tune of $3.3 million), with opposition led by attorneys. The public focused on the idea of preventing drunks and felons from profiting from accidents, even though what excited the insurance companies was the uninsured driver provision, which would save them a lot of money.[24] To many voters, Proposition 213 continued the trend of anti-crime legislation and merited support for that reason.

The relationships in voting for these six initiatives are shown in Table 6.3.

Correlations among the vote on the three anti-attorney Propositions 200, 201, and 202 were extremely high, as one might expect. Interestingly, all three of these votes also related very strongly to that on Proposition 213, which almost everyone ended up supporting. Despite the fact that the first three were beaten, while Proposition 213 was overwhelmingly successful, the pattern of the vote for all four measures across the 58 California counties was consistent (the better each of the first three propositions fared, the higher its correlation with Proposition 213). One thing that Propositions 200, 202, and 213 had in common was opposition from Harvey Rosenfield, the author of the first successful insurance rate reform (Prop. 103) in 1988. He had since become a kind of full-time consumer rights advocate in the initiative business, and had fairly wide support.

Voting on Propositions 207 and 211 did not have the expected negative relationships with the above four initiatives; indeed, the two attorney-sponsored initiatives did not even have a significant relationship with one another. The vote for 207 and 211 did not rise where that for 200–201–202 fell, or vice-versa. Despite the commonalty of their financing, Propositions 207 and 211 appear not to have been tightly linked in the minds of most voters.[25] There was no reason, with all of this, for the public not to be confused.

There were several economic issues apart from insurance and attorneys in 1996, including a continuation of the now long-term Jarvis–Gann efforts to tighten every possible loophole in Proposition 13. Richard Gann, head of his father's Paul Gann's Citizens Committee, and Joel Fox, head of the Howard Jarvis Taxpayers Association, constantly monitored any government practices that potentially undercut the tax-limiting effects of Proposition 13 and its successors. In 1996 they focused on local government taxes and fees.

Proposition 62 of 1986 had been one effort to protect and expand Proposition 13, by requiring a two-thirds vote by the public for new special taxes, and a two-thirds vote by the respective legislative body plus majority public endorsement for new general taxes. But for almost ten years that law had been tied up in the courts. It was finally ruled constitutional in 1995, but to the Jarvis and Gann forces, that was not enough: local governmental agencies were getting around limitations on taxation by using "fees" rather than taxes. Proposition 218 in the 1996 general election sought to firm up these controls and put them in the state constitution. It reiterated the principles of Proposition 62 (a statute), and extended them to local government "fees" (e.g., for trash collection, sewer maintenance, etc.) as well. It was also designed to be retroactive in part to the previous year, and would, for example, require a vote on a 1995 Los Angeles County increase in hotel and business license taxes. It also, uniquely, would require that any property-based new fees or increases be submitted to a mail vote by property owners only, whose ballots would be weighted by the amount of their assessments. Thus, the owner of an expensive home would have a vote that counted more than the owner of a lower-priced one, and the owners of highly assessed business property would have a vote that counted even more.[26] Proposition 218 would definitely eliminate a key way that local agencies had gotten partially around the Proposition 13 limits on raising needed revenue.

The Jarvis organization, especially, continued to have considerable appeal: it raised $3.1 million of the total $3.6 million spent by the pro-218 forces. Unlike the big companies involved in the six insurance/attorney battles, the great majority of these funds came in donations of less than $10,000. The opposition was led by the California Teachers Association and other public employee groups, but raised only $873,000, almost all of it in contributions above $10,000.[27] In a way, then, the Jarvis and Gann forces, and the idea of limiting all governments' ability to raise taxes, continued to have strength with a broad spectrum of the middle class. In a late October poll, for example, the strongest supporters of Proposition 218 were those with either a high school or some college education; those with more or less education had majorities against the initiative. However, only about one-third of respondents were even aware of Proposition 218, so many minds were not made up until the very last days of the campaign.[28]

Proposition 218 passed with 57 percent of the total vote, and it had the effect its authors sought. In the 1997 spring election, for example, there were at least six special taxes (on utilities, hotels, etc.) on the ballots of communities in the greater Los Angeles area that received majority, but less than two-thirds, endorsements from the voters, and were thus defeated.[29]

Another controversial tax-related measure in the 1996 general election was Proposition 217. It, too, related to Proposition 13, in that it was an effort to compensate for the decline in property tax revenues, especially for schools. The initiative statute would have reinstated the higher, temporary 10 percent and 11 percent income tax brackets on the highest earners in the state that had been instituted in 1991 and had expired in 1995. The revenue would be divided between schools and local governments. Proponents, including the League of Women Voters, various public employee unions, and the liberal California Tax Reform Association argued that failure to pass the measure would give a tax break to the wealthiest Californians, and that it would not be a tax increase but the retention of a system that had been in place and was needed to compensate for the channeling of property tax revenues from local government to the state. The opposition, led by the State Chamber of Commerce, other business groups, and the conservative California Taxpayers Association, said that California did not need new taxes, that small business would suffer the most from the proposed statute, and that there was every reason to expect that bureaucrats and politicians would swallow most of the money.[30]

There was no small money involved in this dispute, either. Supporters raised $3.2 million, two-thirds of which came from the California Teachers Association, and the rest from other public employee unions and the campaign bankrolls of several Los Angeles Democratic politicians. The opposition had almost the same amount of money, chiefly from a PAC led by the California Chamber of Commerce ($635,000) and $1.8 million from "Taxpayers Against Frivolous Lawsuits," the anti-Proposition 211 campaign committee that had collected $40 million and obviously had some to spare.[31]

Despite the considerable tax dollars involved, the initiative did not get a lot of attention. The Field Institute, for example, never asked about it in any of its 1996 California Polls, whereas most other propositions were included. Voter participation on the measure was high, however, at 91 percent, and it lost very narrowly, 49 percent to 51 percent.

While the vote against keeping the higher tax rate on California's largest earners can be considered a conservative victory, that on Proposition 210 to raise the minimum wage definitely was not. This initiative statute proposed to raise the minimum wage in all industries from the then-current California and federal rate of $4.25 per hour to $5.00 per hour in 1997 and $5.75 in 1998. The 1998 minimum would put California ahead of the new federal minimum of $5.15, which had just passed Congress and was waiting for the president's signature. The debate that followed was the same one always found with minimum-wage proposals: on the pro side, many workers needed the higher wage desperately and it would benefit the economy; on the con side, small businesses could not afford the increase and it would put people out of work. Proponents included the California Council of Churches, the Congress of California Seniors, numerous unions, and a smattering of liberal academics. On the other side were small businesses and their organizations, plus conservative economists like Milton Friedman. Each side, in fact, had its own Nobel Laureate in Economics, keeping the intellectual ground even.[32]

Proponents managed to raise $1.6 million, almost all of it from individual labor unions and the California Labor Federation, AFL-CIO. Opponents raised $1.1 million, from fast-food companies, restaurants, hotels, car wash companies, and other employers of minimum-wage workers.[33] Proposition 210 tied for the highest number of voters of all fifteen propositions on the 1996 general election ballot with a 94 percent voter participation rate, and won easily with 61 percent of the vote.

In considering Propositions 210, 217, and 218, it seems that California voters continued to be very leery of anything that might raise their taxes, even the taxes of people much richer than themselves. But this did not mean that a majority of voters were for or against business or labor; indeed, this election shows some economic sympathy for both the rich and the poor. Table 6.4 sheds some interesting light on the role of ideology, however.

TABLE 6.4   Correlations of Voting on Three Economic Initiatives, 1996 General Election

|  | Prop. 210: Increase minimum wage | Prop. 217: Reinstate tax on top income brackets | Prop. 218: Voter approval for local tax and fee increases |
|---|---|---|---|
| Prop. 210: Increase minimum wage | 1.000 | | |
| Prop. 217: Reinstate tax on top income brackets | .933 | 1.000 | |
| Prop. 218: Voter approval required for local tax and fee increases | −.876 | −.791 | 1.000 |

NOTE: Pearson product moment correlations, based on percentage voting Yes on propositions, with data aggregated by county and weighted by county population. For clarity, only one-half of table is shown, since the two halves are identical.

While Proposition 210 won and Proposition 217 lost, both measures clearly appealed to the same voters, albeit with varying intensity; the positive correlation of .933 is extremely high. Conversely, the Jarvis–Gann Proposition 218 to impede the ability of local governments to raise taxes or fees has almost as strong negative correlations with both of these initiatives. Its appeal was to a different set of voters and to conservative principles, whereas Propositions 210 and 217 were essentially liberal. Once more, consistency of ideological position among many California voters appears quite strong.

The 1996 primary election included what may prove to be the most radical political change in modern California history. This was Proposition 198, the "open primary" initiative statute. Until 1959, California had permitted "cross-filing," wherein an individual candidate could have his or her name placed on the primary ballots of more than one party; thus, popular Governor Earl Warren was nominated by both the Republican and Democratic parties when he ran for reelection. But even then, only voters registered in a given party could vote in its primary election. After cross-filing ended, California's primary system resembled that of most other states, but its anti-party tradition never died, and the controversies over campaign financing and "special interests" heightened these sentiments in the 1980s and 1990s.

Proposition 198 offered what has more accurately been called a "blanket primary." Generally, in an "open primary," the voter chooses which party's ballot (Democratic or Republican or any other) he or she wants to mark; no prior party registration is required. But Proposition 198 went well beyond that: it set up a system of only one ballot, with the names of all candidates and their party affiliations mixed randomly under the office they were competing for. Thus, a voter could, in effect, participate in the Republican primary for governor, the Democratic primary for Attorney General, and so on — selecting any candidate he or she wanted for each office on the ballot.[34] This was a truly radical approach, and one that endangered the political parties considerably more than even a traditional open primary would. Not surprisingly, the heads of both major parties signed the ballot argument against this proposition.

The initiative was popular from the start and involved, for the time, relatively little money. Supporters raised just under $1 million, with over $400,000 of that coming from William R. Hewlett, David Packard, and the Hewlett Packard Company, interrelated and longtime contributors to Republican and conservative causes. The opposition, despite the potentially dire consequences of Proposition 198's passage for party integrity, raised just under $100,000, all of it from just two sources: the California Republican Party and conservative press baron Rupert Murdoch.[35] The Democrats seem to have shied away from outspoken opposition because they realized from the start that the proposition would pass.

A public opinion poll one month before the election found that 58 percent of voters were not familiar with the proposition. However, once it was explained to them, all demographic groups responded favorably. There was little difference across party or ideological lines, although, logically, those who defined themselves as ideologically "middle-of-the-road" or as "independent" in terms of party were even more in favor of Proposition 198 (70–80 percent Yes) than those with some party and/or ideological commitment (over 60 percent Yes). The respondents' ages also made little difference. Support for the initiative did decline as level of education rose (from 72 percent for those with less than a high school education to 63 percent for college graduates and 59 percent for those with a post-baccalaureate education), and as income rose (from 81 percent for incomes under $20,000 down to 56 percent for incomes above $80,000). However, a majority of each subgroup was nonetheless in favor of Proposition 198.[36]

Proposition 198 won easily, with 60 percent of the vote, while the four other direct legislation measures in the spring 1996 primary election were defeated. Thus, without much fanfare, California voters implemented a drastic change in their state's politics. Their action reflected the suspicion of political parties which has been consistently present in California since the Progressive Era.

The fall general election resembled the bitter 1988 primary, with two rival reform groups submitting initiatives for campaign finance reform. In 1988 both campaign finance reform propositions (68 and 73) had been successful (although they were largely invalidated later by the courts), but in 1996 Proposition 208 won handily, while Proposition 212 lost by the barest of margins.

It was not easy for voters to distinguish between the two initiatives, since their differences were fairly subtle. Proposition 208 sought to limit campaign contributions by individuals to $250 for local offices and $500 for statewide ones, but these amounts would be doubled if the candidate voluntarily accepted overall spending limits. Proposition 212 was a tougher measure that would have permitted $100 individual contributions for local offices and $300 for statewide, but placed mandatory limits on total spending.[37] Both propositions would ban contributions from lobbyists or other candidates, limit political party contributions to insignificant amounts, and place strict limits on contributions by businesses, labor organizations, and PACs. For Proposition 208, limitations were $250 for local offices and $500 for statewide offices, whereas Proposition 212 prohibited such contributions entirely (although campaign support apart from direct contributions to candidates was not limited). While Proposition 212 was overall the more stringent measure, it also would have removed existing legal restrictions on honoraria, gifts, and free travel for elected officials, a point its critics stressed.

There were other provisions as well, since these were complex statutes that had to take into consideration existing legislation going back at least to the political reform act (Proposition 9) of 1974. Trying to compare the two via the official summaries and pro and con arguments in the official ballot pamphlet was a daunting prospect for most voters. And the actual text (at the end of the ballot pamphlet) of Proposition 208 ran to five pages of very small print; Proposition 212 was even longer, by one and one-half pages.

Advocates of the two reform measures spent as much time badmouthing one another as they did extolling the virtues of their own propositions. For Proposition 208 there was an alliance of the League of Women Voters, the American Association of Retired Persons, Common Cause, and United We Stand America, plus endorsements from groups ranging from the American Lung Association of California and the National Council of Jewish Women to United Anglers and the Howard Jarvis Taxpayers Association. Proposition 212's forces were led primarily by the California Public Interest Re-

TABLE 6.5 Correlations of Voting on Three Political Reform Propositions and Census Characteristics, 1996 Primary and General Elections

| | Prop. 198: Open primary | Prop. 208: Campaign reform | Prop. 212: Campaign reform | Mean family income | Percentage of college graduates | Percentage urban |
|---|---|---|---|---|---|---|
| Prop. 198: Open primary | 1.000 | | | | | |
| Prop. 208: Campaign reform | .282 | 1.000 | | | | |
| Prop. 212: Campaign reform | .372 | .526 | 1.000 | | | |
| Mean family income | −.310 | .201 | .026 | 1.000 | | |
| Percentage of college graduates | −.384 | .458 | .007 | .846 | 1.000 | |
| Percentage urban | −.604 | −.254 | −.207 | .568 | .473 | 1.000 |

NOTE: Pearson product moment correlations are based on percentage voting Yes on propositions and on 1990 U.S. Census data, with data aggregated by county and weighted by county population. For clarity, only one-half of table is shown, since the two halves are identical.

search Group (CALPIRG) and former governor Jerry Brown, with a major assist from the California Teachers Association (there was a way in which unions would be somewhat more able to make meaningful donations under 212 than under 208).[38]

The matter of financing is somewhat difficult to evaluate because of the multi-proposition campaign committees previously mentioned. The main Proposition 208 groups had a combined Pro-208/Anti-212 campaign committee that raised $1.7 million. The Proposition 212 interests had a campaign committee of their own that raised $4.7 million, of which $3.9 million came from CALPIRG and $600,000 came from the California Teachers Association PAC. Additionally, two of the big money conservative committees opposing the trial attorney's Propositions 207 and 211 also listed opposition to both 208 and 212 in their names; how much money they actually devoted to either or both of these measures, however, cannot be determined.[39]

Unfortunately, the California Poll did not ask voters about Propositions 208 and 212 in 1996, masking the attitudes that led to almost 100,000 more voters casting ballots on 208 than on 212, and, even more, to the twelve-point difference in their approval by the voters: 61 percent in favor of 208 and 49 percent in favor of 212. Table 6.5 shows that voting for neither of these fall initiatives had much of a relationship with voting for the other political "reform" measure, the open-primary proposition of the previous March. The fairly strong correlation (.526) for the vote between Propositions 208 and 212 suggests that many voters simply supported campaign finance reform, and perhaps also did not see important differences between them.

Correlations with data from the 1990 census are only marginally significant. All three measures of "sophistication" correlated negatively with voting for Proposition 198, with the percentage of urban voters having the strongest such correlation. As the percentage of the college-graduate population — and, more weakly, family income — rose, the relationship with supporting Proposition 208 did increase, whereas that was not the case with Proposition 212. This difference offers a modest indication of the two initiatives' relative rates of success: the more educated and wealthier voters were possibly supporting 208 but not 212. That is important, because these voters were those most likely able to recognize the differences between the two measures, and the most likely to vote as well. And survey data indirectly reinforce this conclusion.[40] Another source of Proposition 208's appeal was probably the broad range of large, powerful groups that supported it.

As had become typical for major initiatives, Proposition 208 was soon in the courts. Backers of the measure had seen their success as the start of a national trend, but that was not to be. Both major parties filed lawsuits against the fund-raising and spending limits on First Amendment grounds.

Major Democratic Party contributors, including the California Teachers Association, filed a suit of their own.[41] The new statute took effect in 1997, even as the lawsuits progressed, with the result that fund-raising was limited that year. But there were no limits on spending, since that part of the new law had been invalidated by a federal judge almost as soon as it had taken effect in January 1997.[42] The measure also suffered from unenthusiastic administration: Ravi Mehta, Governor Pete Wilson's appointee as chair of the Fair Political Practices Commission, made no bones about his dislike for the new law, coached lobbyists on how to get around it, and boasted of being the "eviscerator" of Proposition 208.[43] Finally, in January 1998, much of the rest of the new law was struck down by a federal judge who saw the contribution limits as a violation of the First Amendment free-speech rights of both individual candidates and political parties.[44]

The 1996 general election also saw the return of proposed initiatives for controlling health care costs. More ambitious health care propositions had lost in 1992 and 1994 (Props. 166 and 186), but the national and local health care debate had continued unabated, so it was not surprising to see two new measures on the ballot. The November 1996 proposals were more modest than their predecessors; they were aimed at the most criticized aspects of health delivery in America: costs and patient rights, particularly within health maintenance organizations (HMOs). But, as seems to have become increasingly the case with California initiatives, these were two rival reform proposals from groups that spent too much time bickering with one another, confusing voters in the process.

Both Proposition 214 and Proposition 216 were initiative statutes that would have prohibited financial incentives for physicians or nurses to deny care, outlawed "gag orders" wherein HMO member doctors could not express disagreement with HMO administrative decisions, and required that a second opinion be provided if treatments recommended by a doctor were denied by the HMO or other insurer. Proposition 216 included new taxes on health care businesses to defray costs and required a two-thirds vote of the legislature for amendment; Proposition 214 did not have a taxing feature and required only a majority legislative vote for amendment.[45] The differences were much less significant than the similarities, except to the backers of each measure; in particular, the split was most pronounced between unions and consumer groups, which had originally worked together. Proposition 214 became largely a union-backed measure, with additional support from the AARP and a number of medical groups. Proposition 216, on the other hand, represented consumer groups, with support from Ralph Nader, Harvey Rosenfield, the California Nurses Association, and also some medical groups. The former group raised $1.5 million for their campaign, which was almost entirely union money, whereas Proposition 216 supporters raised about twice that, with 84 percent of the total coming from the California Nurses Association.[46]

While proponents were impressed with the differences between the two initiatives, the same was not true for opponents, who saw them both as dire threats to HMOs and health insurance companies in general. The main No group was Taxpayers Against the Government Takeover, A Coalition of Nurses, Business, Seniors, Taxpayers, Insurers and Hospitals (Oppose Propositions 214 and 216). The name was a euphemism, to be sure, since its $8 million in contributions came almost entirely from health insurers and HMOs, with some support from general business groups. Their cause also received some undisclosed contributions from two of the multi-proposition campaign committees that were mainly focused on defeating the trial attorneys' Propositions 207 and 211, but who had enough cash (over $42 million between them) to help this effort as well.[47]

Neither of the proposed initiatives registered strongly with voters, despite the timeliness of the issue and the money being spent to advertise them. A week before the election, less than half of the respondents to a poll of registered voters remembered seeing, hearing, or reading anything about Propositions 214 and 216. Moreover, responses to questions about the two measures were almost identical, even when their provisions were explained by the pollster. Just under 30 percent planned to vote Yes, while 47 percent planned to vote No and the rest were Undecided. It is difficult to give too much weight for this opposition to the effect of the anti-214 and 216 publicity, since so many voters were basically unaware of the propositions. Certainly, publicity had some effect, but there was also the innately negative response to things one is unaware of. However, there was a clear relationship between increasing wealth and opposition to both of these measures, and a similar relationship between wealth and one's sureness that he or she would vote in the upcoming election.[48] Thus, in this election, as in almost all voting on initiatives, wealthier people had an influence well beyond their numbers, which in this case definitely worked against health care reform.

The vote followed the public opinion polls: Proposition 214 won only 42 percent of the vote, and Proposition 216, perhaps because of its taxing provision, did even worse, with 39 percent. Even modest cost-control proposals for health care reform could not command the support of a majority of voting Californians; as in 1992 and 1994, they remained leery of government intervention in the area of medical care.

As noted at the head of this chapter, the 1996 election year was a prototype of the modern state of direct legislation. Not only were there a lot of initiatives, but many of them were quite complicated. Some were not well understood by many voters, as witnessed by respondents not taking a position on initiatives in public opinion polls until follow-up questions clarified just what was involved. The public's infatuation with tax cutting, and with the related belief that government at all levels could function adequately with decreasing financing, continued unabated. Its enthusiasm for cracking down on crime and criminals also continued, as seen in Proposition 213 and in several legislative propositions (194, 195, and 196) that are not considered here.

But, as usual, it is hard to pin a general ideological tag, or any other simple explanation, on the 1996 election results. Californians voted to kill affirmative action but also to increase the minimum wage; they defeated health care reform but supported serious campaign-finance reform. They voted overwhelmingly in Proposition 213 to punish drunk drivers, but also passed perhaps the most liberal marijuana law in the nation. And they responded to the hugely funded multi-proposition rivalry between big business and insurance companies, on the one hand, and wealthy trial lawyers on the other, by rejecting both sides. There are some patterns in these votes, but those patterns by no means explain all the reasons the public voted as it did.

The 1998 primaries continued both the tensions and some of the confusion of contemporary direct legislation. As with the medical marijuana Proposition 215 in 1996, this year too saw a blatantly unconstitutional measure both reach the ballot and gain the support of the voters. Even more bizarre, the measure's sponsors advised voting against it in the *California Ballot Pamphlet* because they recognized its unconstitutionality, a unique development in the history of direct legislation in California. The initiative constitutional amendment was Proposition 225, which tried once again to apply term limits to members of the House and Senate. It would have declared that the "official position of the People of the State of California" was that its elected officials should support a federal constitutional amendment limiting congressional terms. Further, candidates for federal or state office who did not support the amendment would be identified as "non-supporters" on the ballot.[49]

After Proposition 225 qualified, but before the ballot pamphlet was prepared by the secretary of state, court decisions in other states convinced its backers that it would definitely fail in the courts. So Sally Reed Impasto, a board member of U.S. Term Limits, went on record in the ballot pamphlet against her own initiative, promising a better one for the fall election.[50] Even so, the proposition passed with 53 percent of the vote, reflecting the continuing enthusiasm of Californians for the term-limits idea, and perhaps also the fact that voters didn't read the ballot pamphlet very carefully.

There were four other direct legislation propositions on the 1998 primary ballot, two of which were important and very divisive. Proposition 227 was a logical extension of the ending of affirmative action via Proposition 209 in 1996; effectively, it would end California's 30-year program of bilingual education, replacing it with an intensive one-year "English immersion" program instead. It also would appropriate $50 million per year for funding the English instruction program, and permit parental lawsuits against failure to enforce this law. Proposition 227 was developed and sponsored by Ron K. Unz, a millionaire businessman and unsuccessful candidate for the Republican gubernatorial nomination in 1994, with considerable funding from outside the state. Opponents included the major teachers and state employees unions, the state PTA, the California League of Women Voters, and the California Labor Federation, among others. They complained that the program was too inflexible, took authority away from local school districts and parents and teachers, and took money from academic programs, including bilingual ones.[51]

The initiative definitely existed on two levels. The first was the question itself, which certainly merited debate because there was no doubt that California's bilingual programs had not been successful. Many students never mastered English, there were never enough qualified teachers, and there was a bilingual bureaucracy which often seemed more concerned with its own well-being than that of the students. But there was serious question whether the proposed program would be an improvement, if one year would be enough time to master English for many students, and whether this program, like the current one, would result in unqualified people doing the teaching. There had been considerable debate in California and nationally about how to deal with the increasing numbers of non–English speakers entering the public schools. On this basis, Proposition 227 was opposed by President Clinton and all four major candidates in the gubernatorial primary, Republican Dan Lungren, and Democrats Gray Davis, Jane Harman, and Al Checchi (who distinguished himself by spending forty million of his own dollars in a losing campaign). California voters were obviously not impressed.

There was also a sociocultural element to Proposition 227, which connected it to the anti–illegal alien Proposition 187 of 1994 and the anti–affirmative action Proposition 209 of 1996. This relationship is illustrated in Table 6.6. Some Mexican-American groups, especially, saw the measure as discriminatory and vowed to fight it; a court challenge was instituted the day after the election by the Mexican American Legal Defense and Education Fund, the Southern Christian Leadership Conference, and others.[52]

As the table shows, there was a striking positive relationship in voting for Propositions 187, 209, and 227; between voting to end affirmative action and voting to end bilingual education, the correlation was .940, about as

TABLE 6.6  Correlations of Voting on Sociocultural and Ideological Propositions, and Census Characteristics, 1994–1998

| | 1994: Prop. 187 Illegal aliens | 1996: Prop. 209 Affirmative action | 1998: Prop. 226 Union dues | 1998: Prop. 227 Bilingual education | 1990: Percentage urban | 1990: Percentage with college degree | 1990: Mean family income | 1990: Percentage foreign born |
|---|---|---|---|---|---|---|---|---|
| 1994: Prop. 187 Illegal aliens | 1.000 | | | | | | | |
| 1996: Prop. 209 Affirmative action | .889 | 1.000 | | | | | | |
| 1998: Prop. 226 Union dues | .781 | .933 | 1.000 | | | | | |
| 1998: Prop. 227 Bilingual education | .915 | .940 | .919 | 1.000 | | | | |

| | | | | | | | | |
|---|---|---|---|---|---|---|---|---|
| 1990:<br>Percentage<br>urban | −.391 | −.492 | −.352 | −.379 | 1.000 | | | |
| 1990:<br>Percentage<br>with college<br>degree | −.690 | −.436 | −.193 | −.398 | .473 | 1.000 | | |
| 1990:<br>Mean<br>family<br>income | −.464 | −.320 | −.083 | −.214 | .568 | .846 | 1.000 | |
| 1990:<br>Percentage<br>foreign<br>born | −.390 | −.674 | −.547 | −.495 | .606 | .183 | .352 | 1.000 |

NOTE: Pearson product moment correlations, based on percentage voting Yes on propositions and responses to 1990 U.S. Census, with data aggregated by county and weighted by county population. For clarity, only one-half of table is shown, since the two halves are identical.

close to a perfect relationship as one will ever see in the real world. (There was also a very strong relationship between each of these three measures and the anti-union Proposition 226, which will be discussed below.) The table also suggests that increased wealth, increased education, and urban residence made one less likely to support these sociocultural measures, as did foreign birth, which is to be expected; those relationships are not nearly as strong but are statistically significant.[53]

Proposition 227 won by 61 percent to 39 percent, which was a somewhat lower level of support than had existed earlier in the campaign. Indeed, both Propositions 227 and 226 (below) are examples of the fact that voter initiative decisions over time have more and more been made in the last days of campaigns. In mid-April, for example, all demographic groups in a *Los Angeles Times* poll favored Proposition 227, including slightly over one-half of Latino voters, but on election day two-thirds of the latter voted against it. Also, according to exit polls, slight majorities of blacks, Democrats, and liberals opposed 227.[54]

Another significant aspect of the Proposition 227 campaign was that, as with Proposition 13 in 1978, the legislature responded to the popular opposition to the status of bilingual education by passing a more moderate law which it hoped would make 227 unnecessary and defeat it. The legislation gave flexibility in programs for non-English speakers to individual school districts, evaluating their success with required achievement in core subjects. But Governor Wilson, who had stayed out of the Proposition 227 campaign until just two weeks before the election, vetoed the law and then announced his support for 227.[55] The obvious popularity of the initiative, plus Wilson's continuing desire to endear himself to the Republican right, led him to jump in before it was too late.

The other controversial initiative in the 1998 spring primary, Proposition 226, was part of a national effort by conservatives to deal a critical blow to the political power of organized labor. This initiative statute would have required "all employers and labor unions" to receive their employees' written permission before withholding wages or using union dues for political purposes. The "employers" part was phony, since wage withholding for political purposes essentially does not exist; rather, such wording permitted supporters to present it as a "neutral" measure that was not simply anti-labor.[56] Since unions, and particularly the California Teachers Association, were again and again the main sources of campaign finance for the left in California politics, this measure would have had a cataclysmic effect. There would be no reliable sources of big money to contest the economic weight of organized business and right-wing interests in both candidate and proposition elections, and the nature of California politics would have been dramatically changed.

The movement was triggered in Orange County, when Frank Ury lost his bid for reelection as school trustee. As he saw it, he and other conservatives were being hurt by the political spending of the California Teachers Association. Thus, this initiative would remove that liberal influence. Ury and his associates were also allied with the religious right, as strong supporters of the voucher system for private and public school choice for parents, and they saw the liberal unions, especially the CTA, as their chief opponents, which indeed had been the case with Proposition 174 of 1993 (see Chapter 5). By 1998 the movement had gone national, with about 30 states having groups supporting similar measures. The qualification of Proposition 226 in California was financed with $441,000 from Americans for Tax Reform, an out-of-state organization run by conservative Grover Norquist. It was also taken up by Governor Wilson, as part of his now-habitual search for conservative support for his presidential ambitions. This made the battle partisan as well as ideological.[57]

The campaign on this initiative was bitterly contested and very expensive, ultimately costing at least $25 million, primarily for radio and television advertising. Governor Wilson tried to get anti-Proposition 226 advertisements removed from television by threatening legal action; he also transferred $1.2 million of his own campaign money to the battle, and got major contributions from conservatives in and out of California, plus groups like the California and American Restaurant Associations, which were very bitter at the unions for the 1996 increase in the minimum wage (Prop. 210). A number of wealthy Orange County individuals also made contributions of up to $150,000. For their part, the California Teachers Association and the National Education Association, along with numerous other union groups, led in the fund-raising that gave opponents about $22 million versus the $4 million or so available to proponents.[58]

As seen in Table 6.6, there were very strong correlations between the votes on Propositions 187, 209, and 227 with that on Proposition 226. While this initiative dealt with labor relations rather than ethnic issues, it still elicited a conservative-versus-liberal response. To the voters and to a number of conservative contributors, the initiatives were indeed related (for example, Richard Scaife, who gave $100,000 for Prop. 209, also gave $50,000 to the campaign for Prop. 226).

The fate of Proposition 226 changed as the primary campaign progressed. At the very beginning of the campaign it was ahead by 50 points, and as late as May, in a *Los Angeles Times* poll of "likely voters," it was winning by a 51 percent to 37 percent margin. But that turned around toward the campaign's end, so that it lost fairly decisively: 53.5 percent No to 46.5 percent Yes. The extremely effective organization and vast sums employed by the unions, primarily on radio and television, had their effect — again showing that money can generally guarantee defeat of an initiative. It was additionally speculated that the large turnout of Democrats due to the bitter and unprecedentedly expensive race for the gubernatorial nomination, plus an unusually high turnout of Mexican-American voters, also contributed to the measure's defeat.[59] The issue has likely not died, but for the present conservatives have not been able to stifle the one moneyed source for liberal political positions in California.

The fall 1998 election offered seven direct election measures, and also marked the beginning of periodic renumbering for propositions. The most impressive measure offered was Proposition 5, which would expand the rights of California Indian tribes with respect to gambling on tribal land. Gambling involves enormous profits, and the Proposition 5 battle ended up as the most expensive direct election campaign in American history, with about $80 million in expenditures. The campaign pitted a large number of Indian tribes against Governor Wilson, who once again involved himself in an initiative campaign, and the Las Vegas casinos, which feared losing business to expanded Indian gaming.

Leading casino operators like Circus Circus Enterprises, Inc., Hilton Hotels, and Mirage Resorts, Inc. each contributed over $4 million to the No campaign. But the Indian tribes outspent them three-to-one, anticipating huge potential wealth from the expanded gambling rights. The San Manuel Tribal Administration alone spent $22 million, and the Morongo Band of Mission Indians almost half as much.[60] Both sides waged huge television and direct mail campaigns, but what registered with the voters was the Native Americans' stress on Indian self-reliance. The idea of the Indians "deserving" this chance on their own land struck Californians as just, particularly since it wasn't going to cost the taxpayers any money. Proposition 5 won 63 percent of the vote, with the Indian tribes spending over $13 per vote.[61]

Proposition 9, a highly complex measure relating to electric utilities, was also extremely expensive. It was a "consumer's measure," sponsored by Harvey Rosenfield and Consumers Union, that tried, among other things, to force rate reductions that had been promised but were not forthcoming with the industry's deregulation in 1996 and 1997.[62] What was most notable about the measure was its opposition, which ranged from utility companies all over the United States, to numerous other businesses, to organized labor, to the leadership of both political parties in California. Indeed, it seemed that everyone but the sponsors opposed Proposition 9. Huge sums were raised, and big money was once again successful in a No campaign; 73 percent of the voters opposed the intiative.[63]

The tobacco companies were not as successful in financing the destruction of the anti-smoking Proposition 10, which proposed raising cigarette taxes by 50 cents a pack to create commissions in each county to promote child development and anti-smoking programs. The initiative was promoted by Rob Reiner, the popular actor and motion picture director, who was also a prime contributor to the campaign. The anti-smoking forces' strength was not in finances, however, since they were greatly outspent by the opposition: Philip Morris Co.'s $20 million spending was almost four times the entire Yes side's budget.[64] Tobacco money was not quite enough to defeat a popular measure, and Proposition 10 squeaked by with 50.1 percent of the vote.

Pete Wilson continued to fumble and stumble in his effort to use direct legislation to forward his own career. He supported Proposition 8 in the fall 1998 election, a school-support measure with several aims, including reduced class size. It was very controversial, however, particularly in its creation of a new Chief Inspector of the public schools. The Democratic legislature fought back with its own proposal, Proposition 1A, a $9 billion bond act for reducing class size and improving school facilities. Sixty-three percent of the voters rejected Wilson's initiative, and 62 percent supported 1A. This was another major defeat for Wilson, as was the almost-total sweep by the Democrats of state office from governor on down. The governor had become a master at gaining rejection by both the left and the right.

One other legislative measure, Proposition 3, showed the continued California antipathy to political parties and partisan politics. Proposition 198 in the 1996 primary election had created the new open-primary system, as we have seen. That raised a question of whether Californians would be able to vote in the year 2000 presidential primaries, where it might well be legal for political parties to restrict the vote to registered members only. If true, this would permit the parties to refuse to honor balloting in California's open-primary system and possibly use a caucus system instead. Proposition 3 was the legislature's effort to modify Proposition 198 so as to avoid this danger by making an exception to the open-primary system solely for presidential primaries. But the public was unimpressed, and 54 percent voted to risk the danger and keep the nonpartisan system as broad as possible. Few things were as consistent in the twentieth century as Californians' disdain for political parties.

In 1990, Joel Fox, who had succeeded Howard Jarvis as the head of the Howard Jarvis Taxpayers Association, and Richard Gann, who had succeeded his father as head of Paul Gann's Citizens Committee, responded to criticisms of the direct legislation process by qualifying an initiative constitutional amendment to protect it. Proposition 137's aim was to impede the legislature from making any changes in the laws regulating the initiative or referendum. Specifically, it said that any changes in state law relative to either state or local initiatives or referendums must be submitted to a vote of the people. From the sponsors' standpoint, this would impede the legislature from making the process more difficult through an increase in the number of required signatures or other devices. It would also help ensure that further tax-limitation initiatives would not be kept off the ballot (they actually had another one, Prop. 136, on the same ballot, which was discussed in Chapter 5). Opponents, including the former chairpersons of the Fair Political Practices Commission and the Constitutional Revision Commission, argued that Proposition 137 was "special interest" legislation masquerading as reform: it would keep the legislature from instituting such campaign-finance reform measures as requiring more complete disclosure of who was paying for an initiative campaign.[65]

Interestingly, Proposition 137 had the lowest voter participation rate (88 percent) of the thirteen direct legislation measures on the 1990 general election ballot, despite the fact that the Jarvis–Gann forces had almost $3 million for their campaign and there was no organized opposition. (They also raised over $8 million for their tax limitation Prop. 136.)[66] Proposition 137 lost, gaining only 45 percent of the vote. This was a modest step in keeping initiatives from virtual unassailability, but it did not signify any important change in the public's attitude toward the initiative process.

In 1997 the Field Institute did one of its occasional in-depth polls on public attitudes toward the direct legislation process and toward proposed changes therein.[67] This was a poll of California adults, with a sample size of 1,007. Its results offer meaningful insights into the views of Californians after almost ninety years of experience with the process, 300 direct legislation propositions, and far more legislative ones.

On some things, there was strong agreement. For example, responding to the question of whether ballot propositions were "a good thing," "a bad thing," or "don't make much difference," 72 percent of respondents said that they were a good thing for the state. There was very little difference from the overall percentage when responses were broken down by region of the state, gender, ethnicity, education, age, political ideology, political party identification, religion, or income. "Strong Conservatives" at 83 percent "a good thing," and "Strong Liberals" at 63 percent showed the greatest difference, which is consistent with previous examples of political ideology as a key variable in divergent positions on issues. However, despite the twenty-point gap, both groups still had decisive majorities in general favor of the process. The general approval of the initiative process was echoed on another question, where 61 percent of the respondents favored the idea of creating a national direct legislation process.

When asked what they thought was the best thing about proposition elections, and given a list of eight possible answers, the first response ("Gives people a voice [choice]/chance to give their opinions, to vote, to participate, to show how they feel") was selected by 41 percent of the total and approximately the same percentage for various subgroups. None of the other responses (empowers concerned citizens, diverts power from legislature, forces people to inform themselves, etc.) were chosen by more than about 5 percent of the respondents, except for "Don't know," which was the choice of about 30 percent of respondents. Los Angeles residents, non-citizens, women, Latinos, the less educated, the least wealthy, and renters selected "Don't know" more often that respondents in other subgroups. To some degree, those subgroups are also consistently less likely to vote, which makes their response more understandable.

When given the opportunity to make choices about "the worst things" characteristic of proposition elections, respondents chose a wide variety of answers. The most common was the idea that too often initiatives, once passed, were not put into effect or were overturned.

An important concern with initiatives is that they have become so complex that many voters don't really understand them, something the poll reinforced. Only 5 percent of respondents said "All [propositions] are understandable," 23 percent said "Most are understandable," 41 percent said "Only some are understandable," and 28 percent said "Only a few are understandable." There was almost no variation in these responses across income, educational, or other subgroupings. When over two-thirds of adult Californians find at least a majority of propositions not understandable, the question of just how they determine their ultimate ballot choices becomes troublesome. If nothing else, this suggests why most propositions fail and why disproportionate financing can usually succeed in raising enough doubt to defeat a proposition.

A majority of respondents (54 percent) said that they usually voted on all the propositions on a given ballot, while another 30 percent said they voted on "most of them." Here, there were some significant differences among subgroups, again consistent with correlates of likelihood of voting in general: voting on all or most propositions increased with greater education, with age, with extremes of ideology ("strongly" conservative or liberal), and with income.

Table 6.7 provides information on the important question of where voters get their information about propositions. The question was worded very carefully to avoid suggesting a preferred response, and respondents were permitted only one response to force them to pick the one that was most important.[68]

There are some significant, if not necessarily surprising, differences in primary sources of information across group lines. Reliance on television as a main source of information is very much inversely related to income and education. That explains, in part, the greater reliance on television of ethnic

TABLE 6.7  Main Source of Information About Ballot Propositions, 1997 (percentage making each choice)

| | Television | Newspapers | Radio | Ballot pamphlet | Mailers | Friends and relatives | Internet |
|---|---|---|---|---|---|---|---|
| Total | 22 | 17 | 3 | 36 | 7 | 6 | 4 |
| Party registration | | | | | | | |
| Democrat | 30 | 19 | 2 | 28 | 6 | 6 | 4 |
| Republican | 15 | 13 | 5 | 42 | 9 | 7 | 2 |
| Ethnicity | | | | | | | |
| White (non-Hispanic) | 20 | 15 | 3 | 40 | 8 | 7 | 3 |
| Latino | 29 | 22 | 4 | 26 | 6 | 4 | 3 |
| Black | 28 | 39 | — | 16 | 2 | 1 | 7 |
| Education | | | | | | | |
| High school or less | 36 | 15 | 2 | 28 | 6 | 5 | 5 |
| Some college/trade school | 18 | 14 | 6 | 37 | 7 | 7 | 4 |
| College graduate | 5 | 30 | 3 | 40 | 6 | 9 | 2 |
| Postgraduate work | 6 | 21 | 2 | 51 | 10 | 5 | 2 |
| Age 60 or older[a] | 36 | 18 | 3 | 27 | 3 | 7 | 1 |
| Household income | | | | | | | |
| Under $20,000 | 19 | 5 | 3 | 16 | 4 | 3 | 3 |
| $20,000–$40,000 | 13 | 16 | 3 | 23 | 5 | 5 | 3 |
| $40,000–$60,000 | 13 | 13 | 2 | 44 | 6 | 4 | 2 |
| $60,000–$80,000 | 9 | 12 | 5 | 42 | 6 | 9 | 4 |
| Over $80,000 | 6 | 24 | 3 | 43 | 4 | 4 | 1 |

SOURCE:  Based on responses to Field Institute poll f19703 (12–24 August 1997).
NOTE:  Rows do not add up to 100 because of rounding and because "Other" and "No answer" responses are excluded.

minorities and Democrats as well. The reliance on television is important because televised information on propositions tends to be less objective than other sources; it is where the major expenditure of campaign funds is made, where the greatest part of the "information" is advertisements for one side or another, and where negative advertising is most forcefully presented. Newspapers have proportionately more information, as opposed to advertising, and the ballot pamphlet is the most objective source of all, since it has summaries and evaluations by the legislative analyst, plus clearly labeled arguments for each side. Thus, those who rely more on newspapers and the ballot pamphlets are likely to be more informed; they are also, as seen above, the groups most likely to vote. The relatively low reliance on direct mail as a main source of information is interesting because this type of advertising has been used more and more extensively in recent years. After television (and radio), direct mail is the foremost media for negative advertising, but, as represented by these respondents, it may be less productive than its users believe.

Presented in the above way, the data may understate the breadth of use of the ballot pamphlet. Even though it was listed in the question in the middle of the choices, to avoid its too-easy selection as a response, the ballot pamphlet was nonetheless the most frequently cited "most useful source" — mentioned by 301 respondents, as opposed newspapers by 138 and television by 125. Respondents were also asked their "next most useful source of information." Putting the two responses together, 398 mentioned the ballot pamphlet, 360 mentioned newspapers, 268 mentioned television, 142 mentioned friends and relatives, and fewer than 100 mentioned the other media.[69] Californians do access a variety of sources of information when voting on initiatives, but there are decided differences among subgroups of the voting population.

Californians were not naive about the origins of specific initiatives. When asked whether the issues on statewide ballots "generally reflect the concerns of the average voter or those of organized special interests," 56 percent of all respondents and 59 percent of registered voters said it was interest groups, whereas only 21 percent of all respondents and 19 percent of registered voters believed the propositions represented "ordinary individuals." This breakdown was quite consistent across ethnic, partisan, educational, and other lines. However, respondents who identified themselves as "strongly conservative" were more optimistic, only 44 percent of them selecting interest groups. Why that was the case is unclear, except perhaps that conservatives identified more with the dominant special interests of the time.

This relates to an equally important question about voters' sense that they knew which interests were behind the measures they voted on.[70] Responses to this question are displayed in Table 6.8. The differences are not

TABLE 6.8 Awareness of Interests Behind Ballot Propositions, 1997
(percentage making each choice)

| | All of the time | Most of the time | Some of the time | Rarely | Never |
|---|---|---|---|---|---|
| Total | 6 | 29 | 40 | 16 | 3 |
| Party registration | | | | | |
| Democratic | 5 | 26 | 47 | 17 | 2 |
| Republican | 5 | 42 | 36 | 12 | 1 |
| Ethnicity | | | | | |
| White (non-Hispanic) | 5 | 35 | 37 | 17 | 2 |
| Latino | 10 | 18 | 44 | 11 | 5 |
| Black | <1 | 19 | 56 | 20 | 5 |
| Education | | | | | |
| High school or less | 6 | 22 | 43 | 15 | 5 |
| Some college/trade school | 5 | 33 | 43 | 16 | 2 |
| College grad | 7 | 41 | 26 | 21 | 4 |
| Postgraduate work | 8 | 38 | 36 | 15 | <1 |
| Age group | | | | | |
| 18–24 | 2 | 22 | 50 | 19 | 5 |
| 25–29 | 6 | 29 | 31 | 23 | 2 |
| 30–39 | 8 | 24 | 47 | 13 | 4 |
| 40–49 | 6 | 33 | 34 | 18 | 4 |
| 50–59 | 6 | 33 | 38 | 15 | 5 |
| 60 or older | 7 | 35 | 38 | 11 | <1 |
| Household income | | | | | |
| Under $20,000 | 7 | 21 | 38 | 16 | 6 |
| $20,000–$40,000 | 4 | 31 | 45 | 12 | 2 |
| $40,000–$60,000 | 6 | 40 | 34 | 17 | 2 |
| $60,000–$80,000 | 10 | 28 | 37 | 18 | 5 |
| More than $80,000 | 7 | 39 | 36 | 17 | 1 |

SOURCE: Based on responses to Field Institute poll fi9703 (12–24 August 1997).
NOTE: Rows do not add up to 100 because of rounding and because "No opinion" responses are excluded.

great, but they are nonetheless worth some discussion. Differences in feeling the extremes — that they never or always knew who was behind propositions — were quite minor. However, all but two groups — Republicans and people age 60 or older — had a majority saying they were aware of the interests involved "Some of the time" or less often; and for the total sample, this was true for 59 percent. Given the wording of the choices, it appears that Californians believe that for a majority of the propositions on their ballots, they don't really know who the supporting and opposing interests are.

Democrats are more suspicious on this account than Republicans, blacks more so than whites or Latinos, and the less educated somewhat more suspicious than the more educated. But education does not have a linear relationship here, nor does age. The youngest respondents do recognize their own ignorance; given that they are the group least likely to vote, or to seriously follow politics, this seems appropriate.

It appears, then, that voters, while seeing initiatives as a positive force, are nonetheless aware of some basic weaknesses in the system. How they reconciled this conflict was pursued with a number of questions asking for respondent opinions on some frequently suggested reforms of the direct legislation process. Responses to these questions are presented in Table 6.9.

Given the almost overwhelming number of propositions on the ballots of the 1980s and 1990s, it is noteworthy that a slight majority of respondents did not want to enforce a maximum number of propositions per election. This response was quite consistent across groups, with a couple of exceptions: African-Americans favored (61 percent) limiting the number of propositions; and Latinos, while about average in favoring a limit, had a uniquely high level of "No opinion" (22 percent), so that their "Oppose" rate was also unusually low (40 percent). There is logic in this, in that the initiative process has consistently tended to follow middle-class, white values, and had just eight months before passed the anti-affirmative action Proposition 209. College graduates were the strongest opponents of this proposed reform (79 percent), while those aged sixty and over favored the reform even more than African-Americans (62 percent). Given that college graduates are disproportionately white and middle class, their response is not surprising. The reason for the disproportionate support for this change by older voters is not obvious; they had not, for example, been unusually strong in favoring the two losing health reform propositions the previous November.

Perhaps more important, there were no other significant variations in responses on this measure among other groupings — political party, political ideology, family income, and so on. Among those who did favor this limitation, two-thirds chose either "5 to 9" or "10 to 14" as the proper maximum number.

TABLE 6.9   Public Opinion on Proposed Changes in Direct
Legislation, 1997 (percentage making each choice)

| Proposed change | Favor | Oppose | No opinion |
| --- | --- | --- | --- |
| 1. Limit number of propositions in any single election | 43 | 53 | 4 |
| 2. Require two-thirds rather than majority vote for passage of ballot propositions | 51 | 43 | 6 |
| 3. Use indirect initiative (proposition goes first to legislature; if it fails to pass measure in acceptable form, sponsors can then get it on ballot) | 45 | 46 | 9 |
| 4. Permit legislature to amend laws passed by proposition | 28 | 65 | 7 |
| 5. Require that proposition be submitted to secretary of state, who can comment on its conformity to present law and its clarity of language before it is circulated for signatures | 73 | 22 | 6 |
| 6. Limit the amount of money that can be spent by supporters or opponents of propositions | 79 | 15 | 6 |
| 7. Disallow paid signature gathering to qualify propositions[a] | 38 | 46 | 8 |
| 8. Should there also be a national ballot proposition process? | 61 | 32 | 7 |

SOURCE: Based on responses to Field Institute poll fi9703 (12–24 August 1997).
    NOTE: The numbers before each proposal are for clarity of reference in text; they have no relationship to the numbers of the questions in the actual Field Institute poll.

    [a]The actual question was: "Do you think it is a good thing or bad thing to permit paid signature gatherers to help qualify an initiative for the ballot." In this table, those who responded "good thing" are entered as "Oppose" disallowing, and those who responded "bad thing" are entered as "Favor" disallowing. Nine percent of respondents answered "Mixed," which explains why this row does not add to 100 percent.

Californians were considerably more open to the idea of requiring a two-thirds vote for the passage of propositions than they were to limiting their number. On the face of it, this was a more straightforward measure and a more meaningful reform. It may be that voters were used to the idea of two-thirds votes since they had recently supported them in propositions that sought to eliminate avoidance of the anti-tax system established by Proposition 13. This proposed reform had significant regional variations: southern Californians were 60 percent in favor of the two-thirds rule, while northern Californians actually had a plurality opposed (49 percent to 45 percent). Among registered voters, there was an even greater variation, with Democrats 67 percent in favor while Republicans favored the two-thirds reform at only a 43 percent level. This was not a function of political ideology, however, since self-identified conservatives and liberals were both evenly divided on the issue, although those who defined themselves as "middle-of-the-road" felt more strongly about it, with 59 percent favoring the reform. Blacks (77 percent) were overwhelmingly in favor of the two-thirds idea, and Hispanics (60 percent) were also above the average in support. Similarly, both the less educated and the less wealthy favored the change more than their opposites. What opinions on these first two proposed changes seem to suggest is a consistent relative leeriness of the direct legislation process by those lower on the socioeconomic scale.

That does not hold true on all measures, however, particularly those that include greater power for the state legislature. The proposal for return to the indirect initiative, which had been repealed in 1966, was not too threatening, since it empowered the sponsors of the proposition to put it on the ballot if they were unhappy with the legislature's action or inaction. Even so, opposition had a tiny lead among respondents. Again, Democrats were more in favor (53 percent) of the change than Republicans (46 percent); liberals (54 percent) favored and conservatives (45 percent) opposed it by similar rates. On this measure there were no significant differences by race or ethnicity, nor by income or education, nor by age, except that, for some reason, those aged 25–29 favored the idea by a much higher percentage (65 percent) than all others.

The fourth proposal in Table 6.9 is more controversial because it would give the legislature power to amend laws passed by direct legislation without any of the guarantees contained in the third proposal.[71] And the public does not trust the legislature any more now than it did during the Progressive Era. There is little variation by group on this measure. Blacks were somewhat more supportive of the legislature than the average (46 percent in favor but 51 percent opposed), and Democrats only slightly more so (35 percent in favor to 65 percent opposed). But only self-identified liberals, at 62 percent, had an actual majority in favor of giving this power to their elected representatives. This is a strong indication of the degree to which respect for representative democracy is questioned in contemporary California; in part, that is traditional, but some also see it as an effect of the increasing importance of direct legislation since Proposition 13.[72] Some people may be willing to let the legislature intervene, as in the indirect initiative, but only with an absolute guarantee that initiators of the proposition can still take it to the people.

Californians are more prone to trust an enhanced role for the secretary of state. This is for two reasons. First, secretaries of state, of both parties, have generally done a good job in California and have had widespread approval. Second, this proposal is closer to the third proposal than to the fourth: the secretary of state could comment and instruct (as his or her representatives and the legislative analyst do for each election in the *California Ballot Pamphlet*), but could not halt the initiative process. There was very little variation in response to the question by ideology, wealth, ethnicity, or any other variable. It suggests broad appeal for the idea of clarification and explanation, not surprising when voters see how often initiatives, after passing, languish for years in the courts.

Even stronger agreement is seen in the sixth item, limitation on the amount of money that can be spent in initiative elections. It would have been hard indeed to avoid the publicity over the vast sums in recent California elections, for both candidates and propositions. Thus, four-fifths of the respondents were in favor of such limitation, although they did not necessarily know how it should be done. There is little variation among groups on this question, except for the ideological and political variables: liberals favored it by 88 percent, conservatives by 79 percent, and Democrats favored it also by 88 percent compared to 78 percent for Republicans. Everyone, it seems, had learned something from the 1996 campaigns.

Curiously, respondents did not relate excessive campaign spending to the one expenditure that had been widely criticized since the time of John R. Haynes: paid signature gathering. Their responses were a great surprise, since the practice is such a blatant denial of the whole idea of direct legislation as a vehicle for "the people." But many contemporary Californians appear to realize, or perhaps sense (since they see them all the time), that paid signature gatherers are an integral part of the initiative system.[73]

There were some curious correlates of taking one position or another on this issue. For one thing, it was unusual in that party identification and political ideology made no difference at all. Education did make a difference, with higher levels of education associated with lower levels of approval of paid signature gatherers (54 percent of those with less than high school education saw the practice as a "good thing," while that figure steadily declined to a low of 42 percent among those with more than a bachelor's degree). Income was similar: 56 percent of those with household incomes under $20,000 saw no need to reform the procedure, and that declined to 42 percent among those earning more than $80,000 (those with incomes between $60,000 and $80,000 were an exception to the linear shape of the relationship).

Age operated similarly, with a steady line of approval of paid signature gathering declining from a high of 64 percent for those under 29 down to just under 40 percent for those 65 and over. And finally, blacks and Hispanics were among those least opposed to paid signature solicitation: 57 percent of each group classified it as a "good thing."

In general, then, the poorest Californians were least disturbed by the fact that those with money were more likely to qualify propositions than those without. Perhaps they viewed any type of job in positive terms, or perhaps it was something else. However, the fact that all of these groups responded similarly suggests that they understood the question they were asked.

The survey results leave little doubt that most Californians continue to support the existence of direct legislation. Most of them, as seen in the last item in the table, even support the idea of expanding the process to the national level. They would likely support changes in the system, particularly in terms of cutting back on the huge sums involved in all types of political campaigns in California. Other proposals might find a positive response as well, since these represent only a few of the many reforms currently under discussion. But the citizens still are leery of the legislature, unpersuaded that representative democracy is sufficiently responsive to their needs. Their enthusiasm for term limits, both state and national, reflects the same beliefs.

Looking back at the development of direct legislation over the course of the twentieth century, with 300 ballot propositions proposed via public petition, out of which 100 were adopted, one is left with a few conclusions plus a good many questions. That the direct legislation process is having a greater-than-ever effect on current California and even national affairs has led to a great deal of analysis and proposals for reform.[74] For a historian, the direct line from the Progressive Era to the present is striking. "The people," a term that more often than not includes special and often very rich interests, do not get what they want from the legislature, or get what they don't want — in either case, they can circumvent the legislature via direct legislation. It is such a simple and logical concept, but at the same time one that has gone in many directions, some of which have not served the state well.

One obvious problem with the direct legislation process is the question of who is making the decisions. Part of this is a function of turnout. Proposition 13 electrified the state and led an unusually large number of voters to the polls for an off-year election. While the voter participation rate on Proposition 13 was extremely high at 97 percent, that still represented only 66 percent of the state's registered voters and 45 percent of its eligible voters. And that was a high point. The past generation has seen a steady decline in voting in America, for candidates and all other ballot decisions. (And the fact that initiatives have appeared on primary as well as general election ballots since 1960 has compounded the problem.) In November 1996, for example, when Californians voted decisively on the very controversial issue of affirmative action, the state had just under twenty million eligible voters, of whom about 80 percent, or just under sixteen million, were registered to vote. Proposition 209 was tied with the minimum wage measure (Prop. 210) for the largest number of votes cast; each had voter participation rates of 94 percent. But that amounted to 49 percent of the eligible voters and 62 percent of the registered ones; and if we look only at the winning vote, the 5.3 million people who voted to end affirmative action comprised only 27 percent of the state's eligible voters and 34 percent, just one-third, of its registered voters. Turnout that year for the other propositions, such as Proposition 218, which drastically extended the effects of Proposition 13, was slightly less.[75]

Not only is the number of people actually deciding these propositions quite small — it is also, as we have seen, hardly a representative cross-section. The wealthier, better-educated, older, and white vote in considerably larger numbers than the poor, ill-schooled, young, and minority group members.[76] But is this a weakness of the initiative system? Defenders of the system will argue that the low turnout is characteristic of candidate elections as well, so that members of the legislature are similarly chosen by a minority of the public. Likewise, they can argue that low turnout of any group is that group's problem — nothing is stopping these people from participating in the election process.

There is some merit to this argument, but it ultimately fails. Candidates may well be elected by similarly small majorities, but most cannot avoid considering their future campaigns, which requires some attention to those who may decide to vote the next time. Elected representatives also have some obligations to their political party and some concern relative to their place in the legislative hierarchy. Thus, they do represent nonvoters, to some degree. (Term limits, which Californians embraced via initiative with great enthusiasm, may well result in candidates becoming less, rather than more, responsive to their constituents.) Moreover, the fact that people voluntarily fail to vote does not negate the fact that their actions are a problem in a democratic polity, minimizing, for a large part of the public, their sense of connection to the political system.

A less debatable charge against legislation by initiative is that it tends to create bad legislation. That is demonstrated by the frequency with which initiatives, despite careful drafting by the new professional political law firms, end up in the courts and are often qualified or invalidated there. Neither the success rate of initiatives nor their immunity from legal challenge has improved, despite the professionalization of the process. Indeed, the proportion of initiatives that ends up in the court system has greatly increased in recent years.[77] In the final analysis, initiatives still present voters with a "take it or leave it" situation, where there is no room for compromise. The people who put up millions of dollars to get a measure on the ballot are not prone to compromising their positions—that is not why they mount the campaigns in the first place. Thus, the main difference between legislation by representative democracy and that by popular initiative remains: the former has options for debate and compromise, and for redrafting laws so that they are likely to survive. The latter has neither.

For a contemporary example of the "bad law" idea, one need only look at the "3 Strikes" Proposition 184 of November 1994, which reflected the public's consistent support of almost any measure that appeared to be against crime. Critics, including judges and civil libertarians, expressed concern from the start that the statute could force judges to either rule unfairly against minor offenders or dismiss cases in order to avoid so doing. In 1998, one Russell Benson, who had been convicted fifteen years previously of two felonies for a single knife attack, was caught stealing a carton of cigarettes. This felony comprised the "third strike," and he received the mandatory 25-years-to-life sentence. That decision was upheld by the state Supreme Court, which ruled that Proposition 184 had overturned the 1872 law that prohibited multiple punishments for a single act.[78] Thus "3 Strikes" could actually be only two, and—two strikes or three—one of them could be a very minor theft, with preposterously long prison sentences as a result. California prisons are currently bursting at the seams, and producing rapidly escalating costs for the state's budget.

Because the laws and amendments proposed by direct legislation are so often complex, and rendered even more so by the campaigns of proponents and opponents, voter response frequently revolves around simplifications—a focus on one part of a complex piece of law (lower taxes, punishing criminals, etc.). It has been suggested, for example, that if an initiative uses the word "environment" it will likely be supported by most liberals and Democrats, whereas if it says "punish criminals" it can generally count on support from conservatives and Republicans.[79] Certainly, this was the case with Proposition 215 of 1996, which was officially titled "Medical Use of Marijuana." Once its supporters were able to get the secretary of state to accept that "medical use" wording for the ballot pamphlet title, they were in very good shape indeed, and were able to obtain an extraordinarily broad legalization of marijuana, until the courts intervened.

Similarly, there is no evidence that voters make much distinction between an initiative that is a statute and one that is a constitutional amendment. This has long resulted in an "amalgamation of constitutional and statutory law" that is perhaps unique in California.[80] Any group that thinks it can raise the 8 percent signatures required, may as well go for a constitutional amendment rather than a statute — its initiative, if successful, will be that much more difficult to change or undo.

For the Progressives in the early twentieth century, direct legislation was a way around what they saw as a corrupt and unresponsive legislature. It was also, along with the direct primary and departisanization of many offices, a reflection of the traditional American suspicion of professional politics and, especially, of political parties. It is of no small significance that direct legislation has flourished where political parties are least powerful, where they were diminished by the Progressives in the American Midwest and West. California has been plagued or blessed — depending upon one's own biases — by a weak party system that has become even weaker in the past twenty years or so; the great popularity of term limits is but one strong indication of that continuing trend. This has facilitated the development of candidate independence, but also of single-issue politics, of a system where candidates associate their political fortunes primarily with one or two given issues, often ones being decided by initiative.

Without strong parties to develop voter loyalty, and to provide voters with a permanent institution to blame for government that does not do what they want, this kind of single-issue and centrifugal politics becomes stronger and stronger. That has clearly happened in California: voter loyalties are issue-specific and short-term. The parties become even weaker, losing control of candidate selection, and single-issue interest groups replace the parties as the main source of power in all aspects of the political process. The result is an ad hoc kind of politics where direct legislation is increasingly relied on as a replacement for legislation by representative democracy. The public is being ruled by an uncertain process indeed.[81]

Has direct legislation become more frequent and draconian because state legislatures have avoided basic issues, or is it the opposite — that state legislatures have become more inactive because they have been preempted by direct legislation? This chicken-and-egg argument has been around for a long time, indeed since Progressivism.[82] It might be either, both, or neither; the evidence is in truth arguable. Legislatures in all places and at all levels have been known to pass bad laws — racist, restrictive of civil liberties and civil rights, prejudiced in favor of one group or against another, suborned by money or power. Neither institution, certainly, has a patent on legislative wisdom nor an immunity to occasional stupidity and shortsightedness. But the weaknesses of direct legislation are greater: any group, if it is willing to spend a million dollars or so, can get an initiative on the ballot; and, with enough money, almost any group can usually make sure a proposition is defeated.[83] Even one person, with enough money, can play a dominant role in creating or defeating an initiative, which seems less likely to be the case in candidate elections.[84] Most initiative measures are ultimately decided by a small and unrepresentative body of voters. The laws they pass are often badly drawn, extreme, and subject to judicial revocation. They are, like Proposition 13, reflections of immediate crises, with little concern for long-term effects.[85]

Direct legislation has had profound effects on every aspect of California life over the past 90-plus years. There is no question that it has long since been institutionalized in California and that Californians are committed to its retention. But its weaknesses are real, as we have seen. There seems little question that Californians will continue to view direct legislation as an irreplaceable balance to an unresponsive legislature, just as the Progressives concluded in 1912. Whether they will ultimately become sated with the frequency of the process, or its excesses, and respond to any of the reforms currently recommended by experts inside government and out, remains to be seen.

I concluded a study of a very different kind of politics quite some years ago with an observation that strikes me as equally pertinent to the subject of this book. In a democratic polity, whether decisions are made by representatives or by direct legislation, those decisions are a reflection of that society — its strengths and its weaknesses, its virtues and vices. Whether we are legislating through representatives or directly, it is the people — voters and non-voters alike — who are responsible for what happens. The trouble is not so much with the "system" or the "interests," but with the public, who tend to get the government they deserve.[86]

APPENDIX A

# Direct Legislation
# Propositions, 1912–1998

The following table contains a chronological listing of all direct legislation measures on California ballots since 1912.[1] It gives the election date, the proposition's number, the type of proposition, its topic, and whether it was approved or defeated. The topic given here is not the same as the official title because titles are often not very informative; I have tried, instead, to provide brief but useful descriptions of major provisions. These abbreviations are used in the "Prop. Type" column: R = Referendum; IS = Initiative Statute; ICA = Initiative Constitutional Amendment; IBA = Initiative Bond Act; and ITL = Indirect Initiative.

For referendums one must turn one's mind upside down to understand the results, which officially relate to its effect on the law passed by the legislature. When a referendum is "Approved," therefore, the supporters of the referendum have failed — the legislation under consideration remains in effect. Conversely, when a referendum is "Defeated," the supporters have been successful — the legislation has been overturned.

TABLE A.1    Direct Legislation Propositions, 1912–1998

| Date | Prop. Number | Prop. Type | Topic | Result |
|---|---|---|---|---|
| Nov. 1912 | 3 | R | Law for appointment of a Registrar of Voters | Defeated |
| Nov. 1912 | 4 | R | Law on salaries and fees of county officers, creating Registrar of Voters | Defeated |
| Nov. 1912 | 5 | R | Law creating additional county officers | Defeated |
| Nov. 1912 | 6 | ICA | Consolidate city and county government | Defeated |
| Nov. 1912 | 7 | IS | Prohibit bookmaking, appoint racing commission | Defeated |

| Date | Prop. Number | Prop. Type | Topic | Result |
|------|------|------|------|------|
| Nov. 1912 | 8 | ICA | Taxation by counties, cities, towns | Defeated |
| Nov. 1914 | 2 | ICA | Prohibition | Defeated |
| Nov. 1914 | 3 | IS | 8-hour workday, 48-hour work-week | Defeated |
| Nov. 1914 | 4 | R | Law for abatement of nuisances (prostitution) | Approved |
| Nov. 1914 | 5 | R | Blue sky law to regulate investment companies, create Commissioner of Corporations | Approved |
| Nov. 1914 | 6 | R | Law to create state Water Commission | Approved |
| Nov. 1914 | 9 | IS | Regulate investment companies | Defeated |
| Nov. 1914 | 10 | ICA | Abolish poll tax | Approved |
| Nov. 1914 | 11 | IBA | Bonds for University of California, Berkeley | Approved |
| Nov. 1914 | 13 | ICA | Only property owners to vote on questions of bonded indebtedness | Defeated |
| Nov. 1914 | 14 | IS | Permits absentee voters | Defeated |
| Nov. 1914 | 15 | ICA | Rights of banks holding public moneys | Defeated |
| Nov. 1914 | 18 | R | Law prohibiting most sales of wild game | Defeated |
| Nov. 1914 | 19 | ICA | City-county consolidation, annexation of contiguous territory | Approved |
| Nov. 1914 | 20 | IS | Regulate prize fighting | Approved |
| Nov. 1914 | 21 | ICA | Consolidation and annexation rights of chartered cities | Defeated |
| Nov. 1914 | 22 | IS | Land title law, County Recorder as registrar of titles | Approved |
| Nov. 1914 | 38 | IBA | Los Angeles state building bonds | Defeated |
| Nov. 1914 | 39 | ICA | Extends time to get out of liquor business if Proposition 2 passes | Approved |
| Nov. 1914 | 45 | IS | Day of rest: no business can be open more than six days per week | Defeated |
| Nov. 1914 | 46 | IS | Creates state board for drugless physicians; permits them to treat all illnesses | Defeated |
| Nov. 1914 | 47 | ICA | Prohibits state elections on prohibition matters for eight years | Defeated |

| Date | Prop. Number | Prop. Type | Topic | Result |
|------|------|------|-------|--------|
| Oct. 1915 | 1 | R | Law for direct primaries of 1913 | Defeated |
| Oct. 1915 | 2 | R | Law for form of ballot, including omission of party designations | Defeated |
| Nov. 1916 | 1 | ICA | Enacts prohibition in California | Defeated |
| Nov. 1916 | 2 | ICA | Enacts prohibition in public places | Defeated |
| Nov. 1916 | 4 | R | Law amending Direct Primary law of 1913; permits partisan vote | Defeated |
| Nov. 1916 | 5 | ICA | Taxation on land only (single tax) | Defeated |
| Nov. 1916 | 6 | ICA | Forbids being elected official and member of executive department of government | Approved |
| Nov. 1918 | 1 | IS | Prohibits keeping of saloons and sale of liquor | Defeated |
| Nov. 1918 | 3 | IS | Restricts and regulates interest rates and commissions on loans | Approved |
| Nov. 1918 | 17 | R | Law that regulated county tax levies | Defeated |
| Nov. 1918 | 18 | IS | Creates Board of Authorization; limits on county and school taxation | Defeated |
| Nov. 1918 | 19 | ICA | Taxation on land only (single tax) | Defeated |
| Nov. 1918 | 21 | IS | Regulates Board and Dental Examiners and dental practice | Defeated |
| Nov. 1918 | 22 | IS | Prohibits sale of intoxicating liquors | Defeated |
| Nov. 1920 | 1 | IS | Alien land law | Approved |
| Nov. 1920 | 2 | R | Law for prohibition enforcement | Defeated |
| Nov. 1920 | 3 | ICA | Increase salaries of justices | Defeated |
| Nov. 1920 | 4 | ICA | Initiatives on taxes to require 25 percent rather than 8 percent signatures | Defeated |
| Nov. 1920 | 5 | IS | Regulation of chiropractic practice | Defeated |
| Nov. 1920 | 6 | IS | Prohibits compulsory vaccination for schools or employment | Defeated |
| Nov. 1920 | 7 | IS | Prohibits vivisection for experimental purposes | Defeated |
| Nov. 1920 | 8 | R | Law that regulated use of poisons and drugs | Approved |
| Nov. 1920 | 9 | ICA | Highway bond regulations | Approved |

| Date | Prop. Number | Prop. Type | Topic | Result |
|------|--------------|------------|-------|--------|
| Nov. 1920 | 12 | ICA | New tax on property to be used for University of California | Defeated |
| Nov. 1920 | 13 | R | Law revising community property regulations and taxation | Defeated |
| Nov. 1920 | 14 | R | Law prohibiting state banks from operating insurance companies | Defeated |
| Nov. 1920 | 15 | R | Law to allow organization of irrigation districts on majority vote | Approved |
| Nov. 1920 | 16 | ICA | Adds kindergartens to public school system, sets minimum per-pupil expenditures | Approved |
| Nov. 1920 | 20 | ICA | Taxation on land only (single tax) | Defeated |
| Nov. 1922 | 1 | ICA | Validates legislation for state aid to veterans of wartime service | Approved |
| Nov. 1922 | 2 | R | Law to make Prohibition Amendment and Volstead Act law in California (Wright Act) | Approved |
| Nov. 1922 | 5 | R | Law to specify fire-resistant materials for buildings in incorporated areas | Defeated |
| Nov. 1922 | 10 | ICA | Permits taxation of public land used for public utility service | Defeated |
| Nov. 1922 | 11 | ICA | Regulation of publicly owned public utilities | Defeated |
| Nov. 1922 | 12 | ICA | Regulation of state budget process | Approved |
| Nov. 1922 | 16 | IS | Regulates practice of chiropractic | Approved |
| Nov. 1922 | 19 | ICA | Water and Power Board to issue bonds for water and power development | Defeated |
| Nov. 1922 | 20 | IS | Regulates practice of osteopathy | Approved |
| Nov. 1922 | 24 | R | Law that regulated the practice of law | Defeated |
| Nov. 1922 | 28 | IS | Prohibits vivisection for research purposes | Defeated |
| Nov. 1922 | 29 | ICA | Taxation on land only (single tax) | Defeated |
| Nov. 1922 | 30 | ICA | Railroad Commission to grant franchises for street and interurban rail, etc. | Defeated |
| Nov. 1924 | 1 | ICA | Tax on highway transportation companies in lieu of all other taxes | Defeated |

| Date | Prop. Number | Prop. Type | Topic | Result |
|------|--------------|------------|-------|--------|
| Nov. 1924 | 7 | IS | Regulation of boxing and wrestling contests | Approved |
| Nov. 1924 | 11 | IS | Creates Klamath River Fish and Game District | Approved |
| Nov. 1924 | 16 | ICA | Creates board to acquire land for water and electric power development | Defeated |
| Nov. 1926 | 3 | R | Law that regulates manufacture and sale of oleomargarine | Defeated |
| Nov. 1926 | 4 | IS | Additional tax on gasoline dealers, some funds going to highway construction | Defeated |
| Nov. 1926 | 6 | IS | Regulation of horseracing, pari-mutuel betting permitted | Defeated |
| Nov. 1926 | 8 | ICA | Commits funds to highway construction | Defeated |
| Nov. 1926 | 9 | IS | Repeals prohibition enforcement (Wright Act) | Defeated |
| Nov. 1926 | 17 | ICA | Permits study and reading of Bible in public schools | Defeated |
| Nov. 1926 | 18 | ICA | Creates board to acquire land for water and electric power development | Defeated |
| Nov. 1926 | 20 | ICA | Reapportionment Commission to act if legislature does not adjust districts | Defeated |
| Nov. 1926 | 28 | ICA | Requires legislature to reapportion based on 1920 Census | Approved |
| Nov. 1928 | 1 | R | Law for reapportionment according to Proposition 28 of 1926 | Approved |
| Nov. 1928 | 5 | IS | Repeals law created by Proposition 7, Nov. 1924, to leave prize fighting illegal | Defeated |
| Nov. 1928 | 8 | R | Law that increased vehicle registration fees for buses and trucks | Approved |
| Nov. 1928 | 21 | IS | Prohibits wild animal racing, bull riding, etc. | Defeated |
| Nov. 1930 | 7 | IS | Creates daylight-saving time | Defeated |
| Nov. 1930 | 10 | IS | Usury law; written agreements for interest rate not required | Defeated |

| Date | Prop. Number | Prop. Type | Topic | Result |
|---|---|---|---|---|
| Nov. 1930 | 11 | ICA | Fish and Game Commission created to establish districts, issue licenses | Defeated |
| Nov. 1930 | 14 | IS | New state registration of voters, to be continuous | Approved |
| Nov. 1930 | 26 | IS | All businesses must close on Sundays | Defeated |
| May 1932 | 1 | R | Law that created Conservation Commission to monitor waste of oil | Defeated |
| May 1932 | 2 | R | Law that removed power of Director of Finance to lease state-owned oil tidelands | Approved |
| Nov. 1932 | 1 | IS | Repeals Wright Act that enforced Eighteenth Amendment and Volstead Act | Approved |
| Nov. 1932 | 2 | ICA | If Proposition 1 passes, wine and beer can be served; legislature can permit liquor | Approved |
| Nov. 1932 | 3 | IS | Regulation of mortgages and trust deeds | Defeated |
| Nov. 1932 | 5 | IS | Creates Racing Board to regulate horse racetrack licensing and wagering | Defeated |
| Nov. 1932 | 11 | ICA | To grant to City of Huntington Beach tidal and submerged lands | Defeated |
| Dec. 1933 | 1 | R | Law that created Water Project Authority for Central Valley Project | Approved |
| Nov. 1934 | 2 | ICA | Permits possession, sale, consumption of all liquors except in saloons | Approved |
| Nov. 1934 | 3 | ICA | Nomination and selection of Supreme and Appellate Court Justices | Approved |
| Nov. 1934 | 4 | ICA | Regulates office of Attorney General | Approved |
| Nov. 1934 | 5 | ICA | Court may comment on evidence and failure of defendant to testify | Approved |
| Nov. 1934 | 6 | ICA | Defendant may plead guilty before magistrate if crime not punishable by death | Approved |

| Date | Prop. Number | Prop. Type | Topic | Result |
|------|--------------|------------|-------|--------|
| Nov. 1934 | 7 | ICA | Regulates state civil service, appointments and promotions on merit, examinations | Approved |
| Nov. 1934 | 9 | IS | Creates State Chiropractic Association to regulate chiropractic | Defeated |
| Nov. 1934 | 11 | IS | Creates elective State Board of Education, abolishes office of Superintendent of Instruction | Defeated |
| Nov. 1934 | 13 | ICA | Local option — cities or counties can prohibit alcoholic beverages | Defeated |
| Nov. 1934 | 17 | IS | Regulates naturopathic colleges, sets educational requirements for naturopathy | Defeated |
| Nov. 1936 | 2 | ICA | Sets requirements for income tax; repeals 1935 Personal Income Tax Act | Defeated |
| Nov. 1936 | 3 | ICA | Creates new Alcoholic Beverage Commission, appointed by governor | Defeated |
| Nov. 1936 | 4 | IS | Prohibits tideland surface oil drilling, permits slant drilling | Defeated |
| Nov. 1936 | 7 | ICA | Civil service regulations for county, district, and municipal appointments | Defeated |
| Nov. 1936 | 9 | ICA | Local option — cities or counties can prohibit alcoholic beverages | Defeated |
| Nov. 1936 | 10 | ICA | Motor vehicle license fees to be used for highway purposes and vehicle regulation | Defeated |
| Nov. 1936 | 11 | ICA | Creates State Tenure Board to deal with tenure, dismissal of teachers | Defeated |
| Nov. 1936 | 18 | R | Law that provided excise tax on oleomargarine | Defeated |
| Nov. 1936 | 22 | R | Law that required retail businesses to pay licensing fee based on number of stores | Defeated |
| Nov. 1938 | 1 | IS | Regulates picketing and boycotting, prohibits seizure of private property | Defeated |
| Nov. 1938 | 2 | IS | Regulates dog pounds, sale of animals for experimental purposes | Defeated |

| Date | Prop. Number | Prop. Type | Topic | Result |
|------|--------------|------------|-------|--------|
| Nov. 1938 | 4 | ICA | Creates Highway and Traffic Safety Commission, grants specific powers | Defeated |
| Nov. 1938 | 5 | IS | Regulates commercial fishing in state waters | Approved |
| Nov. 1938 | 10 | R | Law for bidding on state-owned tidelands at Huntington Beach for oil drilling | Defeated |
| Nov. 1938 | 13 | R | Law that created local Public Utilities Commissions, authorized sale of revenue bonds | Defeated |
| Nov. 1938 | 20 | ICA | Revokes sales and other taxes, repeals limits on property tax (single tax) | Defeated |
| Nov. 1938 | 24 | R | Law for bidding on state-owned tidelands at Huntington Beach for oil drilling | Defeated |
| Nov. 1938 | 25 | IS | Retirement payments for life to those over age 50 ("Ham and Eggs") | Defeated |
| Nov. 1939 | 1 | ICA | Retirement payments for life to those over age 50 ("Ham and Eggs") | Defeated |
| Nov. 1939 | 2 | IS | Amends Chiropractor Act, expands regulation | Defeated |
| Nov. 1939 | 3 | R | Law that regulated practice of personal property brokers/money lenders | Approved |
| Nov. 1939 | 4 | R | Law that regulated practice of personal property brokers/money lenders | Approved |
| Nov. 1939 | 5 | R | Law that created Oil Conservation Commission to regulate production of gas and oil | Defeated |
| Nov. 1940 | 5 | IS | Creates daylight-saving time | Defeated |
| Nov. 1942 | 1 | R | Law that outlawed hot cargo, secondary boycott for duration of "national emergency" | Approved |
| Nov. 1942 | 3 | IS | Science exam required to practice medicine, dentistry, chiropractic, etc. | Defeated |
| Nov. 1942 | 4 | ICA | Sets requirements for income tax; repeals 1935 Personal Income Tax Act | Defeated |

| Date | Prop. Number | Prop. Type | Topic | Result |
|------|------|------|-------|--------|
| Nov. 1942 | 10 | ITL | Regulates building and loan associations | Defeated |
| Nov. 1944 | 9 | ICA | Increases amount to be raised and spent for elementary schools | Approved |
| Nov. 1944 | 11 | ICA | Retirement payments age 60 and over, changes tax structure (Townsend Plan) | Defeated |
| Nov. 1944 | 12 | ICA | Right to work, no requirements to join labor union | Defeated |
| Nov. 1946 | 2 | IS | Permits greyhound racing with pari-mutuel betting | Defeated |
| Nov. 1946 | 3 | ICA | Minimum salaries for teachers and minimum state support per pupil | Approved |
| Nov. 1946 | 11 | IS | Fair employment practices, no racial or other discrimination in hiring | Defeated |
| Nov. 1948 | 2 | ICA | Local enforcement of liquor regulations regarding minors and women | Defeated |
| Nov. 1948 | 3 | IS | Public Utilities Commission to specify number of brakemen on railroad trains | Approved |
| Nov. 1948 | 4 | ICA | Aged and blind pensions, control by state rather than counties | Approved |
| Nov. 1948 | 6 | IS | Regulates commercial fishing in San Francisco Bay and connecting waters | Defeated |
| Nov. 1948 | 12 | ICA | Local option — cities or counties can prohibit alcoholic beverages | Defeated |
| Nov. 1948 | 13 | ICA | Reapportionment of state senate, removes limit of one senator per county | Defeated |
| Nov. 1948 | 14 | ICA | Creates state Housing Agency, commits state funds to subsidize public housing | Defeated |
| Nov. 1948 | 15 | IS | Regulates purse net and round haul nets fishing in certain areas | Defeated |
| Nov. 1949 | 2 | ICA | Aged and blind, removes changes of Proposition 4, Nov. 1948 | Defeated |
| Nov. 1949 | 12 | IS | Creates daylight-saving time | Approved |
| Nov. 1950 | 1 | ICA | Forbids taxation of personal property | Defeated |

| Date | Prop. Number | Prop. Type | Topic | Result |
|---|---|---|---|---|
| Nov. 1950 | 6 | ICA | Legalizes off-site gambling on horse races in licensed places | Defeated |
| Nov. 1950 | 10 | ICA | Voter approval required for any state low-rent housing project to be established | Approved |
| Nov. 1952 | 2 | ICA | Increase in per-student public school funds | Approved |
| Nov. 1952 | 3 | R | Property tax exemption for nonprofit religious, hospital, charitable schools | Approved |
| Nov. 1952 | 10 | ICA | Forbids public money to any organization that tries to influence legislation | Defeated |
| Nov. 1952 | 11 | ITL | Old-age pensions increased, state rather than county administration | Defeated |
| Nov. 1952 | 13 | ITL | Ends cross-filing | Defeated |
| Nov. 1954 | 4 | ICA | Increases aid to needy aged, legislature cannot decrease amount | Defeated |
| Nov. 1956 | 4 | IS | Creates California Oil and Gas Commission to prevent waste, monitor pools | Defeated |
| Nov. 1958 | 16 | ICA | Removes property tax exemption of religious and private schools | Defeated |
| Nov. 1958 | 17 | IS | Decreases sales tax, makes income tax more progressive | Defeated |
| Nov. 1958 | 18 | ICA | Forbids closed shop; union membership voluntary, not condition to hiring, etc. | Defeated |
| Nov. 1960 | 15 | ICA | Reapportions state senate, districts based on population and other factors | Defeated |
| Nov. 1962 | 23 | ICA | Increases size of state senate, districts based on population and other factors | Defeated |
| Nov. 1962 | 24 | ICA | Regulates Communists and subversive organizations, requirements to testify | Defeated |
| Nov. 1964 | 14 | ICA | Landlord's right to decline to sell or rent; abrogates Rumford Act of 1963 | Approved |

| Date | Prop. Number | Prop. Type | Topic | Result |
|------|-------------|-----------|-------|--------|
| Nov. 1964 | 15 | IS | Prohibits subscription television; television sent to homes must be free of charge | Approved |
| Nov. 1964 | 16 | ICA | Creates state lottery | Defeated |
| Nov. 1964 | 17 | IS | Applies federal ruling for size of train crews, abrogates earlier state law | Approved |
| Nov. 1966 | 16 | IS | Prohibits obscene matter and conduct, redefines obscenity | Defeated |
| Nov. 1968 | 9 | ICA | Reduces property taxes to maximum 1 percent of market value | Defeated |
| June 1970 | 8 | ICA | At least 50 percent of school costs, 90 percent of welfare costs from other than property taxes | Defeated |
| June 1972 | 9 | IS | Environmental controls on fuels, air quality standards, tidelands oil, etc. | Defeated |
| Nov. 1972 | 14 | ICA | Property tax limitation, two-thirds vote required for tax increases | Defeated |
| Nov. 1972 | 15 | ICA | State employees to be paid prevailing rates in private and public employment | Defeated |
| Nov. 1972 | 16 | ICA | Sets salaries of California Highway Patrol, two-thirds vote for modification | Defeated |
| Nov. 1972 | 17 | ICA | Reaffirms statutes on death penalty, death penalty not cruel or unusual punishment | Approved |
| Nov. 1972 | 18 | IS | Redefines obscenity, removes "redeeming social importance" defense, etc. | Defeated |
| Nov. 1972 | 19 | IS | Permits cultivation, processing, transporting, possessing, using marijuana | Defeated |
| Nov. 1972 | 20 | IS | Creates state and regional coastal protection commissions, defines coastal areas | Approved |
| Nov. 1972 | 21 | IS | Ends mandatory busing, repeals statute that sought racial and ethnic school balance | Approved |

| Date | Prop. Number | Prop. Type | Topic | Result |
|------|--------------|------------|-------|--------|
| Nov. 1972 | 22 | IS | Rules for agricultural labor relations; outlaws certain strikes, boycotts, etc. | Defeated |
| Nov. 1973 | 1 | ICA | Limits state expenditures, mandates use of surplus for tax reductions, etc. | Defeated |
| June 1974 | 9 | IS | Regulates campaign expenditures, lobbyists, disclosure; creates FPPC | Approved |
| Nov. 1974 | 17 | IS | Adds parts of Stanislaus River into Wild and Scenic Rivers Act of 1972 | Defeated |
| June 1976 | 15 | IS | Prohibits new nuclear power plants, regulates existing ones | Defeated |
| Nov. 1976 | 13 | IS | Permits greyhound racing with pari-mutuel betting | Defeated |
| Nov. 1976 | 14 | IS | Agricultural Labor Relations Board, rights of union organizers, penalizes unfair practices | Defeated |
| June 1978 | 13 | ICA | Property tax reduction and limitation, two-thirds vote required for increases | Approved |
| Nov. 1978 | 5 | IS | Prohibits smoking in specified areas, restaurants must have non-smoking areas | Defeated |
| Nov. 1978 | 6 | IS | School employees can be fired for homosexuality | Defeated |
| Nov. 1978 | 7 | IS | Changes criteria and penalties for first-degree murder; death penalty authorized | Approved |
| Nov. 1979 | 4 | ICA | Appropriation limits for state and local government, return of excess revenues | Approved |
| June 1980 | 9 | ICA | Lowers income tax rates, increases to be limited to change in consumer price index | Defeated |
| June 1980 | 10 | ICA | Rent control to be done only at local level and by popular vote | Defeated |
| June 1980 | 11 | IS | Ten percent surtax for oil, gas, coal, and uranium businesses | Defeated |
| Nov. 1980 | 10 | IS | Smoking and non-smoking sections in public places, employment places, etc. | Defeated |

| Date | Prop. Number | Prop. Type | Topic | Result |
|------|--------------|------------|-------|--------|
| June 1982 | 5 | IS | Prohibits gift and inheritance taxes (Proponent Miller) | Approved |
| June 1982 | 6 | IS | Prohibits gift and inheritance taxes (Proponent Rogers) | Approved |
| June 1982 | 7 | IS | Income tax indexing based on consumer price index | Approved |
| June 1982 | 8 | IS, ICA | Criminal procedure and sentencing, victims' rights, bail, plea bargaining, etc. | Approved |
| June 1982 | 9 | R | Law that established water facilities including peripheral canal | Defeated |
| June 1982 | 10 | R | Law that revised boundaries of congressional districts | Defeated |
| June 1982 | 11 | R | Law that revised boundaries of state senatorial districts | Defeated |
| June 1982 | 12 | R | Law that revised boundaries of state assembly districts | Defeated |
| Nov. 1982 | 11 | IS | Beverage containers must have refund value of at least five cents | Defeated |
| Nov. 1982 | 12 | IS | Governor must write to President of the United States in re dangers of nuclear war, testing | Approved |
| Nov. 1982 | 13 | IS | Water conservation programs, wildlife and recreation, water storage | Defeated |
| Nov. 1982 | 14 | ICA | Removes legislature's power over redistricting, creates commission and procedures | Defeated |
| Nov. 1982 | 15 | IS | Requires registration of concealable firearms, protects gun ownership | Defeated |
| June 1984 | 24 | IS | Regulation of legislature's committees, 30 percent decrease in its support appropriation | Approved |
| Nov. 1984 | 35 | IS | Balanced federal budget — removed from ballot by state Supreme Court | No vote |
| Nov. 1984 | 36 | ICA | Forbids new property tax, specifies majorities needed for other tax legislation | Defeated |

| Date | Prop. Number | Prop. Type | Topic | Result |
|---|---|---|---|---|
| Nov. 1984 | 37 | ICA, IS | Establishes state lottery, at least 34 percent of profits for public education | Approved |
| Nov. 1984 | 38 | IS | Governor must request of U.S. government that voting materials be in English only | Approved |
| Nov. 1984 | 39 | ICA, IS | New criteria for redistricting assembly, senate, congressional, equalization districts | Defeated |
| Nov. 1984 | 40 | IS | Limits campaign contributions for state offices, limited public funding | Defeated |
| Nov. 1984 | 41 | IS | New Public Assistance Commission, limits on expenditures for benefits | Defeated |
| June 1986 | 51 | IS | Limits tort liability when multiple defendants are involved | Approved |
| Nov. 1986 | 61 | ICA, IS | Limits salaries of public officials, popular vote required for increases | Defeated |
| Nov. 1986 | 62 | IS | Regulates new and increased taxes by local governments and districts | Approved |
| Nov. 1986 | 63 | ICA | Establishes English as official state language, legislature to enforce | Approved |
| Nov. 1986 | 64 | IS | Declares AIDS an infectious disease, carriers to be placed on reportable disease list | Defeated |
| Nov. 1986 | 65 | IS | Forbids toxic discharge into drinking water, requires disclosure by those doing it | Approved |
| June 1988 | 68 | IS | Limits campaign contributions for state legislative offices, limited public funding | Approved |
| June 1988 | 69 | IS | Declares AIDS an infectious disease, carriers to be placed on special list | Defeated |
| June 1988 | 70 | IBA | Bond issue for wildlife, coastal, and parkland conservation | Approved |
| June 1988 | 71 | ICA | Updates state and local appropriation limit (revises Prop. 4, Nov. 1979) | Defeated |

| Date | Prop. Number | Prop. Type | Topic | Result |
|------|------|------|-------|--------|
| June 1988 | 72 | ICA | Creates emergency reserve, specifies majorities for raising fuel tax | Defeated |
| June 1988 | 73 | IS | Limits campaign contributions (overrides parts of Prop. 68 in same election) | Approved |
| Nov. 1988 | 95 | IS | Support for hungry and homeless, funds to come from fines | Defeated |
| Nov. 1988 | 96 | IS | Mandatory tests for AIDS when crime may involve bodily fluid transfer | Approved |
| Nov. 1988 | 97 | IS | Provides funds to enforce state occupational health and safety plan | Approved |
| Nov. 1988 | 98 | ICA, IS | Establishes minimum level of funding for public schools and community colleges | Approved |
| Nov. 1988 | 99 | ICA, IS | Additional tax on cigarette distributors; funds to be used for research, treatment | Approved |
| Nov. 1988 | 100 | IS | Reductions in auto insurance rates, good-driver discounts | Defeated |
| Nov. 1988 | 101 | IS | Reductions in auto insurance rates, limits attorney contingency fees | Defeated |
| Nov. 1988 | 102 | IS | Requires reporting patients with AIDS; AIDS tests permitted for employment, etc. | Defeated |
| Nov. 1988 | 103 | IS | Reductions in auto insurance rates, elected Insurance Commissioner | Approved |
| Nov. 1988 | 104 | IS | No-fault insurance established for auto accident injuries; some rate reductions | Defeated |
| Nov. 1988 | 105 | IS | Mandatory disclosure to consumers, voters, investors on various matters | Approved |
| Nov. 1988 | 106 | IS | Limits contingency fees of attorneys in tort claims | Defeated |
| June 1990 | 115 | ICA, IS | Changes criminal law, judicial procedures, expands capital offences | Approved |

| Date | Prop. Number | Prop. Type | Topic | Result |
|------|--------------|------------|-------|--------|
| June 1990 | 116 | IBA | Authorizes bonds for passenger and commuter rail systems | Approved |
| June 1990 | 117 | IS | Establishes fund for wildlife protection, habitat acquisition | Approved |
| June 1990 | 118 | ICA, IS | Changes procedures for redistricting, requires legislative and popular approval | Defeated |
| June 1990 | 119 | ICA, IS | Creates citizen commission for redistricting | Defeated |
| Nov. 1990 | 128 | IS | Regulates chemicals in foods and pesticides; air pollution standards; water quality | Defeated |
| Nov. 1990 | 129 | ICA, IS | Creates drug superfund, authorizes bonds for prison construction | Defeated |
| Nov. 1990 | 130 | IS | Authorizes bonds for forest acquisition and job retraining, regulates logging | Defeated |
| Nov. 1990 | 131 | ICA, IS | Term limits for state officials, changes campaign finance laws, some public funding | Defeated |
| Nov. 1990 | 132 | ICA | Establishes marine protection zone within three miles of coast; regulates fishing | Approved |
| Nov. 1990 | 133 | IS | Increases sales tax to fund drug enforcement and education, prisons and jails | Defeated |
| Nov. 1990 | 134 | IS | Increases tax on alcoholic beverages to fund alcohol and drug-abuse programs | Defeated |
| Nov. 1990 | 135 | IS | Pesticide regulation, hazardous materials regulation | Defeated |
| Nov. 1990 | 136 | ICA | Regulates new or increased state or local taxes, specifies majorities for passage | Defeated |
| Nov. 1990 | 137 | ICA | Requires voter approval for changes in initiative or referendum process | Defeated |
| Nov. 1990 | 138 | IS | Revises regulations of logging, mandates study of greenhouse gases | Defeated |
| Nov. 1990 | 139 | ICA, IS | Permits prison inmate work for private businesses, regulates the practice | Approved |

| Date | Prop. Number | Prop. Type | Topic | Result |
|------|--------------|------------|-------|--------|
| Nov. 1990 | 140 | ICA | Term limits for state officials, limits on legislature's salary and operating expenses | Approved |
| Nov. 1992 | 161 | IS | Permits physician-assisted death for terminally ill | Defeated |
| Nov. 1992 | 162 | ICA | Gives boards of public employee retirement systems full control of assets | Approved |
| Nov. 1992 | 163 | ICA, IS | Ends sales tax on candy, snack foods, bottled water | Approved |
| Nov. 1992 | 164 | IS | Term limits for California's U.S. Senators and Representatives | Approved |
| Nov. 1992 | 165 | ICA, IS | Lets governor reduce some expenditures to balance budget, cuts welfare payments | Defeated |
| Nov. 1992 | 166 | IS | Requires employers to provide health care coverage, limits employee contribution | Defeated |
| Nov. 1992 | 167 | IS | Raises top income tax rates, repeals 1991 sales tax hike, renters' tax credits | Defeated |
| Nov. 1993 | 174 | ICA | State education vouchers usable for public or private schools | Defeated |
| June 1994 | 180 | IS | Authorizes bonds for parklands, historic sites, wildlife and forest conservation | Defeated |
| Nov. 1994 | 184 | IS | Increased sentences for repeat criminal offenders ("3 Strikes") | Approved |
| Nov. 1994 | 185 | IS | Additional 4 percent gasoline tax, funds for specified public transportation applications | Defeated |
| Nov. 1994 | 186 | ICA, IS | Establishes state-operated health system to replace existing health insurance | Defeated |
| Nov. 1994 | 187 | IS | Illegal aliens ineligible for public social and health services, public education | Approved |
| Nov. 1994 | 188 | IS | Overrides local smoking laws, permits regulated smoking | Defeated |
| Mar. 1996 | 198 | IS | Open blanket primary — one ballot with all candidate names | Approved |
| Mar. 1996 | 199 | IS | Phases out rent control on mobile homes | Defeated |

| Date | Prop. Number | Prop. Type | Topic | Result |
|------|--------------|------------|-------|--------|
| Mar. 1996 | 200 | IS | No-fault automobile insurance | Defeated |
| Mar. 1996 | 201 | IS | Attorney's fees in class action and shareholder suits in re securities laws | Defeated |
| Mar. 1996 | 202 | IS | Limits on attorneys' contingency fees in tort cases | Defeated |
| Nov. 1996 | 207 | IS | Prohibits restrictions on right of attorneys to negotiate fees | Defeated |
| Nov. 1996 | 208 | IS | Campaign contribution and spending limits | Approved |
| Nov. 1996 | 209 | ICA | Ends affirmative action in California | Approved |
| Nov. 1996 | 210 | IS | Increases state minimum wage | Approved |
| Nov. 1996 | 211 | IS | Prohibits restrictions on right of attorneys to negotiate fees | Defeated |
| Nov. 1996 | 212 | IS | Campaign contribution and spending limits | Defeated |
| Nov. 1996 | 213 | IS | Limits some auto accident recovery benefits to felons or drunk drivers | Approved |
| Nov. 1996 | 214 | IS | Regulates HMOs and other health care businesses | Defeated |
| Nov. 1996 | 215 | IS | Permits growing, possession, and use of marijuana for health-related reasons | Approved |
| Nov. 1996 | 216 | IS | Regulates HMOs and other health care businesses | Defeated |
| Nov. 1996 | 217 | IS | Reinstates expired higher tax rates on top incomes | Defeated |
| Nov. 1996 | 218 | ICA | Requires majority voter approval of local tax and fee increases | Approved |
| June 1998 | 223 | IS | School districts to spend no more than 5 percent of all funds for administrative costs | Defeated |
| June 1998 | 224 | ICA | Regulates state-funded design and engineering contracts | Defeated |
| June 1998 | 225 | IS | California legislators must support term limits for U.S. Representatives and Senators | Approved |
| June 1998 | 226 | IS | Union member's permission required to use dues for political contributions | Defeated |

| Date | Prop. Number | Prop. Type | Topic | Result |
|------|------|------|-------|--------|
| June 1998 | 227 | IS | All public education to be conducted in English; ends bilingual education | Approved |
| Nov. 1998 | 4 | IS | Prohibits certain animal traps | Approved |
| Nov. 1998 | 5 | IS | Expands gambling casino rights of Indian tribes | Approved |
| Nov. 1998 | 6 | IS | Forbids transfer, sale, possession of horse meat for human consumption | Approved |
| Nov. 1998 | 7 | IS | Tax credits to companies that reduce air emissions | Defeated |
| Nov. 1998 | 8 | IS | School class size reduction; creates Office of Chief Inspector of public schools | Defeated |
| Nov. 1998 | 9 | IS | Modifies deregulation of electric industry, mandates rate reductions | Defeated |
| Nov. 1998 | 10 | ICA, IS | Raises taxes on tobacco; commissions for child development, tobacco education | Approved |

# Definitions of Statistics and Terms

When dealing with subjects like voting, where numeric data are an important source of information, the use of statistics can help considerably in both description and analysis. The statistics do not have to be particularly arcane. They have purposely been kept simple in this book both because they are appropriate for the data being used and in order to help rather than hinder the reader's understanding of the material. With a few definitions in hand, the reader should be able to follow them without difficulty and to make productive use of the many tables provided.

The great majority of the data is expressed as simple percentages. This is at one and the same time one of the most easily comprehensible and one of the most useful of statistics. Other measures are used only when they can make a more significant contribution to description or analysis.

*Correlation.* There are many correlation coefficient tables in the text, based on the Pearson product moment correlation. This is a widely used statistic for seeking the relationship between two numeric variables (e.g., the percentage voting Yes for one proposition and the percentage voting Yes for another proposition, or percentage urban and percentage voting Yes or No on any given proposition). Correlation measures the extent to which an increase in one variable is related to an increase or decrease in another variable.

Correlation can also be plotted graphically in a scatter plot, as seen in Figure B.1. The figure plots the correlation between voting on affirmative action and voting to end bilingualism in each of California's 58 counties. For each county, a dot (data point) has been placed where its vote to end affirmative action (represented by the horizontal, or x-axis) intersects with its vote to end bilingualism (represented by the vertical, or y-axis). The solid line is the line of best fit, mathematically calculated from the 58 data points for the 58 counties. From this fit, the numeric correlation coefficient is calculated. The scatter plot provides a nice visual representation of what the numeric expression tells us.

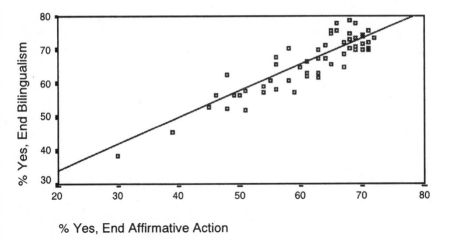

FIGURE B.1. Scatter plot of Propositions 209 and 227: end affirmative action and end bilingualism in schools; weighted for total population, 1990 Census. Pearson correlation coefficient = .940.

The correlation coefficient ranges from +1 to −1, where the former indicates complete positive relationship, and the latter indicates the opposite — that is, as one variable increases the other decreases. For example, in Table 1.1 we saw that the relationship for 1911 voting in favor of creating the initiative process and voting in favor of creating the recall process was .945, very close to a perfect relationship; as voting on one issue rose or fell, so did voting on the other, and in the same direction. On the other hand, the correlation between voting for Hiram Johnson in 1910 and voting in favor of women's suffrage in 1910 was −.557, which indicates a fairly strong negative relationship; as voting for one went up, voting for the other went down. Negative relationships are as important as positive ones; when the relationships are strong in either direction, there is something to be learned.

This statistic measures *relationship*, not *causation*, although causation can be inferred when the statistical data are reinforced by logic and/or substantiating non-quantitative sources, such as campaign materials, memoirs, public opinion polls, and so on. At just what level, positive or negative, a correlation coefficient becomes significant, is a matter subject to interpretation; statistics programs can "tell" us, but only in a mathematical sense that may not relate to the real world we are studying. For the kind of data studied in this book, a level of .400 or higher, positive or negative, points to a significant statistical relationship worth considering. When we get to about .750 or higher, the relationship is strong.

The nature of the data plays an important role in the persuasiveness and significance of any pair of variables. The data in this book are county-level; that is, they are aggregated on relatively large units. Because of their size and diversity, counties are much less likely, for example, than precincts, to be dominated by any one background variable (such as wealth, race, or ethnicity). For that reason, census data were used in this study less frequently than I would have liked; statistical relationships between social and economic variables on the one hand, and voting on the other, were only rarely discernible with county-level data.

*Weighting.* Disproportionate county population explains why all the correlation tables use weighted data. If each county were given the same weight, Alpine County, with a 1990 population of 1,113, or Sierra County with 3,318, would each count for 1/58th of the data under analysis, just as Los Angeles County, with its 1990 population of almost 9 million, would also count for 1/58th of the data. In this scenario, the final results would be terribly skewed and misleading. Therefore, in the correlation tables, each county is given a weight based on its population in the census closest in time to the voting data in that table. This provides a truer picture of the meaning of the data than if each of the 58 counties were given the same weight.

*Cross-Tabulation.* This simple statistical procedure is used for public opinion data. I use it here primarily for relating two variables, although it is easy with cross-tabulation to control for one or more additional variables if the population being studied is large enough. Unlike the voting or census data in correlation tables, which is *interval* in nature (e.g., percentages, ranging from 0 percent to 100 percent), the data in public opinion polls are generally *categorical* (Democrat, Republican, Independent; Favor Proposition X, Oppose Proposition X; etc.), for which correlation is inappropriate. Simple cross-tabulation handles such data neatly and clearly. Everyone, for example, who is a Democrat and who favors a proposition is counted in one box, everyone who is a Democrat and opposes that proposition is counted in another box, in a matrix of boxes, with the information displayed in a simple format, generally in percentages. In most cases, I have extracted the more interesting data from such matrices into tables, as in Tables 5.4 and 5.5.

*The Term 'Voter Participation'.* I have made a distinction in the text between the more commonly used term *turnout* and my alternative of *voter participation*. *Turnout* generally means the percentage of registered voters (or of eligible voters) who participate in a given election. I was more often interested in the percentage of those voting in any given election who also took the trouble to vote for a specific proposition on the same ballot. Therefore, the use of the separate term *voter participation* seemed worth the trouble. Occasionally, I do refer to *turnout*, in which cases its standard meaning is intended.

*Current Dollars.* In several places, I have tried to make the figures for spending in initiative campaigns more meaningful by converting them to current dollars. These conversions were based on the Bureau of Labor Statistics' "Consumer Price Index — All Urban Consumers," for the Los Angeles–Long Beach–Anaheim area, with the base period being 1982–1984.

# Notes

The following shortened references are used throughout the Notes:

Campaign Statements. These are official filings of money raised and spent by all campaign organizations. Campaign statements have been required by law since 1922, and are filed with the office of the California Secretary of State. They are organized by election year, and then by name of the campaign organization; they are not organized by Proposition. They are available at the California State Archives.

Campaign Statement Summaries. These summaries are organized by election year and then by Proposition starting in 1976. From 1976 to 1990, they were published, under varying titles, by the Fair Political Practices Commission. Since 1990, they have been published by the Political Reform Division of the Secretary of State's office, also with varying titles, but recently consistently entitled *Financing California's Statewide Ballot Measures: xxxx Primary and General Elections* (the "xxxx" stands here for the actual year). They are available at various libraries and in the California History Room of the California State Library.

Dickson Papers. Edward A. Dickson Papers, UCLA Research Library.

Gann Papers. Paul Gann Papers, California State Library.

Haynes Papers. John Randolph Haynes Papers, UCLA Research Library.

Hichborn Papers. Franklin Hichborn Papers, UCLA Research Library.

IGS Campaigns File. Files of miscellaneous political campaign materials, Institute of Governmental Studies Library, University of California, Berkeley.

Jarvis Papers. Howard Jarvis Papers, California State Library.

Johnson Papers. Hiram Johnson Papers, Bancroft Library, University of California, Berkeley.

Lissner Papers. Meyer Lissner Papers, Stanford University Library.

Rose Papers. Alice M. Rose Papers, Stanford University Library.

Rowell/B Papers. Chester Rowell Papers, Bancroft Library, University of California, Berkeley.

Rowell/LA Papers. Chester Rowell Papers, UCLA Research Library.

Stimson Papers. Marshall Stimson Papers, Huntington Library, San Marino.

UCLA Campaigns File. Files of miscellaneous political campaign materials, Henry T. Bruman Library, Maps and Government Information, University Research Library, University of California, Los Angeles.

UC Berkeley Oral Histories. These are a series of published oral histories, which were conducted under the auspices of the University of California, Berkeley. Published by: Regional Cultural History Project, The General Library, University of California, Berkeley.

UCLA Oral Histories. These are a series of published oral histories, which were conducted under the auspices of the University of California, Los Angeles. Published by: UCLA Oral History Program, University of California, Los Angeles, for itself or for the California State Archives State Government Oral History Program (Sacramento).

### INTRODUCTION

1. There are several types of statutes that are exempted by the California constitution from the referendum process, notably those involving taxation and appropriations.

2. An excellent description and analysis of Athenian democracy is Mogens Herman Hansen, *The Athenian Democracy in the Age of Demosthenes*, trans. J. A. Crook (Oxford: Basil Blackwell Ltd., 1991).

3. Ibid., 60, 94.

4. On the general background of direct legislation, see Elias P. Oberholtzer, *Referendum in America: A Discussion of Law-Making by Popular Vote* (Freeport, N.Y.: Books for Libraries Press, 1893); Laura Tallian, *Direct Democracy: An Historical Analysis of the Initiative, Referendum, and Recall Process* (Los Angeles: People's Lobby, Inc., 1977); Thomas E. Cronin, *Direct Democracy: The Politics of Initiative, Referendum, and Recall* (Cambridge, Mass.: Harvard University Press, 1989).

5. In modern New England towns, there is a very strong inverse relationship between town size and percentage of the population that participates in annual town meetings. See Joseph F. Zimmerman, *Participatory Democracy: Populism Revived* (New York: Praeger, 1986), 21–22.

6. Oberholtzer, *Referendum in America*, chap. 2; Cronin, *Direct Democracy*, chap. 3.

7. Swiss tradition and the Swiss system are less suspicious of political parties than is the case in the United States, which explains the existence of proportional representation there, and of term limits (see Chapters 5 and 6) here.

8. Cronin, *Direct Democracy*, 50–54.

9. For a general overview of direct democracy in California, and some national information as well, see League of Women Voters of California, *The Initiative and Referendum in California: A Legacy Lost?* (Sacramento: The League, 1984).

10. For example, a recent biography of Hiram Johnson barely mentions direct legislation, and one of Earl Warren ignores it completely: Richard Coke Lower, *A Bloc of One: The Political Career of Hiram W Johnson* (Stanford, Calif.: Stanford University Press, 1993); Ed Cray, *Chief Justice: A Biography of Earl Warren* (New York: Simon & Schuster, 1997).

11. Daniel H. Lowenstein, "Campaign Spending and Ballot Propositions: Recent Experience, Public Choice Theory and the First Amendment," *UCLA Law Review* 29 (February 1982): 508–9.

12. For a recent argument along these lines, see Peter Schrag, *Paradise Lost: California's Experience, America's Future* (New York: New Press, 1988).

13. A good expression of varying interpretations of Progressivism can be found in John D. Buenker, John C. Burnham, and Robert M. Crunden, *Progressivism* (Cambridge, Mass.: Schenckman Publishing Co., 1977). For a convenient summary

of theories of Progressivism, see Judith Sealander, *Grand Plans: Business Progressivism and Social Change in Ohio's Miami Valley, 1890–1929* (Lexington: University Press of Kentucky, 1988), chap. 1.

14. George Mowry, in his seminal and influential *The California Progressives* (Chicago: Quadrangle Books, 1951), is most often cited for his description of the aggregate social characteristics of the Progressives in California. Less frequently noted was his observation that they were "a group of supreme individualists" whose original interests were quite local (and, I would add, personal). Ibid., 22.

CHAPTER 1: PROGRESSIVISM AND THE
ORIGINS OF DIRECT LEGISLATION

Portions of this chapter originally appeared in John M. Allswang, *California Initiatives and Referendums, 1912–1990: A Survey and Guide to Research* (Los Angeles: Edmund G. "Pat" Brown Institute of Public Affairs, California State University, Los Angeles, 1991), and in "The Origins of Direct Democracy in Los Angeles and California: The Development of an Issue and Its Relationship to Progressivism," *Southern California Quarterly* 78 (summer 1996): 178–98.

1. The best overviews of Haynes and his career are Tom Sitton, *John Randolph Haynes: California Progressive* (Stanford, Calif.: Stanford University Press, 1992), and "California's Practical Idealist: John Randolph Haynes," *California History* 67 (March 1988): 2–17.

2. Haynes to *Philadelphia Public Ledger*, 12 June 1905, Haynes Papers.

3. Sitton, "California's Practical Idealist," 3–4, and personal interview with Sitton, Los Angeles, Calif., January 1991; Kevin Starr, *Inventing the Dream: California Through the Progressive Era* (New York: Oxford University Press, 1985), 211–12.

4. Sitton, "California's Practical Idealist," 4–5; Starr, *Inventing the Dream*, 211–12.

5. See miscellaneous 1911 letters, Haynes Papers.

6. *Los Angeles Express*, 25 June 1904; *Pacific Defender*, 19 December 1929; Haynes, "Higher Education and Child Labor," *Western Collegian* 2 (May 1914); and miscellaneous articles and speeches, Haynes Papers. Haynes's environmentalism prevailed primarily in the socioeconomic sphere; like others of his time, he was interested in the role of heredity and was actively involved in eugenics for many years (Tom Sitton, letter to the author, 12 February 1991). There were, of course, other more or less radical social reformers in and around Progressivism, such as Jane Addams and Oswald Garrison Villard. But that does not gainsay the validity of the observation so far as "mainstream" Progressivism was concerned.

7. Untitled, undated speech [1907], and notes on typescript of article on sterilization, Haynes Papers.

8. "Origins and Future of the Recall, the Initiative, and Referendum," typescript of 1909 lecture to University Club, Haynes Papers.

9. See, e.g., Haynes's address to the Joint Constitutional Committee of the California legislature, 20 January 1905; typescript of address to "Friends and Members of the Economic Club," 8 June 1901; miscellaneous notes and clippings, all in Haynes Papers.

10. Extensive perusal of the papers of many Progressives, including Hiram John-

son, Franklin Hichborn, Chester Rowell, Edward Dickson, and Meyer Lissner, convinces me of the accuracy of this generalization. See, for example, Lissner to Johnson, 14 February 1911 and 14 February 1912, including list of Progressive leaders, Johnson Papers. Haynes was an important figure in the Progressivism of the 1920s, but that was really a different movement, involving different people and issues.

11. The Progressives, generally, were too moderate in their politics for Haynes to feel really close to them; he was also somewhat older than most Progressive leaders, which may have increased his sense of separateness. The result was that he and the Progressives mutually used one another, to the advantage of both. See Starr, *Inventing the Dream*, 211.

12. Mowry, *California Progressives*, 135.

13. Haynes, "History of the Recall," typescript in Haynes Papers; Eric F. Peterson, "Prelude to Progressivism: California Election Reform, 1870–1909" (Ph.D. diss., UCLA, 1969), 146–49.

14. It is probable that there was more than one organization of that name, although with an overlap of members. Socialist H. Gaylord Wilshire organized one in 1898, and Haynes started an organization of that name in 1900 for local action, and perhaps a second one in 1902 for statewide action. By the latter date, there seems to have been just one organization; it was definitely under Haynes's leadership. Sitton, "California's Practical Idealist," 5–6, and Sitton, letter to the author, 12 February 1991.

15. J. W. Park, "The Adoption of the Recall in Los Angeles," typescript, Haynes Papers; Haynes, "History of the Recall," typescript, Haynes Papers; Janice Jaques, "The Political Reform Movement in Los Angeles, 1900–1909" (Master's thesis, Claremont Graduate School, 1948), 13–15, copy in Hichborn Papers.

16. Sitton, "California's Practical Idealist," 5–6; V. O. Key and Winston Crouch, *The Initiative and Referendum in California* (Berkeley: University of California Press, 1939), 428 and 428 n. Increased empowerment of the larger cities does not seem to have been very controversial, or partisan, at the time. *Los Angeles Herald*, 23 January 1903.

17. Park, "Adoption of the Recall in Los Angeles" and Haynes, "History of the Recall," Haynes Papers; Sitton, "California's Practical Idealist," 6–7; *Los Angeles Times*, 8 November 1902. The state Supreme Court upheld the legality of the Los Angeles measures in 1906 (*Los Angeles Express*, 15 October 1906). This is also a good example of Haynes's practicality as a politician; in pursuit of direct democracy, he was quite willing to work with the Southern Pacific in these years, and had important SP officials as officers in the Direct Legislation League. Fred W. Viehe, "The First Recall: Los Angeles Urban Reform or Machine Politics?", *Southern California Quarterly* 70 (spring 1988): 3–4.

18. Haynes, undated typescript [1910?], "The Recall of Councilman Davenport," and undated, unsigned typescript, Haynes Papers. Haynes felt that Harper's narrow election was in part due to the Southern Pacific machine's support. He also believed that the recall effort against Davenport led to a reversal of the position of Harrison Gray Otis and the *Times*, in that it made Otis realize that "these measures had shown a capacity for interfering with his personal designs upon the public treasury" (Ibid.). It is true that the main charge against Davenport was his participa-

tion in giving a city printing contract to the *Times* at exorbitant rates. See Grace H. Stimson, *Rise of the Labor Movement in Los Angeles* (Berkeley: University of California Press, 1955), 281–86; Viehe, "First Recall," 9–13. Interestingly, Davenport's recall was later overturned by the courts on the basis of an insufficient number of valid signatures, which anticipated the extremely litigious nature of direct democracy from that time to the present (Viehe, "First Recall," 23).

19. Key and Crouch, *Initiative and Referendum*, 428; *San Francisco Star*, 9 November 1910.

20. Handbills, postcards; J. Rensselaer to Haynes, January 1903; letters from nominees to Haynes and Guy Lathrop of California Federation of Labor; copies of letter from California Federation of Labor to member unions, and of form sent by unions to candidates; R. F. Howard to Haynes, 21 October 1902; P. A. Stanton to Haynes, 29 October 1902, all in Haynes Papers.

21. *Los Angeles Herald*, 5 December 1902.

22. Copy of broadside dated 20 December 1902; U'Ren to Haynes, 9 December 1908; both in Haynes Papers; *Los Angeles Times*, 15 January 1903. It was common for organizations ranging from good government to horticulture to have public-issues committees at this time, and the Direct Legislation League focused on all of them.

23. Haynes supported Preble in Sacramento for about eight weeks. Haynes to Preble, n.d.; Preble to Haynes, 17 March 1903 and 29 March 1903, Haynes Papers. See also *Los Angeles Times*, 19 February 1903; *Los Angeles Herald*, 22 February 1903.

24. N. K. Foster, M.D., to Haynes, 27 October 1902, Haynes Papers; *Los Angeles Herald*, 27 February 1903; *Los Angeles Express*, 14 March 1903. The question of the political power of the Southern Pacific is central to the history of California Progressivism. Certainly, the Progressives believed this power was overwhelming, a conclusion shared by leading students like Mowry (*California Progressives*, 38–39) and Key and Crouch (*Initiative and Referendum*, 423), but the quantity of hard evidence is not huge. There are demonstrable cases where Parker and William F. Herrin directly forced, bribed, and otherwise promoted or stymied actions by public officials (e.g., see affidavit from H. J. Lelande, Los Angeles City Clerk, published in *Pacific Outlook*, 4 December 1909, and *Los Angeles Herald*, 27 and 28 November 1909; and E. T. Earl [publisher of *Los Angeles Express*] to Edward A. Dickson, 8 July 1907, Dickson Papers). Viehe, in "First Recall," 15–21, describes the Southern Pacific's infiltration of the Good Government League in Los Angeles and perversion of the recall election of 1904. But, overall, this is not an easy phenomenon to pin down.

25. Alice M. Rose interview of Frank R. Devlin, 6 January 1937, Rose Papers; Haynes, "The Birth of Democracy in California," typescript [1912?], Haynes Papers. Haynes concluded that "the absolute domination of the Southern Pacific Railroad" was the key factor in this failure, although he probably underestimated the role of lack of interest among many legislators. See also Franklin A. Hichborn, *Story of the Session of the California Legislature of 1909* (San Francisco: J. H. Barry, 1909); Hichborn, "Sources of Opposition to Direct Legislation in California," pt. 2, *The Commonwealth: Official Journal of the Commonwealth Club of California* 7 (3 March 1931): 512–39; and Hichborn, "California Politics, 1891–1939," typescript — all in Hichborn Papers.

26. The Revs. Ervin S. Chapman and J. H. Scott of the Anti-Saloon League worked for Haynes. Chapman to Haynes, 22 August 1904, Haynes Papers.

27. U'Ren to Haynes, 12 January 1909, 18 February 1901, 24 February 1901, 6 March 1901, 9 March 1909, Haynes Papers.

28. They shared the common belief that the Southern Pacific machine's influence made the 1907 session of the legislature the most venal ever, and that the railroad had been the real force behind the election of James N. Gillett as governor in 1906. See Alice M. Rose interview of Dickson, 27 December 1937, Rose Papers; see also Mowry, *California Progressives*, 58.

29. Alice M. Rose interview of Dickson, 27 December 1937, Rose Papers; Ida Tarbell interview of Rowell, 24 March 1911, both in Rose Papers; Jaques, "Political Reform Movement in Los Angeles," 71–72; Dickson, "History of the Lincoln-Roosevelt League," Dickson Papers.

30. *Los Angeles Record*, 17 March 1909; Sitton, "California's Practical Idealist," 7; Royce D. Delmatier, Clarence F. McIntosh, and Earl G. Waters, *The Rumble of California Politics, 1848–1970* (New York: Wiley, 1970), 155; Rose interview of Dickson, 27 December 1937, Rose Papers; Hichborn, *Session of the California Legislature of 1909*, 192–201.

31. See, e.g., letters received, 2 September 1909–19 November 1909, Dickson Papers; Dickson, "History of the Lincoln-Roosevelt League," Dickson Papers; *Fresno Republican*, 31 October 1907; miscellaneous 1908 letters, Lissner Papers.

32. Ida Tarbell interview of Rowell, 24 March 1911, Rose Papers; "Report of Section on Public Laws" and "The Referendum in State Legislation," *Transactions of the Commonwealth Club of California* (January 1905), copies in Haynes Papers; and U'Ren to Dickson, 15 December 1908, Haynes Papers; see also, F. L. Fairbanks to T. R. Bard, 18 April 1908, Rose Papers. On the recall, see below and Delmatier et al., *Rumble of California Politics*, 170–71.

33. When the Direct Legislation League was approached by Franklin Hichborn about subscribing to his proposed study of the 1909 session of the legislature, U'Ren asked him how much coverage the League would get in the book. The League wanted 100 copies, but "perhaps this can be enlarged. . . . " Such hardball was not unusual for Haynes and U'Ren (U'Ren to Hichborn, 20 March 1911, Hichborn Papers).

34. Hichborn, *Session of the California Legislature of 1909*; Hichborn to Sen. Marshall Black, 4 March 1909, both in Hichborn Papers. The U.S. Senatorial primary, however, would be advisory only, since direct election of Senators was yet to come. The Southern Pacific forces were very well organized, led on the floor by Grove Johnson (Hiram Johnson's father), and they were able to defeat a large number of league-supported proposals (Mowry, *California Progressives*, 82).

35. A. H. Spencer [Spence?] of the *Oakland Evening Mail* to Haynes, 10 July 1910, 16 August 1910, Haynes Papers (emphasis added). The *Evening Mail* was a Scripps paper, all of which supported direct democracy in 1910, as did a large number of other papers across the state. Equally important, by 1911 Haynes had managed to get a large part of the Progressive leadership officially enrolled as members of the Direct Legislation League, including Lissner, Weinstock, Dickson, former Governor Pardee, Rudolf Spreckels, Senator Works, and others.

36. Copies of the platforms are in the Haynes Papers. There was some conflict

between the Direct Legislation League and the Lincoln–Roosevelt League (now, actually, the state Republican Party), in that the latter found the former in its way. U'Ren told Haynes that, with the formal adoption of direct democracy, Lissner, now Republican Party chairman, "rather intimated that the League ought to go off and quietly die" (U'Ren to Haynes, 22 November 1910, Haynes Papers).

37. Johnson to J. H. Davis, 11 July 1910; Johnson to Haynes, 12 April 1910; typescript of Johnson campaign speech of 14 October 1910, all in Johnson Papers. A perusal of Johnson's correspondence throughout 1910 shows very little concern with individual issues. Indeed, Johnson was probably one of the least ideological of the Progressives, with his own personal agenda, which helps explain his relatively early split from other Progressives, and then from Progressivism itself. See Lower, *Bloc of One*, chaps. 1–2; Spencer C. Olin, Jr., *California's Prodigal Sons* (Berkeley: University of California Press, 1968), 170; and Mowry, *California Progressives*, 120–21, 135.

38. *Los Angeles Express*, 25 November 1910; Hichborn, *Session of the California Legislature of 1911*, 12–16.

39. Hichborn, *Session of the California Legislature of 1911*, 25–27; Dickson, "History of the Lincoln–Roosevelt League," Dickson Papers; *Los Angeles Times*, 4 December 1910. The *Times*, adamantly opposed to the Progressives and their program, charged that Lissner (whom the paper had earlier characterized in anti-Semitic terms) was the new "boss," whose program would "turn the political system . . . upside down." There was some truth to both of the charges; the Progressives would dispute only the first.

40. Like many of his contemporaries, Johnson just could not persuade himself that women had any proper place in politics. He supported the Progressives' pledge to propose a suffrage amendment and later acknowledged that he would vote for it, but he never specifically or openly supported the proposal (see Lower, *Bloc of One*, 29 n.).

41. On the inaugural, see Ibid., and Hichborn, *Session of the California Legislature of 1911*, i–xvi, and Delmatier et al., *Rumble of California Politics*, 165. On issues: Johnson to Hichborn, 19 June 1911; Johnson to Fremont Older, 19 June 1911; Johnson to A. E. Yel of the Asiatic Exclusion League, 18 May 1911, all in Johnson Papers.

42. Johnson to: Lissner, 16 February 1911; Matt I. Sullivan, 8 June 1911; Mr. Wolcott (of Commonwealth Club), 9 June 1911; Lissner, 12 June 1911; U'Ren, 22 August 1911; Dickson, 11 September 1911; Rowell, 13 September 1911, all in Johnson Papers. See also Lissner to U'Ren, 6 October 1911, and Lissner to Haynes, 14 October 1911, both in Lissner Papers. The fact that each of these proposals had its own constituencies, and that direct democracy was far from high on Johnson's list of priorities, is exemplified by its bare mention in Lower's recent Johnson biography (*Bloc of One*, chap. 1).

43. "Recall," *Transactions of the Commonwealth Club of California*, vol. 6 (1911); Hichborn, "Sources of Opposition," pt. 2, 515–16; Key and Crouch, *Initiative and Referendum*, 437–38; Hichborn, *Session of the California Legislature of 1911*, 102–38; *Los Angeles Sunday Tribune*, 9 July 1911; Haynes telegram to Dickson, 1 January 1911, Dickson Papers; Johnson to Haynes, 17 January 1911, Haynes

Papers; Lissner to Editor, *Santa Barbara Independent*, 17 February 1911, Lissner Papers. The recall proposed for California was a rather powerful one, since it combined a Yes/No vote on recall with another vote on those nominated to succeed the officeholder if he or she was recalled. Only those who voted on the recall itself would have their votes on the successor candidate tallied, and the successor required only a plurality. The legislature also passed two statutes in this session that permitted non-charter (smaller) cities and counties to implement direct democracy.

44. U'Ren to Lissner, 5 May 1911, Lissner Papers; Hichborn to Johnson, 23 June 1911 and 27 June 1911, Johnson Papers.

45. On the decline of California Progressivism, see Mowry, *California Progressives*, chap. 11.

46. In the case of the direct democracy measures, we have seen that both major parties, plus the Socialists and many other groups, endorsed them. Thus, it is misleading to see direct democracy as simply a "Progressive measure" and the lack of strong statistical relationships becomes quite understandable.

47. For example, both the San Francisco and Los Angeles Chambers of Commerce opposed the measure, as did leading Progressives such as Chester Rowell and Meyer Lissner (*Los Angeles Times*, 3 and 4 November 1912, p. 2).

48. In 1912 and 1914, for example, the official *California Ballot Pamphlet* offered no explanation of the voting options. Only in the late 1920s did the pamphlet begin to specify the meaning of Yes and No votes on referendum measures.

49. I must acknowledge having contributed to the confusion in my own earlier book (*California Initiatives and Referendums*). The descriptions of each referendum are correct but misleading. By not clarifying that "Approved" and "Rejected" applied to the law being reconsidered rather than to the referendum itself, and by not clearly specifying just what a Yes or No vote meant, it easily misinforms the reader.

50. The term *voter participation* refers to the percentage of voters who vote on any proposition (see Appendix B). The anti-prostitution measure was a referendum on a law to that effect passed by the legislature; the law was upheld by the voters. The eight-hour day and mandatory day of rest were initiative statutes that were decisively rejected. See Lewis Bohnett oral history, pp. 58–59, and Herbert C. Jones oral history, p. 170, both in UC Berkeley Oral Histories.

51. On the consistent strength of cultural issues in American politics, see John M. Allswang, *A House for All Peoples: Ethnic Politics in Chicago, 1890–1936* (Lexington: University Press of Kentucky, 1971).

52. George V. Streep to Haynes, 9 September 1914, and Mrs. Seward Simons et al. to Mrs. Haynes, 23 October 1914, Haynes Papers.

53. Hichborn, "Sources of Opposition," pt. 2, 519–20.

54. See, e.g., *Los Angeles Times*, 29 July 1916, sec. 2, p. 1.

55. *Los Angeles Times*, 4 November 1916, sec. 1, p. 7, and 4 November 1916, sec. 2, p. 1.

56. Herbert C. Jones oral history, pp. 33–36, UC Berkeley Oral Histories; *Los Angeles Times*, 8 November 1918, sec. 2, p. 2; *San Francisco Chronicle*, 4 November 1918, p. 6.

57. *Los Angeles Times*, 2 November 1916, sec. 2, p. 3.

58. *Los Angeles Times*, 3 November 1912, p. 12; 4 November 1912, pp. 1, 2; and

5 November 1912, p. 1; Haynes to Rowell, 28 December 1918, Rowell/B Papers; *Los Angeles Times*, 31 October 1920, sec. 2, p. 9; *Los Angeles Record* and other 1920 press clippings, Haynes Papers; Allswang, *California Initiatives and Referendums*, 46. See Chapter 2 on Haynes's creation of the League to Protect the Initiative that helped kill this measure.

59. Herbert C. Jones oral history and Lewis D. Bohnett oral history, both in UC Berkeley Oral Histories.

60. *Los Angeles Times*, 5 October 1915, sec. 2, p. 1; 8 October 1915, sec. 2, p. 1; and 20 October 1915, sec. 2, p. 1ff.

61. For example, see "Extracts from Monthly Financial Letters of Farmers and Merchants National Bank of Los Angeles," 1915 and 1916, which advocated doing away with the direct primary as well as direct legislation as a way to lower taxes (typescript carbon copy in Haynes Papers).

62. E.g., 2, 3, 6, 10, and 12 October 1915.

63. See, e.g., *San Francisco Chronicle*, 17 March 1916, p. 11; 21 March 1916, p. 18; 29 March 1916, p. 9; and 4 April 1916, p. 6.

64. League of Women Voters of California, *Initiative and Referendum in California*, 38; *Los Angeles Express*, 20 February 1912; *Los Angeles Times*, 21 February 1912.

65. *Los Angeles Times*, 17 July 1912; Haynes to Harry Chandler, 14 December 1916, Haynes Papers.

66. *San Francisco Chronicle*, 19 January 1917, p. 16; and 14 March 1917, p. 16. See also Hichborn, "Sources of Opposition," pt. 2, 521–27.

67. *San Francisco Chronicle*, 27 November 1918, p. 9; Herbert C. Jones oral history, UC Berkeley Oral Histories.

68. Haynes to Senate Judiciary Committee, 29 March 1915, and Haynes to E. A. Dickson, 9 March 1915, both in Haynes Papers; Haynes to Sen. W. F. Chandler, 4 February 1915, Rowell/B Papers. Haynes urged Dickson to proceed carefully with Johnson, whose commitment he did not entirely trust, and when Dickson did not quickly respond he wrote again, saying that his ally was "treating me very shabbily" (22 March 1915, Haynes Papers).

69. Haynes to Fremont Older, Franklin Hichborn, E. T. Earl, and others, 2 December 1914; Haynes to Hichborn, 15 March 1915; Haynes, "Abuses of the Initiative Referendum, and Recall and the Remedies," 12 December 1914; all in Haynes Papers.

70. A good brief introduction to these questions is Buenker et al., *Progressivism*.

71. Rowell to Johnson, 26 August 1911, Johnson Papers.

72. Lissner to Short Ballot Organization, 5 December 1910, and to League of Justice, 22 December 1910, Lissner Papers. Lissner was not immune to personal preferences either, noting in 1907 that he was "not particularly interested" in a primary law, but that he felt that ballot reform was important (Lissner to W. R. Leeds, 7 February 1907, Lissner Papers). Rowell also complained that "pet reforms" were dividing supporters and interfering with focus on the "main issue" of the Southern Pacific. But he, too, had pet issues, favoring the direct primary but being ever leery of direct legislation (Rowell to Congressman S. C. Smith, 21 January 1910, copy in Rose Papers; see also *San Francisco Star*, 22 February 1908).

73. Peterson, "Prelude to Progressivism," 236–37, 238–50; see also Isidor Jacobs to Dickson, 23 December 1908, and other letters, Dickson Papers.

74. The socialists, also, were represented in the Direct Legislation League from its origins, and as late as 1908 the League had asked the state Socialist Party to provide a member for its Executive Committee. At the same time, recognizing the controversiality of this connection, U'Ren was assuring the mainstream Progressives that the League "had no intention of making them [the socialists] a power in the League." See Sitton, "California's Practical Idealist," 5–6; U'Ren to Haynes, 9 December 1908, and U'Ren to Dickson, 15 December 1908, in Haynes Papers; and Stimson, *Labor Movement in Los Angeles*.

75. E. T. Earl to Dickson, 8 July 1907, and other letters received, June–July 1907, Dickson Papers; Weinstock to Johnson, 16 December 1910 and 11 January 1911, Johnson Papers; Franklin Hichborn, "Points of Difference between Organized Labor and the Better America Foundation" [n.d., ca. 1921–22], Hichborn Papers. On the development of the general fear of labor and Socialists among Progressives, see Mowry, *California Progressives*, 25, 46, 200–5. In contrast, an early argument stressing the mutually supportive relationship between labor and the Progressives is John L. Shover, "The Progressives and the Working Class Vote in California," in Michael P. Rogin and John L. Shover, *Political Change in California* (Westport, Conn.: Greenwood Publishing, 1970), 62–89.

76. Lissner to J. J. Harper, 8 May 1908, Lissner Papers; Marshall Stimson, "The Way the 'Machine' Does Politics" (speech to City Club, 9 May 1908), Stimson Papers; Delmatier et al., *Rumble of California Politics*, 180–81; Walton Bean, *California: An Interpretive History*, 3d. ed. (New York: McGraw-Hill, 1978), 283–85.

77. A. P. Cochran to Johnson, 30 July 1910, Johnson Papers; Rowell to Hugh A. Gilchrist, 30 November 1907, Rowell/B Papers; Lissner to Dickson, 20 September 1910, Dickson Papers; A. J. Wallace, typescript autobiography, 62–63, 74, Rose Papers.

78. Hichborn, "Anti-Japanese Legislation in California," typescript, Hichborn Papers; *Los Angeles Examiner*, 13 October 1907; Asiatic Exclusion League folder, Johnson Papers; Mowry, *California Progressives*, 46, 127. Dickson and Lissner were particularly supportive of Weinstock's nomination for governor if Johnson would not run. Lissner noted that "we discussed the race questions and while they were of the opinion that it would have some effect, it was not serious enough to bother with." See Rowell to Dickson, 10 February 1910; Lissner to Dickson, 11 February 1910 and 15 February 1910; and Dickson, "History of the Lincoln–Roosevelt League," all in Dickson Papers.

79. Rowell to W. B. Taylor, 16 May 1928, Rose Papers; *Fresno Republican* editorials, 14 July 1908, and 2 January 1910, in Rowell/LA Papers; miscellaneous Rowell letters, 1912, Rowell/B Papers.

80. Buenker et al., *Progressivism*, 47–49, 75.

81. A recent Ohio study also stresses this aspect of Progressivism and sees it as a clearly better explanation than the older one of the Progressives as defenders of an established economic order. See Sealander, *Grand Plans*, chap. 6. The concept of moral or religious values as a key explanation of Progressivism was also suggested by Crunden in Buenker et al., *Progressivism*, 75–76.

82. As expressed, for example, in William Miller, "American Historians and the Business Elite," and "The Recruitment of the Business Elite," in Miller, ed., *Men in Business: Essays on the Historical Role of the Entrepreneur* (New York: Harper, 1962). As Samuel P. Hays put it, "One cannot explain the distinctive behavior of people in terms of characteristics which are not distinctive to them," "The Politics of Reform in Municipal Government in the Progressive Era," *Pacific Northwest Quarterly* 55 (October 1964), reprinted in A. M. Wakstein, *The Urbanization of America: an Historical Anthology* (Boston: Houghton-Mifflin, 1970), 289.

83. Examples would be the power of large corporations like the Southern Pacific in the economic sphere, and of urban political machines in the political one. See Hays, ibid., 301; Olin, *California's Prodigal Sons*, 181; and Arthur Mann, "The Progressive Tradition," in John Higham, ed., *The Reconstruction of American History* (New York: Harper, 1962), 163-64.

84. John E. Sawyer, "The Entrepreneur and the Social Order," in Miller, *Men in Business*, 7-22.

85. E.g., Olin, *California's Prodigal Sons*, 174-75.

86. It is not inappropriate to point out, in our own day, the very large numbers of successful, wealthy, quite secure people who line up seeking positions in the administrations of every new president, governor, and mayor. They do so for the reasons noted here, and there is no reason to think the same was not true during the Progressive Era.

CHAPTER 2: DIRECT LEGISLATION IN
GOOD TIMES AND BAD, 1920-1939

1. Legislative measures have continued to be generally more successful down to the present. A study of the "All-Time Most Popular Ballot Measures" found that each of the 44 most popular, with majorities above 80 percent, were legislative. See Tony Miller, comp., *A Study of California Ballot Measures, 1884-1993* (Sacramento: Secretary of State, 1994), 7-8. Note that this definition of "popular" relies solely on percentage voting Yes, not on voter participation rate, where legislative measures do less well than direct legislation.

2. An analysis of one referendum, Proposition 13 of 1938, concluded that "the committee go on record as favoring the referendum of the act, thereby expressing opposition to the act." It never used the words Yes or No, although it was in fact recommending a No vote, perhaps because the author was a bit confused. Anonymous typescript, UCLA Campaigns File, 1938.

3. *Los Angeles Times*, 7 November 1922, sec. 2, p. 8.

4. *Los Angeles Times*, 31 October 1926, sec. 1, p. 2; Campaign Statements, 1926: Wright Act Repeal Association.

5. Campaign Statements, 1926 and 1932; see also brochure of Wright Act Repeal Association, UCLA Campaigns File, 1932.

6. The anti-saloon measure, Proposition 2, had strong business support in both northern and southern California. Business saw it not so much as increased regulation but rather as a more moderate successor to earlier Prohibition laws, now that federal Prohibition had ended. See Campaign Statements, 1934: Northern California

Business Council, Southern California Business Council, Northern California Hotel Association; *Los Angeles Times*, 6 November 1934, sec. 1, pp. 12, 13.

7. See Campaign Statements, 1936, for Propositions 3 and 9; and *Los Angeles Times*, 1 November 1936, sec. 2, pp. 2, 3.

8. See Mowry, *California Progressives*, 154–55; and Lewis Bohnett oral history, pp. 51–54, UC Berkeley Oral Histories.

9. Mowry, *California Progressives*, 154–55.

10. Herbert C. Jones oral history, pp. 99–101, UC Berkeley Oral Histories.

11. "Facts in the Case: A Statement Based upon the Report of the State Board of Control" (San Francisco: Japanese Association of America, n.d. [1920]); copy in IGS Campaigns File. See also *Los Angeles Times*, 1 November 1920, sec. 2, p. 8.

12. The Pearson product moment relationship between a Yes vote on Prop. 13 (i.e., a vote to uphold the community property law) and a Yes in favor of two Prohibition measures (Prop. 2 of 1920 and Prop. 2 of 1922) was .709 and .585, respectively; the correlation with a Yes on women's suffrage was a meaningless .068.

13. A "Racing Board Campaign Committee" had raised $81,000 for Prop. 6 in 1926, and the California Breeders Association spent $60,000 in support of Prop. 5 in 1932; the former is the equivalent of about $700,000 in 1995 dollars, a not inconsiderable sum. (For an explanation of dollar conversions, based on the Consumer Price Index, see Appendix B). See Campaign Statements, 1926 and 1932; and *San Francisco Chronicle*, 14 December 1926, p. 12 (campaign-statement laws were not rigorously enforced in these years, and the statements themselves are not always complete). See also Herbert C. Jones oral history, UC Berkeley Oral Histories.

14. *Los Angeles Times*, 2 November 1924, sec. 2, p. 2; Campaign Statements, 1924: Boxing and Wrestling League; UCLA Campaigns File, 1928.

15. On the background, see Norris Hundley, Jr., *The Great Thirst: Californians and Water, 1770s–1990s* (Berkeley and Los Angeles: University of California Press, 1992), 234–40.

16. Louis Bartlett oral history, pp. 155, 157–72; Herbert C. Jones oral history, pp. 190–91, both in UC Berkeley Oral Histories; *Los Angeles Times*, 6 November 1922, sec. 1, p. 9, and 30 October 1926, sec. 2, p. 1; Campaign Statements, 1924 and 1926: California State Water and Power League.

17. *Los Angeles Times*, 2 November 1922, sec. 2, p. 3, 3 November 1922, sec. 2, p. 2; Campaign Statements, 1924: Pacific Gas and Electric.

18. Louis Bartlett oral history, pp. 182–85, UC Berkeley Oral Histories; *Los Angeles Times*, 12 December 1933, sec. 2, p. 1.

19. Hundley, *Great Thirst*, 243–53.

20. Campaign Statements, 1938: Pacific Gas and Electric, California Debt Relief Association; *Los Angeles Times*, 7 November 1938, sec. 2, p. 4. Professional campaign management was first done by advertising agencies, like Clem Whitaker Advertising; in Whitaker's case, that led to a separate organization, Campaigns, Inc., one of the first companies specializing exclusively in campaign management (see, for example, Campaign Statements, 1934: California State Employees Association). Prop. 13 was to some degree a business-versus-labor issue, with labor on the losing side (see UCLA Campaigns File, 1938).

21. *Los Angeles Times*, 1 May 1932, sec. 2, pp. 1–2.

22. See arguments in *California Ballot Pamphlet*, 1932.

23. Ibid.

24. Opposition to both measures was very broad-based: the Pearson correlation coefficient for voting on the two referendums was .960. See *Los Angeles Times*, 1 November 1938, sec. 2, p. 4.

25. Florence Clifton interview, pp. 23–24, in "California Democrats in the Earl Warren Era" oral history; Robert Clifton interview, pp. 31–33, in "California Democrats in the Earl Warren Era" oral history, both in UC Berkeley Oral Histories; Ralph C. Dills oral history, p. 85, UCLA Oral Histories; Campaign Statements, 1939: Independent Petroleum And Consumers Association, Atlantic Oil.

26. *Los Angeles Times*, 6 November 1939, sec. 1, p.4; sec. 2, p. 4; and Campaign Statements, 1939: Yes on 5 Committee.

27. Robert Clifton interview, pp. 31–33, in "California Democrats in the Earl Warren Era" oral history, UC Berkeley Oral Histories; *California Ballot Pamphlet*, 1939.

28. Herbert C. Jones oral history, pp. 67–70, UC Berkeley Oral Histories; *Los Angeles Times*, 31 October 1920, sec. 2, p. 5.

29. *Los Angeles Times*, 5 November 1922, sec. 2, p. 8.

30. See the *California Ballot Pamphlets* for each of these elections, where the arguments and endorsements for each position leave one quite confused.

31. *Los Angeles Times*, 4 November 1934, sec. 1, pp. 12, 13; Campaign Statements, 1934: Public Health League of California.

32. Campaign Statements, 1934: California Medical Association. As would become increasingly common, following the money was not easy. The Public Health League of California contributed to the California Medical Association campaign, and vice-versa.

33. UCLA Campaigns File, 1939; *Los Angeles Times*, 2 November 1939, sec. 2, p. 4; Campaign Statements, 1939: Affiliated Chiropractors of California, Public Health League of California, California Medical Association.

34. See *California Ballot Pamphlet* for the election of November 3, 1936.

35. *San Francisco Chronicle*, 27 June 1948, TW2. Robinson claimed that 98 percent of all initiatives that had made it to the ballot since 1918 had done so with his help.

36. The Chain Stores Association's $1,052,000 expenditure was the equivalent of $12,000,000 in 1995 dollars, and this in the midst of the Depression. Interestingly, this highly professional referendum campaign did better among less urban and less well-educated voters. Correlations between voting Yes (i.e., supporting the existing legislation against the wishes of the chain stores) were .767 for urban voters and .615 for those age 21–24 who were still in school. Moreover, by the 1930s the per capita costs of initiative campaigns reached a level that would not be exceeded down through the 1980s. See John R. Owens and Larry L. Wade, "Campaign Spending on California Ballot Propositions, 1924–1984," *Western Political Quarterly* 39 (December 1986): 679.

37. David R. Magleby, *Direct Legislation: Voting on Ballot Propositions in the United States* (Baltimore: John Hopkins University Press, 1984), 147.

38. *Los Angeles Times*, 6 November 1932, sec. 2, p. 2; see also *California Ballot Pamphlet*, 1932.

39. See Von T. Ellsworth, "Facts . . . Arguments . . . Questions . . . Answers on Proposition #1: SALES TAX SINGLE TAX [and] Proposition #2: INCOME TAX Applying to BALLOT ISSUES, General Election, November 3, 1936," Bulletin No. 18, 1 August 1936 (Berkeley: California Tax Equalization League, 1936).

40. *Los Angeles Times*, 28 October 1926, sec. 2, p. 1, 1 November 1926, sec. 2, pp. 1, 12; Campaign Statements, 1926: Auto Club of Southern California, California State Automobile Association, Good Roads Gas Tax Committee, All-California Highways Campaign Committee; *San Francisco Chronicle*, 14 December 1926, p. 12. These two propositions, along with the horseracing Prop. 6, are also examples of a constant in initiative politics: while disproportionate funding can usually defeat a proposition, it will often fail to pass one. In all three, the better-financed position failed. See *San Francisco Chronicle*, 14 December 1926, p. 12.

41. UCLA Campaigns File, 1938; Campaign Statements, 1938: California State Automobile Association, Public Affairs, Inc., Insurance Exchange of Los Angeles.

42. *Los Angeles Times*, 31 October 1926, sec. 2, p. 1, and 1 November 1936, sec. 2, p. 3.; *San Francisco Chronicle*, 14 December 1926, p. 12. The *Chronicle* estimated that almost $600,000 had been spent in this election on 11 of the 28 propositions on the ballot.

43. See Chapter 1 and *California Ballot Pamphlets*, 1920 and 1922.

44. A good summary of Ralston and the 1930s movement is James Echols, "Jackson Ralston and the Last Single Tax Campaign," *California History* 58 (fall 1979): 256-62.

45. See above and Ellsworth, "Facts . . . Arguments . . . Questions . . . Answers"; California Farm Bureau Federation and California Tax Equalization League materials in UCLA Campaigns File, 1936; Harold W. Kingsley, "How Repeal Measures and Single Tax Plans Menace Public Schools: A Survey of Tax Proposals on California's November [1936] Ballot for a Study by Friends of Education" (Los Angeles: California Teachers Association, [1936]); Echols, "Jackson Ralston," 256-62.

46. *San Francisco Chronicle*, 3 December 1938, p. 4; *Los Angeles Times*, 1 November 1938, sec. 2, p. 1, and 3 November 1938, sec. 2, p. 1; UCLA Campaigns File, 1938; Campaign Statements, 1938: Campaigns, Inc.

47. Campaign Statements, 1938: California State Chamber of Commerce, California Teachers Association, California State Employees Association.

48. A good brief overview of management-labor conflict in this period is David F. Selvin, *A Place in the Sun: A History of California Labor* (San Francisco: Boyd and Fraser, 1981), chap. 3.

49. Ibid.; see also Cray, *Chief Justice*, 73-76.

50. Pro- and anti-Prop. 1 documents are filed in UCLA Campaigns File, 1938.

51. *Los Angeles Times*, 2 November 1938, sec. 1, p. 9, and 4 November 1938, sec. 2, p. 4.

52. Campaign Statements, 1938.

53. Ibid.

54. Philip Bancroft oral history, pp. 414, 446-47, UC Berkeley Oral Histories; *Los Angeles Times*, 4 November 1938, sec. 2, p. 4.

55. For a brief summary of the plan and of its political ramifications, see William E. Leuchtenburg, *Franklin D. Roosevelt and the New Deal* (New York: Harper, 1963), 103-6, 179-82.

56. An overview of the movement can be found in Tom Zimmerman, " 'Ham and Eggs, Everybody!' " *Southern California Quarterly* 62, no. 1 (1980): 77–96. See also Kevin Starr, *Endangered Dreams: The Great Depression in California* (New York: Oxford University Press, 1996), 202–11.

57. A good summary of their arguments is in a 128–page booklet published for the campaign: *Life Begins at Fifty: $30 a Week for Life: Questions and Answers: California State Retirement Payments Act* (Hollywood: Petition Campaign for Thirty Dollars a Week for Life California State Pension Plan, 1938). See also *California Ballot Pamphlet*, 1938, Proposition 25. This type of very defensive wording of propositions would become quite common in the 1980s and 1990s.

58. Petition Campaign for Thirty Dollars a Week, *Life Begins at Fifty*; Zimmerman, "Ham and Eggs," 80; Starr, *Endangered Dreams*, 206.

59. Philip Bancroft oral history, pp. 414, 446–47, UC Berkeley Oral Histories.

60. The *Los Angeles Times*, for example, saw Proposition 25 and the single tax Proposition 20 as the key issues of the election (6 November 1938, sec. 1, p. 1).

61. Zimmerman, "Ham and Eggs," 82–84; Starr, *Endangered Dreams*, 209–11.

62. Zimmerman, "Ham and Eggs," 85–87. They were even investigated by Martin Dies's House Committee on Un-American Activities on the basis of "evidence" that Communists were trying to achieve control. See also UCLA Campaigns File, 1939, including pamphlet, "Upton Sinclair Speaks."

63. Zimmerman, "Ham and Eggs," 88–89. McLain would reemerge as the controversial leader of his own equivalent of Ham and Eggs in the 1940s; see Chapter 3.

64. UCLA Campaigns File, 1939; *Los Angeles Times*, 3 November 1939, sec. 2, p. 4, and 5 November 1939, sec. 1, p. 1ff.

65. See *San Francisco Chronicle*, 9 November 1939, p. 11.

66. One critic argued that the 1940 proposal was different from the earlier ones in that the pension scheme was not central; rather, its replacement of all other taxes with one on *gross* income would serve the interests of large businesses and property owners to the detriment of small business. It was now an "immoral attempt to curry the favors of the upper income groups." See Luther E. Eggleston, "The Tragedy of 'Ham and Eggs' in 1940" (Los Angeles: California Merchants Council [1940]), copy in IGS Campaigns File.

67. The problem went even further than relative population: Los Angeles County's number of registered voters doubled between 1920 and 1926, and southern California then had more than 50 percent of the state's registered voters (*Los Angeles Times*, 27 October 1926, sec. 1, p. 2, and 29 November 1926, sec. 1, p. 8).

68. John W. Caughey, *California: History of a Remarkable State* (Englewood Cliffs, N.J.: Prentice-Hall, 1982), 322; *Los Angeles Times*, 29 October 1926, sec. 1, p. 8, and 31 October 1926, sec. 2, p. 8.

69. *Los Angeles Times*, 2 December 1928, sec. 2, pp. 1, 2. Los Angeles County voted 82 percent against Prop. 20 and 72 percent for Prop. 28.

70. Campaign Statements, 1928: All Parties Reapportionment Committee, California Farm Bureau Federation, California Statewide Committee for the Federal Plan Reapportionment, San Francisco Chamber of Commerce, Agricultural Legislative Committee; *Los Angeles Times*, 4 November 1928, sec. 2, pp. 1, 2.

71. See press clippings from *Los Angeles Record* and other newspapers, in "Initiative" scrapbooks, Haynes Papers.

72. Ibid.

73. A. J. Pillsbury, "A Study of Direct Legislation in All of Its Forms . . . ," pt. 3 (San Francisco: Commonwealth Club of California, 1931), typescript copy in Hichborn Papers; see also Misc. Papers, League to Protect the Initiative, Ibid.; *Los Angeles Times*, 5 November 1922, sec. 2, p. 2; and *California Ballot Pamphlet*, 1922.

74. *San Francisco Chronicle*, 9 April 1924, pp. 6, 26; and 27 May 1924, p. 22.

75. *San Francisco Chronicle*, 28 June 1927, p. 26, and 8 August 1927, p. 18.

76. "Chester Rowell's Comment," *San Francisco Chronicle*, 29 June 1927, p. 17.

77. *San Francisco Chronicle*, 3 December 1938, p. 4; 10 November 1939, p. 1; 22 November 1939, p. 28.

78. *San Francisco Chronicle*, 6 October 1920, p. 20, and 21 December 1921, p. 22; Sitton, "California's Practical Idealist," 10.

79. Hichborn, "Sources of Opposition to Direct Legislation in California," pt. 3, 529–30.

80. Haynes was the heart and the pocketbook of the organization, but it did have many supporters. One list of members in the 1920s ran to 50 pages (Hichborn Papers).

81. Haynes to Mrs. F. G. Law, 18 February 1922, Haynes Papers.

82. "Haynes" folder, Hichborn Papers. His reimbursed expenses for January to March 1920 were $1,257.

83. Pillsbury, "Study of Direct Legislation," pt. 3; see also Pillsbury to Haynes, 14 September 1930, copy in Hichborn Papers; Haynes, "The Sponsor System as Applicable to Direct Legislation," in Pillsbury, "Study of Direct Legislation," pt. 3, 476–81.

84. "Chester Rowell's Comment," *San Francisco Chronicle*, 14 November 1938, p. 14, and 24 December 1938, p. 14.

85. *San Francisco Chronicle*, 12 November 1938, p. 5; 16 November 1938, p. 2; 21 November 1938, p. 24; 10 November 1939, pp. 5, 6.

86. Statistically, this is not nearly as easy as correlating two elections with one another, or one election with census data. The nature of the data in this case is irregular and problematic. In Table 2.6, only a minority of correlations are statistically significant, even including some with relatively high coefficients; this is almost never the case with the rest of the correlation tables in this book (see Appendix B for more explanation). For example, long-term (1884–1993) data compiled by the California Secretary of State suggest a strong relationship between ballot position and success rate, which is calculated by simply listing the success rate of each proposition position. That seems confirmed by my own correlation of data for positions 1–20 (Pearson = $-.815$). However, the data are questionable because of the number of measures that vary over the years from one position to another (85 have had position 1, 18 have had position 20; if one goes beyond position 20, the data are even more confused). Additionally, starting with 1958, legislative measures have been at the top of the ballot (with just a few exceptions), and since, as we have seen, legislative measures have a higher rate of success than direct legislation propositions, regardless of position on the ballot, this also skews the data. See Miller, *Study of California Ballot Measures*, 5, 6; and Magleby, *Direct Legislation*, 54–55, 167. A more recent study concludes that ballot position is not really important in either the number voting or the voting result (see Cronin, *Direct Democracy*, 68–70).

CHAPTER 3: OLD ISSUES AND NEW, 1940–1969

1. There were individual years when many propositions failed to qualify, but the rate of failures definitely rose in the 1960s, probably because the rapidly increasing California population made gathering the required signatures more and more difficult and expensive (see Magleby, *Direct Legislation,* 66–67). For a list of proposals and their success in qualifying, see Jones, *California Initiative Process,* 20–72 (Sacramento: Office of the Secretary of State, 1996).

2. An indirect initiative was created by the same petition process as a standard one, but it went to the legislature rather than directly to the voters. If the legislature failed to act on it, or appreciably changed it, the proposition then went to the voters. Interestingly, one or another variant of the indirect initiative is one of the frequently suggested "reforms" for the direct legislation process in our own day.

3. Through 1993, there were only twenty legislative initiative amendments, of which seventeen passed, and two legislative statute amendments, both of which passed (see Miller, *California Ballot Measures,* 3–4). The procedures were created by a legislative constitutional amendment, Proposition 12, in the November 1946 general election; the proposition was approved by 57 percent of the voters, but with the lowest voter-participation rate (only 69 percent) among the seventeen measures on that ballot. Given voter commitment to the initiative process and voter suspicion of the legislature, this suggests ignorance rather than apathy.

4. Eleanor Wagner oral history, p. 127, UC Berkeley Oral Histories; Campaign Statements, Propositions 2 and 12, 1948; League of Women Voters, "Pros and Cons of the 1948 Ballot Measures," 2–6, 27–30, UCLA Campaigns File; UCLA Campaigns File, 1948; *Los Angeles Times,* 20 September 1948, sec. 2, p. 4.

5. An evaluation of the 1946 issue can be found in a Town Hall (Los Angeles) report, a copy of which is in the UCLA Campaigns File.

6. James Roosevelt interview, pp. 61–63, in "California Democrats in the Earl Warren Era" oral history, UC Berkeley Oral Histories; Campaign Statements, 1950, especially Californians Against the Gambling Combine; UCLA Campaigns File, 1950; *Los Angeles Times,* 24 September 1950, sec. 2, p. 4, and 3 November 1950, sec. 2, p. 4; *San Francisco Chronicle,* 1 November 1950, p. 22.

7. See miscellaneous campaign materials in UCLA Campaigns File, 1964. This tendency for the authors of propositions to determine the membership of administrative commissions would recur in the future.

8. Campaign Statements, 1962: California Committee to Combat Communism and Bryan Hardwick Associates. The latter company raised $286,000, $186,000 of which came from Frawley's Eversharp, Inc. and Schick Electric Co. See also *San Francisco Chronicle,* 4 November 1962, p. 5; *Los Angeles Times,* 1 November 1962, sec. 2, p. 6; *Sacramento Bee,* 28 October 1962, p. B2. On the role of the extreme conservatives in the 1962 election, including Prop. 24, see Gladwin Hill, *The Dancing Bear: An Inside Look at California Politics* (Cleveland: World Publishing Co., 1968), 181–82.

9. Based on Field Institute polls fi6203 (12–19 July 1962) and fi6205 (13–19 September 1962).

10. Ibid.

11. UCLA Campaigns File, 1966.

12. C. L. Dellums oral history, pp. 116–17, 161, UC Berkeley Oral Histories; Tarea Hall Pittman oral history, pp. 96–97, 120, in Earl Warren Oral History Project, UC Berkeley Oral Histories. Dellums was International President of the Brotherhood of Sleeping Car Porters, and Pittman was an official of the NAACP. See also *San Francisco Chronicle*, 10 October 1946, p. 12. An indication of Governor Warren's lack of interest in the issue is that it is not even mentioned in a recent comprehensive scholarly biography of his career (see Cray, *Biography of Earl Warren*, *passim*).

13. Town Hall of Los Angeles, "Report on Proposed Amendments . . . 1946" (Los Angeles: Town Hall, 1946), 20–25; and "Recommendations of Los Angeles Chamber of Commerce on State Ballot Measures" (Los Angeles: The Chamber, 1946), 18–19, both in UCLA Campaigns File.

14. *San Francisco Chronicle*, 10 October 1946, p. 12.

15. Campaign Statements, 1946, especially Committee for Tolerance, Women of the Pacific, and California Committee for Fair Employment Practices.

16. James Roosevelt oral history, p. 63, in Earl Warren Oral History Project, UC Berkeley Oral Histories; C. L. Dellums oral history, pp. 115–16, UC Berkeley Oral Histories; Tarea Hall Pittman oral history, p. 93, in Earl Warren Oral History Project, UC Berkeley Oral Histories.

17. Assemblymen Augustus Hawkins and Byron Rumford took turns introducing FEPC legislation in every session of the legislature after 1946 (see C. L. Dellums oral history, pp. 115–116, UC Berkeley Oral Histories).

18. One should take care not to confuse the 1948 Proposition 14 with the initiative of the same number in 1964; both involved fair housing, but the latter is the more famous and important.

19. Campaign Statements, 1948, especially Committee for Home Protection; *San Francisco Chronicle*, 31 October 1948, p. 17.

20. Los Angeles Chamber of Commerce, "Recommendations of the Los Angeles Chamber of Commerce"; California Chamber of Commerce, *California — Magazine of the Pacific*; "Committee for Home Protection" brochure; California Taxpayers Association postcard — all in UCLA Campaigns File, 1950. See also Campaign Statements, 1950: Committee for Home Protection and Northern California Committee for Home Protection. Professionals were used both for signature solicitation and the running of the campaign.

21. *San Francisco Chronicle*, 1 November 1950, p. 22; Miscellaneous campaign materials, UCLA Campaigns File, 1950. Organized Labor's Committee for Representative Government raised $101,000 for the anti-10 campaign: see Campaign Statements, 1950.

22. Gerald Horne, *Fire This Time: The Watts Uprising and the 1960s* (Charlottesville: University Press of Virginia, 1995), 223–27; Caughey, *California*, 401–3.

23. William Byron Rumford oral history, pp. 112–28, in Earl Warren Oral History Project, UC Berkeley Oral Histories; Marvin L. Holen oral history, pp. 180–83, UCLA Oral Histories; Frances Mary Albrier oral history, p. 174, UC Berkeley Oral Histories. See also Caughey, *California*, 392–93, 401–2.

24. Flyer, League of Women Voters of Los Angeles, copy in UCLA Campaigns File, 1964; William Byron Rumford oral history, pp. 127–28, in Earl Warren Oral

History Project, UC Berkeley Oral Histories. In 1963 an open housing city referendum in Berkeley, a famously liberal city, had been narrowly defeated (Frances M. Albrier oral history, pp. 202–3, UCLA Oral Histories).

25. Campaign Statements, 1964: Committee for Home Protection. See also William Byron Rumford oral history, pp. 120–26, in Earl Warren Oral History Project, UC Berkeley Oral Histories. A total of almost $1.7 million was raised and spent on this campaign, mostly by the opponents of open housing: see State of California, Fair Political Practices Commission, "Campaign Costs: How Much Have They Increased: A Study of State Elections, 1958–1978" (Fair Political Practices Commission, 1980), 9–11.

26. Miscellaneous documents, UCLA Campaigns File, 1964; Marvin L. Holen oral history, p. 184, UCLA Oral Histories. There were numerous groups raising money to defeat Prop. 14, but they included no important economic interests and raised much less money. See Campaign Statements, 1964: Young Californians Against Prop. 14, Californians Against Prop. 14, California Social Welfare Against Prop. 14, etc. See also Horne, *Fire This Time*, 223–24.

27. Horne, *Fire This Time*, provides very good coverage of the riots and their context.

28. This was because the length of a petition drive was not then limited by law, and the total vote for governor in 1942 was much lower than that of 1938, meaning that the number of signatures that had been gathered, while insufficient for the 1940 election, was sufficient to qualify the initiative for 1944. See California Commission on Campaign Financing, *Democracy by Initiative: Shaping California's Fourth Branch of Government* (Los Angeles: The Commission, 1992), 45–46 n. This led to legislation in 1943 limiting the circulation period to two years. The law was appealed by the then-still-existing Ham and Eggs organization, the Townsend Plan, and several other interests, but was not overturned. Ibid., and *San Francisco Chronicle*, 30 August 1946, p. 9.

29. Abraham Holtzman, *The Townsend Movement* (New York: Bookman Associates, 1963), 194–97; *Los Angeles Times*, 5 November 1944, sec. 1, p. 1ff, and sec. 2, p. 3; Campaign Statements, 1944: Townsend National Recovery Plan, Inc., Downtown Business Men's Association, etc.

30. *San Francisco Chronicle*, 21 October 1945, pp. 15, 22. This led the former Ham and Eggers to commence a recall petition against one of the justices, John W. Shenk. According to Allen, they aimed to "make an example" of Shenk to warn the rest of the court (Ibid.). This action, and the other aged and blind propositions of the period, led to statutory and constitutional changes that limited propositions to dealing with only one subject and forbade individuals from being appointed to office via initiative. See Magleby, *Direct Legislation*, 45–46; California Commission on Campaign Financing, *Democracy by Initiative*, 46–47.

31. *San Francisco Chronicle*, 31 October 1948, p. 15. The same argument was made by the California Association for Social Welfare; see official statement in IGS Campaigns File, 1948.

32. James Roosevelt interview, pp. 43–44; George Outland interview, pp. 21–23; Langdon Post interview, pp. 24–25 — all in "California Democrats in the Earl Warren Era" oral history, UC Berkeley Oral Histories.

33. California Council for the Blind flyer; and *The Tax Digest* 27 (January 1949): 3–4; both in IGS Campaigns File, 1948.

34. *Los Angeles Times*, 1–2 and 4–6 November 1949, all on sec. 2, p. 4; *San Francisco Chronicle*, 6 November 1949, p. 1; see also California Council for the Blind campaign flyer and "The Association Fights for Repeal of Proposition 4," *The Bulletin* (California Association for Social Welfare) 32 (August 1949): 32—both in IGS Campaigns File, 1949.

35. Campaign Statements, 1949: Northern California Committee for Sound Pension Aid, Aid to Aged and Blind Yes #2. McLain's Citizens Committee for Old Age Pensions took in $171,0000 and spent $230,000; that virtually all of this money came in donations of less than $25 testifies to McLain's organizing ability.

36. *San Francisco Chronicle*, 7 November 1949, p. 1ff, and 9 November 1949, p. 1ff.

37. There was another indirect initiative in this election, Proposition 13, to end cross-filing in primaries. These two measures have the distinction of being the last indirect initiatives in California; the device was repealed in 1966. It was used only three times, never successfully. See Jones, *California Initiative Process*, 3, 13. On McLain's tactics, see UCLA Campaigns File, 1952.

38. See *California Ballot Pamphlet*, November 1952 general election.

39. *San Francisco Chronicle*, 3 November 1952, p. 8; UCLA Campaigns File, 1952; Eleanor Wagner oral history, p. 130, in Women in Politics Oral History Project, UC Berkeley Oral Histories.

40. *Los Angeles Times*, 1 November 1954.

41. See *California Ballot Pamphlet* for the November 3, 1942 general election.

42. For example, fund-raising for the law was not extensive and was local; see Campaign Statements, 1942: San Joaquin Valley Committee to Suspend Hot Cargo — Secondary Boycott During the War, California Farm Bureau Federation.

43. See California State Federation of Labor pamphlet, UCLA Campaigns File; Campaign Statements, 1942: California State Federation of Labor; *Los Angeles Times*, 2 November 1942, sec. 1, p. 8.

44. Campaign Statements, 1944: Northern (and Southern) California Committee for the Right to Work; *Los Angeles Times*, 4 November 1944, and 5 November 1944, sec. 2, p. 3; UCLA Campaigns File, 1944, materials from May Co. department stores, Town Hall, Los Angeles Chamber of Commerce, etc.

45. California State Federation of Labor, *Weekly News Letter*, 13 September 1944, copy in IGS Campaigns File.

46. Ibid., 6 September 1944, 27 September 1944, all of October 1944, and 1 November 1944 — all in IGS Campaigns File. The California State Federation of Labor raised $325,000 for the campaign, and many individual unions all across the state also raised money; see Campaign Statements, 1944: California State Federation of Labor. (This also illustrates the difficulty of following the "money trail" with Campaign Statements. Small or local organizations raise money and therefore must file a statement. But often they give much of their funds to statewide organizations, which also file statements. So it is very possible for total contributions to be overstated. Since the specificity of reports, especially before recent times, was not great, it is often impossible to determine exactly how much money was raised and spent.)

47. Campaign Statements, 1948: California Committee Against Featherbedding and California Committee for Railroad Safety. See also California Legislative Conference report, p. 127, in Eleanor Wagner oral history, in Women in Politics Oral History Project, UC Berkeley Oral Histories; *Los Angeles Times*, 31 October 1948, sec. 2, p. 3; miscellaneous materials in UCLA Campaigns File, 1948.

48. Jackson K. Putnam, *Modern California Politics*, 2d. ed. (San Francisco: Boyd & Fraser, 1984), 43–44.

49. Hill, *Dancing Bear*, 155–56.

50. *Los Angeles Times*, 1 November 1958, sec. 1, p. 1ff. There were huge sums spent on this campaign by both sides. The Campaign Statements are voluminous and difficult to follow, but labor had already raised over $600,000 by mid-September, and provided an eighteen–page list of relatively small contributors. The main supporters of Proposition 18 had spent $500,000 by late October; they also provided a long list of contributions from large and small companies. In total, $3.2 million was spent by the two sides. See Campaign Statements, 1958: California Federation of Labor and Citizens Committee for Democracy in Labor Unions; see also Fair Political Practices Commission, "Campaign Costs . . . 1958–1978," 9–11.

51. *Los Angeles Times*, 2 November 1958, sec. IA, p. 17 (full-page ad by opponents); *California Ballot Pamphlet* for the November 4, 1958 general election; and California State Federation of Labor, *Weekly News Letter*, 11 July 1958, 1 August 1958, 15 August 1958, 20 October 1958, 10 November 1958 — all in IGS Campaigns File, 1958.

52. Based on data from Field Institute polls fi5803 (4–10 July 1958), fi5804 (6–11 September 1958), and fi5805 (4–8 October 1958).

53. The interest groups had almost identical names to those of 1948. The California Committee to Preserve Railroad Safety raised over $500,000, almost all of it from the three railroad brotherhoods — engineers, firemen, and trainmen; and the California Committee to Eliminate Railroad Featherbedding had already raised almost $2 million by the end of October, with contributions like $617,000 from the Southern Pacific and $236,000 from the Atchison, Topeka and Santa Fe. See Campaign Statements, 1964; and Fair Political Practices Commission, "Campaign Costs . . . 1958–1978," 9–11.

54. See miscellaneous materials in UCLA Campaigns File, 1964.

55. Ibid.

56. The Southern California Theater Owners Association had already contributed almost $200,000 to the California Crusade for Free TV by late September (see Campaign Statements, 1964: California Crusade for Free TV and Southern California Citizens Committee for Free TV).

57. *Orange County Bulletin*, editorial, 6 April 1964, p. B6.

58. Ibid.; see also miscellaneous campaign documents in UCLA Campaigns File, 1964.

59. Campaign Statements, 1964; see also Magleby, *Direct Legislation*, 46.

60. See *California Ballot Pamphlet* for the 1940 general election; and *Los Angeles Times*, 3 November 1940.

61. Contributors to the anti-Prop. 12 campaign included movie theaters, brokerage houses, and a variety of others. But their total collections for the campaign

amounted to only about $100,000, no longer an impressive sum (see Campaign Statements, 1949).

62. *Los Angeles Times*, 3 November 1949, sec. 2, p. 4, and sec. 2, p. 2.

63. League of Women Voters, *Pros and Cons of 1956 Ballot Measures*, copy in UCLA Campaigns File; *Los Angeles Times*, 4 November 1956; *California Ballot Pamphlet* for the 1956 general election.

64. See miscellaneous brochures, flyers, etc. in UCLA Campaigns File, 1956.

65. See form letters from American Federation of Labor, assemblymen Edward Elliott, and Harold K. Levering, UCLA Campaigns File, 1956.

66. Fair Political Practices Commission, "Campaign Costs . . . 1958–1978," 9–11.

67. See *California Ballot Pamphlet* for the 1942 general election.

68. *San Francisco Chronicle*, 3 November 1950, p. 18; Campaign Statements, 1950: California Committee for Repeal of the Personal Property Tax and California Committee Against Prop. No. 1.; Miscellaneous campaign documents in UCLA Campaigns File, 1950.

69. UCLA Campaigns File, 1952: reports of State and Los Angeles Chambers of Commerce, of Los Angeles Town Hall, and miscellaneous political party campaign materials.

70. *Los Angeles Times*, 2 November 1958, sec. 1, p. 5; Robert L. Morlan, "Analysis of the Measures on the California Ballot" (Haynes Foundation, 1958), 18–19, copy in UCLA Campaigns File, 1958.

71. Fair Political Practices Commission, "Campaign Costs . . . 1958–1978," 9–11.

72. Based on Field Institute polls fi5804 (6–11 September 1958) and fi5805 (4–8 October 1958).

73. California State Federation of Labor, "Analysis: Tax Revision Initiative (Prop. 17 on November Ballot)," submitted to Interim Tax Committee of California legislature; and *Weekly News Letter* (19 September 1958, p. 4); copies of both in IGS Campaigns File, 1958. See also Morlan, "Analysis of the Measures on the California Ballot," 19–21.

74. California Taxpayers Association, "CAL-TAX OPPOSES TAX INITIATIVE" (15 May 1958), copy in IGS Campaigns File, 1958.

75. See pamphlets, brochures, and flyers in UCLA Campaigns File, 1958; and *California Ballot Pamphlet* for the 1958 general election.

76. Based on Field Institute polls fi5804 (6–11 September 1958) and fi5805 (4–8 October 1958).

77. Ronald B. Welch oral history, pp. 72–75, UC Berkeley Oral Histories. There had been some scandals relative to county assessors adjusting rates favorably on the basis of campaign contributions; see David O. Sears and Jack Citrin, *Tax Revolt: Something for Nothing in California*, enlarged ed. (Cambridge, Mass.: Harvard University Press, 1985), 19–20.

78. Assessed value was 25 percent of market value, the ratio having been set by the legislature for all real property in 1967. One effect of this market-value basis was that the property tax burden increased proportionately more for urban homeowners than for other property owners. See Jack Citrin and Frank Levy, "From 13 to 4 and

Beyond: The Political Meaning of the Ongoing Tax Revolt in California," 3, in *The Property Tax Revolt: The Case of Proposition 13*, ed. George G. Kaufman and Kenneth T. Rosen (Cambridge, Mass.: Ballinger Publishing Co., 1981).

79. See *California Ballot Pamphlet* for the 1968 general election; also Welch, Ibid.; UCLA Campaigns File, 1968; "Ballot Propositions for November, 1968," *The Commonwealth: Transactions of the Commonwealth Club of California* 62 (17 June 1968), 2:27–31.

80. Ronald B. Welch oral history, pp. 72–75, UC Berkeley Oral Histories (Welch was on the State Board of Equalization); Philip E. Watson oral history, pp. 88–98, UCLA Oral Histories; UCLA Campaigns File, 1988; *San Francisco Sunday Examiner & Chronicle*, 3 November 1958, p. B2; Campaign Statements, 1968, especially Californians Against the Tax Trap Initiative.

81. John A. Fitzrandolph oral history, p. 5, in State Government Oral History Program, UC Berkeley Oral Histories; Philip E. Watson oral history, pp. 88–98, UCLA Oral Histories; Citrin and Levy, "From 13 to 4 and Beyond," 4.

82. *California Ballot Pamphlet* for the 1968 general election. The ballot also contained another legislative constitutional amendment, Proposition 7, that authorized the legislature to allocate state funds to cities and counties for local as well as state purposes, something which the constitution did not then permit. Proposition 7 was adopted.

83. Los Angeles County voted 43 percent in favor of Proposition 9, the highest approval percentage of any county in the state.

84. *Los Angeles Times*, 4 November 1944, sec. 2, p. 4; *California Ballot Pamphlet* for the 1944 general election.

85. *California Ballot Pamphlet* for the 1944 general election; Campaign Statements, 1944: California Teachers Association, Campaigns, Inc., California Council of Education.

86. *Los Angeles Times*, 3 November 1944, sec. 2, p. 4; UCLA Campaigns File, 1944.

87. Town Hall (Los Angeles) "Report" (October 1946), 3–6; *San Francisco Chronicle*, 3 November 1946, p. TW2; Campaign Statements, 1946: California Teachers Association; and Von T. Ellsworth, "Analysis of An Initiative Constitutional Amendment . . . Prop. 3" (California Farm Bureau Federation), 9 September 1946 — copy in IGS Campaigns File, 1946.

88. Campaign Statements, 1952: State Committee for Proposition 2 and Statewide Citizens Committee Against Prop. No. 2; see also UCLA Campaigns File, 1952.

89. Campaign Statements, 1952, State Committee for Proposition 2 and Statewide Citizen's Committee Against Prop. No. 2.

90. Elizabeth Snyder oral history, p. 63, in Women in Politics Oral History Project, UC Berkeley Oral Histories.

91. Ibid., 64–69.

92. Campaign Statements, 1952; UCLA Campaigns File, 1952; *San Francisco Chronicle*, 3 November 1952, p. 14.

93. Ibid. The Legislative Statute amendment was one of the two devices available to the legislature to put forward propositions to change or undo initiatives (see Note 3 above).

94. Elizabeth Snyder oral history, pp. 69–71, 130–31, in Women in Politics Oral History Project, UC Berkeley Oral Histories. Democratic leaders asked the Supreme Court about such a possible conflict and were advised that whichever had the most votes would prevail (Ibid.).

95. See UCLA Campaigns File, 1948, for a very large collection of mailers, broadsides, etc.; *Los Angeles Times*, 31 October 1948, sec. 2, p. 3.

96. See "Town Hall Ballot Measures Report" (Los Angeles, September 1960) and other campaign materials, in UCLA Campaigns File, 1960. A total of about $550,000 was spent by the two sides: see Campaign Statements, 1960: Californians Against Prop. No. 15, Californians Against Inequitable Reapportionment, Committee for Senate Reapportionment — Yes on 15; see also Fair Political Practices Commission, "Campaign Costs . . . 1958–1978," 9–11.

97. *California Ballot Pamphlet* for the 1962 general election; Campaign Statements, 1962: Californians Against Proposition No. 23, California Labor Federation; and UCLA Campaigns File, 1962.

98. Based on Field Institute polls fi6204 (13–19 September 1962) and fi6205 (9–14 October 1962).

CHAPTER 4: HOWARD AND PAUL TO THE RESCUE, 1970–1982

1. Citrin and Levy, "From 13 to 4 and Beyond," 4–6.

2. Ibid.; William H. Oakland, "Proposition 13: Genesis and Consequences," in Kaufman and Rosen, *Property Tax Revolt*, 40–41.

3. Jim Schultz, *The Initiative Cookbook: Recipes and Stories from California's Ballot Wars* (San Francisco: The Democracy Center, 1996), 2–3; Magleby, *Direct Legislation*, 5.

4. Campaign Statements, 1970 primary election: Californians for Responsible Property Tax Reform, California Taxpayers Association, Californians Against the Tax Hoax.

5. *California Ballot Pamphlet*, 1972 general election; *Los Angeles Times*, 6 November 1972, sec. 2, p. 6; miscellaneous materials, 1976 general election, UCLA Campaigns File; "November 1972 Ballot Proposals," pt. 2, *The Commonwealth: Official Journal of the Commonwealth Club of California* 66 (16 October 1972): 28–34.

6. For example, the members of the Governmental Finance Section of the 12,000–member strong business and professional Commonwealth Club of San Francisco voted 114–8 against the proposition ("November 1972 Ballot Proposals," *The Commonwealth*, 33).

7. Philip E. Watson oral history, pp. 130–44, UCLA Oral Histories.

8. See *California Ballot Pamphlet*, special election, November 1973, especially analysis by Legislative Analyst A. Alan Post; League of Women Voters, "Comprehensive Pros and Cons . . . Proposition 1" (October 1973), copy in UCLA Campaigns File, 1973.

9. *California Ballot Pamphlet*, special election, November 1973; William A. Niskanen, *Tax and Expenditure Limitation by Constitutional Amendment: Four Perspectives on the California Initiative* (Berkeley: Institute of Governmental Stud-

ies, University of California, Berkeley, 1973), 1–6; see also editorials in the *Sacramento Post*, 2 May 1973, sec. 1, p. 3, and the *Sacramento Bee*, 1 May 1973, p. 7.

10. "A Proposal to Limit Government Spending (Prop 1 November 6, 1973 Ballot)," *Cal-Tax Research Bulletin* (Sacramento: California Taxpayers Association, 1973), especially p. 8; John A. Fitzrandolph oral history, p. 118, in State Government Oral History Program, UC Berkeley Oral Histories; Magleby, *Direct Legislation*, 174–75; miscellaneous pamphlets, UCLA Campaigns File, 1973.

11. Paul Gann oral history, p. 17, UC Berkeley Oral Histories.

12. For a general background to the development of Proposition 13 and its immediate state and national effects, see Sears and Citrin, *Tax Revolt*; Kaufman and Rosen, *Property Tax Revolt*; Robert Kuttner, *Revolt of the Haves: Tax Rebellions and Hard Times* (New York: Simon & Schuster, 1980); Lester A. Sobel, ed., *The Great American Tax Revolt* (New York: Facts on File, 1979). A recent book that sees Prop. 13 as a crucial and destructive turning point is Peter Schrag, *Paradise Lost: California's Experience, America's Future* (New York: The New Press, 1998).

13. Sears and Citrin, *Tax Revolt*, 26–27.

14. Gann biography, in Gann Papers; Gann to Lyn Nofziger, 15 October 1981, Gann Papers; Magleby, *Direct Legislation*, 14–17.

15. Paul Gann oral history, pp. ii–iii, 17, 31, UC Berkeley Oral Histories.

16. Philip E. Watson oral history, pp. 310, 424–28, UC Berkeley Oral Histories.

17. See *California Ballot Pamphlet*, 1978 primary; also Sears and Citrin, *Tax Revolt*, 22.

18. While the percentage requirements for initiative statutes and constitutional amendments remained constant at 5 percent and 8 percent, respectively, of the most recent gubernatorial vote, the rapid increase in the California population made the absolute number of required signatures larger and larger. That meant that without enough money to hire professional signature solicitors, it would be just about impossible to qualify an initiative. At a usual charge of $1 per signature, solicitation firms would charge anywhere from $500,000 to $1 million to get a proposition on the ballot. Even mass-based groups like the California State Education Association could no longer get sufficient signatures on its own. And given the money to be made, more and more firms entered the business to create some competition for Joe Robinson. See Magleby, *Direct Legislation*, 61, 64.

19. See *Sacramento Bee*, 22 May 1978, clipping in Gann Papers.

20. Ibid.

21. Ibid.; and *Long Beach Press Telegram*, 27 November 1979, copy in Jarvis Papers. This was also the first year that the Secretary of State's office, in deference to the size of California's voting population, used sampling techniques to validate signatures. If the validation of the sample indicated that the proposition would have 110 percent or more of the required number of signatures, the proposition was qualified; if it indicated something between 90 percent and 110 percent, then all signatures would be checked. I am not sure, however, whether Proposition 13 signatures were validated by the old system or the new one.

22. Campaign Statements, 1978 primary election: Yes on 13 Committee, Yes on 13 — No on 8, People's Advocate, Inc., No on Proposition 8, Yes on 13 Committee of Gilroy, and others. Several of these organizations shared the same address and paid

out money to one another. See also Betty H. Zisk, *Money, Media, and the Grass Roots: State Ballot Issues and the Electoral Process* (Newbury Park, Calif.: Sage Publications, 1987), 93.

23. Miscellaneous clippings, Jarvis Papers; UCLA Campaigns File, 1978 primary; Sears and Citrin, *Tax Revolt*, 25-26. The Los Angeles County Supervisors declared this approach "too little—too late," and argued that if the tax cut were not raised much higher than 30 percent, Proposition 13 would win (*Los Angeles Times*, 3 March 1978, sec. 1, p. 18).

24. Paul Gann oral history, pp. 20-24, 26-27, UC Berkeley Oral Histories; *Long Beach Independent*, 14 April and 18 April 1978, clippings in Jarvis Papers.

25. See, for example, "People's Amendment to Control Taxation" flyer from United Organization of Taxpayers and People's Advocate, UCLA Campaigns File, 1978 primary.

26. John A. Fitzrandolph oral history, pp. 189-91, in State Government Oral History Program, UC Berkeley Oral Histories.

27. Magleby, *Direct Legislation*, 169; John A. Fitzrandolph oral history, pp. 154-55, in State Government Oral History Program, UC Berkeley Oral Histories.

28. UCLA Campaigns File, 1978 primary: CSEA anti-13 "newspaper"; memo by president of California Federation of Teachers; state PTA memo, etc.; John A. Fitzrandolph oral history, pp. 154-55, 189-90, 193-95, in State Government Oral History Program, UC Berkeley Oral Histories.

29. *Los Angeles Times*, 30 April 1978, sec. 5, p. 4; UCLA Campaigns File, 1978 primary.

30. In the last pre-election Field Institute California Poll, 99 percent of respondents had heard of Proposition 13 and 93 percent had heard of Proposition 8 (poll fi7806, variables 21 and 24).

31. Still, while both turnout and voter participation on Prop. 13 were clearly high, the fact remains that the total vote on this initiative represented only 66 percent of registered voters and 45 percent of eligible voters in California. Or, to put it another way, the 4,280,689 people who voted Yes on Proposition 13 represented 43 percent of the registered and 29 percent of the eligible voters of the state. This is characteristic of the operation of direct legislation.

32. For additional analysis of poll responses to this and other Jarvis and Gann measures, see Sears and Citrin, *Tax Revolt*, chap. 4.

33. On the spread of Proposition 13's ideas and principles to initiatives in Massachusetts and Colorado, for example, see Daniel A. Smith, *Tax Crusaders and the Politics of Direct Democracy* (New York: Routledge, 1998); see also John M. Allswang, review of Smith book for H-Pol on H-Net ⟨http://www.h-net.msu.edu/pol/⟩.

34. Gann Papers.

35. He would determinedly protect Proposition 13, as in his joining a lawsuit against the city of Arcadia in early 1979 over its increasing sewer and other fees to compensate for revenue losses from the initiative's passage. As Gann put it, "This case is another battle in the war." (*Antelope Valley Press*, 25 January 1979.)

36. See *California Ballot Pamphlet*, special election, November 1979; Sears and Citrin, *Tax Revolt*, 34-35; and Raymond K. O'Neil, "The Gann Initiative and Local Government," internal memo dated October 1979 of Bartle Wells Associates, Municipal Financing Consultants, in UCLA Campaigns File, 1979.

37. Paul Gann oral history, pp. 42–43, UCLA Oral Histories; Gann campaign letter, copy in UCLA Campaigns File, 1979.

38. Memo from Hay on letterhead of Dobbs and Neilsen, a Sacramento legal firm, which firm, Hay noted, "serves as treasurer and legal counsel to Spirit of 13, Inc." (copy in Gann Papers); see also quotas of signatures assigned to various groups and to "Paid Circulators," untitled document, Gann Papers.

39. *Los Angeles Herald Examiner*, 15 July 1979, p. A1ff; Jarvis form letter, no date, UCLA Campaigns File, 1979.

40. *California Ballot Pamphlet*, special election, 1979; miscellaneous documents, Gann Papers.

41. *Long Beach Independent Press Telegram*, 27 November 1979, copy in Jarvis Papers; Robert Kuttner notes that while Proposition 13 ended up costing about 5 cents per signature, for Proposition 9 the cost was $2.53 per signature (*Revolt of the Haves*, 27). The total budget for Prop. 9 was $3.6 million — more than double that of the opposition (see Zisk, *Money, Media, and the Grass Roots*, 93).

42. Kuttner, *Revolt of the Haves*, 325–26.

43. "Higher Education and the Public Interest: Proposition 9, An Interview with David S. Saxon, President, University of California," pamphlet in UCLA Campaigns File; miscellaneous campaign materials, IGS Campaigns File, 1980.

44. *Los Angeles Herald Examiner*, 17 April 1980, *Sacramento Union*, 26 March 1980, *Long Beach Independent Press Telegram*, 16 January 1980 and 27 January 1980 — copies in Jarvis Papers; *Sacramento Bee*, 13 February 1980 — copy in IGS Campaigns File, 1980; *Los Angeles Times*, 25 May 1980, sec. 5, p. 4.

45. Answers on Field Institute California Poll fi8003 (May 1980).

46. Jarvis form letter to "Dear Fellow Taxfighter," 30 March 1981, copy in Gann Papers.

47. League of California Cities, "Fact Sheet on Propositions 5, 6, and 7" (24 May 1982), copy in IGS Campaigns File, 1982 primary; *California Ballot Pamphlet*, 1982 primary election.

48. Kuttner, *Revolt of the Haves*, 276–77.

49. Sobel, *Great American Tax Revolt*, 126; Kuttner, *Revolt of the Haves*, 288–90.

50. Jarvis speech at University of Cincinnati, 1 November 1979, Jarvis Papers. Tom Hazlett, "What Ever Happened to Proposition 13," *Reader's Digest* (October 1981), copy in Jarvis Papers.

51. *Los Angeles Times*, 1 July 1978, 7 July 1978, 9 March 1979 — clippings in Jarvis Papers.

52. Tom Bradley oral history, p. 265, UCLA Oral Histories; *Los Angeles Herald Examiner*, 12 April 1979 — clipping in Jarvis Papers.

53. *Los Angeles Herald Examiner*, 15 April 1979 — clipping in Jarvis Papers. The rise of rent control led to a June 1980 initiative, Proposition 10, which was misrepresented as a defense of the process but actually would have made implementation more difficult. A huge number of contributors, mainly real estate interests, spent $4.6 million, while the opponents raised and spent only $178,271. Nevertheless, the measure was defeated 65 percent to 35 percent. This is one of many examples of money (and untruthful advertising) not necessarily being able to win an initiative election. See Campaign Statement Summaries, 1980 primary election; and Daniel

Lowenstein, "Campaign Spending and Ballot Propositions: Recent Experience, Public Choice Theory and the First Amendment," *UCLA Law Review* 29 (February 1982): 524-26.

54. *Palm Springs Desert Sun*, 18 April 1988 — clipping in Jarvis Papers; Debora Vrana, "Recession Drives Local Developer Bonds to the Brink," *California Journal* 23 (January 1992): 37-38.

55. John A. Fitzrandolph oral history, p. 199, in State Government Oral History Program, UC Berkeley Oral Histories. The fact that Congress was also responding to the Watergate scandal with its own Federal Election Campaign Act of 1974 demonstrated the public enthusiasm, at that time, for campaign-finance reform.

56. Walter A. Zelman oral history, pp. 117-18, UCLA Oral Histories, (Zelman became head of Common Cause in 1978); Daniel H. Lowenstein oral history, pp. 74-79, UCLA Oral Histories (Lowenstein was the principal author of Proposition 9); Carla L. Duscha, "It Isn't a Lobby . . . and the People Are Few," *California Journal* 6 (March 1975): 83-85, which is based on an interview with Ed Koupal.

57. Magleby, *Direct Legislation*, 60; People's Lobby, *Proposition 9, The Political Reform Act: A Fact for California, A Proposal for America* (Los Angeles: People's Lobby Press, 1974); Daniel H. Lowenstein oral history, p. 92, UCLA Oral Histories.

58. *California Ballot Pamphlet*, 1974 primary election; Rico J. Nannini oral history, pp. 119, 132-33, UC Berkeley Oral Histories; miscellaneous materials, UCLA Campaigns File, 1974 primary.

59. People's Lobby, *Proposition 9*, 16-17.

60. Vigo Nielsen, Jr., oral history, pp. 67-68, UC Berkeley Oral Histories. The laws were, respectively, S.B. 716 and A.B. 703, 1973. See also *Sacramento Bee*, 30 September 1973, *San Francisco Examiner*, 23 August 1973, *Los Angeles Times*, 5 October 1973 — all clippings in Proposition 9 file, IGS Campaigns File.

61. People's Lobby, *Proposition 9*, 23; Proposition 9 file, IGS Campaigns File; Daniel H. Lowenstein oral history, pp. 107-12, UCLA Oral Histories.

62. Proposition 9 file and miscellaneous press clippings, IGS Campaigns File.

63. Ibid.; John A. Fitzrandolph oral history, pp. 127-28, State Government Oral History Program, UC Berkeley Oral Histories.

64. Walter A. Zelman oral history, pp. 130-34, UCLA Oral Histories.

65. Notes by interviewer Carlos Vasquez, pp. 121-24, and Walter A. Zelman comments, pp. 130-34, Zelman oral history, UCLA Oral Histories.

66. Vigo Nielsen, Jr., oral history, pp. 67-69, 72-73, 76-77, UC Berkeley Oral Histories.

67. "Anti-Obscenity Reporter," copy in UCLA Campaigns File, 1972; *San Francisco Chronicle*, 15 September 1972; *Los Angeles Times*, 2 October 1972, sec. 2, p. 6; copy of letter from [Democratic law firm] Wyman, Bautzer, Rothman & Kuchel on consequences of passage, UCLA Campaigns File, 1972; Rosalind Weiner Wyman oral history, pp. 99-100, UC Berkeley Oral Histories (Wyman ran the anti-18 campaign). For an example of middle-class arguments on both sides, see "November 1972 Ballot Proposals," *The Commonwealth*, 48-50.

68. A pro-Proposition 19 flyer named the San Francisco Bar Association, the American Civil Liberties Union, liberal Democratic members of the State Assembly,

and various business leaders and medical personnel (copy in UCLA Campaigns File, 1972 general election); see also "November 1972 Ballot Proposals," *The Commonwealth*, 54–59.

69. *California Ballot Pamphlet*, 1972 general election; "November 1972 Ballot Proposals," *The Commonwealth*, 64–67; miscellaneous documents, UCLA Campaigns File, 1972 general election.

70. Miscellaneous documents, UCLA Campaigns File, 1972 general election. Members of the "Administration of Justice" section of San Francisco's Commonwealth Club, whose membership drew from the business and professional class, voted 100–65 in favor of the proposition, a figure almost as high as the vote by the public at large (see "November 1972 Ballot Proposals," *The Commonwealth*, 44).

71. John C. Bollens and G. Robert Williams, *Jerry Brown in a Plain Brown Wrapper* (Pacific Palisades, Calif.: Palisades Publishers, 1978), 140–44; Putnam, *Modern California Politics*, 81.

72. *California Ballot Pamphlet*, 1978 general election; League of Women Voters of California, *State Ballot Measures, General Election, November 7, 1978, Pros and Cons* (San Francisco: The League, 1978), 2–5.

73. Field Institute polls fi7807 (12 –28 August 1978), fi7808 (17–24 September 1978), and fi7809 (30 October–1 November 1978).

74. It may well be that there was not so much a lack of emotion as a lack of publicity and information. Compared to other propositions in the same election, relatively little money was spent on Prop. 7: $657,000 by supporters, $12,000 by opponents (Campaign Statement Summaries, 1978 general election). This would also explain why, in the polls, fewer people had heard of Prop. 7 than of the better-financed initiatives.

75. *San Francisco Chronicle*, 23 April 1981, p. 14. Gann's files contained hundreds of clippings of news stories about various crimes in California (see Gann Papers).

76. Paul Gann oral history, pp. 72–75, UC Berkeley Oral Histories. Gann used both his established organization, People's Advocate, Inc., and a new one, Citizen's Committee to Stop Crime, Paul Gann, Chairman, for this campaign (see Gann Papers). The "specific and primary purpose" of the committee was "to educate the public on issues involving crime and the criminal justice system" (see copy of incorporation papers, undated, Gann Papers).

77. *California Ballot Pamphlet*, 1982 primary election.

78. *(San Fernando) Valley Daily News*, 30 September 1981, sec. 2, p. 1; *Los Angeles Times*, 18 January 1982, sec. 2, p. 1ff.

79. See, for example, a letter from Assemblyman Richard Mountjoy, with 4,485 signed petitions "collected by persons in my district" (Gann Papers). Copies of form letters and responses are in Gann Papers.

80. *Sacramento Union*, 21 February 1982, p. B2; Paul Gann oral history, pp. 28–29, UC Berkeley Oral Histories; Proposition 8 folder, IGS Campaigns File; Gann Papers.

81. *Los Angeles Times*, 5 May 1982 and 17 May 1982; *San Francisco Examiner*, 30 May 1982; *San Jose Mercury News*, 23 May 1982; *Sacramento Bee*, 17 May 1982 — all clippings in Proposition 8 folder, IGS Campaigns File.

82. Bill Blum and Gina Lobaco, "The Proposition 8 Puzzle," *California Lawyer* 5 (February 1985): 28ff.

83. *California Ballot Pamphlet*, 1982 general election; Campaign Statements, 1982: Californians Against Street Crime and Concealed Weapons, and Citizens Against the Gun Initiative; and miscellaneous campaign materials and *Los Angeles Times*, 16, 19, 22, 24, 25 October 1982 — all in IGS Campaigns File.

84. Field Institute poll fi8206 (1–4 October 1982).

85. Major contributors against Prop. 5 were the tobacco companies: R. J. Reynolds, $1.7 million; Philip Morris, $1.5 million; Brown and Williamson, $882,000; and Lorillard, $638,000 (see Campaign Statement Summaries, 1978 general election).

86. Field California Polls fi7808 (17–24 September 1978) and fi7809 (30 October–1 November 1978). For an argument that opposition was stronger earlier in the campaign, see Lowenstein, "Campaign Spending," 537–38 and 538 n.

87. *California Ballot Pamphlet*, 1980 general election.

88. *Los Angeles Times*, 9 October 1980, sec. 1, p. 3ff.

89. *Los Angeles Times*, 2 October 1980, sec. 1, p. 23; *The Commonwealth* 74, no. 80 (1980): 16–17.

90. Eighty-eight percent of the opposition funds came from the four big tobacco companies (Campaign Statement Summaries, 1980 general election).

91. The relationships among these three variables also bear this out, with one exception: mean family income correlates above the .600 level with both percentage high school graduates and percentage urban. Only the relationship between percentage of high school graduate and percentage of urban voters is non-significant, although it is positive, at .289.

92. For general background on this issue, see Leonard Pitt, *California Controversies: Major Issues in the History of the State*, 2d. ed. (Wheeling, Ill.: Harlan Davidson, 1989), 321–42.

93. "November 1972 Ballot Proposals," *The Commonwealth*, 68–75. Interestingly, the Industrial Relations Section of the Commonwealth Club divided almost evenly, 60–47, in favor of Proposition 22, whereas the Agriculture Section voted 278–17 in favor of the measure.

94. *California Ballot Pamphlet*, 1972 general election; miscellaneous flyers, UCLA Campaigns File, 1972 general election.

95. Fair Political Practices Commission, *Campaign Costs: How Much Have They Increased and Why? A Study of State Elections, 1958–1972* (Sacramento: FPPC, 1980), 9; Lowenstein, "Campaign Spending," 522–24.

96. *The (La Crescenta-Montrose) Ledger*, 5 November 1972 — clipping in UCLA Campaigns File, 1972 general election; Lowenstein, "Campaign Spending," 522–24.

97. UCLA Campaigns File, 1972 general election; Lowenstein, "Campaign Spending," 523–24. After the election, sixteen people were charged with fraud in connection with the signature solicitation process.

98. *Los Angeles Times*, 16 October 1972, sec. 2, p. 6; miscellaneous campaign documents in both English and Spanish, UCLA Campaigns File, 1972 general election.

99. *California Ballot Pamphlet*, 1976 general election; and Town Hall (Los Angeles) of California, "Ballot Measures Report, 1976" — copy in UCLA Campaigns File, 1976 general election.

100. Field Institute (California) Poll fi7605 (24 July–2 August 1976).

101. "Ballot Propositions for June 1972," *The Commonwealth*, 19.

102. Ibid.; *California Ballot Pamphlet*, 1972 primary election.

103. Fair Political Practices Commission, *Campaign Costs*, 9; and League of Women Voters, "Primary Election Extra" [in English and Spanish] and *Santa Monica Evening Outlook*, 24 May 1972—both in UCLA Campaigns File, 1972 primary election.

104. Paul A. Sabatier, *Can Regulation Work? The Implementation of the 1972 California Coastal Initiative* (New York: Plenum Press, 1983), 14–17, 38; Magleby, *Direct Legislation*, 60.

105. *California Ballot Pamphlet*, 1972 general election; "November 1972 Ballot Proposals," *The Commonwealth*, 61.

106. James W. Moorman [attorney for the Sierra Club Legal Defense Fund] oral history, pp. 76–77, UC Berkeley Oral Histories; William F. Siri oral history, pp. 187–90, UC Berkeley Oral Histories; miscellaneous campaign documents, UCLA Campaigns File, 1972 general election.

107. Sabatier, *Can Regulation Work?*, 293–97.

108. Fair Political Practices Commission, *Campaign Costs*, 9; Sabatier, *Can Regulation Work?*, 40–45, 293–97; William F. Siri oral history, pp. 187–90, UC Berkeley Oral Histories (Siri concluded that the Whitaker and Baxter campaign was "so dishonest and distorted" that it backfired).

109. Miscellaneous campaign materials, UCLA Campaigns File, 1972 general election. There was some business support for the initiative; for example, the Commonwealth Club's Environmental Crisis Section voted 141–84 in favor, and its Natural Resources Section voted 107–92 in favor ("November 1972 Ballot Proposals," *The Commonwealth*, 61, 63).

110. Sabatier, *Can Regulation Work?*, 293–97.

111. Hundley, *Great Thirst*, 353–57. The battle over the dam would continue for almost ten more years, in the courts and in Congress.

112. *California Ballot Pamphlet*, 1976 primary election; and League of Women Voters of Los Angeles, "Election Extra" (2 April 1976), p. 3—copy in UCLA Campaigns File, 1976 primary election.

113. David R. Brower oral history, pp. 287–90, UC Berkeley Oral Histories; Magleby, *Direct Legislation*, 57, 143.

114. William F. Siri oral history, pp. 160–63, UC Berkeley Oral Histories; Magleby, *Direct Legislation*, 169.

115. Campaign Statement Summaries, 1976 primary election. Californians for Nuclear Safeguards raised over $1 million of this sum; two other large committees were Project Survival to Californians for Nuclear Safeguards ($502,000) and Simpatico to Californians for Nuclear Safeguards ($300,000). The vagueness of their names and the fact that these groups transferred money back and forth is an indication of one of the difficulties of really finding out exactly who finances initiative campaigns. Additionally, an unspecified amount of this money was spent on signature solicitation, even if it was done by volunteers, so the pro-15 campaign had even less available than this sum suggests.

116. Ibid.

117. Field Institute poll fi7604 (31 May–5 June 1976), variable 162.

118. For an overview of the issue, see Pitt, *California Controversies*, 298–320, and Hundley, *Great Thirst*, 309–28. The peripheral canal would have looped around the Sacramento–San Joaquin delta to facilitate the movement of northern California water to the south. Northern California voters had been instrumental in the passage of a legislative constitutional amendment on the 1980 general election ballot (Prop. 8) to protect the delta and north coast rivers.

119. Citizens for Water — Yes on 9, campaign materials, in Proposition 9 folder, IGS Campaigns File.

120. Campaign Statements: Californians for a Fair Water Policy, California Coalition to Stop the Peripheral Canal, Californians against Higher Water Bills. Hundley estimates a total of $6 million spent on the campaign (*Great Thirst*, 324).

121. Pitt, *California Controversies*, 300.

122. Campaign Statements, 1982 general election: Californians against Waste Campaign, Californians for Recycling and Litter Clean-Up.

123. Campaign Statements, 1982 general election: Californians for Sensible Laws (the Coors beer company alone donated $108,000); *Los Angeles Times*, 24 October 1982, sec. 1, p. 1ff; Proposition 11 folder, IGS Campaigns File. In the early October California Poll, 87 percent of registered voter respondents were aware of this initiative: see Field Institute poll fi8206 (1–4 October 1982).

124. *California Ballot Pamphlet*, 1982 general election; see also Californians for a Bilateral Nuclear Freeze, and Town Hall of California, "Ballot Measures Report" (n.d. [1982?]) — both in UCLA Campaigns File, 1982 general election. On the congressional vote, see *Los Angeles Times*, 15 and 16 August 1982, clipping in Proposition 12 folder, IGS Campaigns File.

125. Campaign Statements, 1982 general election: Californians for a Bilateral Nuclear Freeze.

126. Field Institute poll fi8206 (1–4 October 1982).

127. Campaign Statements, 1982 general election: Californians for a Balanced Water Policy. This was the main opposition group, spending $2 million to defeat the measure.

128. Duscha, "It Isn't a Lobby . . . and the People Are Few," 83. The speaker was Ed Koupal, head of People's Lobby.

129. Fair Political Practices Commission, *Campaign Costs*, 9.

130. Lowenstein, "Campaign Spending," 518, 550.

131. For another discussion of this topic, see Magleby, *Direct Legislation*, 80–81, 84–92, 121.

132. Respondents were also asked what were their most important sources of information for proposition campaigns (with multiple responses permitted): 75 percent mentioned television, 96 percent radio, 73 percent the "voter information pamphlets," 70 percent newspapers, 96 percent "word of mouth," and 96 percent direct mail. Since the poll results do not indicate which were mentioned first, this information is not analytically useful.

CHAPTER 5: INITIATIVES ALL OVER THE PLACE, 1984–1994

1. Jones, *California Initiative Process*, 46–65. By contrast, the 1920–1939 period had only 47 proposed initiatives that did not qualify, but the immediately pre-

ceding 1970–1982 period, only slightly longer, had 218. Clearly, the process has seemed more and more attractive to more and more interest groups in recent times. That rate would continue in 1994, when there were 27 non-qualifiers.

2. For the first time since 1982, a referendum has qualified for the March 2000 primary election. It relates to the Indian gaming controversy discussed in Chapter 6.

3. In the 1984 general elections, both Prop. 36, on taxation, and Prop. 39, on reapportionment, had total expenditures above $10 million (see Campaign Statement Summaries, 1984 general election). Actually, spending on the smoking regulation, Prop. 5 of 1978, if converted to 1984 dollars, was just over $10 million as well.

4. In the 1990 general election, Prop. 129, which dealt with drug enforcement and prison construction, is categorized as both a Health and Welfare and a Sociocultural measure; Prop. 133, which also dealt with drug enforcement, is listed under both Health and Welfare and Taxation. In the 1992 general election, Prop. 161, physician-assisted death, is listed under both Sociocultural and Health and Welfare; and Prop. 165, which dealt with both budget powers and reduction of welfare, is listed under both Government and Elections and Health and Welfare. In the 1994 general election, Prop. 185, which taxed gasoline, is listed under both Environment and Taxation; and Prop. 187, dealing with illegal aliens, is listed under both Sociocultural and Health and Welfare.

5. *San Francisco Examiner*, 3 June 1984; Proposition 24 folder, IGS Campaigns File; Town Hall of California, "Ballot Measures Report, June 5, 1984," 20–24, in UCLA Campaigns File, 1984 primary.

6. Paul Gann oral history, pp. 44–45, UC Berkeley Oral Histories.

7. Gann Papers. Gann's correspondence was enormous, and very well filed and responded to; he also lectured constantly all over the state. His People's Advocate organization was central to all of this, as a mass-based permanent political movement. See ibid.

8. Copies of letters, Gann Papers; "Information Package," ibid.

9. Field Institute polls fi8401, fi8402, fi8403, fi8404 (February–June 1984). The February poll also asked a number of questions relating to attitudes toward the state legislature (variables 68–87), which did demonstrate a good deal of skepticism and distrust.

10. *Sacramento Union*, 30 November 1984, p. A1ff; *Sacramento Bee*, 3 January 1985, p. A14; Gann Papers.

11. Gann Papers.

12. Gann to Butcher-Forde Advertising, 6 April 1983; John T. Hay to Gann, 22 June 1984 and 18 July 1984, both in Gann Papers.

13. People's Advocate, Inc., *Report* (May 1983), copy in Gann Papers.

14. Jarvis and Laffer form letters, undated [1984], copies in UCLA Campaigns File, 1984 general election.

15. *California Ballot Pamphlet*, 1984 general election.

16. Field Institute polls fi8405 (4–9 September 1984) and fi8406 (8–12 October 1984).

17. *California Ballot Pamphlet*, 1986 general election; UCLA Campaigns File, 1986 general election. The definition of "general" and "special" taxes was never entirely clear. Also, the measure was less inclusive than Jarvis thought; the state legislative analyst said that since this was an initiative statute rather than a constitutional amendment, it could not apply to the 82 chartered cities. See also *Los Angeles*

*Times,* 12 October 1986, sec. 5, p. 4, and *San Francisco Examiner,* 21 October 1986, copies in Proposition 62 folder, IGS Campaigns File.

18. Campaign Statements, 1986 general election: Taxpayers Voting Rights Committee; Campaign Statement Summaries, 1986 general election.

19. Field Institute poll fi8604 (24 July–2 August 1986).

20. Field Institute polls fi8604 (24 July–2 August 1986), fi8605 (24 September–7 October 1986), fi8606 (27 October–30 October 1986).

21. *Los Angeles Times,* 2 March 1997, p. B1ff.

22. Campaign Statement Summaries, 1986 general election. Gann acknowledged that they had to pay for signature gathering for this proposition (Paul Gann oral history, p. 40, UC Berkeley Oral Histories).

23. Campaign Statement Summaries, 1986 general election; Proposition 61 folder, IGS Campaigns File; UCLA Campaigns File, 1986 general election; *California Ballot Pamphlet,* 1986 general election.

24. *California Ballot Pamphlet,* 1988 primary election; miscellaneous campaign materials in Propositions 71 and 72 folders, IGS Campaigns File; Jarvis Papers; "League of Women Voters of California Stands on State Ballot Initiatives, June 1988," typescript copy in UCLA Campaigns File, 1988 primary election.

25. Campaign Statements, 1988 general election: Californians for Quality Government, California Tax Reduction Movement; see also Campaign Statement Summaries, 1986 general election.

26. See miscellaneous documents in UCLA Campaigns File, 1988 primary, especially Commonwealth Club of California, "1988 State Ballot Propositions," *Transactions of the Commonwealth Club* 82 (2 May 1988): 13–14; Jarvis Papers; Paul Gann oral history, p. 13, UC Berkeley Oral Histories; Propositions 71–72 folders, IGS Campaigns File.

27. *San Francisco Examiner,* 27 May 1988, copy in Jarvis Papers.

28. Field Institute poll fi8803 (16–22 May 1988).

29. Campaign Statement Summaries, 1988 general election; "California's Pride: Our Public Schools," copy in Proposition 98 folder, IGS Campaigns File.

30. *San Francisco Chronicle,* 13 October 1988; *San Francisco Examiner,* 20 October 1988 and 28 October 1988; *Tuolumne County Union Democrat,* 11 October 1988; *Oakland Tribune,* 6 November 1988—copies in Proposition 98 folder, IGS Campaigns File.

31. The funding aspects of this measure were made less absolute by a legislative constitutional amendment, Proposition 11, in the June 1990 primary.

32. Field Institute poll fi9006 (26–30 October 1990). When asked the same question about themselves rather than the "average voter," respondents discerned a considerably higher level of comprehension.

33. *Los Angeles Times,* 4 November 1990, p. M4; "Californians for Safe Streets" bulletin, UCLA Campaigns File, 1990 general election; *California Ballot Pamphlet,* 1990 general election.

34. Campaign Statement Summaries, 1990 general election.

35. Field Institute poll fi9006 (26–30 October 1990).

36. See miscellaneous flyers, mailers, etc. in UCLA Campaigns File, 1990 general election, and Propositions 126 and 134 (combined) folder, IGS Campaigns File.

37. The decision was particularly important because it could apply to up to seven of the propositions on the November 1990 ballot, to say nothing of the future. *Los Angeles Times*, 2 November 1990, sec. 1, p. 1ff.

38. Campaign Statement Summaries, 1990 general election.

39. Jim Schultz, *The Initiative Cookbook: Recipes and Stories* (San Francisco: The Democracy Center, 1996), 8. The $27 million figure, as we have seen, was an underestimation, which also illustrates the increasing difficulty of establishing just how money was distributed among various initiative campaigns in the same election.

40. The legislative analyst's analysis was that a *special* tax was one earmarked for a specific purpose, whereas a tax that raised money for the state general fund was a *general* tax. This was a topic that had been subject to some debate and interpretation. *California Ballot Pamphlet*, 1990 general election.

41. Ibid. To the legislative analyst, "The legal effect of these provisions is uncertain." He well knew it would end up in the courts.

42. *Los Angeles Times*, 25 September 1990. See also Jarvis Papers, and miscellaneous campaign materials in Proposition 136 folder, IGS Campaigns File.

43. Campaign Statement Summaries, 1990 general election. The largest single donation, $1.2 million, was from the Howard Jarvis Taxpayers Association.

44. See clippings from *San Francisco Chronicle*, 28 November 1991, and *Oakland Tribune*, 26 December 1991, plus miscellaneous campaign materials in Proposition 163 folder, IGS Campaigns File.

45. See documents and clippings in UCLA Campaigns File, 1992 general election, and Proposition 167 folder, IGS Campaigns File.

46. *Sacramento Union*, 9 October 1992, plus other clippings and campaign materials, UCLA Campaigns File, 1992 general election.

47. *California Ballot Pamphlet*, 1994 general election.

48. Miscellaneous brochures and reports in UCLA Campaigns File, 1992 general election.

49. Data available on request.

50. *Los Angeles Times*, 10 September 1984, sec. 1, p. 3. These were Propositions 10, 11, and 12 on the 1982 primary election ballot.

51. Form letter [undated] by Governor Deukmejian, UCLA Campaigns File, 1984 general election; *Los Angeles Times*, 10 September 1984, sec. 1, p. 3, 19 October 1984, sec. 1, p. 2ff; Commonwealth Club of California, "1984 November State Ballot Propositions," *Transactions of the Commonwealth Club* 78, pt. 2 (October 1, 1984): 19–20; César Chávez form letter [undated], in Proposition 39 folder, IGS Campaigns File.

52. "News Release," Secretary of State March Fong Eu, 18 July 1989; *Los Angeles Times* editorial, 6 August 1989, sec. 5, p. 4.

53. *California Ballot Pamphlet*, 1990 primary election.

54. Californians for Political Reform brochure, Sierra Club postcard, and California Federation of Labor form letter—copies in UCLA Campaigns File, 1990 primary election; League of Women Voters memo, 21 February 1990, and *San Francisco Examiner*, 30 April 1990—copies in Propositions 118 and 119 folders, IGS Campaigns File.

55. *Los Angeles Times*, 20 September 1990, *Oakland Tribune*, 27 September

1990—clippings in Propositions 131 and 140 folders, IGS Campaigns File; *California Ballot Pamphlet,* 1990 general election.

56. *California Ballot Pamphlet,* 1990 general election; *Los Angeles Times,* 31 October 1990, clipping in Propositions 131 and 140 folders, IGS Campaigns File.

57. Campaign Statement Summaries, 1990 general election.

58. Ibid.

59. *Los Angeles Times,* 24 April 1997, p. A1ff; 8 September 1997, p. A1ff; 15 October 1997, p. A3ff; 20 December 1997, p. A1ff. The Supreme Court actually did consider the case in 1998 and upheld the appeals court ruling that the vote of the people of California should be the determining factor (see *Los Angeles Times,* 24 March 1998, p. A3ff).

60. California Secretary of State, *History of Initiative Process,* 59–60; *San Francisco Chronicle,* 20 November 1991, clipping in Proposition 164 folder, IGS Campaigns File.

61. Field Institute poll fi9208 (25–30 October 1992); see also *San Francisco Chronicle* editorial, 27 October 1992, and other campaign materials, in Proposition 164 folder, IGS Campaigns File.

62. Peter F. Schabarum, *Enough is Enough: Term Limits in California* (Los Angeles: Peter F. Schabarum, 1992); the entire book and copies of many other campaign flyers and mailers are in UCLA Campaigns File, 1992 general election; see also Campaign Statement Summaries, 1992 general election.

63. The case was *U.S. Term Limits, Inc.* v. *Thornton,* 1995; the Court's decision invalidated 23 state laws for congressional term limits that had been passed since 1990. See also *Los Angeles Times,* 20 December 1997, p. A1ff.

64. Susan Heavey, "Term Limits Take Effect," *Washington PostCom* (http://www.washingtonpost.com/wp-srv/politics/special/termlimits/termlmits.com), 20 May 1998. The same Internet site also provides additional information on term limits and links to other sources. Equally useful is the Internet site of the major national pro-term limits organization, U.S. Term Limits (http://www. termlimits.org/research/fact.htm).

65. *California Ballot Pamphlet,* 1984 general election; Commonwealth Club of California, "1984 State Ballot Propositions," *Transactions of the Commonwealth Club,* 78, pt. 2 (1 October 1984): 20–22.

66. Campaign Statement Summaries, 1984 general election.

67. Field Institute polls fi8406 (8–12 October 1984) and fi8407 (27–30 October 1984).

68. *California Ballot Pamphlet,* 1988 primary election.

69. Ibid., and press release entitled "Taxpayers to Limit Campaign Spending," copy in Propositions 68 and 73 folders, IGS Campaigns File. The spending limits applied only to those candidates who wanted to receive public funding.

70. See, e.g., typescript, "League of Women Voters of California Stands on State Ballot, June 1988," copy in UCLA Campaign Files, 1988 primary; see also Walter A. Zelman oral history, pp. 145–48, UCLA Oral Histories.

71. *Los Angeles Times,* 14 April 1988 and 14 May 1988, clippings in Propositions 68 and 73 folders, IGS Campaigns File.

72. Campaign Statement Summaries, 1988 primary election. Amounts reported

were "No on Props. 68 and 73" ($1.1 million) and "Committee to Protect the Political Rights of Minorities" ($71,000). Willie Brown and David Roberti were among the largest donors to the former.

73. Ibid.

74. Field Institute polls fi8802 (6–10 April 1988) and fi8803 (16–22 May 1988).

75. *Los Angeles Times*, 18 June 1989, sec. 1, p. 3ff, and 4 August 1989, sec. 1, p. 1ff. Most of what remained of Prop. 68 was invalidated by a California Supreme Court decision in 1990, and the contribution limits and certain other parts of Prop. 73 were thrown out by a U.S. District Court decision in September 1990. See also *Los Angeles Times*, 6 October 1996, p. A3ff.

76. Vigo Nielsen, Jr., oral history, p. 90, UC Berkeley Oral Histories.

77. *California Ballot Pamphlet*, 1990 general election; Jarvis Papers.

78. Campaign Statement Summaries, 1990 general election. About $1.6 million of the total came from the Howard Jarvis Taxpayers Association. In fact, they had somewhat more money than $3 million, because Gann's Spirit of 13 Committee for Proposition 136 (tax limitation) on the same ballot gave some of its money to the Prop. 137 campaign. Ibid.

79. Commonwealth Club of California, "1984 State Ballot Propositions," *Transactions of the Commonwealth Club* 78, pt. 2 (1 October 1984): 16–17; *California Ballot Pamphlet*, 1984 general election.

80. *Sacramento Union*, 21 February 1982, p. B2; Dena Cochran, "A Victim's Bill of Rights or a Lawyer's Employment Act," *California Journal* 13 (April 1982): 133–34; Gann Papers.

81. Gann Papers.

82. Field Institute polls fi8604 (24 July–2 August 1986), fi8606 (27–30 October 1986), fi8607 (4 November 1986).

83. *California Ballot Pamphlet*, 1990 primary election.

84. Wilson, who had his eye very much on the White House, from this time forward would continuously advocate initiatives to solidify his position with conservatives. His initiatives did not always fare well in the courts, however. Proposition 115, for example, was invalidated by the California Supreme Court in December 1990 on the basis that it was a "revision" rather than an "amendment" of the state constitution, and therefore could not be accomplished by initiative.

85. *California Ballot Pamphlet*, 1994 general election.

86. Ibid., and miscellaneous documents, UCLA Campaigns File, 1994 general election.

87. Ibid.

88. Campaign Statement Summaries, 1994 general election.

89. Field Institute poll fi9407 (21–30 October 1994).

90. In 1975 Congress had amended the 1965 Voting Rights Act to specify that voting materials should be offered in alternative languages in given areas of the United States. That law had recently been extended to 1992. See "The Constitutional Future of the All-English Ballot," *Pacific Law Review* 16 (1985), copy in Proposition 38 folder, IGS Campaigns File. The *California Ballot Pamphlet* has been available in Spanish and Chinese since 1979.

91. E.g., John H. Tanton to Gann, 25 April 1983, 10 August 1983, 17 August

1983, all in Gann Papers. It was a testament to Gann's popularity at the time that Proposition 38's sponsors courted him so vigorously; the Gann Papers have four folders of correspondence with U.S. English.

92. *San Francisco Chronicle*, 16 February 1984, p. 9.

93. *California Ballot Pamphlet*, 1984 general election; Commonwealth Club of California, "1984 November State Ballot Propositions," *Transactions of the Commonwealth Club* 78, pt. 2 (1 October 1984): 18; miscellaneous campaign materials, in Proposition 38 folder, IGS Campaigns File.

94. See, e.g., statement of Hispanic lawyers, *Los Angeles Daily Journal*, 23 October 1984, p. 1ff.

95. Stanley Diamond, who shared leadership with Hayakawa, said in a San Francisco speech, "This is the first time in American history where one ethnic group, the Hispanics, do have an agenda that is different" (*Oakland Tribune*, 15 October 1986, p. A5).

96. See miscellaneous campaign materials, UCLA Campaigns File, 1986 general election; *California Ballot Pamphlet*, 1986 general election.

97. Campaign Statement Summaries, 1986 general election.

98. According to Field poll results published in the *San Jose Mercury News*, 17 October 1986, p. 1F.

99. Ibid., 23 September 1986, p. 1B.

100. *Los Angeles Times*, 25 October 1986, sec. 1, p. 1ff.

101. Susannah D. A. MacKaye, "California Proposition 63: Language Attitudes Reflected in the Public Debate," *Annals of the American Academy of Political and Social Science* 508 (1990): 135–46. The Arizona law, a constitutional amendment passed in 1988, was invalidated by the Arizona Supreme Court, and that decision was upheld by the U.S. Supreme Court in early 1999. See *Sacramento Bee*, 12 January 1999 (electronic Internet copy, UMI Company, ⟨http://www.Northernlight.com⟩).

102. "A California Journal Analysis: 1993 November Ballot Propositions," special insert in *California Journal* 24 (September 1993): 4–5; "Citizens Against 174" brochure and miscellaneous documents, UCLA Campaigns File, 1993 general election; *California Ballot Pamphlet*, 1993 special election.

103. Associated Press dispatch in *Oakland Tribune*, 10 September 1993, clipping in Proposition 174 folder, IGS Campaigns File. This is not to suggest that there wasn't support for the measure based on purely educational issues; see Laura A. Locke, "The Voucher Initiative: Breakthrough or Break-up for California Schools," *California Journal* 24 (October 1993): 9–14.

104. See numerous campaign documents in UCLA Campaigns File, 1993 special election, and Proposition 174 folder, IGS Campaigns File. Governor Wilson wanted the issue resolved in a 1993 special election so it wouldn't cloud his campaign for reelection in 1994; he skirted the issue for a long time, but finally, "reluctantly," opposed it because of its potential diversion of money from the public schools. *Oakland Tribune*, 3 June 1993, *San Francisco Chronicle*, 21 May 1993 and 24 September 1993 — clippings in IGS Campaigns File.

105. Campaign Statement Summaries, 1993 special election, especially "Citizens Against 174, Sponsored by the Education Coalition."

106. Field Institute poll fi9304 (8–15 October 1993).

107. Legislative analyst's analysis, Proposition 187, *California Ballot Pamphlet*, 1994 general election.

108. *California Ballot Pamphlet*, 1994 general election; "A California Journal Analysis: 1994 November Ballot Propositions," special insert in *California Journal* 25 (September 1994): 9-10.

109. "A California Journal Analysis: 1994 November Ballot Propositions," special insert in *California Journal* 25 (September 1994): 9-10.

110. Ibid.; UCLA Campaigns File, 1994 general election.

111. Miscellaneous documents, UCLA Campaigns File, 1994 general election.

112. Campaign Statement Summaries, 1994 general election, especially: Citizens for Legal Immigration Reform/Save Our State, and Taxpayers Against 187, Sponsored by Education, Healthcare, Labor and Business.

113. Field Institute poll fi9407 (October 21-30 1994).

114. *Los Angeles Times*, 28 November 1996, p. A1.

115. *Los Angeles Times*, 19 March 1998, p. A3ff and editorial, p. B8. For a more complete chronology of the history of Judge Pfaelzer's rulings on Prop. 187, see *Los Angeles Times*, 9 November 1997, p. A1ff. When Gov. Gray Davis and civil rights groups came to agreement in 1999 not to appeal further, accepting Judge Pfaelzer's ruling, the initiative was pretty well dead. The issue, however, was not. Former Governor Wilson, among others, was ready to try again (see *Los Angeles Times*, 29 July 1999, p. A1ff and 30 July 1999, p. A1ff).

116. *California Ballot Pamphlet*, 1986 general election and 1988 primary election.

117. Among other things, Larouche was noted for his accusations that former Vice President Walter Mondale was a Soviet agent and Queen Elizabeth of England a drug pusher (*San Jose Mercury News*, 30 September 1986, p. 1A). On his role in the 1986 campaign, see Ibid., 2 November 1986, p. 3H.

118. League of Women Voters of California, *Comprehensives: State Ballot Measures, General Election, November 4, 1986* (The League, August 1986), 1-7.

119. *San Jose Mercury News*, 30 September 1986, p. 16B.

120. Ibid., 3 September 1986, p. 1A, and 23 October 1986, p. 18A. The same groups and arguments also prevailed with Prop. 69 in 1988 (see *Los Angeles Times*, 24 April 1988, and 24 May 1988; *San Francisco Chronicle*, 20 May 1988 — copies in Proposition 69 folder, IGS Campaigns File).

121. Campaign Statement Summaries, 1986 general election and 1988 primary election.

122. Field Institute polls fi8606 (27-30 October 1986) and fi8803 (16-22 May 1988).

123. *California Ballot Pamphlet*, 1988 general election; Reese Erlich, "The Tragedy of the 'Other' AIDS Initiative," *San Francisco Bay Guardian* 23 (23 November 1988): 13-14.

124. Erlich, "'Other' AIDS Initiative," Ibid.; Paul Gann oral history, pp. 77-79, UC Berkeley Oral Histories; and *San Francisco Examiner* 6 November 1988, *Oakland Tribune*, 19 September, 3 October, and 5 October 1988; *San Francisco Chronicle*, 10 September 1988 — all in Propositions 96 and 102 folder, IGS Campaigns File.

125. Campaign Statement Summaries, 1988 general election. The "Stop Danne-

meyer" money came from primarily small donations from a large number of individuals and small groups.

126. Field Institute poll fi8807 (31 October–2 November 1988).

127. The correlation coefficients for the vote on these four AIDS initiatives were very high, ranging from .715 to .972. A considerable number of Californians had fixed attitudes about the dangers of AIDS.

128. *California Ballot Pamphlet*, 1984 general election; *San Francisco Chronicle*, 14 September 1984, p. 14.

129. *Los Angeles Times*, 27 September 1984, p. A1ff; *Vacaville Reporter*, 13 September 1984, p. 3; Commonwealth Club of California, "1984 State Ballot Propositions," *Transactions of the Commonwealth Club* 78, pt. 2 (1 October 1984): 23–24; miscellaneous clippings and campaign materials, UCLA Campaigns File, 1984 general election, and Proposition 41 folder, IGS Campaigns File.

130. Miscellaneous clippings and campaign materials, UCLA Campaigns File, 1984 general election, and Proposition 41 folder, IGS Campaigns File; Campaign Statement Summaries, 1984 general election.

131. *California Ballot Pamphlet*, 1988 general election; *Northern California Real Estate Journal* (18 July 1988) and *San Francisco Chronicle*, 2 November 1988 — copies in Proposition 95 folder, IGS Campaigns File.

132. Campaign Statement Summaries, 1988 general election. The opposition money was primarily from grocery and restaurant interests.

133. Field Institute polls fi8806 (10–16 October 1988) and fi8807 (31 October–2 November 1988).

134. *California Ballot Pamphlet*, 1992 general election; *Los Angeles Times*, 25 October 1992, p. T5.

135. *San Francisco Chronicle*, 24 April 1992, and *San Francisco Examiner*, 16 June 1992 — clippings in Proposition 165 folder, IGS Campaigns File.

136. *San Francisco Independent*, 15 February 1992; *San Francisco Chronicle*, 12 February 1992, and 7 July 1992; *San Francisco Examiner*, 1 August 1992 — all clippings in Proposition 165 folder, IGS Campaigns File. See also miscellaneous campaign flyers, etc., in ibid. and in UCLA Campaigns File, 1992 general election.

137. Campaign Statement Summaries, 1992 general election.

138. Field Institute poll fi9208 (25–30 October 1992).

139. *California Ballot Pamphlet*, 1992 general election; Richard F. Corlin, M.D. [President of the California Medical Association], "ABC Plan for Californians Without Health Coverage," *Sacramento Bee*, 9 April 1992 — copy in UCLA Campaigns File, 1992 general election.

140. *California Ballot Pamphlet*, 1992 general election.

141. Bill Ainsworth, "Derailing Initiatives (Before They Reach the Ballot)," *California Journal* 23 (January 1992): 47–50.

142. "A California Journal Analysis: 1992 November Ballot Propositions," special insert in *California Journal* (September 1992): 7–8; *California Ballot Pamphlet*, 1992 general election; *Bay Area Reporter*, 22 October 1992, clipping in Proposition 166 folder, IGS Campaigns File; miscellaneous campaign materials, UCLA Campaigns File, 1992 general election; Campaign Statement Summaries, 1992 general election.

143. Campaign Statement Summaries, 1992 general election.

144. *California Ballot Pamphlet,* 1994 general election; "A California Journal Analysis: 1994 November Ballot Propositions," special insert in *California Journal* 25 (September 1994): 7–9.

145. Campaign Statement Summaries, 1994 general election. The California Teachers Association, at $348,000, was the largest single donor to the pro-186 side. State Farm Insurance alone almost tripled that, with its $1 million contribution to the opposition; and numerous other insurance companies also made contributions in the $200,000–$500,000 range. See also *Los Angeles Times,* 9 September 1994, p. A18; Richard Reeves, "Surgeons Get It," op-ed piece in *San Jose Mercury News,* 14 February 1994; and miscellaneous documents, UCLA Campaigns File, 1994 general election.

146. *California Ballot Pamphlet,* 1988 general election; *The California Senior* 1 (October 1988), and other anti-99 materials, copies in Proposition 99 folder, IGS Campaigns File; see also Campaign Statement Summaries, 1988 general election.

147. Field polls fi8805 (6–13 September 1988) and fi8807 (31 October–2 November 1988). There is some evidence from recently uncovered secret tobacco company memos that the companies tried to undermine implementation of Prop. 99 by getting the new tax revenues switched to other purposes. There is no current proof of action on the memos, but the Wilson administration and the legislature in the mid-1990s did divert over $100 million to health care programs other than anti-smoking ones (*Los Angeles Times,* 21 January 1998, p. A3ff).

148. See miscellaneous campaign materials, and *San Francisco Chronicle* editorial, 11 May 1994 — both in UCLA Campaigns File, 1994 general election.

149. Campaign Statement Summaries, 1994 general election. On the support of some other groups, see "A California Journal Analysis: 1994 November Ballot Propositions," special insert in *California Journal* 25 (September 1994): 10–12.

150. Walter A. Zelman oral history, pp. 161–65, UCLA Oral Histories.

151. Some observers thought the insurance companies put Prop. 106 on the ballot mainly to distract the attorneys from the insurance initiatives (*San Francisco Chronicle,* 10 October 1988, clipping in Proposition 106 folder, IGS Campaigns File).

152. Walter A. Zelman oral history, pp. 161–65, UCLA Oral Histories; John A. Fitzrandolph oral history, p. 208, in State Government Oral History Program, UC Berkeley Oral Histories. This was in fact the case with Proposition 103, at least parts of which were in the courts and unimplemented eight years later; see, e.g., *San Francisco Chronicle,* 9 March 1989, and *Oakland Tribune,* 8 March 1989, both clippings in Propositions 100–104 folders, IGS Campaigns File.

153. *San Francisco Chronicle,* 2 November 1988; *San Francisco Examiner,* 20 September 1988; Californians Against Unfair Rate Increases, "Why Should We Pay More So Los Angeles Can Pay Less" — all in Propositions 100–104 folders, IGS Campaigns File.

154. Field Institute polls fi8804 (22–29 July 1988), fi8805 (6–13 September 1988), fi8806 (10–16 October 1988), and fi8807 (31 October–2 November 1988).

155. See lists of specific expenditures in Campaign Statement Summaries, 1988 general election, especially those in favor of Prop. 104; see also UCLA Campaigns File, 1988 general election.

156. Rosenfield proved a master at generating a great deal of publicity with relatively little money, as when he shipped a truckload of manure to the Los Angeles offices of Farmer's Insurance Co. (Schultz, *Initiative Cookbook*, 48).

157. See Campaign Statement Summaries, 1990 general election; some of the money for and against "Big Green" (Prop. 128) was transferred to other proposition contests in this election. The other propositions were: Prop. 130, forest acquisition; Prop. 132, marine resources; Prop. 135, pesticide regulation; and Prop. 138, forestry programs. Proposition 128 is also an example of the increasing number of lengthy, complex, multisubject propositions that were making it to the ballot despite the "one subject" rule. They proved fodder for the courts and a frustration to the creation of policy. See *California Ballot Pamphlet*, November 1990 general election, and Hundley, *Great Thirst*, 417.

158. Reporting was often somewhat misleading. "Professional management" does not specify just how those managers spent the money given to them. Therefore, the data here are essentially suggestive, certainly not definitive.

CHAPTER 6: NOT QUITE HISTORY,
BUT MORE OF THE SAME, 1996 AND BEYOND

1. The California Secretary of State estimated that two-thirds of the total $141 million spent on propositions in 1996 could not be linked to specific measures, whereas before 1996 the "vast majority" of contributions were directly linked to individual ballot measures (California Secretary of State, "Financing California's Statewide Ballot Measures: 1996 Primary and General Elections," report posted on Secretary of State Internet site ⟨http://www.ss.ca.gov/⟩).

2. Campaign Statements for the respective years; totals calculated by office of the Secretary of State.

3. *California Ballot Pamphlet*, 1996 primary election and 1996 general election; *Los Angeles Times*, 3 November 1996.

4. Personal telephone interviews and E-mail exchanges by the author with administrators of several World Wide Web sites. For example, Sean Garrett of the PBN campaign consulting firm, managing the campaign against Prop. 210 (minimum wage increase), said that they had little sense of people using their site to help evaluate the issue; moreover, they received only about 25 E-mail responses from people who wanted to get involved in their campaign (telephone interview, 15 November 1996).

5. A thorough recent study of the entire Proposition 209 battle is Lydia Chávez, *The Color Bind: California's Battle to End Affirmative Action* (Berkeley: University of California Press, 1998).

6. *Los Angeles Times*, 13 August 1996, p. A3. Both Field Institute and *Los Angeles Times* polls found that wording on describing the measure had a significant influence; using the language of the proponents without the term *affirmative action* in the question resulted in considerably higher Yes responses; see *Los Angeles Times*, 31 October 1996, p. A20; and Field Institute poll fi9606 (25–28 October 1996), especially Questions 21–23A.

7. Campaign Statements, 1996 general election; and California Secretary of

State, "Financing California's Statewide Ballot Measures: 1996 Primary and General Elections," (http://www.ss.ca.gov/).

8. *Los Angeles Times*, 16 September 1996, p. A1. Connerly, who could be aggressive at times, and who was convinced that in their hearts both businesses and average workers were on his side, was quoted as saying, "When the chips are down, big business is a coward" (ibid.).

9. *Los Angeles Times*, 28 October 1996, p. A1, and 29 October 1996, p. A1ff. The Republicans had hoped and expected that they could ride Proposition 209 to a broad-based victory in California in 1996, but it did not work that way: pro-209 candidates did not fare particularly well, and the Democrats bounced back at all levels from their 1994 losses.

10. *Los Angeles Times*, 25 September 1996, p. B1, and 29 October 1996, p. A3ff.

11. A *Los Angeles Times* poll in late September found that registered voters favored the measure by 60 percent to 25 percent (19 September 1996, p. A18). The Field polls found that registered voters gave very similar responses when asked the question "unaided," and even with an explanation, their responses were 45 percent Yes to 37 percent No in late October, and 50 percent Yes to 45 percent No a week later (see Field Institute polls fi9606 [25–28 October 1996] and fi9607 [29 October–3 November 1996]).

12. The history of the litigation can be followed in the *Los Angeles Times*: 20 November 1996, p. A3ff; 28 November 1996, p. A1ff; 24 December 1996, p. A1ff; 9 April 1997, p. A1ff; 4 November 1997, p. A1ff.

13. *California Ballot Pamphlet*, 1996 general election.

14. Campaign Statement Summaries, 1996 general election, Proposition 215. The source of funding was somewhat unusual: almost two-thirds of the total came from the contributions of four individuals (Peter Lewis, $500,000; George Soros, $550,000; John Sperling, $200,000; George Zimmer, $260,000).

15. Miscellaneous radio and television advertisements throughout the campaign; *Los Angeles Times*, 7 November 1996, p. A3.

16. Field Institute polls fi9604 (29 August–7 September 1996), fi9606 (25–28 October 1996), and fi9607 (29 October–3 November 1996).

17. The lower court had ruled that Proposition 209 could protect the right of an individual to use marijuana for medicinal purposes only. It did not protect marijuana clubs, nor the right to sell marijuana, nor the right of a commercial enterprise acting as a primary caregiver to furnish it. The aims of the authors of the initiative were almost entirely undone. This was reified by a 1998 federal court decision that ordered six "cannabis clubs" in northern California to be closed because they were in violation of federal law. The U.S. Justice Department advised other such clubs to close as well (*Los Angeles Times*, 15 May 1998, p. A2).

18. The ideological factor was also demonstrated in responses to public opinion polls. Self-described "strong conservatives" favored Prop. 209 by 80 percent and opposed Prop. 215 by 63 percent, whereas "strong liberals" opposed Prop. 209 by 82 percent and favored Prop. 215 by 92 percent. Those who defined themselves as "not very strong" conservatives or liberals were not quite so adamant, but they also divided on the same basis as their more ideological kin (Field Institute poll fi9607 [29 October–3 November 1996]).

19. *Sacramento Bee*, 12 December 1996, p. A3.

20. Kelly Kimball, former president of Kimball Petition Management, in remarks to Workshop on Direct Democracy, University of California, Riverside, 26 June 1997. Their success in aiding the defeat of Propositions 207 and 211 led the high-tech group to create a new organization for political action, headed by John Doerr, a leading Silicon Valley venture capitalist (see *Los Angeles Times*, 8 July 1997, p. A3ff).

21. Campaign Statement Summaries, 1996 primary and general elections.

22. *Los Angeles Times*, 31 October 1996, p. A37, and 15 October 1996, p. B6. There were also ubiquitous billboards and radio and TV spots devoted to this proposition. A *Los Angeles Times* article (2 October 1998, p. A1ff) stated that an all-time-high record $57.5 million had been spent on Prop. 211, but, as noted, much of this money was combined and in fact cannot be so directly traced to an individual proposition.

23. Field Institute polls fi9604 (29 August–7 September 1996) and fi9607 (29 October–3 November 1996).

24. The Consumer Attorneys Issues PAC, while primarily involved in the five "big initiatives," did devote some of their $38 million bankroll to opposing Prop. 213 (see also *Los Angeles Times*, 9 October 1996, p. A3ff, and 16 October 1996, p. A1ff). Moreover, while Prop. 213 was the only one of these initiatives to pass, it was immediately embroiled in lawsuits from several interests and appeared very likely to lose some of its parts (*Los Angeles Times*, 18 December 1996, p. A3, and 6 April 1997, p. A3ff).

25. This is reflected in the fact that one major attorney-driven campaign committee (Citizens for Retirement Protection and Security), which raised about $13 million, supported Prop. 211 only (and opposed 200–201–202); another campaign committee (Frivolous Lawsuit Reform) raised $10 million to support Prop. 207 only (and opposed 200–201–202). It is also worth noting that none of these six initiatives had strong relationships with such census data as family income, education, level of unemployment, or being recent arrivals in California.

26. *Los Angeles Times*, 8 October 1996, p. A1ff, 25 October 1996, p. B8, 2 March 1997, p. B1ff; *California Ballot Pamphlet*, 1996 general election.

27. Campaign Statement Summaries, 1996 general election.

28. Field Institute poll fi9606 (25–28 October 1996). Those who defined themselves as "Conservatives" and as Republicans tended to favor Prop. 218 in the poll, whereas "Liberal" and Democratic identifiers did not.

29. *Los Angeles Times*, 2 March 1997, p. B1ff, 6 March 1997, pp. A1ff and B5.

30. *California Ballot Pamphlet*, 1996 general election; *Los Angeles Times*, 29 October 1996, p. B8.

31. Campaign Statement Summaries, 1996 general election.

32. *California Ballot Pamphlet*, 1996 general election.

33. Campaign Statement Summaries, 1996 general election.

34. *California Ballot Pamphlet*, 1996 primary election.

35. Campaign Statement Summaries, 1996 primary election.

36. Field Institute poll fi9601 (21–25 February 1996).

37. The proposed Prop. 208 voluntary limits were: $200,000 for state assembly, $400,000 for state senate, $2 million for statewide offices other than Governor, and

$8 million for Governor. The respective Prop. 212 mandatory limits were $150,000, $235,000, $1.75 million, and $5 million. The authors of Prop. 212 tried to cover possible legal problems by also specifying that if the mandatory spending limits were invalidated by the courts, they would automatically become voluntary (see *California Ballot Pamphlet*, 1996 general election).

38. Ibid.; *Los Angeles Times*, 8 October 1996, p. A3ff, 21 October 1996, p. A30, 29 October 1996, p. A3ff.

39. Campaign Statement Summaries, 1996 general election.

40. For example, an early fall 1996 poll found that the better educated and wealthier respondents would be: (1) much more likely to have voted in statewide elections in the past and to be sure that they would vote in the upcoming November election; (2) more likely to report that they carefully reviewed ballot propositions; and (3) much more likely to rely for information on the ballot pamphlet and newspapers, and much less likely to rely on television. Interestingly, education and income had relatively little effect on respondents' feelings about how understandable ballot propositions were (Field Institute poll fi9604 [29 August–7 September 1996]). The greater likelihood of those who are better educated and wealthier to vote is well known, and was recently confirmed by a study by the Committee for the Study of the American Electorate, U.S. Census Bureau (see *Los Angeles Times*, 4 May 1998, p. A5).

41. *Los Angeles Times*, 7 November 1996, p. A3ff, 7 February 1997, p. A1ff. One immediate effect was for potential 1998 gubernatorial candidates to raise as much money as possible before the law went into effect in January 1997. Republican Attorney General Dan Lungren and Democratic Lt. Gov. Gray Davis did just that, which left them in strong positions against their opponents, except for the case of very wealthy individual opponents, which is what Davis encountered in 1998.

42. *Los Angeles Times*, 7 January 1997, p. A1ff. The federal judge who issued the ruling was particularly concerned with how the spending limits would hurt "ordinary candidates," since there were no limits on how much of his or her own money a wealthy candidate could spend. He urged the state FPPC to take the case to the California Supreme Court to try to separate the legal parts of the statute from the unconstitutional ones.

43. *Los Angeles Times*, 24 June 1997, p. A3ff.

44. *Los Angeles Times*, 16 March 1998, p. A3. In early 1999, a federal appeals court ordered a full trial on Proposition 208, upholding the earlier injunction pending final disposition. The appeals court did not, however, express an opinion for or against the district court ruling (*Los Angeles Times*, 6 January 1999, p. A3ff).

45. *California Ballot Pamphlet*, 1996 general election; *Los Angeles Times*, 6 October 1996, p. A1ff.

46. See *California Ballot Pamphlet*, 1996 general election; and Campaign Statement Summaries, 1996 general election.

47. Campaign Statement Summaries, 1996 general election.

48. Field Institute poll fi9606 (25–28 October 1996).

49. *California Ballot Pamphlet*, 1998 primary election.

50. Ibid., and *Los Angeles Times*, 26 April 1998, p. A3ff. The initiative's sponsors failed by a small margin to obtain enough signatures to put their revised con-

gressional term-limits proposition on the fall 1998 ballot. They vowed to try again in the year 2000.

51. *California Ballot Pamphlet*, 1998 primary election; and flyer from Citizens for an Educated America, No. on 227 (in author's possession). Opponents were not short of money, either: they received $1.5 million from A. Jerrold Perenchio, billionaire chairman of Univision Communications. This was about double what Unz put into the pro side (*Los Angeles Times*, 27 May 1998, p. B1ff, and 3 June 1998, p. A24).

52. *Los Angeles Times*, 4 June 1998, p. A1ff; Kathleen Les, "No Mas for Bilingual," *California Journal* 29 (July 1998): 24.

53. The *Los Angeles Times* exit poll found quite the opposite so far as wealth was concerned: the greater the family income, the more people supported Prop. 227. What seems to be true with data aggregated at the county level is not so for data from the 100 selected precincts used by the *Times* (4 June 1998, p. A30).

54. *Los Angeles Times*, 13 April 1998, p. A1ff, and 4 June 1998, p. A30.

55. *Los Angeles Times*, 19 May 1998, p. A1ff. The state's bilingual law had lapsed in 1986 and had not been renewed, although funding continued. This had resulted in a situation similar to what the new legislation proposed.

56. Supporters of Proposition 226 used extensive radio advertising, paid for by the conservative Claremont Institute, that always used the word "employer" and never used the word "union" (e.g., advertisement broadcast on radio station KNX, 23 May 1998, and other dates).

57. See *Los Angeles Times*, 8 June 1998, p. A1ff; and Steve Scott, "Proposition 226: Labor's Big Victory," *California Journal* 29 (July 1998): 22–23.

58. See California Secretary of State, "Committees Formed Primarily to Support or Oppose Proposition 226," ⟨http://www.ss.ca.gov/⟩, 10 September 1999; also, *Los Angeles Times*, 23 March 1998, p. A1ff, 6 April 1998, p. A3ff, 29 May 1998, p. A3ff, and 3 June 1998, p. A1ff. Calculations of exact expenditures are difficult to gauge, as was becoming increasingly the case, because of transfers of funds from one campaign committee to another; for Proposition 226, this was particularly the case for the initiatives supporters.

59. *Los Angeles Times*, 8 June 1998, p. A1ff. Perhaps even more influential in Prop. 226's failure was voter confusion, induced by the negative nature of the measure itself and the persuasive advertising of the initiative's opponents. It appears that many voters simply did not understand just what the effects of a Yes or No vote would be, and that at least some concluded that a No vote would weaken the unions (see David S. Broder, "Voter Confusion on a Hot Controversy," *Washington Post*, 31 May 1998, p. A4; and Scott, "Proposition 226," 22–23).

60. Campaign spending data can be found at California Secretary of State, ⟨http://www.Vote98.ss.ca.gov/lcrV98/⟩; and Compaq Computer and California Voter Federation ⟨http://www.calvoter.org/98general⟩ or ⟨http://www.digital.com⟩. See also *Los Angeles Times*, 24 October 1998, p. 1ff; *California Journal* 29 (December 1998): 5. This campaign came under new regulations requiring campaign-finance committees to file their reports electronically; the process is still being developed, however.

61. That is the total pro-Prop. 5 expenditure of about $60 million divided by the

4,518,824 voters who supported the proposition ($13.28 per vote). As might be expected in 1998, the measure was immediately taken to court and was blocked by the state Supreme Court one month after the election, pending a resolution of its constitutionality. Then, in August 1999, the state Supreme Court overturned Proposition 5 on the basis that its permitting "casino" games like blackjack and slot machines was in violation of the state constitution (*Los Angeles Times*, 3 December 1998, p. A1ff, and 24 August 1999, p. A1ff; and *New York Times*, 24 August 1999, p. A1ff). Another initiative, which hoped to undo earlier Indian gaming agreements with Governor Wilson, qualified well ahead of time for the March 2000 ballot. Meanwhile, Governor Davis and the Indian tribes involved in Proposition 5 were trying to work out a compromise that would pass constitutional muster, but, at the same time, the tribes began the process of getting an unassailable initiative constitutional amendment on the March 2000 ballot (*Los Angeles Times*, 25 August 1999, p. A3ff).

62. Legislative analyst's analysis, *California Ballot Pamphlet*, 1998 general election.

63. Opponents raised about $40 million, with Southern California Edison and Pacific Gas and Electric together contributing well over half of the total (Compaq-Digital "Campaign Contribution Database," ⟨http://ca98.election.digital.com/cgi-bin/summary⟩, 4 November 1998; California Voter Foundation, "Top Ten Contributors," ⟨http://www.calvoter.org⟩, 6 November 1998.

64. Ibid.; see also *Los Angeles Times*, 24 October 1998, p. 1ff.

65. *California Ballot Pamphlet*, 1990 general election; Jarvis Papers; Propositions 136–137 folders, IGS Campaigns File.

66. Campaign Statement Summaries, 1990 general election.

67. Field Institute poll fi9703 (14–24 August 1997). The questions in this poll were written by myself and Professor Ted Lascher of California State University, Sacramento, with assistance from Mark DiCamillo of the Field Institute.

68. Question 52: "In deciding about statewide ballot propositions, voters look to various sources of information, such as television, newspapers, the Secretary of State's ballot pamphlets, the advice of friends and relatives, mailings sent to you, as well as information on the Internet. What is the most useful source of information for you?"

69. One conclusion we might draw from these responses is that the "experts" may be wasting money on the extensive amount of radio advertising they currently do. Unless they are looking for very specific target audiences, it appears that much of that money might well be applied elsewhere.

70. Question 55: "In general, how much of the time do you feel you know which groups or organized interests are supporting or opposing individual propositions that appear on statewide ballots—all of the time, most of the time, some of the time, rarely or never?"

71. California is the only state where the legislature cannot amend initiatives (remarks of Robert M. Stern, California Commission on Campaign Financing, at the Workshop on Direct Democracy, University of California, Riverside, 26 June 1997).

72. A very strong representation of that view is in Schrag, *Paradise Lost*.

73. The signature gathering process was further "commercialized," in the words of California Secretary of State Bill Jones, by a U.S. Supreme Court decision in early 1999. The Court invalidated any laws that required signature gatherers to be registered voters in the state in which they are working. This nullified laws in California and eighteen other states, but the Court ruled 8–1 that it was an exercise in "political speech" (*Los Angeles Times*, 13 January 1999, p. A3ff).

74. Probably the most comprehensive study of the current state of direct legislation in California, and the most complete set of suggestions for reform, can be found in California Commission on Campaign Financing, *Democracy by Initiative*; see also Magleby, *Direct Legislation*, and Dubois and Feeney, *Lawmaking by Initiative*. A persuasive recent condemnation of the whole system and its effects, which overly idealizes representative government, is Schrag, *Paradise Lost*.

75. The *Los Angeles Times* predicted (4 May 1998, p. A5) that this trend would continue, with almost two-thirds of the electorate not voting in the fall 1998 election.

76. Ibid.

77. On the current sophisticated process of developing an initiative, see *Los Angeles Times*, 16 April 1998, p. A1ff; See also, remarks of Craig Holman, Center for Governmental Studies, at Workshop on Direct Democracy, University of California, Riverside, 26 June 1997.

78. *Los Angeles Times*, 29 May 1998. Justice Ming W. Chin, speaking for the minority, argued that trial judges would likely often dismiss charges to avoid such a situation. But Gov. Pete Wilson, one of Proposition 184's main sponsors, said he was very pleased.

79. Column by Peter H. King, *Los Angeles Times*, 20 October 1996, p. A3.

80. Key and Crouch, *Initiative and Referendum*, 459.

81. On this idea, see Magleby, *Direct Legislation*, 15–16, 25; and *Los Angeles Times*, 16 April 1998, p. A1ff.

82. An extensive discussion of the issue can be found in Schrag, *Paradise Lost*. Longtime Secretary of State March Fong Eu was convinced that legislators "very frequently" wanted measures put on the ballot in order to avoid having to go on record on the controversial issues themselves (see March Fong Eu oral history, pp. 87–88, UC Berkeley Oral Histories). An alternative argument, that direct legislation has become less used because state legislatures "have steadily improved" and professionalized, is made by Cronin, *Direct Democracy*, 197. Cronin's idea of diminished use certainly does not apply to California.

83. See Schultz, *Initiative Cookbook*, 34–35; and remarks of Kelly Kimball, former president of Kimball Petition Management, at Workshop on Direct Democracy, University of California, Riverside, 26 June 1997.

84. Examples of the latter are the spectacular recent failures of Michael Huffington, who spent almost $30 million of his own money in his effort to defeat Diane Feinstein for the U.S. Senate in 1994, and of Al Checchi, who spent almost $40 million of his own money in search of the Democratic gubernatorial nomination in 1998.

85. A lengthy contemporary analysis of the pros and cons of the long-term effects of Proposition 13 can be found in *Los Angeles Times*, 26 May 1998, p. A1ff. Nine months before the 2000 primary election, four direct legislation measures had already qualified for the ballot and another nineteen were at one or another stage of the

qualification process. These included four separate initiative constitutional amendments by Ron Unz of Proposition 227 fame, all of them combining campaign finance reform, reapportionment, and other matters, in an effort to find a combination that the public would adopt. No one had ever tried quite so brazen an approach to get his way via the initiative. Once again, there are many sociocultural measures, for example, those dealing with crime, the outlawing of homosexual marriage, prayer in the public schools, and even two measures from the same sponsor that would make marital infidelity a crime, which would not ease California's crowded-jail problem. Old issues like public support for private schools have returned. And California's disdain for politicians is reflected in a "None of the Above" initiative, which would let voters vote against everybody. Good or bad, sublime or ridiculous, the role of direct legislation in California is definitely not on the wane. (See California Secretary of State, "2000 Ballot Initiative Update," (http://www.ss.ca.gov), 10 September 1999.)

86. John M. Allswang, *Bosses, Machines, and Urban Voters*, rev. ed. (Baltimore: The Johns Hopkins University Press, 1986), 167.

APPENDIX A

1. Sources: Tony Miller, Acting California Secretary of State, *A Study of California Ballot Measures, 1884–1993* (Sacramento: Office of the Secretary of State, 1994); John M. Allswang, *California Initiatives and Referendums, 1912–1990: A Survey and Guide to Research* (Los Angeles: Edmund G. "Pat" Brown Institute of Public Affairs, California State University, Los Angeles, 1991); *California Ballot Pamphlet* (issued by the Secretary of State before each election). The Miller book lists information for legislative propositions as well as popular ones. For a listing of proposed direct legislation measures that failed to qualify, see Bill Jones, Secretary of State, *A History of the California Initiative Process* (Sacramento: Office of the Secretary of State, 1996).

# Bibliographical Essay

The literature on direct legislation in California is less voluminous than one might expect, given the length of time that the institution has been around, its controversiality, and the number of measures involved. With the exception of the past twenty years, the secondary literature is quite limited — confined primarily to studies by political scientists, often devoted to single measures or campaigns, and only occasionally of long-term usefulness. My fellow historians have been particularly lax in studying this problem, and longitudinal studies are rare.

Manuscript collections are particularly productive for the origins and early history of direct legislation, particularly the monumental John Randolph Haynes collection at UCLA. Also useful are the Edward A. Dickson, Franklin Hichborn, and some of the Chester Rowell papers, all at UCLA. Another part of the Rowell papers, along with those of Hiram Johnson, are at the Bancroft Library at UC Berkeley. The Meyer Lissner and Mary Rose papers are at Stanford, and the marginally useful Marshall Stimson papers are at the Huntington Library.

For more recent history, the Paul Gann and Howard Jarvis papers, both at the California State Library in Sacramento, are worth using. Also, for the period from the 1930s to the present day, a major source of information is the extensive number of book-length oral histories, in two series, one done by the University of California, Berkeley, and the other by UCLA. These were sometimes sponsored by the universities themselves and sometimes implemented by them for outside sponsors, such as the California State Archives. Guides to these interviews are Suzanne B. Riess and Willa K. Baum, eds., *Catalogue of the Regional Oral History Office, 1954–1979* (Berkeley: Bancroft Library, 1980); Constance S. Bullock, comp., *The UCLA Oral History Program: Catalog of the Collection* (Los Angeles: UCLA, 1982); and, Teresa Barnett, comp., *The UCLA Oral History Program: Catalog of the Collection: Second Edition, Supplement* (Los Angeles: UCLA, 1996).

Government documents are also useful to any student of California direct legislation. Two regularly updated compendiums of information from the California Office of the Secretary of State are *A History of the California Initiative Process* (Sacramento, 1996), which contains summary data and is unique in including information on propositions that failed to qualify as well as those that made it to the ballot; and *A Study of California Ballot Measures, 1884–1993* (Sacramento, 1994), which contains data similar to Appendix A in this book, but which also includes the vote for and against each measure and some other interesting data as well.

Campaign financing data are obviously important for understanding initiative elections, but the actual obligatory Campaign Statements filed by groups raising money for or against initiatives are not easy to use. They are voluminous, often imprecise or incomplete, and are filed by committee name rather than proposition number, so that it is easy for the researcher to miss important groups. Since 1976, government publications have provided spending summaries by proposition. From 1976 to 1990, this was done, under varying titles, by the Fair Political Practices Commission. Since 1992, the job has been taken over by the Political Reform Division of the Office of the Secretary of State of California for every election, also under varying titles, but most recently, *Financing California's Statewide Ballot Measures* (Sacramento: Office of the Secretary of State, [election date]). Unfortunately, the ability of groups to evade accurate reporting continues, making the scholar's inquiry into this subject often frustrating.

Secondary works on campaign financing are sparse, especially for the earlier years, in part because the collection of accurate data was so difficult. An exception, although general in nature, is John R. Owens and Larry L. Wade, "Campaign Spending on California Ballot Propositions, 1924–1944," *Western Political Quarterly* 39 (December 1986). Historically useful is Fair Political Practices Commission, *Campaign Costs: How Much Have They Increased: A Study of State Elections, 1958–1978* (Sacramento: FPPC, 1980). An analytical contemporary study is Daniel H. Lowenstein, "Campaign Spending and Ballot Propositions: Recent Experience, Public Choice Theory and the First Amendment," *UCLA Law Review* 29 (February 1982): 505–641. See also Betty H. Zisk, *Money, Media, and the Grass Roots: State Ballot Issues and the Electoral Process* (Newbury Park, Calif.: Sage Publications, 1987); John R. Owens and Edward C. Olson, "Campaign Spending and the Electoral Process in California, 1966–1974," *Western Political Quarterly* 30 (December 1977); and California Fair Political Practices Commission, *Campaign Contribution And Spending Report* (Sacramento: FPPC, 1978).

There are some fairly recent national studies on direct legislation, none of them historical, which serve as a useful introduction to the issue and to current academic interests. David R. Magleby, *Direct Legislation: Voting on Ballot Propositions in the United States* (Baltimore: Johns Hopkins University Press, 1984), and Thomas E. Cronin, *Direct Democracy: The Politics of Initiative, Referendum, and Recall* (Cambridge, Mass.: Harvard University Press, 1989), are two good ones by political scientists. Most recent is Philip L. Dubois and Floyd Feeney, *Lawmaking by Initiative: Issues, Options, and Comparisons* (New York: Agathon Press, 1998). Earlier works, also by political scientists, include Hugh A. Bone, *The Initiative and the Referendum* (New York: National Municipal League, 1975); David Butler and Austin Ranney, eds., *Referendums: A Comparative Study of Practice and Theory* (Washington, D.C.: American Enterprise Institute, 1978); Austin Ranney, *The Referendum Initiative Device* (Washington, D.C.: American Enterprise Institute, 1981); and Eugene C. Lee, *750 Propositions: The Initiative in Perspective* (Berkeley: Institute of Governmental Studies, University of California, 1978). Considerably less historical than its title suggests is Laura Tallian, *Direct Democracy: An Historical Analysis of the Initiative, Referendum, and Recall* (Los Angeles: People's Lobby, 1977).

More specialized national studies include Institute of Governmental Studies, *The Initiative: A Brief Bibliography with Emphasis on California* (Berkeley: Institute of Governmental Studies, University of California, 1978); David H. Everson, *Initiatives and Voter Turnout: A Comparative State Analysis* (Springfield: Illinois Legislative Studies Center, Sangamon State University, 1980); Harlan Hahn and Sheldon Kamieniecki, *Referendum Voting: Social Status and Policy Preferences* (New York: Greenwood Press, 1987); and Patrick B. McGulkigon, *The Politics of Direct Democracy in the United States: Case Studies in Popular Decision Making* (Washington, D.C.: Free Congress Research and Education Foundation, 1985). A recent, interesting study by a direct-democracy advocate, largely of California but with some national data, is David D. Schmidt, *Citizen Lawmakers: The Ballot Initiative Revolution* (Philadelphia: Temple University Press, 1989).

Many of the above books have considerable emphasis on California, and there are also general works exclusively focused on California direct legislation, often by advocates of the process and those who would reform it. California Commission on Campaign Financing, *Democracy by Initiative: Shaping California's Fourth Branch of Government* (Los Angeles: The Commission, 1992) is a study in depth, replete with reform proposals. Less thorough are Philip Dubois and Floyd Feeney, *Improving the Initiative Process: Options for Change* (Davis: California Policy Seminar, University of California, 1991); and Nancy Young, *The Initiative Promise in California* (Los Angeles: University of Southern California Law Center Library, 1982). Another is League of Women Voters of California, *Initiative and Referendum in California: A Legacy Lost?* (Sacramento: The League, 1984).

A lighthearted but perceptive view of the present state of direct legislation in California by a fan of the process is Jim Schultz, *The Initiative Cookbook: Recipes and Stories from California's Ballot Wars* (San Francisco: The Democracy Center, 1996). Peter Schrag's *Paradise Lost: California's Experience, America's Future* (New York: New Press, 1998) is a different evaluation that sees the initiative as a key element in the breakdown of representative government in California since the 1960s. A useful summary of California propositions through 1990, with an extensive bibliography, is John M. Allswang, *California Initiatives and Referendums, 1912–1990: A Survey and Guide to Research* (Los Angeles: Edmund G. "Pat" Brown Institute of Public Affairs, California State University, Los Angeles, 1991).

Earlier studies include Winston W. Crouch, *The Initiative and Referendum in California* (Los Angeles: Haynes Foundation, 1950), and its predecessor, V. O. Key and Winston W. Crouch, *The Initiative and Referendum in California* (Berkeley: University of California Press, 1939). For a business perspective, see California Chamber of Commerce, Research Department, *Initiative Legislation in California: History of the Use of the Initiative and Summary of Various Proposals for Amendment of the Initiative Process* (San Francisco: The Chamber, 1950); and *Initiative Legislation of California: History of the Use of the Initiative and Summary of Various Proposals for Amendment of the Initiative Process* (San Francisco: The Chamber, 1961).

Little contemporary work has been done on the origins and early history of direct legislation. The most important work for this period is Tom Sitton, *John Randolph Haynes: California Progressive* (Stanford, Calif.: Stanford University Press, 1992). The works by Key and by Crouch, mentioned above, provide some additional coverage, and George Mowry, *The California Progressives* (Berkeley: University of California Press, 1951) is still useful, as are some more recent works: Spencer Olin, *California's Prodigal Sons: Hiram Johnson and the Progressives, 1911–1917* (Berkeley: University of California Press, 1968); William Deverell and Tom Sitton, eds., *California Progressivism Revisited* (Berkeley: University of California Press, 1994); and Richard Coke Lower, *A Bloc of One: The Political Career of Hiram W. Johnson* (Stanford, Calif.: Stanford University Press, 1993). On progressivism generally, see John D. Buenker, John C. Burnham, and Robert M. Crunden, *Progressivism* (Cambridge, Mass.: Schenkman, 1977). On the California background, see Kevin Starr, *Inventing the Dream: California Through the Progressive Era* (New York: Oxford University Press, 1985); Royce D. Delmatier, Clarence F. McIntosh, and Earl G. Waters, *The Rumble of California Politics, 1848–1970* (New York: John Wiley & Sons, 1970); and Walton Bean, *California: An Interpretive History* (New York: McGraw-Hill, 1978). Also useful is Eric F. Peterson, "Prelude to Progressivism in California: Election Reform, 1870–1909" (Ph.D. diss., UCLA, 1969).

The series of contemporary books surveying the California legislature by Franklin Hichborn, *The Story of the Session of the California Legislature* (San Francisco: J. H. Barry, 1909–1915) was as much reformist as reportorial, but nonetheless is informative relative to the battle to implement direct legislation; this is true also of his "California Politics, 1891–1913" (unpublished typescript at UCLA Research Library), and his "Sources of Opposition to Direct Legislation In California," pt. 2, *The Commonwealth* 6 (March 1931). See also John R. Haynes, "The Adoption of the Initiative and Referendum in California," *West Coast Magazine* 11 (January 1912).

A huge survey of the development of direct legislation through the late 1920s can be found in A. J. Pillsbury, "A Study of Direct Legislation in All of its Forms . . . " (written for *The Commonwealth*, 1931; carbon copy in Hichborn Papers, UCLA).

For the 1930s, additional general background can be found in Kevin Starr, *Endangered Dreams: The Great Depression in California* (New York: Oxford University Press, 1996); John W. Caughey, *California: History of a Remarkable State* (Englewood Cliffs, N.J.: Prentice Hall, 1982); and Gladwin Hill, *The Dancing Bear: An Inside Look at California Politics* (Cleveland: World Publishing, 1968).

There is a real paucity of studies on the topic for the 1930s through the 1970s. General works include J. G. Lapalombara and C. B. Hagin, "Direct Legislation: An Appraisal and A Suggestion," *American Political Science Review* 45 (June 1951): 400–21; and John E. Mueller, "Voting on the Propositions: Ballot Pattern and Historical Trends in California," *American Political Science Review* 63 (December 1969): 1197–1213. James Echols, "Jackson Ralston and the Last Single Tax Campaign," *California History* 58 (fall 1979): 256–63, is good on the finale of that long-term issue; and Tom Zimmerman, "Ham and Eggs, Everybody!" *Southern California Quarterly* 62 (spring 1980): 77–96 is good on that very controversial movement. See also Luther F. Eggleston, *The Tragedy of "Ham and Eggs" in 1940* (Los Angeles: California Merchants Council [1940]); and Abraham Holtzman, *The Townsend Movement: A Political Study* (New York: Bookman Associates, 1963).

On the issue of civil rights and race relations, including the fair employment Proposition 11 in 1946 and open housing (Proposition 14 in 1948, Proposition 10 in 1950, and Proposition 14 in 1964), see the following oral histories: *C. L. Dellums*, Regional Oral History Office (Berkeley, 1973); *William Bryan Rumford*, Regional Oral History Office (Berkeley, 1973); *Tarea Hall Pittman*, Regional Oral History Office (Berkeley, 1974). An good overview of the topic, particularly as it relates to the

Watts riots of 1965, is Gerald Horne, *The Fire This Time: The Watts Uprising and the 1960s* (Charlottesville: University Press of Virginia, 1995).

On the early stages of the property tax issue, including Philip Watson's Proposition 9 in 1968, see David O. Sears and Jack Citrin, *Tax Revolt: Something for Nothing in California* (Cambridge, Mass.: Harvard University Press, 1985); and the following oral histories: *Philip Watson*, UCLA Oral History Program (Los Angeles, 1989); *Ronald B. Welch*, Regional Oral History Program (Berkeley, 1988). Good background on the important issue of water and water policy for the whole twentieth century, with some attention to direct legislation, is in Norris Hundley, Jr., *The Great Thirst: Californians and Water, 1770s–1990s* (Berkeley and Los Angeles: University of California Press, 1992).

Watson's second try at property tax reform, Proposition 14 in 1972, is analyzed in "November 1972 Ballot Proposals," *The Commonwealth: Official Journal of the Commonwealth Club of California* 66 (October 1972). For Governor Reagan's effort to the same end in 1973, see William A. Niskanen, *Tax and Expenditure Limitation by Constitutional Amendment: Four Perspectives on the California Initiative* (Berkeley: Institute of Governmental Studies, 1973); and California Taxpayers Association, "A Proposal to Limit Government Spending (Prop. 1, Nov. 6, 1973 Ballot)," (pamphlet; Sacramento: California Taypayers Association, 1973).

The literature on Proposition 13 of 1978 is vast and still growing. Two early bibliographies are Terry J. Dean and Ronald Heckart, *Proposition 13, 1978 California Primary* (Berkeley: Institute of Governmental Studies, 1979); and Ronald J. Heckart and Terry J. Dean, *Proposition 13 in the 1978 California Primary: A Post-Election Bibliography* (Berkeley: Institute of Governmental Studies, 1981). Among useful works on this critical election and its effects are George G. Kaufman and Kenneth T. Rosen, eds., *The Property Tax Revolt: The Case of Proposition 13* (Cambridge, Mass.: Ballinger Publishing Co., 1981); Robert Kuttner, *Revolt of the Haves: Tax Rebellions and Hard Times* (New York: Simon and Schuster, 1979); and Lester A. Sobel, ed., *The Great American Tax Revolt* (New York: Facts On File, 1979). The accounts by the measure's authors are also worthwhile: Howard Jarvis, *I'm Mad As Hell: The Exclusive Story of the Tax Revolt and Its Leader* (New York: Times Books, 1979); and *Paul Gann*, oral history, UC Berkeley Oral History Office (Berkeley, 1988). One of many longitudinal analyses of the pros and cons of the long-term effects of Proposition 13 can be found in *Los Angeles Times*, 26 May 1998, p. A1ff. A recent national study that sees the tax revolt as primarily serving special interests rather than "the people" is Daniel A. Smith, *Tax Crusaders and the Politics of Direct Democracy* (New York: Routledge, 1998).

On the important Political Reform Act (Proposition 9) of 1974, see People's Lobby, *Proposition 9, The Political Reform Act: A Fact for California, A Proposal for America* (Los Angeles: People's Lobby Press, 1974); Carla L. Duscha, "It Isn't a Lobby . . . and the People Are Few," *California Journal* 6 (March 1975); and two oral histories: *Daniel Lowenstein*, The UCLA Oral History Program (Los Angeles, 1989); and *Walter A. Zelman*, The UCLA Oral History Program (Los Angeles, 1989).

Paul Gann's successful entry into the crime issue, in Proposition 8 of 1982, is discussed in Bill Blum and Gina Lobaco, "The Proposition 8 Puzzle," *California Lawyer* 5 (February 1985). The deep social and economic forces involved in the rise of the United Farm Workers (Proposition 22 of 1972), and the almost equally divisive issue of water policy (Proposition 9 of 1982) are discussed in Leonard Pitt, *California Controversies: Major Issues in the History of the State* (Wheeling, Ill.: Harlan Davidson, 1989). Proposition 22 is also analyzed in Commonwealth Club of California, "November 1972 Ballot Proposals," *The Commonwealth* 66 (October 1972). A good case study of a significant environmental issue handled by the initiative is Paul A. Sabatier, *Can Regulation Work? The Implementation of the 1972 California Coastal Initiative* (New York: Plenum Press, 1983); see also *William F. Siri*, oral history, UC Berkeley Oral History Office (Berkeley, 1979).

The increased interest in California initiatives after Proposition 13 is demonstrated by the publication dates of many of the books listed at the start of this bibliography. The term-limits controversy is presented by its leading proponent in Peter F. Schabarum, *Enough Is Enough: Term Limits in California* (Los Angeles: Modernage Marketing Services, 1992). The crime issue and its relationship to the "purge" of the California Supreme Court in 1986 are dealt with in Dena Cochran, "A Victim's Bill of Rights or a Lawyer's Employment Act," *California Journal* 12 (April 1982). The 1984 beginnings of the "English-only" issue (Proposition 38) are analyzed in "The Constitutional Future of the All-English Ballot," *Pacific Law Review* 16 (1985). The somewhat related issue of school vouchers in 1993 (Proposition 174) is treated in Laura A. Locke, "The Voucher Initiative: Breakthrough or Break-Up for California Schools?" *California Journal* 24 (October 1993): 9–14.

On the combined health-sociocultural issue of AIDS, including Paul Gann's Proposition 102 of 1988, see *Paul Gann*, oral history, UC Berkeley Oral History Office (Berkeley, 1988); and Reese Erlich, "The Tragedy of the 'Other' AIDS Initiative," *San Francisco Bay Guardian*, 23 November 1988, pp. 13–14. The affirmative action controversy, culminating in Proposition 209 of 1996, is summarized in Lydia Chávez, *The Color Bind: California's Battle to End Affirmative Action* (Berkeley: University of California Press, 1998).

# Index